T-DISPATCH

Associated Press News Service.

RIL 16, 1912—28 PAGES. PRICE ONE CENT

HOME EDITION

TANIC" SA... SAVED

h Survivors; None on Other Ships

eeding to New York with about 800. Consulted with Mr. Ismay. So much ice about. con-

Marconi via Cape Race, from Capt. Gambell of the Virginian, that he arrived on the scene of

she has no passengers from the Titanic on board.

ybreak FOUND BOATS AND WRECKAGE ONLY. Titanic sank about 2:20 a. m. in 41:16
gers included. Nearly all saved women and children. Californian remained searching exact

St. Louis woman passenger rescued.

ABOUT 2200 PERSONS WERE ABOARD TITANIC.

Passengers of all classes	1310
Crew	860
Women and children in first cabin	143
Women and children in second cabin	87

White Star line officials say that a small number of passengers may have been taken on after the booking list was made up, and that the crew may be a little larger or smaller than stated.

Lifeboats for Only One-Third on Board

NEW YORK, April 16.

THE Bureau of Inspection of Steam Vessels gives statistics of the life-saving apparatus of the Olympic, the Titanic's sister ship. As the two ships are almost identical in size and capacity, it is not likely that their life-saving equipment differs materially.

The Olympic has 16 lifeboats and four collapsible boats, or rafts, calculated to accommodate 1171 persons. This means about one-third

2-THIRDS WOMEN IN PARTIAL LIST OF THOSE RESCUED

Astor, Butt, Guggenheim and Many Other Famous Men Who Were on Board Not Mentioned Among Survivors---Money Loss Is $20,000,000.

By Associated Press.

ST. JOHNS, Newfoundland, April 16.—All hope that any of the passengers or any members of the crew of the Titanic other than those on the Carpathia are alive was abandoned here this afternoon. All of the steamers which have been cruising in the vicinity of the disaster have continued on their voyages.

HALIFAX, N. S., April 16. — The liner Parisian has reported by wireless that she steamed through much heavy field ice looking for passengers from the ill-fated Titanic. No life rafts or bodies were sighted among the floating wreckage which covered a large area. The Parisian reports that the weather was cold, and that even if any persons had been on the wreckage they would in all probability have perished from exposure before they could have been picked up.

NEW YORK, April 16.—There are among the 868 survivors of Titanic now on the Carpathia steaming for this port, 553 whose

FV

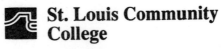

Joseph Pulitzer II
and the
Post-Dispatch

Joseph Pulitzer II
and the
Post-Dispatch

—— A Newspaperman's Life ——

Daniel W. Pfaff

The Pennsylvania State University Press
University Park, Pennsylvania

Frontispiece illustration (p. ii) of Joseph Pulitzer II by Steven Kress. From a photograph taken on September 15, 1912, courtesy of David E. Moore.

The photographs and illustrations herein were provided courtesy of the *St. Louis Post-Dispatch,* Joseph Pulitzer III, Michael E. Pulitzer, Mrs. Elwood R. Quesada, and David E. Moore and are used with their permission.

Library of Congress Cataloging-in-Publication Data

Pfaff, Daniel W.
    Joseph Pulitzer II and the Post-dispatch : a
newspaperman's life / Daniel W. Pfaff.

        p.   cm.
    Includes index.
    ISBN 0-271-00748-6
    1. Pulitzer, Joseph. 2. Journalists—United States—
Biography. 3. St. Louis post-dispatch—History. 4. United States—
History—1865- I. Title.
    PN4874.P8P47 1991
    070.4′1′092—dc20
    [B]   90-49036
                                                              CIP

It is the policy of The Pennsylvania State University Press to use acid-free paper for the first printing of all clothbound books. Publications on uncoated stock satisfy the minimum requirements of American National Standard for Information Sciences—Permanence of Paper for Printed Library Materials, ANSI Z39.48-1984.

For my parents,
Ivan and Ruth Pfaff,
and in memory of my teacher
Bessie M. Savage Baker

Contents

Contents

List of Illustrations

Sources and Acknowledgments

Coincidentally, another man whose initials are J.P. got me started on this project. Jack Pontius, associate librarian and head of the microform and periodical collections of Penn State's Pattee Library, informed me several years ago that the library had acquired the papers of Joseph Pulitzer II on microfilm from the Library of Congress. These papers were by far the richest of the resources I consulted in my research. I am most grateful to Jack and Microforms staff members Mildred C. Allen, Evalyn S. Antenucci, Kalani L. Doll, and Susan H. Hayya for their expert assistance. I am also indebted to Jerry Olsen and the Pattee Library's photoduplication staff for their excellent service.

The second major resource was the Papers of Joseph Pulitzer (I) at the Butler Library, Columbia University, New York City, where I was capably assisted by the staff of Kenneth A. Lohf, librarian for rare books and manuscripts. Elizabeth B. Mason, who has retired as associate director of Columbia's Oral History Research Office, Butler Library, and her successor, Ronald J. Grele, were also extremely helpful. And the late director of the Oral History Research Office, Louis M. Starr, obtained illuminating interviews with Joseph Pulitzer II and former *St. Louis Post-Dispatch* managing editor Benjamin H. Reese in 1954.

Of limited but significant use were the Papers of Joseph Pulitzer (I) at the Library of Congress, where I was generously assisted by David W. Wigdor, assistant chief of the Manuscripts Division. In St. Louis, Frances H. Stadler, formerly archivist for the Missouri Historical Society, provided helpful advice about using collections there, as did Anne R. Kenney, associate director of the Western Historical Manuscript Collection at the University of Missouri at St. Louis. Gladys O'Neil, curator of the Bar Harbor (Maine) Historical Society, located several helpful items during my visit there.

For secondary sources, the thorough "Pulitzer–*Post-Dispatch* Bibliography" prepared in 1976 by Roy T. King, former *Post-Dispatch* librarian, was invaluable. It is included with the Papers of Joseph Pulitzer II. King also prepared a most useful genealogical chart of the Pulitzer family and organized, cataloged, and identified hundreds of family photographs at the *Post-Dispatch*, where most of the photographs in this book were found.

This biography was written with the full cooperation of Joseph Pulitzer III, his brother Michael E. Pulitzer, and their sisters, Mrs. Elwood R. Quesada (the former Kate Davis Pulitzer) and Mrs. Louis H. Hempelmann Jr. (the former Elinor Pulitzer), all of whom granted interviews. I was assisted most of all by Joseph Pulitzer III, who worked with his father for many years before succeeding him as editor and publisher of the *Post-Dispatch* and chairman of the Pulitzer Publishing Company. In his first response to my expression of interest in researching the life of his father, Joseph Pulitzer III wrote: "I am not one who admires or approves of 'authorized' biographies—they smack of too much PR and so are suspect." Accordingly, we readily agreed that I would have full control over the manuscript. At my request, however, he read early drafts of the chapters as they were produced and offered comments and suggestions. He was unfailingly helpful, never demanding, and always willing to allow me the final decision. Without exception, his suggestions served to improve the manuscript. He did not review the revised manuscript submitted for publication. Under the same arrangement and with the same warm cordiality, Michael Pulitzer, Mrs. Quesada, and Mrs. Hempelmann reviewed several chapters. David E. Moore, a nephew of J.P. II, reviewed one chapter and provided several photographs that had belonged to his mother, the late Edith Pulitzer Moore.

Two others read all the chapters as they were drafted: Donald L. Smith, my colleague in the Pennsylvania State University School of Communications, and Julian S. Rammelkamp, recently retired head of the history department at Albion College in Michigan. Smith, primarily a legal scholar, is the author of a recent biography of Zechariah Chafee Jr. of the Harvard Law School. Rammelkamp, a specialist on the history of St. Louis, is author of the highly regarded *Pulitzer's Post-Dispatch, 1878–1883* (Princeton: Princeton University Press, 1967) and is currently working on a comprehensive history of the *Post-Dispatch*. James Boylan of the University of Massachusetts at Amherst and Steve Weinberg of the University of Missouri at Columbia offered a number of excellent suggestions after reading the entire manuscript.

Four former *Post-Dispatch* employees read chapters dealing with events of which they had direct knowledge: Arch R. King, secretary for many years to Joseph Pulitzer II, and Irving Dilliard, Robert Lasch, and James Lawrence, former *Post-Dispatch* editorial writers who became editors of the editorial page. I am sincerely grateful to each of them.

The help of several others was vital as well. First among them was James V. Maloney, secretary of the Pulitzer Publishing Company and administrative assistant to Joseph Pulitzer III. Mr. Maloney attended to countless requests with the greatest patience, care, and promptness. Martha Schomberg, Marie Waterhouse, and Eileen Bertani of Mr. Pulitzer's office also helped in many ways, as did Mary Blackburn of Michael Pulitzer's office. Many others at the *Post-Dispatch* made important contributions, including Joseph Pulitzer IV, now a vice president of the company. He was only five when his grandfather died, but he has been an enthusiastic collector of lore about him, and he assisted me in a substantial way. Gerald Brown and Nancy Stoddard of the *Post-Dispatch* reference department found answers to numerous requests. I encountered nothing but friendly cooperation throughout the *Post-Dispatch* building, from the sixth floor to the sub-basement, and thank everyone there who made my visits so pleasant.

I am most grateful to the many individuals who either granted interviews or wrote me letters: Richard G. Baumhoff, Ben L. Brockman, Asa Bryan, Edward J. Burkhardt, Harry J. Cargas, Marquis W. Childs, Mrs. A. Mervin Davies, Howard Derrickson, Irving Dilliard, Mrs. Frank Doyle, Richard Dudman, Edward A. Dwyer, Mrs. Edward L. Dwyer, A. James Fox, Kathleen E. Gilmore, John A. Gould, Dr. William A. Gould, Evarts A. Graham Jr., Harold O. Grams, Ralph Grayczak, George H. Hall, Gouverneur Morris Helfenstein, Charles J. Hentschell, Arthur W. Hepner, John Hohenberg, Lionel Horton, Norman E. Isaacs, Emily Kimbrough, Arch R. King, Roy T. King, Raymond Kringer, Robert Lasch, James Lawrence, Morris J. Levin, Clarissa Start Lippert, Mrs. Lawrence Lymburner, George McCue, C. Wickham Moore, David E. Moore,

Michael D. Murray, Selwyn Pepper, Mrs. Thomas Pettus, Louis L. Phillips, W. Julius Polk, Mrs. Carl Richards, George N. Sayers, Lester A. Schaffer, Don Schomburg, Mr. and Mrs. Wallace H. Smith, Mrs. Charles Symington, Stuart Symington, Elbert A. Talley, Mrs. Charles A. Thomas, Mrs. Joseph L. Werner, Harry Wilensky, Eugene F. Williams Jr., Mrs. John Gates Williams, Arthur Witman, Amadee Wohlschlaeger.

My university, Penn State, provided much of the financial support for the travel involved in gathering material. I wish particularly to acknowledge the support and encouragement of these Penn State administrators: Robert O. Blanchard and R. Dean Mills, former directors of the School of Journalism; John J. Romano, former acting director of the School of Journalism; Kenneth P. Mortimer, former vice president and vice provost and former acting dean of the School of Communications; Brian N. Winston, dean of the School of Communications; and Joseph W. Michels, former associate dean for research of the College of the Liberal Arts. Stanley Weintraub, director of the university's Institute for the Arts and Humanistic Studies and a biographer of note, generously provided advice on the world of agents and publishers. For cheerfully performing countless tasks, I thank the administrative staff of the School of Communications: Christine L. Templeton, assistant to the dean, and Patricia E. Kidder, Delores J. Vonada, LaDawn H. Dutrow, Penny Snyder, and Cindy Willson. Valuable research assistance was performed by Penn State graduates Mary Reilly, Marilyn Kilbert, and Martha Fisher.

As a gesture to their father's memory, Joseph III and Michael Pulitzer provided a grant through the Pulitzer Publishing Company Foundation to The Pennsylvania State University Press specifically designated to enhance the physical quality of this book and to augment its promotion. This decision was subsequent to and independent of the decision by the Press to publish the book. The grant was not proposed until after the Pulitzers and I had reached the definite understanding about my independence as author and was both offered and accepted with the specific stipulation that it carried with it no conditions as to the book's content. The book itself is, of course, the best testimony to authorial control. No one's life is entirely free of negatives, but some finish with a better record than others, and Joseph Pulitzer II appears to be one of the latter. The best testimony to that is the completeness of the record he left behind. In combing through his papers, I found no evidence of any attempt to sanitize them—for example, letters dictated but never sent were not destroyed, and uncomplimentary or potentially embarrassing references remained. This was a reflection of his strong sense of fairness: he believed that the best journalism is candid and complete, and that this applies to the publicist as well as to the publicized.

Portions of this book appeared in somewhat different form as "Joseph Pulitzer II and the European War, 1938–1945," in *American Journalism* 6, no. 3 (1989), and as "The St. Louis Post-Dispatch Debate over Communism, 1940–1955," *Mass Comm Review* 16, nos. 1 and 2 (1989), Special Issue. I gratefully acknowledge the assistance of the respective editors of those publications, William David Sloan and Diane J. Tillinghast, with that material. The following specific permissions were granted for use of materials herein: from Joseph Pulitzer III, literary executor of the estate of Joseph Pulitzer II, authorization to quote from the archives and oral history held by Columbia University pertaining to Joseph Pulitzer and descendants; from Columbia University Libraries, owner of original letters and manuscripts in the Joseph Pulitzer Papers, Rare Book and Manuscript Library, Columbia University; from the Oral History Research Office, Columbia University, to quote from the oral history memoirs of Joseph Pulitzer II and Benjamin H. Reese; and from the Missouri Historical Society, St. Louis, to publish material from the Clark McAdams and George M. Burbach Papers.

I shall never have better professional help than that rendered by the staff of Penn State Press, in particular, Sanford G. Thatcher, director; Peggy Hoover, copyeditor; Janet Dietz, production manager; Steven R. Kress, designer; and Kate Capps, marketing manager. My agent, Julian S. Bach, and his assistant, Susan Merritt, also provided much wise counsel.

Eileen, my wife, and sons Andrew and Mark, have endured this project for years with patience, forbearance, and genuine interest. My sister-in-law Eleanor Zupp and her husband, Robert, both sustained and saw me through several misadventures in using the metropolitan public transportation system during my research visit to New York City. My neighbors and friends, Stanley and Françoise Rosen, kindly translated a letter from French to English.

The generosity of all those named above is primarily responsible for whatever merit this work may have. Its lapses and imperfections are mine alone.

A Few Words About Names

The subject of this biography, Joseph Pulitzer II, was in fact named and known as a child and young man as Joseph Pulitzer Jr. But in 1922, a decade after his father died, he chose to drop the "Jr." and sign himself "Joseph Pulitzer" or "J.P." In turn, his eldest son — actually Joseph Pulitzer III — signed himself "Joseph Pulitzer Jr." In the text, except when it would create confusion, the name each went by is used, but in the figure captions and the footnotes "II" and "III" are used to identify the son and the grandson of the founding Pulitzer.

Joseph Pulitzer II took pride in the high journalistic standards associated with the family name and was dismayed at its frequent mispronunciation as "PEW-litzer." He complained in 1950 to Carl W. Ackerman, dean of the Columbia University Graduate School of Journalism, which administered the Pulitzer Prizes, that broadcast commentator Elmer Davis persisted in this error. He offered this instruction: "I find the easiest way to explain the proper pronunciation is to tell people to utter the three simple English words, 'pull-it-sir,' with the accent on the 'pull.' Technically the 's' of 'sir' should be pronounced as a 'z'." Whether Ackerman reformed Davis is unknown, but perhaps this repetition of the lesson will reach some other violators.

Joseph Pulitzer II
and the
Post-Dispatch

— 1 —

The Heir Unapparent

"**A** Pulitzer property and baronial in management" and "probably the most effective liberal newspaper in the United States" is how John Gunther described the *St. Louis Post-Dispatch* in his *Inside U.S.A.*, published in 1947. The "baron" of that reference was editor-publisher Joseph Pulitzer II, who had inherited direction of the newspaper on the death of his father, its founder, in 1911. Almost all the achievements that brought the newspaper its importance and distinction came during the forty-three-year tenure of the second Joseph Pulitzer, who assembled and kept an outstanding staff over which he maintained firm but benevolent charge. His associates regarded him as a consummate professional, but to outsiders he was a largely invisible influence.

The first Joseph Pulitzer, a genius with a theatrical flair, was a delicious subject for comment and commentary—"perhaps the most interesting person on the planet," a contemporary observer declared. By contrast, his namesake son, though hardly shy, avoided personal publicity and preferred, with few exceptions, to work anonymously. As a result, relatively little was published about the second J.P. during his lifetime, and almost nothing has appeared since his death in 1955. Others received the considerable credit for his newspaper's accomplishments. There have been biographies of longtime managing editor Oliver K. Bovard and of Washington correspondent, editorial page editor, and Truman press secretary Charles G. Ross. Reporters Paul Y. Anderson and John T. Rogers, editorial cartoonist Daniel R. Fitzpatrick, and syndicated columnist and Washington correspondent Marquis W. Childs are all better known and more often mentioned in texts and histories than J.P. II. He figured importantly during his career in only three national magazine articles: the *American Mercury* in 1931, the *Saturday Evening Post* in 1939, and *Collier's* in 1950.[1] "About right!" one can hear him say from offstage. Whenever he traveled, he instructed hotels, which liked to link widely recognized names with their own, that there was to be "no publicity" about his tenancy. But he prized the letters from U.S. Presidents he received at the paper over the years complimenting the *Post-Dispatch* for special series, symposiums, or campaigns it published.

The articles consistently placed the *Post-Dispatch* among the top five dailies in the nation. They attributed this, in the *American Mercury*'s words, to its having "completely realized the Pulitzer ideal of a newspaper which should be absolutely independent of all party and financial interests, should constantly be fighting vigorous and interesting battles, and should at the same time make a lot of money." The second Joseph Pulitzer's subordinates, no matter how capable or dedicated, could not have achieved these things except at the behest—and willingness to spend—of the editor-publisher. As a newspaper businessman, Joseph Pulitzer II showed that it was possible to place principles ahead of balance-sheet considerations and still come out ahead. He had no ambition to be the wealthiest publisher in the country, and he took no more than ordinary satisfaction from being the most prosperous publisher within the radius served by his newspaper and, in time, by its allied radio and television stations.

He did not come to hold this philosophy—which amounts to considerably more than following a path blazed by his father—gradually over a period of years, but started with it and stuck by it. This is impressively illustrated by his persistent disgust at the large number of newspapers, including his father's newspapers, that carried so-called medical advertising offering worthless and even dangerous advice and products to gullible readers. He protested this to the point of provoking rage—but not reform—from his father. After he took charge of the *Post-Dispatch,* millions of dollars in aggregate in "medical" advertising was turned away. On his strict orders, there was absolutely no self-aggrandizing publicity about this. To him, human decency in the practice of journalism was neither a matter of pride nor an article of trade. It was a norm, even if not widely observed. That he separated himself from the business preoccupations of most newspaper proprietors showed through on occasion, as in a response to his eldest son, Joseph Pulitzer III, who had been asked for an interview by the trade publication *Editor and Publisher* in 1949. "Suit yourself" about granting the interview, he said. "Incidentally, I have always thought of Editor and Publisher as a cash register, business office medium."[2]

The first Joseph Pulitzer had pointed the way toward principled journalism in the commanding language of the paper's platform, a commitment to social and political justice and fair play which he wrote in 1907. But it was his namesake son who so impressively advanced the organization's reach toward those always illusive goals. This feat was achieved by translating the founder's ideals into action under circumstances that even the most brilliant intellect would be unable to foresee. The high quality the *Post-Dispatch* achieved under the administration of Joseph Pulitzer II should be attributed more than anything else to his dedication to unusually high standards of performance and craftsmanship. The period of his tenure—during which the paper won twelve of its seventeen Pulitzer Prizes—might well have been a kind of "golden age" of the *Post-Dispatch.*

They were stirring times, spanning from the ruthlessness of the Gilded Age to the unrelenting distrust of the cold war. Throughout the period, Joseph Pulitzer II had a sure sense that his newspaper had an obligation to help its readers safely and sanely through whatever might happen—be it war, economic depression, or public or private misdeeds. This was almost all grimly serious stuff, and, perhaps more because of that than despite it, Pulitzer insisted that the *Post-Dispatch* provide a leavening of humor and joy in living. Both were evident in his own personality and in his recreational pursuits.

Somewhat less apparent in him was the questioning and even abrasive liberal bias of the *Post-Dispatch*. Proud though he was of this heritage, he was at times a traditionalist. For example, he saw enforcement of a mandatory flag salute law against Jehovah's Witness schoolchildren as nothing more than the requirement of "good manners." More often than his more liberal editorial subordinates, he was inclined to strive for a balanced presentation or to reach for an understanding of the conservative viewpoint on an issue. Similarly, courtesy and respect for others were virtual constants in his administrative dealings. His was as much the last word as his father's had been, but he was not given to bombast or fits of temper, probably because as a young man he experienced more than a sufficiency of such treatment. Through his late teens and early twenties he endured paternal tirades filled with stinging reminders of his shortcomings. These alternated with periods of understanding and encouragement.

Perhaps most interesting is that the effect of his father's mercurial behavior toward this son seems to have been wholly beneficial. He drew upon the considerable positiveness he found in his father's example with confidence and gratitude, and he walked away from the dismissive, overbearing self-righteousness, recognizing it for what it was, the expression of a restless mind and soul for which he and others were blameless, regardless of his father's charges to the contrary. And he did this without lingering resentment, which is suggestive of a mental balance that may well have formed his editorial approach.

Insightful though he was, the evidence indicates that the founding Pulitzer, as his life approached its end in 1911, sensed none of these qualities in Joseph, his middle son. Compared with Ralph (the eldest) and Herbert (the youngest), gregarious, fun-loving Joseph Jr. seemed to him to have the least promise. For that reason, his father assigned him to the *Post-Dispatch*. The journalistic stakes were not nearly so high there as at the New York *World*, which Pulitzer purchased in 1883 and thereafter gave his closest attention. The St. Louis paper, which he founded in 1878, was sound and successful, but the *World* was his dearest possession, whose continuing service of public causes he wanted to be his monument.

It was only briefly to be so. By 1931 the *World* was gone, a casualty of weak management in a troubled economy. Ralph and, for a short time, Herbert were its titular directors, but sadly neither was a leader. In the same period, however, Joseph Jr. proved himself to be one. There is nothing to suggest that this had anything to do with a wish to discredit his father's lower estimate of him or to spite his brothers, who were willed greater shares of the newspapers' dividends than he. (Herbert got 60 percent, Ralph 20 percent, and Joseph Jr. 10 percent. Top editors and managers got the remaining 10 percent.) Nor was there a hint of the internecine feuding that often breaks out among heirs to large fortunes. (In more recent times, the family's third generation did undergo a major dispute, resulting in the company's shift from private ownership to public ownership.)

The second Joseph Pulitzer's introduction to the *Post-Dispatch* had taken place in a few weeks early in 1903, when he was seventeen. Then, after a socially successful but academically subpar year-and-a-half at Harvard in 1905 and 1906, his exasperated father took him out of college and put him into training for some sort of newspaper career, first at the *World* and then at the *Post-Dispatch*. He worked there steadily for the remainder of his career, with the exception of a few stints at the *World* while his father was still living and still mulling the futures of his three sons. In his father's estimate, the main trouble with Joseph Jr. was his apparent lack of intellectual drive. He was bright and for the most part well behaved, but he did not show the probing curiosity and fascination with historical currents and political issues which his father regarded as essential attributes of his successor. His comment on one of the young man's editorials was: "Poor for a beginner, good for a finisher." The available evidence suggests that the father was the most comfortable with the idea of this son working in the business office with little or no authority over news or editorial policy. But Joseph Jr. did not see it this way at all, and he protested. Following a near severing of relations between them, after one of the father's emotional outbursts about the time of Joseph's twenty-fourth birthday in 1909, the son one by one saw all his chief desires fulfilled: to live and work in St. Louis rather than New York, to marry a young St. Louis woman whom he had known since 1906, and to devote most of his time to news and editorial projects and administration.

He ever afterward preferred the editor's role to that of publisher. He was only twenty-six when he took charge of the *Post-Dispatch* at his father's death. The responsibility was not daunting; he had a facility for command, which he developed gradually and used with some reserve in deference to certain older and more experienced men who were now his lieutenants. As a result of his preference for day-by-day oversight of the news and editorial operations, he delegated more authority to those in the advertising, circulation, and business departments. When he did issue directions on the business side, they were often aimed at improving the journalistic product: banning fraudulent and misleading advertising, limiting the total space allocated to advertising in general and giving the managing editor authority to throw out ads to make space for important news, and spending whatever it cost to keep the *Post-Dispatch* technologically current. No one got a wider berth for autonomy than managing editor Bovard. From his first observations of Bovard at work, the young Pulitzer recognized his extraordinary news-gathering talent. He paid the editor accordingly, his salary peaking at $75,000 in 1932, second only to Pulitzer's own. (Bovard's successor started at $20,000 in 1938 and finished at $33,300 in 1951.)

Pulitzer and Bovard parted company in 1938. Bovard went into retirement frustrated that he had not been able to achieve total command over both the news pages and the editorial pages (the latter of which Pulitzer ran with the largest turnover in editors of any major department) and because Pulitzer refused to commit the paper to advocacy of socialism, which Bovard believed was the remedy for the Great Depression. Following Bovard's departure, Pulitzer played an even more dominating role as editor-in-chief. Benjamin H. Reese and Raymond L. Crowley, the managing editors who in turn succeeded Bovard, clearly saw Pulitzer as their superior. Despite professions to the contrary, Bovard had never been able to do this, probably because he had been Pulitzer's exemplar and tutor. He was one of the few longtime working associates who called the editor-publisher "Joe" rather than "Mr. Pulitzer." The only editorial page chiefs who did that were George S. Johns, whose tenure at the *Post-Dispatch* reached well back into the first J.P.'s administration, and Clark McAdams, who was probably the closest of the very few personal friends Pulitzer had among his employees.

Perhaps predictably, the younger Pulitzer found Johns's editorial demeanor stuffy and outdated. He moved that editorship into the younger and much livelier charge of McAdams. But McAdams, an ardent New Dealer, proved too liberally rambunctious for Pulitzer, who replaced him with the more deliberative and analytical *Post-Dispatch* Washington correspondent and bureau chief, Charles G. Ross. Ross, however, swung too far in the other direction. Pulitzer found his measured, low-key style too sedate. While he didn't demand fire and brimstone tirades, he wanted a "fighting" editorial page with a character like that of his father's beloved morning *World*. He found the closest realization of an editor capable of achieving this ideal in Ross's successor, Ralph Coghlan, who almost surely would have held the position throughout the remainder of Pulitzer's life had Pulitzer not been forced to fire him because of alcoholism. Coghlan's successor was Irving Dilliard, who had been on the editorial page since the days of Johns. Dilliard and Pulitzer shared a devotion to the commands of the founder's platform, but sometimes interpreted them differently.

Pulitzer, who was described by a close subordinate as "middle-of-the-road, maybe slightly on the conservative side," frequently found himself at odds with Dilliard's militant civil libertarianism. There had been similar disputes with Bovard, McAdams, Coghlan, and a few others about emphasis and intensity, but these could not be characterized as liberal-conservative clashes; they were more subtly complicated differences of opinion about how various issues should be treated in the newspaper. Their chief importance lies in what they reveal about the tug-and-pull process through which Joseph Pulitzer II ran the *Post-Dispatch*. It seems fair to say that his outlook was closer to what might be called the conventional mainstream than that of his editorial subordinates generally, or it might be said that he was less a doubter and a distruster than they. This is strongly suggested in his relatively rapid movement, compared with his news and editorial executives, from isolationist to interventionist in the developing stages of World War II.

Another basis of at least presumed cleavage between the second Joseph Pulitzer and his subordinates was the assumption by some that the publisher's own wealth and his social associations with the rich and powerful at Bar Harbor, Maine, and elsewhere influenced his social and political philosophy. His editorial endorsements of Republican presidential candidates Alfred M. Landon and Thomas E. Dewey in 1936 and 1948, over most of his editorial staff's objections, were the most frequently cited evidence. But it must be swiftly added that he allowed all his editors a considerable range of freedom of thought and expression—none of the dissenters had to write in favor of Landon or Dewey—and often compromised or deferred to their judgments. However achieved, the result was that throughout his tenure the *Post-Dispatch* was regarded as staunchly independent and politically unfettered. Its strong leadership among newspapers across the nation in unraveling the corruption that became the Teapot Dome scandal of the 1920s—for which reporter Paul Y. Anderson won a Pulitzer Prize—is but one example of this. "I have always been careful to avoid questionable connections such as bank directorships, repeatedly offered me," Pulitzer once pointed out, "and there has never been a sacred cow in this office." It is true, too, that few of the men who came to work under him chose to leave, recognizing, it seems certain, that in nearly all respects this was as professionally fulfilling a place for their careers as they were likely to find.

By current standards, both Joseph Pulitzer II and his top subordinates were definitely illiberal in an important respect: the employment of women and minorities in positions of importance and authority. During his tenure, there were virtually no female reporters, except for the society pages, and only one black reporter. White males filled all the key editorial and business executive positions. The ready explanation is that this was unexceptional for the times: the women's liberation movement, in particular, had yet to develop, and the black civil rights movement was only beginning during his last decade. Pulitzer recognized racial inequality and discrimination as wrong, but he largely accepted the bigotry and racism he had observed all his life as the result of deep-seated attitudes not likely to be overcome anytime soon.

Nevertheless, the editorial page gradually took up the cause of racial integration, following a "go slow" approach he recommended. He expressed a willingness to employ more blacks in the newsroom and other departments if the whites already there would accept them, but when told they would not be accepted he did not press the issue.[3]

His response to the Communist-hunting forays of Senator Joseph McCarthy in the early 1950s was to deplore the senator's tactics, but also to harbor some of the widespread concern about the threat of Communist subversion. He saw no civil liberties obstructions to measures meant to deny subversives access to sensitive positions in government, and he even entertained thoughts of establishing harsher screening of new *Post-Dispatch* employees but was dissuaded by, among others, his son and eventual successor, Joseph Pulitzer III. One of the handful of major editorial disputes of his career was his difference with Dilliard over the tenor of editorial response to court tests of the anti-subversive Smith Act of 1940 and to McCarthy's red-baiting behavior.[4] While he prevailed by virtue of his position, it is the dialogue in which he was willing to engage in fashioning the newspaper's responses to events of the times that makes this historically significant.

The lighter vein in Pulitzer's life also helps define and explain the man. From childhood on, he enjoyed outdoor activities: sailing, bird-shooting, and fishing became his special favorites. He also enjoyed the company of friends, particularly at dinner parties, of which he hosted many over the years both in St. Louis and at Bar Harbor. Because he was less enthusiastic about taking part in the rituals of wealthy high society, he avoided much of it. His eyesight was limited and gradually worsened — most likely a genetic factor, for his father became virtually blind — but this never took away his ability to sight a mallard on the wing or a beautiful woman across the dance floor. Despite that, it was so difficult for him to recognize the faces of even close friends in crowded settings that he avoided much active participation in conventions and gatherings of editors and publishers. This, in turn, contributed to his being less well known than such contemporary fellow publishers as Robert R. McCormick and William Randolph Hearst. It may have caused some to assume, mistakenly, that he was cold and aloof when in fact he was quite social and gregarious.

His first wife died from injuries suffered in a car accident in 1925, and he remarried the following year. There were a son and two daughters from the first marriage and a son from the second. As is often the case, he was an imposing and stern figure to his sons, whose role he hoped would be, as it has become, to assume charge of the company, and a softer, more affectionate being to his daughters. But, unlike his own father, he played no testamentary favorites. Each child was willed precisely the same sum, taking into account that control of the business remained with the male descendants.

It is, however, the intangibles he left behind which form the core of this biography. Unforeseeable twists of fate influence the course and outcome of any life, and the response of each individual to the forces and events of his days defines that life's interest and importance. To be sure, Joseph Pulitzer II started out under conditions that predisposed him to achieving some degree of journalistic significance, be it good or ill. In his case, he was the inheritor of a set of ideals fully as subject to defeat as to realization. The differing fates of the *World* and the *Post-Dispatch* demonstrate this. It is too much to claim the ability to fully explain one paper's success against the other's failure, except to suggest that it almost certainly had something to do with the quality of their leadership. In turn, leadership itself is always influenced by unpredictable mental and physical forces. If there is a particular character trait to credit for the success of Joseph Pulitzer II, it was identified by his father in 1908 when in one of his better moods. After getting reports on how well his son had performed as temporary managing editor during Oliver Bovard's vacation that summer, he wrote Joseph: "What I liked most in you was the enthusiasm, ambition and *love of work* you showed. No man can do much without the latter no matter what his talent and no man can help doing something and perhaps considerable with it."[5]

— 2 —

Life with Father

"The skies are bright and clear and the day auspicious," proclaimed the front-page story in the senior Joseph Pulitzer's *New York Evening World* on October 10, 1889. That afternoon, the cornerstone was to be laid for the ultramodern $1.6 million *World* building on a site at the corner of Park Row and Frankfort Street in New York City for which Pulitzer had paid $630,000 in cash the previous year. It would house the *World* newspapers—morning, evening, and Sunday—and would be completed a year later at an actual cost of $2.5 million. No matter. Six years earlier, Pulitzer had bought the moribund morning *World* from railroad magnate Jay Gould for $346,000 and turned it almost instantly into a circulation and profit-making success. In 1886, the *World* earned more than $500,000.[1] In 1887, Pulitzer established the

Evening World, confident that even better years were ahead. One of the seven decks of headlines declared that the new edifice would be "a fitting habitation for the people's champion newspaper."[2]

The story boasted of the "six elevators, giants in size and very fast," and the burnished copper dome 50 feet in diameter "in which the news, editorial and special writers will have their lair" atop "the highest office building in the universe" and "the highest building of any description in America." Although the publisher himself was in Europe too ill to attend, the story reported that his second son, "Master Joseph Pulitzer, jr., a lad of four years of age, will handle the trowel, laying the cornerstone."

When the time came for the boy's part in the proceedings, young Joseph, dressed in a blue-and-white sailor suit and a visored officer's cap, patted the cornerstone into place with a silver trowel and proclaimed three times: "It is well done." Had his father lived four decades into the next century, he might have pronounced the same benediction on the journalistic achievements of this his middle son. It was Joseph Jr.—about whom his father had the gravest doubts—who kept Pulitzer journalism alive and flourishing in the United States by building the *St. Louis Post-Dispatch* into a newspaper of national and international importance. The *World,* under his two brothers, faltered and in 1931 died.

Among the dignitaries listed by the *New York Times* as watching the "bright-looking youngster" at the cornerstone-laying were New York mayor Hugh J. Grant, New York governor David B. Hill, inventor Thomas A. Edison, and former U.S. president Grover Cleveland,[3] who, though narrowly defeated for reelection the previous year, knew how important the *World*'s support had been in 1884—and correctly figured it might be important again. Following an invocation by Episcopal bishop Daniel S. Tuttle of St. Louis, a longtime Pulitzer friend, opening remarks on behalf of the publisher were made by John A. Cockerill, whom Pulitzer had moved up to the *World*'s managing editorship from the same position on his St. Louis paper, the *Post-Dispatch.* Railroad executive (and later U.S. senator) Chauncey M. Depew gave the main address. The next morning's *Times* account included remarks about another rival, Charles A. Dana of the *New York Sun,* and Pulitzer's near blindness, observing that Dana's office "overlooks the foundation of the Pulitzer Building" and that "this will not be the case . . . in a few months. Then, like a certain other eminent gentleman, he, too, will sit in the shade."[4]

In the shade, yes, but hardly out of action. Almost exactly twenty-two restless years lay yet before the senior Pulitzer on that October day in 1889. His years of personally directing his newspapers were behind him, but those of greatest accomplishment—and of greatest worry about the uncertain future—were ahead. He had literally worked himself into invalidism. His eyesight was so dim that his newspapers had to be read to him. He slept poorly, and suffered from asthma, diabetes, and great swings in mood that at times made him seem to be on the verge of suicide. He was extraordinarily sensitive to noise and went to great lengths of architecture and travel to isolate himself from sounds that others would disregard as the hubbub of daily existence. The usual interactions of social and family life were impossible for him in this condition, and he spent long stretches of time away from hearth and home. The family was usually together much of the summer at Chatwold, their palatial estate at Bar Harbor, Maine, where Pulitzer had an imposing soundproofed addition constructed for his use. Out of the master's hearing, his secretaries referred to it as the "tower of silence." From 1889 on, a personal physician always accompanied him, and in the course of his travels he consulted many of the best medical men in Europe and America.

Complete rest was the usual prescription, but the powerful mind of Joseph Pulitzer could not be idle. It took the services of six male secretary-companions to keep it occupied by reading to him and accompanying him on walks and horseback rides, and sometimes to concerts and plays, which he enjoyed even though he could only hear them. He even employed a "musical secretary," whose main job was to be available to play the piano for him, usually in the evening after dinner. The secretaries also took his dictation of countless letters, memorandums, cables, and telegrams to his newspaper subordinates and family members.[5] These are a rich source of information about his life and the basis for two excellent biographies.[6]

Although Pulitzer Sr. had grown up in comfortable circumstances and was educated by private tutors, he had put punishing demands on himself from the time he reached the United States from his native Hungary at the age of seventeen in 1864. He was the second son of Philip Pulitzer, a prosperous grain and produce merchant, and Elize Lujza Berger, both Hungarian Jews. The future publicist, who had experienced anti-Semitism in both Hungary and the United States, did not willingly disclose his Jewish ancestry in his adopted country—even to the woman he married, fearing that her Episcopalian family might oppose the union.[7]

Following his father's death in 1858 after a long illness that considerably diminished the family's wealth, his mother had married a man he did not particularly like. These family circumstances and a certain adventuresome streak led the gangling six-footer, only sixteen years old, to apply in early 1864 for a commission in the Austrian Army. Rejected because of his age, his weak eyes, and his scrawny physique, he then applied to the French Foreign Legion and the British Army, with the same results. Finally, in Hamburg, Germany, he encountered a recruiting agent for the Union Army and signed on for service during the American Civil War, receiving in exchange his passage as well as a bounty when he reached the United States.[8] The regimentation of military life proved disagreeable to him, and he was glad when the conflict ended and he was mustered out in July 1865.

The four military skirmishes in which Pulitzer took part during his short army career were a minor prelude to numerous other challenges, scraps, and battles he faced in the dozen years after his discharge. By the time of his marriage, on June 19, 1878, to Kate Davis, daughter of well-connected Washington, D.C., parents, he had earned U.S. citizenship and clearly demonstrated the ability to succeed in three fields: journalism, politics, and law. Furthermore, he was known in political circles in both Washington and New York City as well as in St. Louis. He had been a dogged worker in the unsuccessful 1872 presidential campaign of liberal Republican Horace Greeley, whose renown as a journalist eventually was equaled if not surpassed by Pulitzer's.

Joseph Pulitzer built the foundation for his wealth and power in a rapidly growing metropolis of 311,000 people, more than half of whom were foreign-born when he arrived.[9] Unable to find work in New York after the war, Pulitzer had migrated to St. Louis, where he held a series of menial jobs, including one as a mule tender. "The man who has not cared for 16 mules doesn't know what work and troubles are," he said of that experience.[10] In 1868 he became a reporter for the German-language *Westliche Post.* St. Louis had never seen anything like him; he produced many columns of copy daily, putting nearly all the city's other reporters to shame. Even though he was writing in German, he recognized the need to learn English and rapidly became as fluent in it as he already was in German, Hungarian, and French. Though underage, he was elected to the Missouri legislature in 1869 and served one year, while continuing to work as a reporter. His·popularity was put to a test when he shot and wounded a dishonest St. Louis County official who publicly called him a liar for accusing the official in print of malfeasance. The official was angered because Pulitzer had proposed a state law to regulate county purchasing practices. Pulitzer's friends paid the $405 fine and costs for his impulsive act, and the law he proposed was adopted. In 1871, he became a part owner of the *Westliche Post,* and in 1872 he was appointed one of three St. Louis police commissioners.

Over the next four years he transacted a series of newspaper purchases and sales, including the sale of his interest in the *Westliche Post,* which left him modestly solvent. At the same time, he read law and was admitted to the bar in Washington, D.C. His interest in national politics had naturally drawn him to Washington, and after failing to find a newspaper he could run there, he was considering practicing law there when he met Miss Davis, who "was very beautiful, highly connected and in no hurry to be captured by an unknown."[11] Her parents were cousins: William Worthington Davis, a distant cousin of former Confederacy president Jefferson Davis, and Catherine Louise Worthington, of a prominent Maryland family. But her determined suitor succeeded. "I have an ideal of home and love and work—the yearning growing greater in proportion to the glimpse of its approaching realization," he wrote in his first love letter. "I am almost tired of this life—aimless, homeless, loveless, I would have said, but for you. I am impatient to turn over a new leaf and start a new life—one of which home must be the foundation, affection, ambition and occupation the cornerstones, and you my dear, my inseparable companion."[12]

Few marriages follow the course of such predictions, and theirs was no exception. After a ten-week European honeymoon, during

which he also gathered information for a series of political articles on England, France, and Germany for publication in the *New
York Sun,* the newlyweds returned in the fall to St. Louis. Pulitzer
was now sure he wanted a newspaper career—with himself in
charge, not working for someone else. He saw an opportunity
when the dilapidated, bankrupt *St. Louis Evening Dispatch* was
offered at a forced sale, and he purchased it for $2,500. Pulitzer
knew well that its main asset was a Western Associated Press
franchise, and, as he probably had foreseen, that fact proved
sufficient bait for John A. Dillon, owner of the struggling *St. Louis
Evening Post,* to propose a merger. Thus the *Post-Dispatch* was
born, its first issue dated December 12, 1878.[13] Thanks mainly to
Pulitzer's dominating ambition and skill, the enterprise wobbled
only briefly before gaining enough circulation and advertising
revenue to turn a profit. Dillon, an able editorial writer with a
quiet temperament, felt overshadowed by his whirlwind partner.
In November 1879, he offered his half-interest to Pulitzer for an
incredible $40,000, which Pulitzer paid. As an investment in his
own self-confidence, it proved a bargain. In less than five years,
the *Post-Dispatch* was doing so well that he could make the down
payment on the *World* out of *Post-Dispatch* profits. *World* profits
paid the rest of the $346,000.

From that point on, the *Post-Dispatch* became a decidedly secondary concern for Pulitzer, and his growth as the "pre-eminent
American press baron" began.[14] Within two years of his arrival in
New York, he increased the *World*'s circulation tenfold, from
15,000 to 150,000, making it "the most widely read daily in the
Western Hemisphere" largely by "concentrating on stories of time-
less appeal—sex, crime, tragedy"—as others had done before, but
without the same skill, energy, and technical brilliance. "It is not
too much to say," wrote the historian of Pulitzer's New York
triumph, "that the moment Joseph Pulitzer entered Jay Gould's
office and deposited his check on the financier's desk marked the
start of a revolution in journalism that eventually worked its
influence upon every metropolitan and rural paper published in
the United States. A great newspaper, what observers recognized
in retrospect as the first modern newspaper, was born that
moment."[15] Its proprietor would accept that conclusion but insist
that public service—not the profits of sensationalism, though

important for political and editorial independence—was his goal. He identified "teaching, teaching, teaching, not only truth per se but puncturing falsehood, humbug, demagoguery, etc.," as his newspapers' purpose, adding, "President-making may be a consequence of this."[16]

By the time Joseph Jr. was born—two years after the move to New York and the stunning success of the *World*—it was apparent that the elder Pulitzer's yearning for home and love were powerfully tempered by his zeal for daily journalism. His was not to be a conventional family circle, partly for that reason, and even more so because of the calamitous decline in his health, starting in 1887, when, with the rupture of a blood vessel, the rapid deterioration of his eyesight began.

Yet as great a preoccupation and strain as the senior Pulitzer's physical ailments became, the ties of family affection were strong. Even though family members might be separated by many miles or even oceans, constant written communication kept them closely in touch. For the two elder sons particularly, who were sent off to prep school at the ages of ten or eleven, it became second nature to record their activities in letters. As for the physical necessities, Pulitzer lived in comfort and style wherever he traveled, and he saw to it that Kate and the children inhabited handsome homes equipped with the latest conveniences and generously staffed with servants, nurses, and governesses. When the family made its annual migration each summer to Chatwold, their lavish "cottage" at Bar Harbor, some help went along, and more was engaged there. Travel, usually to European capitals or spas, was always first class. To some it undoubtedly seemed contradictory that the proprietor of the "people's champion" newspaper was living like the royalty and industrial robber barons his papers often denounced. Pulitzer showed he was aware of this when he wrote his wife: "I decidedly object to your buying any more jewelry out of the large dividends you receive. Very decidedly. . . . It is unbecoming in a woman whose husband is practically blind, a wretched invalid and has a certain public character and position."[17] The tone of that and many other letters bespeaks the nature of Pulitzer's familial relations, which were, in the words of one of his corps of male secretaries, "the strangest mixture of deep affection, anxious solicitude, arbitrariness and caprice."[18]

The first three of the seven Pulitzer children were born in St. Louis: Ralph on June 11, 1879, Lucille Irma on September 30, 1880, and Katherine Ethel on June 30, 1882. Neither of the girls survived to adulthood; Lucille died of typhoid at age seventeen, and Katherine died of pneumonia before she was two. Joseph Jr., the fourth child, was born in New York on March 21, 1885. There were two more daughters, Edith Louise, born on June 19, 1886, and Constance Helen, on December 13, 1888, and another son, Herbert, born on November 20, 1895.[19]

Mrs. Pulitzer and the children generally conformed to the patterns of life of the rich in New York society. The children were either tutored privately or attended private school, and thus came to know the children of other wealthy families. The daughters "came out" in the customary fashion of dinner parties and debutante balls. The sons attended such affairs and were thus at ease and correct in "proper society," though Joseph in later life said he had never cared for "society" in the usual sense,[20] and Ralph, at age thirty-one, published a book that gently satirized New York society.[21] The Pulitzers were in the New York Social Register from 1891 but enjoyed far from universal acceptance among the wealthy upper crust, many of whom did not appreciate the unsympathetic attention they got in the *World.* One of J.P.'s English secretaries who was not yet aware of the source of the objection commented in a letter to his wife in London that "most people here seem to look upon any sort of connection with J.P. as a very malignant form of leprosy and yet they have nothing definite to say against him."[22]

Notoriety did not concern the senior Pulitzer, for the kind of recognition he cared about had little to do with high society. Instead, he cultivated a reputation as a zealot for social reform achieved by democratic means with *his* ideas having a large role in the process. He wanted his sons to perpetuate this, and he believed that education bolstered by travel would best prepare them. He held to the then standard conception of the role of women being essentially domestic and social, which meant his daughters did not need an education beyond finishing school. However, he wanted them to be more than mere adornments, as he made clear in a letter to the headmistress of Edith's school: "I want her to be a good rather than a society woman, with high ideals and intellectual tastes and inclined to interest herself in the serious things of life."[23] The girls were to be well read, a point their father emphasized in a letter urging Kate to monitor Edith's literary selections. He had received a bill from his daughter for books listing "a number of Daudet's stories that are quite unfit for her." He asked his wife to check into this with "the utmost promptness. I would as soon give her strychnine as let her read the average French novel at her formative, impressionable age. You should watch this very sharply and tell the governess to do the same." He admitted, though, that "I did say as far as books were concerned, they could have whatever they wanted; but that naturally meant that the books must be proper and fit, subject to the mother's or governess' approval."[24] This attitude derived from Pulitzer's own literary tastes. "No man was ever quicker to spot and denounce playwright or novelist who used sex and such merely to startle or allure the reader," a secretary recalled. "On the other hand, no man was ever quicker to detect genuine sincerity of aim in even the muckiest book." He was "almost squeamishly clean-minded in the sense that he had no use whatever for smoke-room stories or smut for smut's sake. But he read literally everything in English, German and French — the last usually in German translations — that had the slightest claim to distinction."[25]

Though usually absent, Pulitzer considered himself in charge of the household as much as he was in charge of his newspapers. How faithfully his orders were carried out can only be guessed, but while it is plain that some family members took him more seriously than others, all generally respected his authority despite his frequent complaint that he was seldom obeyed. "You like to emphasize the word 'order,' my order or your order, when you refer to my wishes, or when I refer to them, especially a wish that is habitually trampled upon and disregarded," he wrote to Kate in 1894. "I wish you would not do that, because it reminds me how utterly ignored my wishes are." He complained that she had not written him "one line for over two weeks," apparently the result of a spat. "Don't you think you should have written me, no matter how angry you felt because I interfered with your pleasure? Don't you think you should have written about the children at least? Am I not entitled to that much, or that little? Again, after all it is supposed to be the first business of a wife to be interested in the comfort and condition of her husband who is absolutely without family and as helpless as I am."[26]

The unceasing references to his frailties permeated the senior Pulitzer's correspondence and his relationships. "He was complaining about his health a great deal—day after day, after day," Joseph recalled.[27] He wanted frequent letters from the children, and received many. Invariably, both the children and Mrs. Pulitzer expressed the hope when they wrote that he was feeling better and advised him to "cheer up." They usually omitted or soft-pedaled information about ills of their own, knowing that this would upset him, though there were times when the correspondence between husband and wife showed a certain competitiveness in detailing their aches and pains, as when Pulitzer wrote: "I have frightful rheumatism and have had it for the last six weeks more than in the last six years together. This morning I could hardly sponge my face or eat my bread—rheumatism in the joints of my right hand. I can now fully sympathize with you if you have the thing as badly."[28] One of Joseph's earliest letters to his father, written in the careful script of a beginner, recommended a spa: "Dear Papa, Please [underscored four times] try that place Momma has just been to."[29]

In later life, the second Joseph Pulitzer told his sons that he attributed at least part of their grandfather's preoccupation with his health to hypochondria.[30] In addition to his personal observations, he had some written evidence tending to support that judgment in some poignant, melancholy letters that had been his mother's and that he kept under lock and key. They were written during a world cruise Pulitzer took at the end of 1889 and the beginning of 1890 on the advice of physicians that he make a complete break from his newspaper concerns for the sake of his general health and particularly in order to save his eyes. In his retinue were his physician, Dr. James W. McLane; a companion, Charles B. Fearing; and the first of a long line of English secretaries, Claude Ponsonby. As the ship approached Aden, on the Red Sea, Ponsonby wrote Mrs. Pulitzer, then staying in Paris, that the cruise was having the desired effect: "He is *certainly* better than when he left, but is inclined to take a despondent view of his health and pitches into Fearing and myself when we try to cheer him up by making light of his complaints and telling him that he has already improved. His appetite is *first class.* He sleeps very fairly. Coughs only a little, very little, I may say. But that very little seems to annoy him greatly and still excites a certain amount of nervousness. . . . I can conscientiously say that you would be pleased, were you here, at the change for the better."[31] But her husband's version, written in the large scrawl his handwriting had become as his vision faded, was sharply different:

> Fearing and Ponsonby have written you all about me as it suits their fancy to think I am much better or at least to say so be it so. I am certainly no worse than when I came on ship, though I still have that *cough* in spite of every precaution and for several days felt *very* miserably. Sleep &c are all about as usual and I still continue to lose flesh. Can't wear things that were already taken in 2–3 times and my bones absolutely become melancholy, literally painful.
>
> Still I manage to preserve a little spirit and humor and hope.
>
> I write this solely because I think it may seem like an attention to you and you may like it. But it is horrible scrawling I know. It hurts my eyes and is written under electric light.[32]

In a postscript he added: "Make the children write often."

Writing on New Year's Day from Bombay, he reported that he had not improved at all and continued to sleep poorly. He hadn't been able to shake the cough, and rheumatism was bothering him as well. The voyage itself "could not have been pleasanter in most respects . . . and nearly everybody was happy." But not he. "I arrived here as tired as when I left Brindisi and after 3 nights here (*very* bad ones) have concluded to give up India and go right on by the same steamer which brought us." His companions were terribly disappointed by this decision, he said, "but I am sure that the long RR journeys and miserable noisy hotels throughout India would not have been good for me. It was the dream of my boyhood to see India and now when I am actually here I must give up my dream no matter how great the temptation." Revealing some capacity for enjoyment, he described what he had seen of India as "fascinatingly interesting. . . . If I were only half as well as I was at St. Moritz I would enjoy it greatly. As it is, even I have some pleasure and much interest in the trip." But then he became morose:

> Wish I could write more cheerfully, but I really tried hard and in vain. The year closed with the one before it represent more suffering than all the rest of my life brought me—ten times as much—I honestly think fifty times as much. And the year which opens with this day—I cannot finish the sentence.
>
> I hope before this reaches you I shall be able to cable you I am better. But just now I am not hopeful. I really feel that my health is broken and gone and that I cannot in reason expect to regain it without either that freedom from all business worry and care and the enjoyment of that domestic . . . care and peace which seem beyond my reach. Travel will not cure me. . . . I am miserable. I cannot trust myself to write more. Whatever I feel, however, you are still the only being in this world who fills my heart and mind and hope and receives my love and tenderness and affection.[33]

He seemed doomed to restlessness and worry. He consulted physicians continuously, but nearly always disobeyed their advice to retire and rest. Dr. Weir Mitchell, a New York physician, expressed his exasperation with the publisher in a letter Pulitzer asked him to write at the end of 1891: "I want to say for the hundredth time what I think in regard to your present condition. I say it again because you have asked me about it again, not that it ought to need repetition." Continuing to direct the *World* newspapers, even from afar, "will inevitably result in the total destruction of what remains to you of eyesight," Mitchell advised. Further, "it is quite impossible for you to carry on your paper under present conditions without total sacrifice of your general health." And if that weren't enough, he closed: "The course on which you are now engaged is one of physical and moral disaster."[34]

Of course, the difficulty of his condition complicated the lives of those around him. Felix Webber, Pulitzer's musical secretary in 1894 and 1895, recorded his frustrations in letters to his wife and mother in London. Unlike the physician, he did not see his employer as an invalid, "but merely a great coarse bloated millionaire who thinks that by paying people he can buy immunity from the little self-restraint that comes natural to most people (thank goodness)."[35] Webber didn't mind playing the piano for Pulitzer, but he disliked other assignments, particularly reading to and making conversation with the publisher, who was more comfortable when his mind was busy. Because of this unceasing need for mental exercise, Webber once complained, the publisher could tire out twelve secretaries in twenty-four hours. "It takes me every moment of my time to devour literature enough to keep J.P.'s mind occupied and even then my stock of conversation runs out before we get to the end of our rides and drives and I am barely one novel ahead of him. I have to have two or three in hand to feel comfortable," he wrote from Bar Harbor.[36]

During meals with the family, Webber got some intimate glimpses inside the family circle. As in many marriages, money was a source of friction between husband and wife, and neither of this pair could be described as thrifty. "It is incredible that any man could be so horribly selfish as he is," Webber wrote from New York in December 1894. "We've been going through stormy days partly because it is the beginning of the month and accounts have to be settled up. Mrs. P. says she cannot and will not run the house on $6,000 . . . a month; that it's absurd to ask her to and that . . . she cannot possibly make . . . ends meet on less than double that sum and so when her cheque was given to her for that amount for this month through the business secretary, she returned it and asked, just as the London cabby, what *that* was for, and left the task of making conversation to J.P. at meal time to the unfortunate secretaries."

Webber found the publisher brutish when he happened to be at home at the time Lucille, then fourteen, had surgery ("something cut between her nose and throat"). The first procedure failed, the operation had to be repeated the following day, and there was a considerable loss of blood. "The poor girl after suffering hours of torture fainted away when the second operation was made and then was given morphia to spare her more pain," Webber recounted.

> Mrs. P. was terribly upset with all this — never left the girl, came to meals in a peignoir with hair uncurled (a sign of

terrible anxiety with her), couldn't eat anything and began
to look very ill herself. Meanwhile the great J.P. never even
went up to see his daughter, and at dinner Mrs. P. asked
him why this was, and if he did not pity her. "Pity Lucille!"
he shouted. "No! I'm the one to pity—has no one any pity
for *me!*—does no one realize what *I* suffer! My own house
turned into a hospital! Doctors coming at all hours! You
rushing upstairs in the middle of meals, without a word of
conversation for me. No one pities me and you ask me to
pity Lucille!" After this outburst of eloquence Mrs. P. could
not bring herself to speak to him for a long time. . . . The
next day . . . she gave me instructions that J.P. was not to
be allowed upstairs, that he was to be kept down by main
force if he should want to go up, "but," she added ferociously,
"*he* won't want to come up, he won't even ask after her."
And she was quite right. The next day J.P. seems to have
realized that he had shown what a brute he is when a
message came from Lucille asking why he had not once
been to see her. He went up to her and promised her a pair
of cabs and a carriage for her to drive herself as a reward
for the pluck she had shown. By her bedside he saw piles
of flowers, and when he was told that they had been sent
by different friends of hers, he got quite jealous (jealousy
of the most intense is the only symptom of anything
approaching affection he can feel for anyone, even his own
children) and so he told me to go and order the handsomest
basket of flowers I could get, regardless of price, and have
it sent up to her. But having done so much he thought he
had quite made up for everything and began patting himself on the back for his wonderful generosity and again lost
all interest in the child and seemed bored when I asked
him if he had any preference as to the sort of flowers. "Oh,
any sort," he said impatiently, "as long as they are the
handsomest in New York." So I obeyed instructions and
spent $25 on a basket of roses.

Near the end of the letter, Webber reported that Pulitzer was
intensely interviewing men to fill a vacancy in his secretarial staff
and that a man named Harbord "stands the best chance, simply

because he never stops talking. Dull as ditch water he is, but he somehow manages to keep the ball rolling and that's the chief thing that's wanted so that the times when J.P. and Mrs. P. are not on speaking terms—which mostly happens at the beginning of the month—should be less apparent at meals."[37]

At the beginning of 1895, Pulitzer left New York for his winter retreat at Jekyll Island, Georgia, much to the relief of himself and the others left behind in New York, Webber reported, "especially Mrs. P., who got up out of bed as soon as he was gone and received lying in a chaise lounge in her boudoir in a vieux rose peignoir and a chinchilla fur rug also lined with vieux rose over her legs and plenty of white frou frou all about her. She was sighing over a portrait of J.P.'s which had just come from Paris painted by Bonnat two years ago. 'I suppose I ought to hang it in my boudoir,' she said, *but I won't;* don't you think that a large photograph is enough for me to have in my boudoir?' Then she went on to tell me that she remembered a time when J.P. had quite a sweet expression (many, many years ago)."[38]

On another occasion, Pulitzer dictated a lengthy memorandum to his wife of "rules about money matters which, I hope, you will observe and respect." The six rules, he explained, "are just intended to bring you to your senses and possibly to the appreciation of my intelligence and forbearance in the past, and also to an appreciation of the very large dividends I have made for you and given to you with pleasure on my part for your pleasure." He complained, however, that "the least you could have done would have been to give me a few words of appreciation" and that "instead of getting them I have received only blows, and hurts and injuries." The memo reveals that Mrs. Pulitzer was receiving an allowance of $100,000 a year for all her "clothes and finery, and that of the youngest two children." In addition, he would pay her traveling expenses and her stays at Aix-les-Baines "or anywhere else you go for your health strictly," but not her expenses in Paris, where, he grumbled, she had run up "large dressmakers' bills kept unpaid for a year or two . . . and then dumped upon me."[39] There would be a separate check for Edith's expenses, and the girl was to keep an account of her expenditures. Though the memorandum doesn't mention them, Ralph and Joseph, away at school, also would have been provided for separately and instructed to keep track of their costs. This they did with relative regularity, though Joseph especially needed reminders.

It would be wrong, however, to suggest that Joseph Pulitzer was a tyrant about money or an unyielding autocrat as head of the family. The fact is that he was generous in providing for himself—to the sum of $348,040 in 1897, for example[40]—as well as for his family and employees. When someone pleased him, there was a gift or a bonus. And he conceded in his memorandum of rules to Kate that "strictly speaking you can do with your own money just what you like and disregard my wishes." In St. Louis, when the first three children were quite small and his health much better, neighbors reported seeing him "sitting with his wife in the cool evening air on the front steps. His children had cut their teeth on his gold watch."[41] Joseph's earliest memory of his father was "as a very young child being on his bed, romping and playing with him."[42]

But what stayed with him most emphatically—and surely with the other children—was their father's unceasing lamenting about his health. It was a morbid undertone almost certainly calculated to produce guilt and pity. The available evidence suggests that Joseph Jr. and his sister Edith were the best at managing to achieve independence by recognizing that their father's problems did not necessarily have to become theirs. Nevertheless, as an observer of the family remarked many years later, his impression was that for all the children theirs was "a difficult kind of inheritance, because the first Pulitzer, my God, what a force of nature he was!"[43]

— 3 —

"Make a Real Man
Out of Him"

Because the first Joseph Pulitzer accomplished virtually all he did on his own initiative, he believed his children should develop self-reliance at an early age. "Father spoiled the children outrageously," Edith recalled, "but when they were 12, they were expected to be adults."[1] In 1892, the family (except Ralph, who stayed behind in prep school) went to Paris for an extended stay, mainly in the hope that putting some distance between Pulitzer and the *World* would diminish his restless worry about the coming presidential campaign. He was, he frequently admitted, "crazy about politics." The next year, Joseph, eight years old, was put into Dr. Carter's School, a boarding school in Farmborough, near

London. His only memorable experiences there were of "being
given baths by some very gruff old woman who would stand us up
in a tub and scrub us down" and of being lined up with his
classmates "on the side of a small country road at attention" as
Queen Victoria rode by. Two or three other American boys were
there, including a son of U.S. Senator George Peabody Wetmore of
Rhode Island and a Carnegie.[2]

The family returned to New York in the fall of 1893, after
summering at Bar Harbor. Joseph probably was tutored for a time,
and then he was enrolled at St. Mark's Preparatory School in
Southborough, Massachusetts—where Ralph had preceded him—a
few months short of his tenth birthday. Founded in 1865 by
Joseph Burnett, a wealthy Boston merchant and manufacturer
who came from Southborough and wanted a prestigious school in
his native town, St. Mark's was from its beginning exclusive and
fashionable. It started with only twelve boys but had more than
one hundred by the time Joseph was enrolled. Socially ambitious
parents were said to "move mountains to get their sons admitted,
and the list of the boys' names reads like a rather carefully expur-
gated Social Register of Boston and New York." It was Episcopalian in religious affiliation, and its headmaster for many years
starting in 1894 was the Rev. Dr. William Greenough Thayer.
Daily attendance at chapel was mandatory. In the introduction of
one innovation, St. Mark's became the leader in American prep
school practice: it adapted from English schools a system of
"monitors"—six or seven boys from the eldest, or sixth, form—
who had "a general oversight over the life of the boys," stood "for
the school ideals," and were expected "to exert their influence and
leadership in all school matters."[3]

Joseph was not likely to be so signally honored. "I was a bad
scholar," particularly in mathematics, he recalled. His name was
usually "way down at the bottom of the list" when grades were
posted each month. But, as would ever be the case, he enjoyed
extracurricular activities and made "quite a few friends." He considered himself a poor baseball player, an average football player,
and rather good at boxing, a sport he enjoyed into early adulthood.[4]

Joseph's father was not happy about this son's academic performance but was undoubtedly pleased that he was physically
robust and something of a scrapper. Ralph, in contrast, had always

been frail physically and had suffered particularly from asthma. Though a good student, Ralph was shy and retiring in temperament, not a competitor. Had it been possible to combine the strongest traits of each son into one individual, Pulitzer might well have done it. Ralph lacked stamina and aggressiveness, and Joseph lacked ambition. Herbert, still a child when his brothers reached adulthood, was an unknown quantity. Yet the sons were destined to inherit the newspapers, and their father had strong doubts that either of the older boys could carry on the tradition he had started. He also worried that they would squander their inheritances—as so many rich men's sons had done—rather than be productive workers. There were many examples he could cite: "Just see the Baltimore and Ohio Railroad and its wonderful system. An able father originated it and his son smashed it all to pieces.... The Missouri Pacific. Jay Gould could not educate any of his sons to even preserve what he created and the Goulds are out of it as a matter of fact, although they nominally may be on the board. Nor could Gould keep the Western Union, certainly a wonderful property and institution. They could not conserve, despite the growth of the country, what the father had created."5

Believing that education was the main hope, the senior Pulitzer took a keen interest in his sons' training for careers in journalism. There was no discussion as to whether any of them might want to do something else. "I want it perfectly understood," he instructed one son's tutor, "that I want the boy to be a publicist, not merely a journalist. I want him to be a degree higher. I want him to be interested in public questions, public causes, public welfare, public good. . . . The paper I regard as a public institution. He will be a power in the community." He asked the headmaster at St. Mark's to tailor Joseph's coursework accordingly. He saw no need for Greek, Latin, or trigonometry. "But on the other hand, nothing could be of greater importance than a thorough knowledge of *America* — of his own country, of its resources and its history—of history of every kind, of biography or geography and of the English language." Being a voracious reader himself, with an encyclopedic memory, Pulitzer wanted his sons to develop "the habit or taste for good reading" and strong, disciplined memories.

Joseph adjusted well to the regimentation of St. Mark's, but he suffered "a real jolt" when some of the boys began calling him "sheeny" and making a hissing "Shhh" as he walked by them. It was his first realization of his Jewish ancestry and caught him completely by surprise. When the headmaster, Dr. Thayer, got wind of this, he called Joseph in to reassure him that the name-calling was wrong and that it would stop. Anti-Semitism had never come up at home, but after the incident Joseph did discuss it with his mother, who by this time knew her husband's father had been Jewish—but probably not his mother, who was always identified as an Austro-German Catholic.[6] "She told me there's nothing to be ashamed of," Joseph recalled, "that the Jews were a great people. She pointed to several distinguished names in New York of that day."[7] His father never mentioned the subject to him. Though epithets such as "*Jew*seph Pulitzer" were from time to time published about the elder Pulitzer, he sublimated his irritation. As for religious practice, the Pulitzers were affiliated but relatively casual Episcopalians, Mrs. Pulitzer's denomination. The sons, however, got fairly heavy exposure to the tenets of that faith at St. Mark's. Pulitzer himself rarely attended church, but he did contribute.[8]

Kate Pulitzer's influence was felt in other ways too. When there was a paternal outburst about a child's behavior or the failure to write to their father, or low grades, she would act as a buffer. "I always felt that she stood by me, so to speak," Joseph recalled. That went for the other children as well, and there were strong bonds of affection and understanding between Mrs. Pulitzer and her children and among the children themselves. This was not a conspiracy to disobey Pulitzer so much as an agreement among them that in his nervous condition he could be unreasonably demanding. Sometimes Kate met this attitude directly, as when she answered her husband's complaint that he found Edith cold-natured. "The great trouble is that she is so like you," she wrote. "Your two natures are sure to clash at times. You are both emotional, both dogmatic and both lacking in self discipline, you because you had a man's work to do when still a boy and in disciplining others no time was left to disciplining yourself, she because she is very much your daughter." Then she added, "I assure you living in such a strenuous family is very puzzling to a nature so little complex as mine."[9]

Shortly before his fifteenth birthday in March 1900, Joseph

wrote a lengthy letter from St. Mark's asking if his father would get him a boat known as a "knockabout" to use at Bar Harbor that summer. A used one would cost about $1,300, he said, adding a gentle reminder that Ralph had been given a boat. He also would need a man to serve as skipper and suggested that his father hire one who had worked for them the previous year. He then listed the books he had been reading, which included *The Honorable Peter Stirling* by Leicester Ford and a Richard Harding Davis story, "The Princess Alice," and dutifully commented on the *World,* which was being sent to him. Its editorials "have been quoting or mentioning other papers a good deal," he wrote. "For instance the other day it said something like this: 'We congratulate the Times and Herald in their fight against gambling dens.' Is this not a new idea?"[10]

Joseph's career at St. Mark's came to an abrupt end the next year, when he was sixteen, putting him under a huge cloud in his father's estimation. As a lark, Joseph and several schoolmates had walked the short distance from St. Mark's to the village of Southborough, where they bought beer. When they returned to the school, which was just a single large building, it was locked. They decided to get in by climbing the ivy to an open window, with Joe Pulitzer leading the way. He made it to the window and fell inside. It was the bedroom of Headmaster and Mrs. Thayer. He was expelled.[11]

When this news reached Joseph's father, he exploded. "It is not the incident, but the causes," Pulitzer exclaimed. "The character, the loss of moral sense and loss of honor involved in it. . . . He has very little mind, very little intelligence, very little head but a great deal of the animal instinct, a great deal of the passion for pleasure and nothing else. No respectable aims, no high ambitions, aspirations, ideas, tastes, so far as I can see, except for the physical pleasures."[12] He blamed his wife for spoiling the boy and said he would now take full charge of his upbringing "on the condition that she will not interfere, cannot interfere. Must submit to my judgment. Must aid, help, cooperate with me to save that boy. I would have my right arm cut off to feel sure that boy will have an honorable, happy, useful career, and not disgrace my name." He was ready to give up on formal schooling for Joseph because "no amount of school will reach the root of the trouble, or will touch it even." Instead, "moral education" was the "stern necessity" for one who had "committed a crime against his father, his mother, his sisters and his own good name and future. This should be rubbed into him. That might, with the other circumstances, make a real man out of him, if he has the pride and the strength of character to say: 'Now I will show Mr. Thayer and the world, I will show my mother, that I will overcome and outlive this and be a man of some use in the world.'"

Joseph returned to New York, where he was put in the charge of a tutor, but the main purpose was to bring him into closer contact with the *World*'s editors and managers. Thus his schooling as a journalist, with his father as headmaster, was to begin. Until that was under way, Pulitzer insisted on knowing how his son was using his time: "Riding in the park? Every day how spent from morning to night, hour by hour. How he spends the evening."[13] The answers to those questions do not survive, but one can be sure they were supplied. At Pulitzer's direction, no doubt, Joseph and Mr. Sheafe, his tutor, visited Washington, D.C. "We spent a good deal of time in the House and Senate but unfortunately, heard no good speeches," he reported. "We also went out to Mt. Vernon. I found this place most picturesque and absorbingly interesting. I saw that my cousin, Varina, Mrs. Jeff Davis, has given several old Washington relics to the place."[14] He also ran into Jim Corbett, the boxer, whom he had met previously, "and chatted a few words with him," he related. "He is not as one might suppose, a loudly dressed cheap sport. Instead, he dresses quietly and well and has a very pleasant manner." Sheafe was invited to a party given by Miss Alice Roosevelt, and Joseph got a look at her. "She seemed rather attractive," he wrote, then crossed out "rather" and wrote in "very." He was developing a keen appreciation for the ladies.

He gradually was maturing in other ways as well, particularly in the direction of self-possession and confidence not unlike, ultimately, that of his father's, minus, notably, the strains of ill health. James W. Barrett, a *World* city editor who knew them later in life, described the Pulitzer brothers this way: "Ralph was and perhaps is the idealist, Joseph is the fighter, and Herbert is the stubborn one."[15] Their father embodied all three qualities in Barrett's analysis and recognized that neither of his eldest sons could truly be described in the trite phrase "a chip off the old block." Pulitzer had the highest hopes for Herbert, but died before the boy was old enough either for an accurate assessment of his potential or for a trial under his father's direction. Ralph and Joseph did endure such scrutiny, with harsher effects on the more cerebral Ralph than on the scrappier, more resilient Joseph. Of the two, Ralph comes across as the more diplomatic—if not awestruck—in dealing with his formidable parent. He was more anxious to please and more harshly stung by a reproof or criticism than his brother. "I am sure you would be pleased if you could know how a word of praise from you makes me feel for the rest of the day as though I had just had a big drink of whiskey—so happy and exhilarated, and as if I could surmount any obstacle or perform any task," he once wrote to his father.[16]

Joseph, on the other hand, could challenge, contradict, and at times even poke fun at some of his father's strictures. Acknowledging in a letter from St. Mark's that Pulitzer had "forbidden" his going to Harvard, Joseph responded testily: "I *do* hope you won't object to Yale."[17] Even before his expulsion from prep school, he had been told he would not attend Harvard, presumably because of his lackluster grades. Still, this came as something of a shock, since St. Markers traditionally went to Harvard and Joseph had expected to follow Ralph, who received his degree in 1900.

But, whether because of a certain maturity or lack of it, even as an adolescent Joseph had a sense of mental balance that kept him from brooding at any length about displeasing his father. To do so, after all, was inevitable, and the youth seemed able to accept this as a natural consequence of living in what musical secretary Felix Webber described as "the uncomfortable bosom of the Pulitzer establishment." Webber described "the system the P's go on with their employees" in terms that also fit Pulitzer's relations with his two eldest sons: "If 100 difficult things are done and well-done and one little slip is made; forget the 100 things but remember and rub well in the one slip, and write it down so as to turn to it for future occasions in case once the 100 things should be well done and there should be no slip."[18] This was embellished by Alleyne Ireland, a secretary during the last year of Pulitzer's life, who observed that "so far as the quantity and quality of work were concerned it was an easier task to be one of Mr. Pulitzer's secretaries than to be one

of his sons. I have never seen men put to a more severe test of
industry, concentration and memory than were Mr. Ralph and Mr.
Joseph, Jr." He attributed this to Pulitzer's "love of power and to
his horror of wasted talents. . . . What you knew and what you
were able to do, once you had reached a certain standard, became
secondary in his interest to what you could be made to know and
what you could be taught to do. He was never content that a man
should stand upon his record."[19]

As harsh as that sounds, it comes close to describing what
surely was Ralph's assessment of his father's expectations of him
in shouldering ever greater responsibilities at the *World* after he
finished college. For his efforts he so seldom got a word of praise
that "a big drink of whiskey" was an apt description of his reaction.
His father's explanation of his brusque behavior, according to
Webber, was "that out of all the men who had amounted to anything in this world (Napoleon, J.P. & Co.) not one had had a
tolerable temper and that a good temper was entirely incompatible
with greatness in any line."[20]

Webber also described the publisher in terms that probably
figured in Joseph's interest in going off to college, whether Harvard
or elsewhere: "He's got a way of keeping all your nerves on the
bristle and even if for some time he doesn't say or do anything
disagreeable, there is always the fear that he will. Leaving him is
just like getting up from the dentist's chair and letting all one's
nerves relax again."[21] It is doubtful that Joseph reacted as severely
as that, but he surely felt his father's intensity firsthand in 1901
and 1902, between the time he left St. Mark's and January 1903,
when he was sent to St. Louis for his first intensive course in
newspaper-making. He was an interested and apt pupil, but this
didn't keep him from hoping for a chance at what he envisioned to
be the greater freedom of college life.

Although he never saw his father at work in either the New
York or the St. Louis office, he had essentially the same experience during those two summers at Bar Harbor, where he spent
the mornings on a Chatwold veranda with his father and a secretary while the publisher dictated memorandums. In the afternoons, they went horseback riding for about two hours, something his father handled well, despite his blindness. (There always
was a watchful groomsman riding nearby.) Joseph also was with

his father part of the fall and winter, cruising on Pulitzer's yacht. When they were not together, Joseph was in New York working with his tutor, Sheafe. He reported reading a biography of Benjamin Franklin, Story's *Commentaries on the Constitution* ("an extremely interesting but hard subject"), and *Principles of Argumentation,* a book used in a sophomore course at Harvard.[22] He also was reading the New York papers, and he commented that the comic "Alphonse and Gaston" was a great hit in archrival William Randolph Hearst's Sunday *Journal:* "Everyone says 'After you my dear Gaston,' now."[23]

He knew by this time that his father valued any "talk making" feature for its ability to spread a paper's popularity and increase its circulation, and so would be interested in that observation. In fact, a Hearst-Pulitzer tug-of-war over the "Yellow Kid" comic feature was the source of the "yellow journalism" tag used to describe the sensationalism of the *World* and the *Journal* at the turn of the century,[24] which ended in an infamous duel of shrieking headlines and dramatic illustrations during the Spanish-American War of 1898. By the time Ralph and Joseph were ready to begin their apprenticeships, the morning *World*, which Pulitzer considered his flagship, was using fewer stories of sin and crime and concentrating its attention on crusades for social and economic improvements that would benefit the working classes. While it lost circulation, it remained popular and profitable, and Pulitzer saw that his editors remained fully aware of the relationship between sales and entertainment.[25]

He was, after all, a businessman who knew that a sound financial base was essential for his newspapers to survive and to do good works. Therefore, he wanted his sons to understand first of all the operation of the newspapers as businesses. In January 1903, he sent Joseph to St. Louis with a detailed list of instructions on how he was to learn the operations of the advertising, circulation, and business departments by working in each of them. He wanted his son first to understand "the property side." Then, "As to the ethical side, the paper there is a public institution. . . . You can have your mind and spirit in that direction but can study it later." The object was, he instructed his son's supervisors, "to cultivate the habit of concentration and accuracy and neatness" and "to give practice in figuring in which he is very weak; to compel him particularly to make small calculations in his head." He should "be polite to everybody down to the office-boy" and "consider himself not the proprietor's or the rich man's son, not entitled to luxury, but like any other worker." He was to "study, watch, learn what workers and particularly managers are doing," until he understood that "the life and blood of the property" are "in circulation, which springs from news and advertising, which springs from circulation." On Saturdays he need only report to the paper in mid-afternoon and "stay till the last edition has gone to press." On Sunday, he could "make calls, amuse himself, and see the young ladies so long as he does his work during the week." He was to keep a daily diary of his work in shorthand and write his father twice a week.[26]

On his first morning in St. Louis, after getting a room at the Westmoreland Hotel, Joseph dutifully bought a diary, a fountain pen, and some notebooks and arranged to take an hour-long shorthand lesson five days a week at Barnes Business College. He was introduced to the staff and had "a chat with every one of them, telling them what I'm here for, how little I know, etc." Most "offered their help any time I want it."[27] Two weeks later, his father ordered a change in Joseph's routine. He was to spend two hours every afternoon in the pressroom and in the mechanical and circulation departments "until he knows every machine, every man and every method." He was to be taught to understand the weekly report sent to his father "until he has every comparison and figure at his finger ends." Advertising manager William C. Steigers was to "teach him general business methods and potash principles."[28]

"Potash," meaning "advertising," was one of thousands of code words Joseph Pulitzer sometimes used in his communications. "Nelson" (for "net profit"), "curate" (for "circulation"), and "potash" were three of the most frequently used. There were code names for all the major editors and managers, for family members, and for competing papers and their editors. Pulitzer himself was "Andes," which was used often, and "Marksman," which was not. J.P. Jr. was "Velocity," "Vandalia," or "Pulitjos"; Ralph was "Cybria." The code words for rival publishers began with "G": Adolph S. Ochs of the *New York Times* was "Glucose"; William Randolph Hearst was "Gush." The months of the year began with "T"—January was "Toilet," August was "Tomato," December was "Tonic." There were codes for circulation figures in increments of 1,000, such as "Afraid" for 343,000 and "Afresh" for 344,000. Pulitzer's displeasure could be expressed in one word, "Uneasy," meaning "On the first of the month there was an article, the tone of which I did not like, on the subject of . . . " Perhaps the most used word of all was "sedentary," meaning "a prompt reply is required." It is possible that the publisher's satisfaction with the St. Louis paper's circulation and business success influenced the choice of its code name, "Grasping." The rival *Globe-Democrat* was "Vampire."[29]

Newspaper Apprentice to Harvard Man

Within a few days of Joseph's arrival in St. Louis, Florence D. White, the overseer of the eastern and western newspapers, wrote Pulitzer: "The indications are toward a strong probability that he will become a St. Louisan." White quoted the young man as saying, "The fellows here are a nicer set than in the World office," to which the reply had been that *Post-Dispatch* workers are under less pressure than those at the *World*. "Joseph promptly differed with the view and said that he thought the men are really busier than those in the New York office."[1]

That may have been because he did not want his father to think he was having an easier time of it than Ralph at the *World*. In any case, he enjoyed his work and felt comfortable in his routine. Knowing that his father was a stickler about putting in a full day, he reported arriving at the office seven minutes late one morning because the streetcars had been slow. However, he and Steigers took only fifty minutes for lunch, "so that evens up on my 7 late minutes of this morning and gives me 3 to the good." He particularly enjoyed his time at the want-ad counter, calling it "really more interesting work than it may seem. You're in contact with many different kinds of people on so many errands. There are some really very funny scenes up there, if you watch out for them." The reactions of women who came for replies to their "Personal" ads, some of whom would get forty or fifty answers, amused him. He enjoyed it when "occasionally flirtatious girls float in and ask a few questions in a most amiable manner." There were times, too, "when you see some pathetic things. As . . . when a young girl asked for answers and there were none for her. That she was surprised and hurt was quite evident. I suppose she was in some sort of trouble and put in a personal ad."[2]

Because White spent most of his time in New York, *Post-Dispatch* general manager Frank R. O'Neil became Joseph's immediate supervisor. After Joseph had been at the paper for nearly a month, O'Neil described his routine to Pulitzer in detail. He was literally teaching Joseph the business from the ground up, starting with how steam to run the presses was generated in the boilers of the mechanical department. "This method will characterize his instruction, from basement to mail room," O'Neil wrote, "and will, I think, satisfy him that there is no department of the business which need be considered a mystery, or too intricate in its details for him to investigate, whenever investigation is desirable." He added that Joseph's "performance is not at all perfunctory, but is prosecuted with real interest."[3]

Despite that reassurance, Pulitzer wired Joseph two days later that he didn't think the boy was taking his work seriously. "I most decidedly am 'settled down' and am not thinking of 'getting off' by any means," he responded. "You must know by this time that I *am* determined to learn as much as I can. If I wasn't, I would not be staying down here later than necessary every night, nor would I have been so particular about not arriving later than 8 in the mornings. And furthermore, I flatter myself with the thought that since I've been out here, now one month, I've really been quite sensible. Much more sensible, in fact, than I supposed I would be." He did admit, though, that on occasion an impulse to slack off "hits me like a cyclone. And it's not such an easy job to stop it." He said he hoped to be allowed to stay there "two months more at least."[4]

When it came to Joseph's social life, Pulitzer wanted to direct that too, and he sent his son several letters of introduction to St. Louis friends of some prominence that the boy was to use in his "social campaign."[5] Joseph was slow at getting this under way, but he reported delivering a few letters, including one to former Missouri governor David R. Francis. Francis arranged a country club membership for him and told him that his home and library were always open to him. Everyone Joseph met was "very decent," he reported, and added, "Of course they haven't received me like Prince Henry, but why should they?"[6]

While Joseph's candor and ease of expression suggest a strong streak of independence, he usually kept in mind his father's sensitive condition. He tried, as he knew the secretaries did, to divert Pulitzer's attention from his ills with detailed descriptions of people and places. He also knew the value of humor. When he went to dinner and the theater one evening with a Mr. and Mrs. Carruthers, he described her as "a peach" and "of the same southern type as Mother though much more pronounced, her hair and eyes and skin being much darker and her color brighter." She was "one of the most southern Southerners I've ever met" and became so excited when the orchestra began to play "Dixie" that he thought she "would fall out of the box in her enthusiasm. Luckily the music ended just at that time and thus a horrible catastrophe was averted."[7]

In the same letter he mentioned meeting a woman "whose mother was a Miss Dickson, an old friend of yours, I believe, in the days when you were a Beau Brummell here." He noted, "People still tell me almost every day that I remind them of you. . . . Of course I don't resemble you *now,* but perhaps I do resemble you in your youth, when these men knew you. . . . At any rate I hope so." He then gave a description of St. Louis, comparing it to New York:

> It's an entirely different town from N.Y. and its inhabitants are an entirely different class of people. Here everyone

FIG. 1. Joseph Pulitzer II in 1889, age 4, at the cornerstone-laying for the New York *World* building, Park Row and Frankfort Street, New York City.

FIG. 2.   Front page of the New York *World*, October 11, 1889, reporting the cornerstone-laying for the newspaper's new building.

FIG. 3. Father. Joseph Pulitzer (I), founder of the *St. Louis Post-Dispatch* and proprietor of the New York *World*. Portrait by John Singer Sargent, 1905.

FIG. 4. Mother. Kate Davis Pulitzer. Portrait by John Singer Sargent, 1905. For many years after her death, this portrait was moved each summer to the Pulitzer summer home at Bar Harbor, Maine, with the family of Joseph Pulitzer II. For the remainder of the year, it hung in the St. Louis home with the portrait of Joseph Pulitzer (I).

FIG. 5.   Joseph Pulitzer (I), wearing goggles over his blind eyes, on the arm of a secretary (probably Harold Stanley Pollard). As usual, the secretary was well stocked with material to read to J.P. About 1910.

FIG. 6. Joseph Pulitzer II aboard one of his first yachts, which he sailed between New York City and Bar Harbor, Maine. He is playing "baseball" with a loaf of bread for a bat. The "catcher" may be Ephraim Catlin, a friend from St. Louis. About 1906.

FIG. 7. The steam yacht *Liberty*, built for Joseph Pulitzer (I) in 1907 so that the ill but restless publisher could travel the world unimpeded by the schedules and noisy passengers on commercial liners. There were occasional family gatherings aboard the yacht.

FIG. 8.   Joseph Pulitzer II, age 25, with Norman G. Thwaites, one of the elder J.P.'s secretaries. Thwaites did what he could to shield Joseph from some of his father's emotional outbursts. At Cap Martin, France, 1910. Joseph got permission to marry on this visit to his peripatetic parent.

FIG. 9. Sisters of Joseph Pulitzer II: Constance (left), age 21, and Edith, 23,
at Cap Martin, France, 1910.

FIG. 10.   The gold-domed, ultramodern *World* building at the corner of Park Row and Frankfort Street, New York City. Erected in 1889–90 to house the morning, evening, and Sunday *World* newspapers. The elder Pulitzer's seldom-used office and those of his editorial writers were in the dome. About 1910.

FIG. 11.   The *St. Louis Post-Dispatch* building, 12th Boulevard and Olive Street, St. Louis, about 1917, where Joseph Pulitzer II was editor and publisher until his death in 1955. Open windows provided slight relief from the summer heat.

FIG. 12.   Joseph Pulitzer II and his first wife, the former Elinor Wickham of St. Louis, probably during their wedding trip in the summer of 1910.

FIG. 13.   Kate Davis Pulitzer, mother of Joseph Pulitzer II, in mourning black for her husband, who died the previous year. Seated at a picnic on Turtle Island off Bar Harbor, Maine, between her son and his first wife, Elinor Wickham Pulitzer. September 15, 1912.

FIG. 14.   Elinor Wickham Pulitzer reading to her son, Joseph Pulitzer III (always known as Joseph Pulitzer Jr.), about 5 years old, on the grounds of their St. Louis home. Probably 1918. She and J.P. II also had two daughters, Kate Davis and Elinor. Elinor Wickham Pulitzer died following an automobile accident in 1925.

FIG. 15.   Joseph Pulitzer III, age 9; his mother, Elinor Wickham Pulitzer;
and former French Premier Georges Clemenceau. Clemenceau was a guest
of the Pulitzers in St. Louis in December 1922, for whom they remodeled
a room in their home, known thereafter as the "Clemenceau Room." In later
years the room was used to display works of modern art when J.P. III began
his collection, which became one of the world's finest.

FIG. 16. "Chatwold," the Pulitzer "cottage" at Bar Harbor, Maine, which the family used from 1893 until 1942. It was torn down in 1946. Seen from the ocean side, the first Joseph Pulitzer's so-called "Tower of Silence," specifically built to insulate him from outside sound (which it did not), is at the right; the main house, with 26 rooms and 7 bathrooms, is at the left.

FIG. 17. "Chatwold," as it nestled into the shoreline of Mount Desert Island near the village of Bar Harbor, Maine. The 15-acre site also had a separate servants' dwelling, a caretaker's cottage, and a large stable. The tower, which had an ocean-fed swimming pool in its basement, was removed in 1936.

FIG. 18. Bookplate designed for Joseph and Elinor Wickham Pulitzer depicts the second J.P.'s enthusiasms for fishing, hunting, and sailing and the large home they built on the 100-acre Lone Tree Farm in St. Louis County (now Ladue).

FIG. 19. Rear of house at Lone Tree Farm, the St. Louis County home of Joseph Pulitzer II, about 1924. Seated on the grass are two of the three children of Joseph and Elinor Wickham Pulitzer: Joseph Pulitzer III and Kate Davis Pulitzer.

FIG. 20. Morning room of the house at Lone Tree Farm in 1924. The decor largely reflects the taste of Elinor Wickham Pulitzer. Because her husband liked it, J.P. II's second wife, Elizabeth Edgar Pulitzer, made few changes in the furnishings.

works. You never see a man, except on Sundays, in anything but business clothes. . . . Westerners don't pay much
attention to "style" of which you see so much in N.Y.
They don't dress very well. This applies especially to the
women. Of course the town is a filthy one, though I have
become accustomed to this by now. And the disgusting
filthy habit of spitting prevails everywhere. On one occasion, in a street car, I became so mad at a man that
was making a hog of himself, that I could hardly re-
strain myself from telling him to quit it. Thank the Lord
the Mayor signed an anti-spitting ordinance the other
day which may amount to something; though I doubt it.
I don't think the average Westerner could be happy without spitting.

For exercise, Joseph spent some evenings after work at a gym-
nasium, boxing with a sparring partner, once receiving "an artisti-
cally bruised rib, which I notice occasionally, but which really
doesn't amount to anything."[8] He also enjoyed boxing as a spectator,
and described in colorful detail a bout at the West End Club,
which he saw with advertising manager William Steigers and
editorial page editor George S. Johns, between Billy Schreck and
Cyclone Kelly: "They fought for 4 rounds during which time
Schreck dropped the Cyclone about 8 times. At the end of the 4th
the police sergeant signalled to the referee to stop the fight, which
he very justly did, giving the decision to Schreck. Kelly was yellow
(this means a coward) and at one time lowered his head, turned
tail and ran from one corner to the other, with Schreck in hot
pursuit. The house roared."[9]
Pulitzer was especially interested in hearing about any young
women his son might meet and asked Joseph several times
for word on this subject. The first one he met was Irene Catlin, whose father, tobacco manufacturer and financier Daniel
Catlin, was a friend of the elder Pulitzer—and, as events trans-
pired, the uncle of Joseph's first wife. Miss Catlin was an unlikely match for him, Joseph explained, "as she is no longer
a chicken, having been out, I am told, for 9 years. She's a bit
too old for me, though I've called on her twice and she has
really been very nice to me."[10] Pulitzer asked for a description

of Miss Catlin, including, apparently, the shape of her nose. Joseph obliged:

> In the first place, she is about 25 years old. She is a girl you would notice if you saw her on the street, on account of her height, for she is as tall as Edith. She has a good figure and is really a handsome, well developed woman. She is not at all Western except in her pronunciation. She has been in the East and abroad so much that she has quite an atmosphere of the East about her. She dresses very stylishly, usually in a certain kind of gown that women wear now-a-days which shows their figures off to good advantage. . . . Her nose is not large. Whether it's pretty or not, I don't know. Unless they are ugly, I never seem to notice noses. She has pretty, twinkling, narrow, half-shut eyes, I think blue in color. Not the sleepy kind of half closed eyes, but the bright merry kind.[11]

On another occasion he and a friend found that an attractive Miss Dula, whom they had met at a concert, was not at home when they called, "so her staid, elderly and altogether 'boresome' sister came down and bored us for a while until we could escape."[12] They were more fortunate at the Esponschied household, where they called next and were invited to supper. The father had known Pulitzer many years before and recounted how the publisher had vowed that, while he could never be president because he was a foreigner, someday he would elect a president. "And if you behave yourself and do what I tell you I might consider you as a possibility," he had told Esponschied. The youngest daughter in the family was Joseph's age, having made her debut that year. He thought she was both pretty and unusually bright. She "always chirped into the conversation, whether it was concerning the World's Fair [scheduled to open in St. Louis the following year] or Roosevelt's chances for re-election."[13] He was asked to call again, and planned to, but was summoned back to New York before he got the chance.

On another subject, he showed an awareness of business ethics as well as readiness to advise his father by questioning a claim printed on a *World* envelope that it had the largest circulation of all papers printed in English. "If that's an old statement, once true, and now no longer true, I think it should be changed," he suggested.[14] Though no one but his father and Pulitzer's secretaries knew it, he also began what could rightly be called his first crusade—for more honest advertising—before he had been in St. Louis a month and was still six weeks short of his eighteenth birthday. He objected to the advertising of cure-alls, home remedies, and self-proclaimed medical practitioners, much of which was published in both the *World* and the *Post-Dispatch,* politely asking his father to "please complain about the medical ads on Sunday. They're disgusting."[15] Pulitzer ignored it this time, but Joseph returned to the subject periodically over the next several years.[16]

In fact, Joseph's only frustration during the two months he spent in St. Louis that year was that he heard so seldom from his father and was kept in the dark as to his father's short-range and long-range plans for him. He was quite content to stay, he emphasized, "as I am now well under weigh and I think it would be too bad to cut me away *too* soon. I think they out here want me to stay."[17] In early March, he suggested that Pulitzer have him come to New York for just a few days when Pulitzer expected to be there, and then send him back to St. Louis. He did hope, however, to spend part of the summer at Bar Harbor and asked whether his father would again let him have a boat and hire William Conary— who became a lifelong employee and friend—as his yachtsman, as he had been the previous two summers.[18]

Joseph was slowed down for a time in early March because he was having some difficulty with his vision. "I hope you won't object to my having laid off as I have," he wrote, "but when anything connected with my *eyes* goes wrong I always immediately run to a Dr. For I think I appreciate the value of eyesight better than most people."[19] Following a trip to Chicago for a few days to be with his mother and brother Ralph, who were passing through, Joseph reported: "After having them painted almost every day my eyes are practically well again."[20] It was a temporary reprieve. By the time he was thirty-five, he had lost the vision in his left eye because of a detached retina. There had been a gradual loss to about 50 percent vision in his right eye and, like his father, the paper he edited and virtually everything else he "read" had to be read to him.

In the same letter, he took credit for having done "a little practical work for the paper" by telling managing editor Harry L. Dunlap to telegraph the *World* and ask it to check the accuracy of a story it had sent to St. Louis announcing the engagement of Harold Vanderbilt to Miss Violet Cruger. Joseph said he knew young Vanderbilt "and I know that he is such a bashful, unsophisticated boy that no thought of marriage has ever entered his head." He doubted that Vanderbilt even knew Miss Cruger. *Evening World* city editor Charles E. Chapin made inquiries and found that Joseph was correct.

Within a week, there was a parental command to return to New York, where he saw for the first time the new Pulitzer home at 7 East Seventy-third Street, which his father called "an utter, wretched, miserable failure so far as the main principle is concerned, which is to keep the noises of the main house out of my bed-room."[21] For that reason, Pulitzer's stays there were relatively short.

Before leaving for quieter surroundings he granted a wish of Joseph's, who had become eighteen on March 21, to have a new boat. It was a small yacht capable of cruising from New York up to Bar Harbor. "Let me thank you a thousand times for the boat," he wrote. "She has two staterooms and a cabin for our use, and has crew's quarters and a galley and stove up forward, entirely separated."[22] Joseph used her on weekends and spent the rest of his time in the *World* business offices, which didn't interest him much. "I am progressing gradually," he said of the work, "but I fear I was never cut out for a cashier. I have no more accuracy in me than in a $1.35 watch." He assured his father that he was not being tempted by city pleasures: "With the possible exception of seeing a 'perfect lady' once in a very long while, I feel sure that I can keep straight . . . what with being well occupied all day, not drinking, not having a liking for gambling, not having the money even if I *did* like it, and last but not least, having 6:30 A.M. staring me in the face every morning."

At the end of July, his father—now staying in London—gave him a two-week vacation at Bar Harbor, after which he returned to the *World* business office. There was little communication between father and son until late September, when Joseph asked, "Won't you let me know what you hear about me from the office? I always like to know the unfavorable things people think about me."[23] Characteristically, Pulitzer didn't respond to the question, but he did admit that he had lost touch with what Joseph had been doing at the *World* and asked for a report: "You need not be afraid of giving me any number of details. Sometimes the simplest details suggest light, thought and character." He urged him to study "particularly what other men are doing. If you could simply learn to know who is really doing the real work of direction, suggestion, initiative, from whom the ideas emanate, you would be doing capital work."[24] That the head man always had to know who was doing what became a refrain Joseph heard countless times over the next eight years. The senior Pulitzer regarded it as the foundation of his success. Although he didn't live to see it happen, that injunction—and a good many others—stuck with his namesake son.

Joseph was much happier working at the *Post-Dispatch* than at the *World*. In New York the training program for him was not as structured or as congenial. At the *Post-Dispatch,* Joseph's desk had been only a few feet from O'Neil's, and he regularly spent time with staff members outside of work, but at the *World* he had no assigned space, and instead moved from department to department observing others at work. The New York and St. Louis experiences were alike, however, in concentrating on the business—or publisher's—side of the operation rather than news and editorial work. Joseph's introduction to the journalistic side came in December 1903 when he was assigned, as an observer only, to the *World* newsroom.

In January he asked for a more active role, writing that *World* editor Bradford Merrill "wants me to report": "So do I. It's the only job in sight that will produce that sense of duty and responsibility in me which you desire. I'd either have to toe the mark and 'make good' or be laughed at. I feel confident that the latter would not be the result."[25] He wrote frequently in late January and early February, comparing the relative strengths and weaknesses of the *World* and its competitors and reporting his observations of the newsroom. "The Herald was a better paper than the World today," said one letter. "Their best story, about Harry Lehr, proves a fake. The J's [Hearst's *New York Journal*] pathetic and strikingly pretty picture of the boy beheaded by mother is also a fake. . . . Thayer explained what the City news covers and how it's organized, etc." He conveyed his attitude toward how he was spending his time in this comment: "Day was generally stupid with little to observe."[26]

A week later he suggested using a credit line when a story from another paper was reprinted in the *World,* because "that would look to the ordinary reader like fair honest work, showing him that if we lift a story we are willing to give credit for it. . . . Also, if the story should prove a fake, it would expose the faking paper. This stealing of other men's stories in my opinion is a despicable practice." And as for medical advertising: "Page 9 of this morning's World, the home paper of N.Y., was positively repulsive and disgusting. I showed it to Brad. I enclose the page. For heaven's sake have these medical ads killed. I neither know what they're worth nor do I care."[27] Again the response was silence. Pulitzer knew perfectly well what those ads were worth. Back in his St. Louis days, when he could read the paper himself, he had urged advertising manager Steigers to get more "Eastern business": "There is a regular boom of medical ads of which we have very little. We must get at least those big advertisers to *commence* with us who are in all prominent papers."[28]

Joseph's outspokenness may have had something to do with the fact that he had heard nothing from his father about whether he could do some reporting. In early February he tried again: "I begin to fear that education by observation is theoretically fine but practically useless. Experience is what counts. That's why I think I should report. When may I begin to do so? Please answer soon."[29]

The disappointing answer came two days later in a telegram. The observation method was to continue, but not in the newsroom. He was to return to the business office for further study of advertising rates, circulation figures, and the cost of paper and ink. Joseph thought he had had enough of all that. "I consider the change you propose absolutely unwise," he responded. "If I did not know that in making the change you have my welfare and improvement in mind, I should consider it most unfair." He complained that just as he had gotten to know the editors and reporters "I am to leave them, to take up a new business job and a purely imaginative and unproductive job at that. I tell you, Father, this sort of education is the surest possible means of destroying my ambition and of making me feel disgusted with the whole business. . . . " He offered this proposition: "Don't you think you might give me one chance to 'make good'? Give me a week or two weeks or a month in which to do reporting. Then if I have proved myself a damned fool and a failure, put me at whatever work you desire. That's not demanding more than any ordinary editor's son would demand. And it's the only way, *they all say,* to make an editor out of me."[30]

Four days later, Joseph was both blunt and somewhat sarcastic in a letter that began by asking Pulitzer to review his son's financial situation and "kindly wire me what you decide, for this is already the 8th of Feb. and you know my regard for regularity and method!"[31] As for his work assignment: "I am now resigned to my fate and am determined to plug away again at the business." He had reported to business manager Don C. Seitz. "When we have decided on a sensible, practical job (for the mere studying of reports doesn't amount to a damn), I shall let you know," Joseph wrote his father.

> The reports, you may think, are your key to the whole business, but they are not and cannot be, mine. For you have the knowledge of the business, gained by experience, which *I* have not. To me the reports are but strings of figures, varying slightly perhaps, but that's all. It is for that reason that I contend that your "observation" plan of education is no good. At least for a beginner. The only way I can really learn a thing is by doing it myself. It's for that reason that I know at this moment how to open mail and how to receive wants. They, of course, are unimportant parts of the machine, but that is no reason why I should not learn to operate the important parts in the same manner.

He had not, he wrote a few days later, "entirely dropped the news end of the shop," but usually went up there for "half an hour or so" after lunch to chat with the editors, read the assignment schedules and daily report, and thereby "keep in touch with them all upstairs."[32]

New developments, the origins of which are not clear (Joseph, in later years, suspected his mother's hand was in it),[33] showed that Pulitzer was either approached about or indicated that he would listen to arguments on whether Joseph should attend Harvard. The boy's time at St. Mark's had been far from a total loss. While there, he had earned sixteen of the twenty entrance "points" needed to be admitted to Harvard "with conditions." He would need twenty-six points to be admitted unconditionally. His tutor, Sheafe, recommended that he be given a chance to earn the additional points by examination, saying they would not be difficult if Joseph prepared for them with the help of a tutor. Unable to do it himself, Sheafe recommended another tutor. Sheafe thought Harvard training would give Joseph "poise and self control" and development "he cannot get anywhere else." He thought any length of time there would be beneficial, even one year, but urged that Joseph be allowed to stay three years, which he considered sufficient time to earn a bachelor's degree. He said a man who takes four years "has not enough to do."[34]

The new tutor was W. F. Woodward, Harvard '95, whom Joseph described to his father as "capable, careful and conscientious, to use a little of your favorite alliteration."[35] He worked with Joseph through the spring on geometry and physics, and on Greek, Roman, English, and American history, preparing for exams at the end of June. Pulitzer made passing those exams a condition of letting his son have a vacation at Bar Harbor that summer. While this surely helped motivate him, Joseph was, as usual, candid in his assessment of the work. "American history is the only one that ordinarily would really interest me," he wrote. "English history, until after George I is, I think, very stupid and can be summed up under two heads, Religious throat-cutting and Irish Revolutions. . . . As for algebra and geometry, well, you know how I like them."[36] Nevertheless, he passed, had his break—spent largely on his boat— and went back to work with Woodward to bone up for a second set of exams in September. His father's change of heart about his schooling made this a happy period for him: "I'm perfectly satisfied with everything and everybody. A very fortunate frame of mind and I realize it and try to cultivate it. Of course at my age there's no reason why I shouldn't be entirely happy but still I think that way of looking at things is the best way, and it may come in handy later on."[37] Ordered by Pulitzer, whom they saw at Bar Harbor, to find a quiet place to study for the fall exams, he and Woodward went to Poland Springs, Maine. Fearful that his father would consider the place unsuitable, Joseph wrote that an occasional tennis match was the only distraction and that the main hotel was "filled with the cheapest crowd of people I ever laid eyes on, most of whom range in age from sixty to ninety. . . . I can assure you they look like a pretty sad lot!"[38]

Joseph did well enough on the exams to be admitted to Harvard with two mathematical "conditions." Pulitzer was unhappy about this, and had in fact told Joseph he wouldn't agree to a conditional admission. He relented, however, after they talked at length while riding together at Bar Harbor in late September. To Harvard's conditions, Pulitzer added several of his own. The gravest were that the young man had six months in which to prove himself and that "any misbehavior or slip of any kind" would bring his "instant withdrawal from college." He required Joseph to put their understanding in writing:[39]

> My request that you send me to college was based on the following convictions: I believe that by attending lectures at Harvard University I can learn more during the next three years than I could learn either at the office or under your immediate supervision and instruction. By this I don't mean to imply that I believe that I cannot learn anything from you. On the contrary, I believe I can learn about everything from you, but *not* until I know at least my ABC.
>
> I believe that by hard concentration on those subjects which we have already selected, I can fit myself for a public career as a journalist and politician. And I believe that were I to remain at the office, at the end of three years I might be more familiar with the Want Ad and Circulation figures, but I would not have read anything enlightening or elevating or even directly practical. In other words, I would have an excellent start towards becoming a purely commercial, narrow, selfish, uneducated and inwardly unrefined "businessman." . . .
>
> In other words, I distinctly and unqualifiedly assert that my primary object in wanting to go to college is to become educated and prepared for my future responsibilities. Although I do not pretend to say that the possibilities of making friends and of doing something in athletics and of "having a good time," as you expressed it, do not also appeal to me. That expresses my side of the case as well as

I can express it. I understood your side of the case as follows.

I asked for 3 months in which to prove to you that your convictions and doubts are unfounded. You have given me six months.

If you hear of any misbehaviour or slip of any kind, I must expect instant withdrawal from college.

I am not to leave college without your knowledge.

I am to have an allowance of eighteen hundred dollars per year which is to include all my expenses except doctor's bills, and my room furnishings.

I am to keep a minute and exact expense account, and I am "to live within my income."

I am to keep a diary, in which I must write down my hour of rising and of retiring, any bit of newly acquired learning or thought, and any impression, other than commonplace, which the morning or evening paper (World) may have made.

I am to appeal to you alone for money.

I must remember the St. Mark's expulsion and blot that out by doing well at college.

And I must not expect to remain at college indefinitely, but must certainly graduate at the end of 3 years.

Your loving son,
Joe

Shortly after Joseph settled in at Cambridge, he got a message from his father scolding him for the harsh remarks about businessmen in his statement. He responded that he had been misunderstood: "I realize that it is possible for a man to be keen at business but at the same time to have read something and to be interested in higher ideals than those of dollars and cents. This idea is not original. It came from you when you were complaining last spring about my N.Y. friends who are business clerks and nothing else. So please remember that I did not 'pooh pooh the business man.' On the contrary, I hope I may be one. But at the same time I shall have other interests."

As if to demonstrate this attitude, he described his courses in some detail, mentioning a number of books and several of his assignments, and then concluded the letter with a postscript (presumably not read to J.P.) asking Alfred Butes, one of his father's secretaries, for $30 to get him through the rest of the month. He was taking American and European history, English, German, French, government, and rhetoric. He was keeping an account book and a diary, "though I must say I never was much of a diary keeper. . . . I think I agree with a remark I find here in my rhetoric book by Mr. Stevenson, whoever he was, Robert Louis I suppose, who says he always 'speedily discarded' the diaries he used to try to keep 'finding them a school of posturing and melancholy self-deception.' "[40]

In a month's time he became an enthusiastic Harvard man, "liking it more and more every week, as I absorb the spirit of the place." He went out for the freshman football team with about 150 others and didn't make it, but he became an enthusiastic fan of both the freshman and the varsity teams and greatly enjoyed the cheering and singing at pre-game rallies. "Some of these songs sound wonderful, and I challenge anyone to prevent chills of excitement creeping up his back when everyone rises waving . . . hats and singing the Marseillaise," he wrote.[41] He was pleased to report that his English instructor had told him he wrote better than the average freshman. "After the several complimentary (?) remarks you have made at different times recently about my style, if I may use such an important word, I was surprised and rather amused to hear him tell me this," he remarked. "I suppose you are laughing at this opinion of the instructor's, but personally I was glad to hear it for, call it conceit if you will, I think I have more of a knack for writing than you give me credit for. And what is more, I expect to improve steadily."[42]

German was another matter. Two weeks later, he confessed that the subject didn't interest him and also that "because I am kept decidedly busy . . . my diary and my expense account have been forgotten long ago."[43] To his mother he confided that after some initial fear of "butting in where I wasn't wanted," he had gotten to know at least twenty boys on a first-name basis and could drop into their rooms whenever he wished. "I thoroughly like (I shall soon be saying 'love') Harvard," he added. "I shall never regret having come here."[44]

How good a time he was having became even more evident in

his next letter to his father, which raised "a subject which will prove disagreeable to you." He had only 65 cents in the bank and 29 cents in his pocket, and bills totaling $149.43. "I must plead guilty," he wrote. "As my own financial manager I have proved a failure." He conceded that he had failed to meet one of his father's conditions—living within his means—but pleaded, "If I could start off fresh again, with the past 2 months' experience before me, which have taught me about how much I can afford to 'blow in,' I shall come out all right."[45] His next letter was headed: "P.S. *I have paid all my bills!*" He thanked his father for doing nothing more than sending "two rebukes," which he considered relatively mild. Then he declined an offer of a $250 fur coat, saying few Harvard men wore them and that he would rather have a $50 cloth coat "because my sense of appreciation of the value of money has grown to such a marvelous extent."[46]

That remark did not sit well. Joseph was becoming lackadaisical and, in his father's opinion, rude. Pulitzer directed Ralph to speak with his brother about this during a trip to Cambridge after the Christmas holidays. "I only had a chance for a few words with Joe alone," Ralph reported, "but I spoke to him quite sharply about his rudeness, etc., and I hope it made an impression."[47] Pulitzer also was dissatisfied with the brief comments about the *World* that Joseph had been including in his letters and asked him particularly to read the *Evening World* more carefully. He complied, rather offhandedly pronouncing the paper "improved in tone and in enterprise, Seitz's editorials being something new at least and anyway far better than the old rot."[48] But there were still those medical ads! "For Heaven's sake wire Seitz to stop all Cuticura ads, which we have been printing on the inside col. of the 2nd page where they were bound to strike the eye as it glanced across the page at the headlines," he exclaimed. " 'Baby's Face a Mass of Pimples!' and 'Itching all day long' are some of their fascinating little bon-mots. A paper can hardly be called high toned when it prints such filth as this." Once again there was no reaction, evidently because it was not the sensitive matter to the senior Pulitzer that it was to his son. It is interesting that several months later Florence White, Pulitzer's general overseer, recorded after a conference at Bar Harbor that the publisher's "chief concern" was "the preservation of the character and tone of *all* the editions of the *World* and of the *Post-Dispatch.*" Because he was "removed from close touch with the office, the danger of violations of good taste, even through over-zeal, gave Mr. Pulitzer his greatest anxiety." Furthermore, "the results, however profitable, will not excuse a violation of Mr. Pulitzer's injunctions on this subject."[49] This was a lingering reaction to criticism of the sensational depths to which the *World* had descended in its circulation battle with Hearst's *Journal* during the Spanish-American War. After the war, he turned the morning *World* especially away from this at the sacrifice of many thousands in circulation.[50] But he wasn't about to throw out medical advertising on grounds of poor taste. The fact was that it was a lucrative revenue source for most newspapers and many magazines—so much so that they ignored the bursts of criticism.[51]

As severe as he became on that subject, however, much in Joseph's letters from Harvard was in a lighter vein. At about 2 P.M. on February 15, 1905, while Joseph was attending a French recitation nearby, a fire broke out in a wing of Thayer Hall, a dormitory for "the poorer boys in the college." He reported the event in colorful detail. His class was dismissed, and before long a crowd of about 800 had assembled:

> And a more happy-go-lucky and thoroughly amused crowd you never saw, in spite of the sympathy felt for the poor devils whose clothes and books were burning up inside. Every time a fireman would go up a ladder there would be cheers, and whenever they broke in a window the noise would be deafening. . . . At one time a fearful black column of smoke was pouring out of a window when suddenly a fireman poked his head out and hung over the sill, almost suffocated. Someone in the crowd seeing him yelled "look out boys!" he's going to "lunch!" and that's all the sympathy the poor duck got.[52]

When *World*-supported New York mayor and former Columbia University president Seth Low lectured at Harvard on "The College Man in Politics," Joseph reported: "Among many interesting things, in warning us not to turn up our noses and be always criticizing unfavorably, he said: 'I know of one paper in New York which once had a great influence but has now lost nearly all of it by this fault.' I wonder what paper he meant(?)."⁵³

There also were a few references to young ladies. His father had apparently objected to his seeing one "F.C." during breaks in New York. "I can't see this as you do," Joseph responded. "I suppose you must think that she has had influence on me. If so, you are wrong. Although of course she doesn't know it, she encourages me to work faithfully and to keep straight. A darned sight more, in my opinion, than you can say for the average girl and especially the average N.Y. girl!"⁵⁴ Returning from a trip to Baltimore in April, he called it "a great little town. The men are so hospitable, and the girls — why I declare I've never seen as wonderful a lot of girls as you can see any time down there in the Belvedere Hotel."⁵⁵ His opinion of Boston girls, however, was that they were "with very few exceptions, homely, stupid and dead."⁵⁶

Joseph's social life no doubt interested his father, but he most wanted to know about his son's grades. Explaining that he hadn't reported on them because some hadn't been determined, Joseph reported that the worst news was likely to be his performance in European history, because "old McVane is such a sleepy, uninteresting old ass, and the course is such an extensive one that it hit me pretty hard, I fear." He received a B– in government, a C+ in English, a C in French, and a D in American history, which he said was passing. He had done pretty well, he concluded, "when you consider that eight of the nicest lads in the class . . . have just been dropped out of college for poor marks, including Griswold Lorillard, Fred Cruger, Anson Hard and several others."⁵⁷ He thought most would work with tutors and return as sophomores in the fall. As for himself, his father had him stay in Cambridge over the summer, taking algebra and archeology, which he passed, and architecture, which he did not. Nevertheless, a Harvard official wrote Pulitzer in the fall that his son had done well overall and was making "an intelligent selection of courses to fit him for what you have in mind that he should do in the future."⁵⁸ By December, Joseph could write that he had earned "the required marks for promotion": "I am now a proud sophomore and can smoke a pipe on the street!"⁵⁹

⎯ 5 ⎯

J.P. Takes Charge

Joseph's second year at Harvard started out well enough. He was earning respectable marks—three B's in French, an A and a B+ in German, at least a C in English literature. He was working with tutors on both German and literature. And he was keeping a diary, "though it's an awful nuisance and very easy to forget."[1] The entries were brief: October 31: "Did 10 hrs. of work today, mostly in preparation for a German hour exam on Fri. Tom Jones is getting interesting at last. Got up at 7." November 20: "Got an invitation for Katherine Atterbury's coming out dance on Fri. before Xmas. Accepted. Most of '1908' [his class] will be there. Should be good fun."[2]

Good fun was in ample supply. In late November he wrote his father that he *did* want a fur coat after all and listed the names of seven men in his class who had them. "But if you're worrying about the danger of my appearing over-dressed, why then by all means forget the fur coat," he added, explaining that he would wear it only to football and hockey games and when he went into town—not to classes, to avoid appearing ostentatious.[3] He was taken into Zeta Psi, a social fraternity known as the Spee Club, where it was pleasant, he admitted, to have lunch and "sit in a nice easy chair in front of the fire for a little while before going back to work."[4] He again overspent his allowance, mostly by dining at hotels and attending theater parties, and appealed to secretary Alfred Butes, then in New York while Pulitzer was at his retreat at Jekyll Island, Georgia: "If you could pay off these bills before Father's return I really would feel much relieved, for if he finds that they're still unpaid I fear he will raise hell especially as he has been talking of taking me out of college for some time, as you may know."[5] Butes obliged, advising Joseph to "begin a new system of paying as you go."[6]

Pulitzer probably never learned of that episode, but he had to be told that Joseph did so poorly on his midyear exams that he had been placed on academic probation. He summoned his son to New York on a mid-February weekend. There was a tense discussion in a carriage outside their home among both parents and their son. Pulitzer said he was inclined to withdraw his son from Harvard in one month, on his twenty-first birthday, March 21, 1906. Afterward Joseph produced the usual written memorandum of the session: "You said that if I had a natural bent for learning and reading, or if I were preparing to be a lawyer, a doctor or a scholar, then Harvard would be a good place for me. But as it is, you said that I have shown that I have no taste for reading, that I have disregarded your wishes as to reading the paper and keeping a diary, and that on the whole my mind is now in a less developed, less matured condition than it was . . . two years ago." Instead of wasting time at college, Pulitzer contended, Joseph should be in St. Louis preparing to relieve his father of his responsibilities. "You also went on to impress upon me the importance of my becoming of age on the 21st of next month," Joseph continued,

> and you told me that you had made me a trustee in your
> will and that in such a position I would have it in my

power to ruin not only my own fortune but those of my brother and sisters. You told me that I was quite unfit to hold such a responsible position and in that I entirely agreed with you and in fact said that when the time came I should probably refuse to accept it. . . . I said that I thought I *was* learning something, especially of English literature. And finally asked you to let me remain in college not simply until March 21st, but until after my final exams, my purpose in this request being thus to get an opportunity to improve my midyear grades at the final exams.[7]

Joseph returned to Harvard, thinking he had again won a reprieve. "I appreciate thoroughly and heartily your giving me another chance to stay here, for a while longer, at least," he wrote a few days later.[8] He predicted a "decided improvement" in his final grades. "You may be thinking of your favorite figure of speech now, 'Hell is paved with good resolutions,'" he remarked. "Perhaps it is. But this particular resolution is not going to become an infernal cobbling-stone if I can help it." Pulitzer asked for more detailed diary entries, always to include his son's times of rising and retiring. In them—somewhat curiously in view of his father's comment about his lack of taste for reading—Joseph was as candid as ever, commenting, for example, that he "failed to appreciate any of Milton's much talked of *majestic* sentences" in *Areopagitica*.[9] And after reading 250 pages of *David Copperfield:* "He is still a damned uninteresting, simple-minded, unlovable school-boy. That is what discourages me with most good literature. You don't get anywhere."[10] Fifty pages later, he pronounced the story "disgustingly stupid": "How such a book can appeal to full-blooded able-bodied men . . . is beyond me! I can understand its being a popular and generally read book in an old lady's home or some place of that kind, but nowhere else."[11]

If that didn't damage his father's estimate of his prospects as a scholar, a letter in early March from Harvard dean B. S. Hurlbut explaining the reasons for probation definitely did. Hurlbut reported that in addition to getting unsatisfactory marks in all but one course, Joseph had cut "no less than thirty-seven college engagements" during the first half-year.[12] Still, he urged Pulitzer "very strongly to give him a chance to retrieve himself." After

Pulitzer dispatched Ralph to Cambridge two weeks later to confer with Hurlbut about Joseph, the dean said he was now attending classes faithfully and that it would be "unjust, it seems to me, not to give him the reward of this—the degree will mean much in years to come."[13] This had little effect. In a telegram, Pulitzer demanded an explanation for the cuts and ordered Joseph to repeat what Ralph had told him about their father's condition.[14] His son replied that he had no excuses to offer, but that, on average, he had cut only three out of seventeen hours of recitation each week. As to his father's health:

> Ralph dwelt a good deal on your unfortunate condition . . . saying that you are in a generally lower state of mind and body than you have ever been, and that things have been going worse with you than usual, not only at the office but at home and in fact everywhere. . . . [T]hat your diabetes has unquestionably increased a great deal, that your sight has diminished perceptibly even since last summer at Bar Harbor, and that you are all the time suffering from these terribly gloomy spells during one of which you fear that you may sometime do something desperate, unless you are soon relieved.[15]

Against this, Joseph's plea to his father "to forgive me for the additional pain I have caused you" was to little avail. He was, as he put it, "yanked" out of Harvard in early April and put back to work at the *World*.[16] He had, in effect, summarized his college experience in a letter to his father two months earlier: "There is no doubt about it. Cambridge, Mass., is just about the worst place for work and the best place for indolence in the world."[17]

Yet the place had its uses, and Joseph ever afterward thought of himself as a Harvard man, class of 1908. His experience there seems to be in accord with an observation of Henry Adams, who had attended Harvard almost fifty years earlier: "No one took Harvard College seriously. All went there because their friends went there, and the college was their ideal of social self-respect." And yet, he added, "Harvard College was probably less hurtful than any other university then in existence. It taught little, and that little ill, but it left the mind open, free from bias, ignorant of facts, but docile. The graduate had few strong prejudices. He knew little, but his mind remained supple, ready to receive knowledge."[18] That description fit young Joseph Pulitzer Jr. well. When he left Harvard, his education truly began.

It is not clear why he wasn't immediately sent to St. Louis, but it is plausible that Mrs. Pulitzer prevailed upon her husband not to both take Joseph out of college and banish him from family and friends in one stroke. The blow also was softened by Pulitzer's granting his son's wish of two years earlier to be a reporter. He was put under the supervision of stern, iron-jawed *Evening World* city editor Charles E. Chapin, a man of legendary toughness. Joseph thoroughly enjoyed the work. "Reporting suits me down to the ground and I am learning every day," he wrote his father. "I hope you will not think of transferring me to any other job." He told of being shown by a coroner at a morgue how an autopsy is done: "I expected to faint when I got inside but didn't. I think I must be cold blooded."[19] A few days later he called reporting "such a naturally interesting occupation that, generally speaking, it does not seem like work at all, at any rate not like my idea of work."[20] A week later, he said he was

> convinced that all that newspaper reading and writing of reports that you made me do years ago was of very little good in developing my news instinct, compared to this reporting. This gets me right up against a thing at first hand and it's up to me to decide what I'm going to use and how I'm going to use it. Then again I feel that if I'm ever to occupy an editorial position I shall have far more control over my staff and shall have their respect to a far greater extent than I should have had had I never gone right out and done actual reporting.[21]

Enlarging that theme at the end of three months, he wrote that reporting "has done me a world of good" mainly because of its "moral effect upon the others in the office," who couldn't have been impressed when he was just "hanging around" observing. Their view of him, he speculated, had been, "Gad, what a poor lot that young Pulitzer is. He drops down here . . . and first butts into my business and then butts into the business of the man next to

me, and after doing this for eight hours he goes home, imagining
that he has done a good solid day's work, and tells his Father all he
can find out about me." They couldn't help but think, he concluded,
that he should "actually take a hand in doing some of the practical
work" and wouldn't amount to anything until he did. "That, in my
opinion, is the way they feel about Ralph, and the way they used to
feel about me." He said he also had earned the respect of "outsiders,"
including his friends, their parents, and other newspapermen,
had become a better judge of people, and now knew the ease with
which a reporter, "if he cares to . . . can shirk his work."

Finally, he reported discovering "several very bad tendencies
which exist in the *Evening World* office and which make it the
unreliable newspaper that it is."[22] He probably meant the paper's
tendency to "fake" for sensational effect, which he had complained
of earlier and of which Pulitzer was more tolerant in the *Evening
World* than in the morning paper. Even though the cavernous, desk-
filled newsroom, some 50 feet wide and 100 feet deep, was adorned
with printed posters reading "Accuracy, Accuracy, Accuracy! Who?
What? Where? When? How? The Facts—The Color—The Facts!"
manufactured reports with only a thin underlay of objective truth
were produced there daily. "The Color," budding novelist Theodore
Dreiser discovered during brief employment at the *World* as a
young man, was often the first requisite of a printable story. He
soon learned "that what my city editor wanted was not merely
'accuracy, accuracy, accuracy,' but a kind of flair for the ridiculous or the remarkable even though it had to be invented, so that
the pages of the paper, and life itself, might not seem so dull."
After concluding that he was too new to the city to know enough
of its people and places to stimulate plausible imaginings, he
quit, "realizing," he confessed, "that I was losing an excellent
opportunity."[23]

Joseph came under this influence as well, and in the spring of
1906 produced this "bright," which was headlined "An Old Offender
Refuses to Reform":

> What is probably one of the most remarkable instances of
> inherent and incorrigible criminality that has ever been
> known in the city of New York has recently turned up in
> the Centre Street Court.

Day after day for the last two weeks the Police Magistrate has found himself face to face with a certain offender,
and to-day he is in court again. Magistrate Breen did everything in his power to set this unfortunate on a straight
path, but with no effect. The clerks have done their best,
and so have the court policemen. And now Magistrate
Wahle is after him.

The offender must be about fifty years old and has a face
as hard as marble and utterly devoid of color. He has
caused one lawyer after another to be late in appearing in
court with the consequent postponement of innumerable
cases; he has made trouble for everyone, and is still making it. The general impression about the court-room is
that he is in serious danger of having his face smashed, for
if the truth must be told he is none other than the court-
room clock.[24]

Chapin, who eventually murdered his wife and spent the rest of
his life in Sing Sing prison, took a genuine liking to his new
charge. "He was a lovable lad, with many of his father's characteristics and much of his mother's gentleness," Chapin recalled in
the autobiography he wrote in prison. "Joe loved fun." However,
Pulitzer's instructions to Chapin had been that "there is to be no
partiality shown because he is my son. . . . I know how you handle
young men and I wish you to do the same with him." Chapin didn't
obey these orders at first. He excused a tardiness on the third day
("because the butler neglected to call me") with the suggestion
that Joseph buy an alarm clock. Then he dealt with a whole day's
absence by delivering a stiff scolding. "He was as penitent as an
heir to millions might be expected to be," Chapin recalled,

> and he made a lot of promises that I think he sincerely
> intended to keep.
> But the sting of reprimand is soon forgotten, and prom-
> ises and good resolutions are easily broken when a pretty
> girl beckons from afar. And that is what happened to Joe
> the following week. Despite all I had told him about the
> instructions his father had given me and his own promise
> not again to ask me to disobey them, he came with another

pleading request to get away for a few days and I refused. Joe went without permission and didn't come back for almost a week. When he did come I fired him.

The office gasped with astonishment when it got noised about that I had discharged "Prince Joe," as they called him, but Joe good-naturedly treated it as a joke and took the night train for Bar Harbor, where he fitted out his yacht and sailed it in all of the regattas there that summer, or until his father returned from Europe and sent him out to St. Louis.[25]

When Pulitzer did return, there was a session between father and son, this one aboard a launch, the record of which Joseph committed to paper. "You have decided that I am to go to St. Louis, although you still believe that really the best thing for me to do would be to go off somewhere and shift for myself on my own hook," he began. Once there, he was to work under the direction of Frank O'Neil, telling him: "I am out here to learn something in case something happens to my Father. Teach me as much as possible without my becoming a bore." He noted that his father had told him he had come close to making a new will that excluded Joseph entirely, and had asked him if he had been "in any way impressed" when his father had told him in the spring that he had changed his will to Joseph's disadvantage. His reply: "Yes it did make an impression, but I didn't worry about it." Then he added, "I should have worried about it."

That was not all Joseph had to think about. Pulitzer sent his son back to St. Louis with instructions that he was to keep in mind "two central ideas, apparently, but not really, inconsistent." The first was that he must go out there feeling that someday he "might take possession of that property." The second was that he must read the New York papers "every single day and try to think that your future will be in N.Y. after all. For the paper in N.Y. is bigger, more powerful and has more prestige, character, honor and name."[26] It was typical of the senior Pulitzer to do this. He kept his subordinates always off balance, never quite knowing where they stood or what might happen next and always aware that the final decision was his. He also had the top editors and managers report directly to him about each other's performance, especially those at the

World. He justified it as the only way an absentee publisher could function.[27] Still, while his son could be certain that he would be the subject of frequent reports, he also knew that there was a more congenial atmosphere at the *Post-Dispatch* and less political intrigue than at the *World,* simply because it was secondary in the publisher's concerns.

On his second day in St. Louis, Joseph wrote the first of numerous diary pages that he sent regularly to his father. These were on full-sized sheets he usually filled to their twenty-six-line capacity with no side margins, occasionally going to a second page. They invariably began with the time he reached the office in the morning and ended with the time he departed at night. He also wrote frequent letters, all in a firm, legible hand and relaxed, clear prose. Again he was mostly an observer, but not confined only to the business side, the importance of which he was beginning to appreciate. Within a week of his arrival he reported going over the previous week's financial report with James T. Keller, the paper's treasurer: "To my surprise I found it most interesting."[28]

After his father asked for "more ideas and reflections, not just facts," he readily responded that the "idea that strikes me most forcibly is how terribly dependent we are on lack of competition. As soon as it comes, and that must happen soon, I fear we will have a different story to tell." In 1906, the *Post-Dispatch* had only one evening competitor, the *Star-Chronicle,* with 75,306 circulation to the *Post-Dispatch*'s 140,180. Its Sunday circulation of 214,525 was 41,246 ahead of its nearest competitor, the *Globe-Democrat.* Another evening competitor, the *St. Louis Times,* was founded in January 1907.[29]

It wasn't long before Joseph concluded that the staff member who offered the greatest promise of keeping the *Post-Dispatch* ahead of its rivals was thirty-four-year-old city editor Oliver K. Bovard. He had joined the paper as a reporter in 1898, when the *Post-Dispatch* agreed to publish an exposé of political corruption he had uncovered that the *Star,* for which he had been reporting, refused to print.[30] Joseph was able to observe Bovard during meetings of the morning "council," where plans for the day were discussed. O'Neil and managing editor Harry L. Dunlap also attended. His first, and correct, impression was that the city editor was aloof: "Bovard always takes notes but seldom opens his mouth.

He seems to have an ugly disposition, though pleasant and obliging enough to me."[31] That was sufficient encouragement for him to begin observing and talking to Bovard and to make some story suggestions, which the editor accepted.

Joseph's ready self-assurance quickly took hold. "I am learning a lot," he wrote his father within ten days of his arrival, "and now almost believe that after all I'm not as hopeless a case as you would have me believe and that it's quite possible for me someday to become a successful newspaper proprietor." He had begun to like St. Louis, although "at first I thought it was hell, but now I'm getting accustomed to western ways and have gotten over my first attack of homesickness." Despite the August heat, he was "in a pretty cheerful and optimistic frame of mind,"[32] and for once his mood was matched by his father's. "I cannot help saying that your diaries I read with considerable pleasure and avidity," Pulitzer wrote. But he cautioned his son against spending too much time "following details of advertising, which I certainly never did and should have *hated* to do. . . . I should like to feel that this sort of thing is rather distasteful to you. . . . I am thinking of you all the time, all day and every hour, and hope you will stick to a good beginning with tenacity."[33]

Joseph hadn't yet received his father's advice to pay less attention to advertising when he again registered his dislike of medical advertising: "When I see you, please be ready to receive a strong kick on the disgraceful medical ads that we print. They are not only disgusting but are a mean deception of an ignorant public that can in no way be justified."[34] Ten days later he mailed several clippings of the ads, saying:

> It will be unpleasant reading, I hope, for then it may produce results. I can't believe that you realize what these damned medical ads say, and how much dreadful harm they do. If you did realize it then I'm sure you wouldn't permit them to appear in your newspapers, both of which, as you know, claim to be respectable "home" newspapers intended for the fireside and the home. You don't need the money. Why then do incalculable harm by accepting such filth? I think it is positively criminal. You have my views. I beg you to read the enclosed, which are comparatively

mild, and act accordingly. Or else place the matter in my hands and let me act.

The response came in a sharply worded letter written by secretary Alfred Butes containing "the pith of your father's talk to me yesterday," in which the publisher dodged all responsibility for the ads:

> You were sent out to learn your profession—not to kill the medical ads. You have plenty to do with that study. Leave disagreeable problems of management alone. You are not a competent judge. Even if you are competent, and if your judgment were correct, you would be doing the grossest wrong to your father in laying the responsibility upon him. You know very well that the paper is in charge of competent managers who have the fullest control, and are men of character. The responsibility is *theirs*.
>
> Mr. P. says that when the time comes—if it ever comes—for *you* to take charge of the paper you will be able to kill these ads. He would be glad if that time could come *Soon*. But it will not be brought nearer by irritating letters.
>
> Besides studying the business he suggests also thorough self-examination. Your letter, he says, shows deplorable self-deception. You assume that you have made but *one* mistake, ignoring all that has happened in the past two or rather the past four years—broken promises, pledges and obligations which have caused him grief a thousand times greater than you will ever know. . . .
>
> Your father is also grieved to notice a train of coarseness that has come into your writing, and, he fears, into your mind. For instance, frequent slang like "Hearst's old man"—too frequent oaths and hells. . . . Remember your age and to whom you are writing. . . .
>
> *Absolutely and positively* you must write *no more disagreeable letters.*[35]

Joseph wrote two letters in response, one to Butes and the other to his father. In the first, though he expressed regret at "having caused Father so much irritation," the young man not only held his ground but also disputed the argument that the papers' managers would take appropriate action if necessary. "I knew that none of his managers would feel justified in killing such valuable business," he wrote. "And I therefore brought the matter to his attention, supposing, in fact, heartily believing, that in so doing I was acting in his interest and in the interest of his newspapers. . . . I still believe that what I did was right and you or anyone else can't dissuade me from this belief." Furthermore, "I still contend that my view of this class of business is the only upright, honorable and *refined* one. I hope you will note this word 'refined.' I shall not worry about his views as to my refinement. It's very probably another case of self-deception, either on my part or on his. And I am satisfied that it is on his." He thanked Butes for his letter, because it was "not only sane and logical in expression, but between the lines I could read indications of your apparent liking for me and your desire to smooth things over. I shall do the same for you whenever I get a chance." In a postscript, he gave Butes permission to read the letter to his father "edited or unedited, as you see fit," asking only that if he did not read it he would at least explain Joseph's position and his belief that his intentions were good.[36]

The letter to his father was polite and agreeable, as per instructions. He apologized and attempted to do what probably was impossible—convince his father that he both loved him and sympathized deeply with him. "When I shut my eyes for a while, as I often do, and the full realization comes over me that you actually are blind and can't see, I feel how utterly selfish and inconsiderate I often am," he wrote. "I shall gladly welcome any line from you that will tell me that you have forgotten this new trouble that I have caused you and that you love me."[37]

That may have helped somewhat. At any rate, in late September Pulitzer allowed Joseph a four-day vacation, plus travel time, to visit Ralph and his wife, the former Frederica Vanderbilt Webb, at Shelburne Farms, the 3,500-acre Webb estate near Burlington, Vermont, where they had been married the previous year. Several young people were there, including two men Joseph had known at Harvard, and he wrote his father that he had "really never enjoyed 4 days more in *all my life*," despite suffering a badly sprained left wrist in a fall from a horse the first day. On his return to St. Louis, he wrote his father—now in Vienna, where he could attend some concerts—in detail about his outing. He confessed that he would like to know when he would again be allowed to go east, "even if it's to be in the dim, far future" and only for two or three days. "I feel about it out here just as we used to on getting back to school when we'd begin counting the days, hours and minutes before the next vacation," he explained. "For it *is* lonely out here, . . . and the prospect of a return to home, family and friends *is* very encouraging."38

It was well that he was refreshed, for no sooner did he return than he received an assignment to do a detailed self-appraisal. "Are you aware of your own temperament, character and nature, your limitations, defects, aptitudes, or talents?" his father asked. "If so, tell me exactly what you think of yourself—past, present, prospective. Be self-examining, self-judicial, introspective and self-critical—or self laudatory if you feel like it. Try to get acquainted with yourself—your inner self, your most important self. I don't believe you know him. Self-knowledge, as I have told you before, is necessary to self-mastery."39 Joseph answered at length:

> I think I have, so far, led a pretty useless sort of existence. My purpose in the past has always been to enjoy life. And it strikes me that if I can accomplish my purpose in the future as well as I have succeeded in the past, and in the face of equally unfavorable circumstances, I shall be a success in this little world and prove my right to have been brought into it. . . . I admit that my youth has produced no unusually fine results. But I console myself by thinking that it might have produced worse. After all I am not a drunkard; I am not a degenerate; I am not a gambler, and I am not a rounder—and in these four respects I am superior at least to the average millionaire's son. I have my weaknesses, more of them undoubtedly than I realize. I flatter myself, however, by the thought that I am aware of my worst weakness, which is, in my opinion, to "have a good time" by loafing out of doors and out in the country, by indulging in all sorts of sports—riding, hunting, sailing, and swimming—in other words, looking at life from a point of view which, although not vicious or actually

harmful, is nevertheless frivolous, useless and weak. Then again, I am too fond of the society of my friends, and too willing to loaf simply because they may be loafing. And I am too kind-hearted and afraid of hurting a person's feelings by a direct command or expression of opinion. And I suppose I am also too fond of the ladies, although I really can't see that I have ever suffered much from this failing. Still, it *is* a weakness, I admit, and I put it down as such. . . .

. . . I hope primarily to be a successful journalist and a help to mankind in that way. But it would not surprise me if I eventually landed in politics, though I shant do much in the way of seeking the office but shall rest quiet in the hope that eventually the office may seek me. In other words, I should like to get a nomination, not as Hearst has done but as Hughes has done, without apparently trying very hard for it. . . .

You ask me to put down whatever I can recall about your invalidism and suffering. . . . This is a distressing duty. I know that you are now totally blind, that you are terribly nervous, that you can't sleep, and that you are suffering in other ways. I don't know how to express my sympathy for you on paper. All I can say is that I do feel very sorry for you, a good deal more so than I have ever done in the past.

You ask me "to put down minutely every admonition, warning, criticism, and reproach" that you have addressed to me since my entering Harvard. I fear I shall fail in doing this exactly. . . . You have reproached me for not giving you sympathy, for showing no appreciation of the work that you are doing solely for us boys. You have admonished me for being idle, shiftless and short-sighted, never looking ahead of the day. Or, to cut matters short, you have told me that I am no good and that the best thing I could do would be to get out, leave home, and shift for myself.[40]

There was no immediate reaction to this. For his part, Joseph cheerfully resumed his duties at the *Post-Dispatch* and continued the stream of diary sheets and letters. "I really believe that a fellow doesn't know what real happiness is unless he works," he commented several days later, explaining that the simple diversion of a brisk walk on a Saturday morning, when he didn't have to work, put him in "such exuberant spirits that I was whistling and singing most of the time." The reason, he thought, was the change from being in the close office air all week. "After all," he observed, "life is largely a matter of contrast."[41]

In his self-appraisal, Joseph had mentioned the Hearst–Charles Evans Hughes race for the New York governorship, then in its last weeks before the election. The *World* supported Hughes, and though the paper was relatively polite in its opposition toward Hearst,[42] the rival publisher retaliated by calling the elder Pulitzer, among other things, a pimp. On hearing that, Joseph promised his father: "The next time I happen to meet him, I shall sail in and knock hell out of him." He soon got his chance. Following his defeat, by a 58,000-vote margin, much smaller than Pulitzer had expected, Hearst stopped in St. Louis on his way to Mexico. He needed to send a message via the Associated Press, which occupied a corner of the *Post-Dispatch* newsroom. On seeing him, Joseph strode over, introduced himself, and asked Hearst if he really meant those things he had said about Pulitzer. "I usually mean what I say," was the reply. Joseph took a swing at him, but was grabbed and restrained by a bystander. That the punch hadn't landed, he later said, was "always . . . one of my regrets."[43]

— 6 —

Pleasure and Pain

The Hearst incident, which was reported in newspapers around the nation and as far away as Belgium,[1] may well have raised the publisher's estimate of his most troublesome son, for their long-distance relationship was generally congenial during the last three months of 1906. There had been an infraction, however, though one that need never have caused the trouble it did had Joseph not suffered pangs of conscience and confessed to his father. He had taken a five-day vacation to attend the Harvard-Yale football game in New Haven on November 24 without asking his father's permission. (To make matters worse, Yale made the only score, a touchdown.[2]) He had informed O'Neil, who didn't object. But when he got word a week before Christmas that his father was giving him a week's holiday at home and $500, he felt so remorseful that he declined both and confessed that "I neglected my duty to you and the office" by taking the unauthorized trip.[3] Pulitzer responded by cable: "Amazed. You must certainly stay and recover lost confidence. Had just intended to raise your pay, position, powers, title, handsomely, but first importance I must depend upon you. Grieved."[4] Joseph spent Christmas—his first away from home—in St. Louis. On Christmas Day he traveled around the city with editorial page editor George S. Johns to attend seven "Poor Children's Festivals" supported by funds collected by the *Post-Dispatch*. He was deeply moved by what he saw. "At times I was on the verge of tears," he wrote.[5]

The unauthorized trip notwithstanding, Joseph had done well during those first four months back in St. Louis. He had assumed the role of management apprentice with enthusiasm and interest and was genuinely respected—instead of merely tolerated—by all those in charge. O'Neil and Bovard, in particular, seemed impressed, and to Joseph's surprise Bovard was willing to have long talks with him about how the news machine ran. By mid-October, Joseph was approving requisitions and signing checks and taking an active part in some decision-making, such as one to improve photo reproduction by hiring four new people so the engraving could be done more carefully. He also helped decide the Christmas bonuses and salary increases, which totaled more than $5,000. "I fear my business instinct isn't nearly strong enough, judging from the pleasure this sort of work gives me!" he remarked.[6]

He had few regular assignments, though, and that troubled him. He complained that his work was "too indefinite. In fact, I am always looking for . . . something new to study, and every now and then this freedom strikes me as being too great." He said the only thing that kept him in the office was "the fear of being considered an incompetent ass by the entire staff and a certain amount of pride or whatever you choose to call it." He asked to be "placed in a certain regular position and be given a certain regular title— let it be window cleaner, for all I care." He recalled that during his reporting days at the *World* "the paper did get at least a few feeble stories out of me. In other words, until I own the paper, I'd rather work for *it* than for myself. When I become the proprietor, then of course I'll be satisfied to work for myself."[7]

He received brief but encouraging notes from his father that fall, expressing satisfaction at the quality of his letters and diary. Emboldened by this, Joseph suggested that his father might now be able to think "that after all your two sons are not as hopeless as they have seemed and have some good in them after all, especially myself." He tempered this slightly by adding: "I should very much like to know what you think of my work and also what O'Neil has reported on it. I suppose most of the people in the office still give me credit for not being anything very much more than an ass, but this feeling does not worry me in the slightest. Some day I'll fool 'em."[8]

Three days later O'Neil did send a highly laudatory report to Pulitzer. "Possibly you would not care to put him at it, but Joseph, Jr. would make a capital customs officer," he began. "If anything got by him without a challenge it would be because neither eye nor ear could detect it." He described a daily routine that included time in the circulation, editorial, news, and advertising departments, adding: "My opinion grows stronger . . . that while he will patiently acquire knowledge of the publishing departments . . . his taste and capacity all tend to make him a news and editorial man." Because he had nothing negative to say, he concluded that the report, "barren as it is of black marks, may challenge your credulity; but really the young man has surprised, and in a measure disappointed, me in his failure to disclose some really reprehensible or barbaric characteristics. Every boy has 'em, and I'm waiting."[9]

O'Neil further demonstrated his confidence by delegating some of his troubleshooting chores, letting Joseph try to resolve problems or disputes in various departments. "Herein lies my greatest chance to do the real kind of work that I desire—by suggestion," Joseph reported. "I have been able to straighten out several tangles of various kinds."[10] He also began to consider himself a competent judge of others. When it was discovered that the pressroom foreman had been accepting $100 a month from an ink company, he reported that while O'Neil had sworn by the man, he had "always distrusted him. He's got the shiftiest eye I've ever seen."[11] The foreman was dismissed.

At about the same time, Joseph was put in charge of the midday edition, which had a 10:15 A.M. deadline. He handled everything from headline writing to page layout and supervision in the composing room. He did some writing as well, and showed a special flair in suggesting feature story ideas for the Sunday magazine. When he found that others were getting $2.50 for each idea accepted, he submitted a bill for $12.50, which O'Neil approved. "At last I have something to do and when I go to bed at night I have something to look forward to the next morning," he wrote. "I've had a lot of my ideas in the paper and I feel that I am doing a little something."[12]

At the end of January 1907, O'Neil wrote Pulitzer that Joseph "is becoming more censorious, and, I am glad to report, his criticisms are mainly on behalf of good journalistic standards."

> He, like his father, is somewhat prone to the very quick application of the penalty that fits the crime of neglect or disobedience of orders; but, again like his father, he is entirely willing to hear the evidence later on. He is absolutely opposed to temporizing, after a plan has been laid out, and he does not approve of back talk or any delays incident to "diplomatic" management where a man or department is a little backward in obeying orders. . . . [President Theodore] Roosevelt, who does not hesitate to sweep statutes and even constitutions aside in order to "do things" is the object of his great admiration. He would edit the advertisements through all of the stages from Manhood Restored to 98 cent pure silk shirtwaists, until they fooled nobody; and he would hunt all forms of crime and misconduct into deep, deep holes, with the editorial pitchfork. All of which is admirable. For it is always easier to control speed or aggressiveness than to make it, and experience is the reliable and beneficent brake which develops on all intellectual and moral machines.[13]

The elder Pulitzer "retired" on his sixtieth birthday, April 10, 1907, marking the occasion with banquets in both New York and St. Louis. Though the publisher felt too ill to attend either, the resident son in each city made a brief speech and engaged in a bit of friendly sibling rivalry via telegrams read at each affair. Ralph telegraphed from Delmonico's to his brother at the Southern Hotel: "The greatest American newspaper predicts a still greater future for the 'biggest and best newspaper in the Great Southwest.'"

Joseph responded: "We ... wish you continued success in that valuable public service which distinguishes the *New York World*'s work and honors its parent, the *Post-Dispatch.*"[14] Joseph's contribution to the evening's oratory was to thank the staff for the consideration and kindness shown him during the eight months he had been at the *Post-Dispatch.* In a letter to his father, he admitted having been nervous for two days before he was to speak, but when the time came he was calm and "actually enjoyed the experience." He thought he might become a good speaker, for "I know I have the voice and think I have the necessary self-assurance or conceit, whichever it is, but it's the brains I'm worrying about." He also had enjoyed the chance the dinner gave him "to see the men outside the office under congenial circumstances and thus get to know them better."[15]

The main event of the evening in each city was the reading of a telegram from the publisher announcing pension plans for each newspaper. A portion of the senior Pulitzer's St. Louis message became the editorial "platform" of the *Post-Dispatch,* printed since Pulitzer's death in 1911 on its editorial page:

> I know that my retirement will make no difference in its cardinal principles; that it will always fight for progress and reform, never tolerate injustice or corruption, always fight demagogues of all parties, never belong to any party, always oppose privileged classes and public plunderers, never lack sympathy with the poor, always remain devoted to the public welfare, never be satisfied with merely printing news, always be drastically independent, never be afraid to attack wrong, whether by predatory plutocracy or predatory poverty.[16]

Pulitzer also had it announced at the dinner that Ralph was to be acting head of the *World* and president of the *Post-Dispatch,* apparently believing that Joseph had not yet qualified for any title.

Of course, Pulitzer never retired, but remained very much in charge, from wherever he might be, of both the eastern and the western newspapers. He was often quoted as saying he had no interest in the *Post-Dispatch* beyond its money-making capability, "and I assure you it is a perfect mint,"[17] but his involvement was considerably greater. He would instruct O'Neil and White that he was not to be bothered about details of the paper's operation, but they kept in touch regularly, knowing they ran greater risks by not consulting him and that he invariably had an opinion on any matter at hand. And he was, of course, kept in close touch through his son's communications, one of which clearly showed the extent of the paper's prosperity: "I firmly believe that we should place a limit on the amount of advertising that we will accept. That would get advertising copy in more promptly and we would then not antagonize advertisers by throwing out their ads at the last minute as we now often have to do."[18] Joseph reported that in asking *Post-Dispatch* advertising manager William C. Steigers "what he thought my chances are of ever becoming a great journalist," he got the reply "that it would depend largely on how much I allowed money to distract me. Which, of course, I realize to be very true."[19]

In the meantime, it was clear from the satisfaction he found in putting together the midday edition what aspect of newspapering Joseph liked the most. The work began at 7:15 each morning and entailed his making a series of quick decisions, first at the copy desk and then in the composing room. On his first day on the job, 160 people died in a theater fire in Boyertown, Pennsylvania. He gave the story an eight-column banner headline. The second day "was dull," he noted, "and I had a harder time." He was particularly proud of his suggestion that the paper start agitating for a subway system in St. Louis because, after first rejecting it, Bovard had reversed himself two days later during a meeting of the morning council. That "pleases my vanity and strikes me as a vindication of my original suggestion to him," Joseph wrote. "We must now adopt a battle cry like 'To Harlem in 15 Minutes.' "[20]

A few days later he attended a trial of a treasury clerk on charges of embezzling $61,500 "to observe how our reporters covered the story and also to compare a trial in St. Louis with one in New York."[21] In O'Neil's opinion, the heir apparent worked comfortably with both staff members and supervisors. "Nobody defers to him," O'Neil wrote the publisher, "but everybody gives him the inside of every subject under consideration, and when he makes a good suggestion it is gladly accepted. Some are rejected, which is well, I think."[22]

As those soothing words were being written to Pulitzer at the end of January 1907, a letter from his son that had just the opposite effect was on its way to intercepting him during a Mediterranean cruise. For the first three of its five pages the letter was strictly conversational. Joseph told of having visited former governor Charles P. Johnson, with whom Pulitzer had studied law and who regarded himself as a "staunch friend" of "old Joe." Johnson had recounted to the son the story of how Pulitzer during his days in the Missouri legislature had shot the man who had called him a liar. "Too bad you only caught him in the leg," Joseph commented. He then turned to the question of his own future, saying he looked forward to the time when he and his father could meet to "exchange ideas" about his prospects. "I believe you will find me slightly changed," he suggested, adding that he hoped his father would give him a more definite idea of what lay ahead and of how long he was to stay in St. Louis. He offered two proposals for discussion:

> Personally, this would be my ideal scheme of life. I should get a flat (2 rooms and a bath); a servant, probably a Jap (for they are cheap and good), and a horse and make St. Louis my home for *at least three whole years*. But of course I can do nothing of this kind without a raise in pay. If this plan does not meet with your approval, the only alternative, I think, would be that you should give me six months' or a year's leave of absence, that we should say goodbye to each other in a friendly way with the understanding that neither of us should hear from the other except for some extraordinary illness or something of that kind, and that I should make my own way in this small world howsoever and wheresoever I please. I would get more practical knowledge probably out of the first scheme, but I would get more character training and fortifying out of the second. And it's a question simply of which is the more desirable. It's this sort of thing that I should like to talk to you about and that makes me hope that you will be returning some time soon.[23]

On reflection—and having had no response—Joseph wrote three weeks later, saying he was "struck with an apprehension" that the tone of the earlier letter "might be misleading, and that it may cause you to think that I wrote it in a dissatisfied, resentful and ungrateful spirit." He did not want his father to think the suggestion about their going separate ways was made "in an impulsive or threatening manner," and he emphasized that he would "much prefer remaining in direct communication and sympathy with you and your life." He then revealed that his main fear was of being sent back to work at the *World,* not because of any objection to the paper itself but because of the unwholesome influence of New York City on him. "I am still young and am still sadly lacking in self-control," he confessed. "Everything about N.Y. is distracting. The very air is full of amusement, frivolity and dissipation." But

> in St. Louis, no matter whether a fellow is so inclined or not, he *has to work* to occupy his time. And that is why I think you should keep me in St. Louis and away from New York. And that is also why I told you what I did about our separating and about my going off "on my own hook." Won't you as a great favor, on receipt of this letter, dictate a few lines, telling me in the first place that you have not misunderstood my motives and attitude of mind, and in the second place telling me what your plans for me and my immediate future are? I should very much appreciate it.[24]

Though Pulitzer's "retirement" dinner intervened in April, Joseph had no response to these letters until May. He became so impatient with waiting that in late April he wrote: "To whomsoever it may concern: Please urge Andes to write me immediately! I'm tired of this one-sided correspondence! He need expect no more letters from me until I have received one from him. J.P. Jr."[25] When word did arrive, it was from his mother, then at Aix-les-Bains with his father. Pulitzer had "talked" the letter to her, she explained, because he did not have a shorthand secretary with him. He hadn't written for so long mainly because of "his disposition," as she delicately expressed it. He was still smarting from "your desertion from your post to go to the ball game" and all the professions of hard work and duty that had preceded it. "But your letter suggesting breaking away from him, not communicating with him unless allowed to have a flat, a Japanese servant and a horse, cut him to the heart and greatly angered him." Then came the familiar recital of Pulitzer's woes, concluding: "When he is hurt, he cannot forget. His mind revolves around and around the hurt during all the long hours of night and headachy days." This was followed by the equally familiar refrain that the father's love was not reciprocated by his son's, but still "he loves you and has tried what he considers best for you." Her empathy for her son was apparent in her closing: "Now, my dearest, keep this letter so that you may read it [in the] future should the occasion arise or should I have misunderstood him. I have not read it to him. With a heart full of love, your devoted Mother."[26]

This came as a shock to Joseph. He was especially surprised that his remark about the flat, servant and horse had been transposed into a demand, something he had tried to head off in his second letter. But he replied diplomatically, saying, "I expressed what I wanted to say in an asinine way and I see clearly how it must have irritated and hurt you." The offending remark, he emphasized, was only an expression of an "IDEAL" which he had mentioned "quite incidentally" to his desire to stay in St. Louis. He was sorry he hadn't yet "wiped out the traces" of going to the game, but added, "Nevertheless, I am not discouraged. I shall continue as I have been doing, to work as hard, as diligently and as intelligently as I know how. I am gifted with a strong constitution and can stand plenty of hard work." He pledged to prove this by working all summer without a vacation, except, he hoped, for a brief interruption to see his father when he returned home, "to get the inspiration that I always derive from seeing you in action."[27]

But Pulitzer wouldn't be consoled. From Carlsbad, he responded in a long letter that was highly revealing of the publisher's temperament and of the complexities with which his son had to deal. "To be frank, your Mother's letter was hers, not mine," it began. "It misrepresented my views and perverted my feeling." He hadn't written for so long, he explained, "because I felt hurt and bruised and sore and pained and wounded all over, and did not wish to trust myself until time had, at least, partially healed the wounds you had reopened and added to." Then he went to the heart of the matter:

> You deceive yourself completely, incredibly, in presenting your letter of alarm about the possibility of my taking you to

New York as any excuse whatsoever for the letter in which, after careful consideration, you threaten to leave me and the paper unless I give you a horse, a flat and a Japanese servant. There is not one scintilla of a shadow of a shade or one shade of a scintilla of a shadow of reason for the thought that I ever contemplated your coming to New York last year, this year or next year. It was a pure invention, utter and preposterous, a shallow crazy subterfuge.

But even if not ludicrous as an invention, what has it to do with the regular threat and "hold up" written, as you said, after careful reflection, that unless you could have a horse, a flat and a Japanese servant, *you* would not only leave St. Louis, not only shift for yourself, but have *no communication with me for a year?* There is no logic or consistency anyhow.

. . . It was this threat, a regular hold up, as they say in vulgar commercial phrase, that upset me beyond belief even more than your desertion for the football game. Much more, because the desertion, however unpardonable, had the one mitigating feature of an honorable confession. . . .

. . . I do appreciate fully the regularity and steadiness of your application to work. Indeed it pleased me very much. Ordinarily it would wipe out all ordinary faults or mistakes. I do not expect perfection. Lord knows I am indulgent enough and affectionate enough and weak enough in my children, but I must leave you under no delusion. I must say that if you worked ten times as hard, with one hundred times the talent you possess, it would still be no equivalent or recompense for the constant pain and suffering and distress, mental, moral and consequently, physical, by day and by night and almost every waking hour of the night and of the day you have caused me this winter and the winter before and certainly one winter before that.

. . . I want some love and affection from my children in the closing short span of life that still remains. If I cannot have that love and affection, I may expect to be spared wilful deliberate disrespect, disobedience and insult.

. . . I hope you will be kind enough to come to Bar

Harbor with the intention of staying there some time. How long I cannot now say because I do not know what may happen. Indeed, I do not even know but what you may still want to go away for a year or still insist upon the horse, flat and Japanese servant idea.

He said Joseph was "again laboring under a delusion" in believing he could learn more at the *Post-Dispatch* than under his father's direction. "I am vain enough to think that as far as the vitalities, fundamentals, . . . the creative, life-giving principles, the ideas and ideals of journalism are concerned, I can teach you more in one month than you can learn in any office in a year and perhaps in ten years," he asserted. "I am not talking of details and routine which I do not know myself and never did"—a claim any number of subordinates could dispute. And finally, he complained of being "in a wretched physical and nervous condition, every single element of the so-called cure or treatment having been a failure and having done me more harm than good." He looked forward with dread to "a horrible night" in the noisy harbor at Southampton before sailing on an unfamiliar steamer. "I have to expect a wretched trip and shall arrive in New York in a dreadful condition," he predicted.[28] He said he would need two days to recuperate in bed at Bar Harbor before sending for Joseph to join him.

Perhaps the strangest thing about the reaction of the elder Pulitzer to his son's latest letters was that the idea that Joseph might benefit by going off on his own had come from Pulitzer—as recorded in the obligatory memo by his son—the last time they were together, on the launch at Bar Harbor the previous August. To Joseph, this must have seemed a game with no rules.

7

In Love

As if to keep his son perpetually confused, Pulitzer followed his blistering letter two days later with a highly unusual apology. He had misinterpreted the horse, flat, and servant remark as a threat. "I quoted from memory and was wrong," he admitted. "I am glad I was wrong because it is in your favor." He said he had changed his mind and now wanted Joseph to meet him in New York on his arrival and then go up to Bar Harbor. The letter ended with a tantalizing postscript: "Of course I hope you will be glad to go to Bar Harbor and not show the smallest anxiety about returning to the young lady in St. Louis until I tell you to do so. Perhaps it is of some importance for you to make my acquaintance before you see her."[1]

If this was a hopeful sign to Joseph, it was only momentarily so, for he got a stern dressing-down when he and his father met, as if there had been no apology. The litany of the son's misdeeds again covered everything from his Harvard days to the present, complete with references to the "hold-up" letter. "One consequence is that JP dares not be generous," Joseph recorded in the memorandum of their conversation. "It might ruin me. His object is to cure me. . . . But for these incidents he would have been only too happy to have done something for me at the dinner, giving me some title, position, prestige, like Ralph." Pulitzer set down these terms: "You must regain my confidence and affection. Of course you can have first place in St. Louis, the very first, as soon as you are fit for it. When I feel sure you'll not run away. Confidence much more easily destroyed than regained."[2] This was what Pulitzer wanted him to bear in mind before he again saw "the young lady in St. Louis."

It was a lot to take in. Until this turn, Joseph had thought that at last he was inching upward in his mercurial father's estimate. In the three-month span between the offending letter and the angry response, there had been three indications of this. The first came in early March, when Ralph relayed this message from "Andes" by telegraph: "Joe to start sailing next Tuesday Kaiser Wilhelm for Cherburg. Arrange passage. Give him six weeks pay." He was to "make notes on the journey about his impressions of the office and his judgment of the men and their characteristics, their relative brains and qualities, value and work."[3] A second telegram delayed the departure for several weeks, so that he could sail with his mother. The second indication of confidence was the generous $23 weekly salary Pulitzer approved for Joseph in April, retroactive to the first of the year. He knew O'Neil had recommended only $10, and was greatly pleased that his father had more than doubled the amount. Third, and equally disarming, was the fact that Pulitzer had shown encouraging interest when Joseph formed a group of friends within a short time of his return to St. Louis and began having a busy social life.

That, more than anything else, made the European trip unappealing, but Joseph had couched his argument against going in strictly practical terms. "It is certainly beyond me and I certainly don't think I have deserved it," he wrote. On the one hand, he explained, the prospects of a voyage, a chance to see Europe, and the opportunity "to talk to you and to exchange views and find out what you think of me . . . tempt me strongly." But on the other hand, there was the "more logical, practical and sensible" argument that he should stay in St. Louis to prepare himself to relieve his father of some of his "terrible responsibilities." He had made headway since August, he wrote, "when I arrived here very hot, very miserable and very sorry for myself, but still with a considerable amount of determination and irritation at the thought of being considered a loafer." His main accomplishment, he continued, was that "I have acquired a real sincere liking for work and a veritable love for newspaper work, newspaper men and everything connected with newspapers." But his training wasn't complete: "I am on the verge of accomplishing my purpose and with a few months more time, I will, I feel, be in a position where I can help you and can relieve you of a few at least of your many burdens." He feared losing what he had gained by making a break at this point as well as "the possibility of my falling back into the old life and the old way of looking at things, from the standpoint of self-indulgence and nothing else."[4] He sent a copy of the letter to Ralph, asking him to show it to their mother so she would understand his attitude, and also to wire Butes, "asking him to use his influence in dissuading Andes." He also wanted Ralph to keep him posted "as to which way the wind is blowing, as I am . . . not unnaturally curious to know just where in hell I'm going to be the next minute."[5] He was grateful to hear on his twenty-second birthday, March 21, that his father considered his request both "wise" and "sensible" and had canceled the travel order, cabling through Ralph and adding, "Besides good to represent family name at dinner. Try and make good impression on public end."[6]

Although Joseph did not mention this as another reason for wanting to stay in St. Louis, he had made it plain during the last months of 1906 that Miss Elinor Wickham, daughter of a well-established St. Louis family, had become a powerful attraction. In his letters she became the centerpiece of his circle of friends, and he was rapidly falling in love. He had met her through his closest male friend, Andrew Drew, an up-and-coming *Post-Dispatch* reporter the same age as he, who was well thought of by Bovard and from a comfortably well-off family. Joseph often had Sunday dinner with the Drews and had particularly enjoyed one in October, about two months after his return to St. Louis, when several other young people were guests. Writing to his father the next day, he included in his listing of those present "the following girls: 2 Miss Drews, Emma, the younger extremely clever, a Miss Nugent, a Miss Somebody or Other, and a Miss Wickham, the last a very pretty and very vivacious young lady, next to whom I sat at dinner and with whom I got along reasonably well." He planned to see Miss Wickham again and promised that afterward "I'll write you all about her. But meanwhile don't think that I am forgetting my work for a pretty face."[7]

He kept his word. His letters over the next few months were sprinkled with news of his "social flutterings." Those who gathered at the Drew home became regular companions for dances, theater parties, and other outings, and Joseph virtually forgot about the east. "On the whole, I consider myself very fortunately situated," he wrote at the end of November. "And New York can remain where it is for all I care."[8] He quickly added that this shouldn't be taken to mean "that I'm falling back into my old habits and letting work come after play instead of vice versa." But he was having a very good time. "I find the society of St. Louis an extremely pleasant and hospitable one," he wrote two weeks later.

> Its great charm is its democratic informality. Why there's almost nothing girls can't do here. When they go to balls they are always called for by some man, with whom they drive off in a carriage, and by whom they are accompanied home. . . . A chaperone at a theater party is unheard of. Even at dinner parties the mother simply receives the guests, but when they go in to dinner, . . . the mother calmly disappears and the party takes care of itself. In spite of this unusual liberty, which to a N.Y. girl would seem incredible, the girls here are extremely well behaved and not a bit foolish or giddy. I tell you all this realizing that it's very frivolous but hoping that, from the fact that it's new, it will interest you.

In the same letter he wrote: "One of the strange differences between us two, to my mind, is the fact that you have never come anywhere near learning how to enjoy life whereas I, I fear, have learned the lesson only too well."[9]

That might have annoyed his father, but it hadn't. When Joseph wrote that his descriptions of his "dreadful frivolity" probably were boring, Pulitzer seemed surprised. "How could you . . . be so silly, to use a mild word, as to speak of my being bored with your so-called social frivolities?" he asked. "Your letter . . . certainly did not bore me as you seem to expect."[10] He had written something similar to Ralph the previous year in asking for more information about Ralph's fiancée, Frederica Vanderbilt Webb: "I am interested, always have been, in love affairs."[11]

Before long, Joseph was seeing "Nellie" Wickham, as she was called much to his dismay, almost exclusively. He had shown some interest in Emma Drew, Andrew's sister, whom he described as "decidedly clever and attractive," and Marjorie Thornburg, who was "attractive in spite of her name."[12] But by the end of the year "the fair Nell" was the leading lady in his letters. "How that name grates!" he wrote in December. "But she's a very attractive girl."[13] He dined often with the Wickhams, where the following March he met Elinor's grandfather, "Colonel Ed" Wickham, who told Joseph that he had known his father.

A week before the retirement dinner, Joseph gave a *"Post-Dispatch* party" for his group of friends, who had asked for a tour of the newspaper. It was chaperoned by Mrs. George Drew, wife of Andrew's older brother, and included stops in every department. The high point of the evening came while the group was gathered afterward at Faust's restaurant. "Andrew and I together wrote a fake story about the party," Joseph recounted, "describing my desperate attempt to break into St. Louis Society, had it set and had about 10 proofs pulled. These we suddenly flashed on the party, telling them that the story would appear on Sunday. It was quite an amusing thing and took a hit at everyone at the party."[14] The story, headlined "Mr. Pulshnitzer Tries to Burgle St. Louis Sassiety!" began with a paragraph accurately reflecting the strain at that time between father and son: "Joseph Pulshnitzer, Jr., who came to St. Louis because he had to choose between being disinherited or sent here, made a desperate attempt last night to break into St. Louis sassiety. The attempt failed." It described those in the group—who were in fact from leading St. Louis families—as bumptious nobodies who could do him no good in his quest for social acceptance. The names were only faintly disguised, and his admiration of one "Miss Nellie Sickem" showed through his gentle characterization of her as "the belle of Germantown and the lady of the never quiet brown eyes."[15] He also had a flash photograph taken of the group at the beginning of the tour and had prints delivered to the restaurant less than an hour later.

Coming as it did in the midst of such gaiety, the word that he was to go to Europe had hit Joseph a powerful blow. But doubting that he could change his father's mind, he began saying goodbye to his friends. Then, "when the reverse order came, it jarred him somewhat," O'Neil wrote Pulitzer, "involving as it did a renewal of closed social relations, with some incidental embarrassment, for a boy. But he quickly recovered control, as the automobilists say, and has since been regular and industrious."[16] Joseph's own report lightheartedly reflected his relief: "You would have been amused had you seen the tearful adieu I bade last week. To use the words of the clever Emma Drew, in speaking of me and Miss Wickham, 'You cut more ice with her last week than you ordinarily could have in a month.' . . . I fear the lady thought the whole business was a base deception, designed to get everyone's sympathy and expressions of regard."[17]

As it turned out, the pair was apart over the summer, probably at least partially because Pulitzer thought the romance should cool somewhat. He reassigned Joseph to the *World* — which he had written so emphatically in May that he had no intention of doing — again apparently in the passive role of observer, reading the *World* and its competitors and watching others at work. In late August, Joseph heard from O'Neil. "I have missed you much," he wrote, "because I relied on you to keep me in touch with the atmosphere of the editorial room, which I cannot often visit, and to keep me from a wrong judgment as to the artists and newshunters, whose work I estimate after it is printed, without knowing what brains were back of their doings."[18] Those doubtless were welcome words. It is likely, too, that he took some consolation from a magazine article published in December 1907, which he saved. Titled "Joseph Pulitzer: Father of Modern Journalism," it was full of praise but contained the following line: "There are strange, subtle Oriental twists in his mind."[19]

So Joseph had observed. Writing to Ralph two weeks after the "retirement" fetes, he remarked that in rereading "JP's telegram" he was struck by how " 'sacrifice everything to the public interest' is a pet phrase of his,

> but how can anyone really believe that he and the paper are sincere when we carry this fraudulent, deceptive stuff and make ourselves every day parties to the crime of ruining the fortunes and health of scores of ignorant people who believe in the paper they read, many of them no less fervently than they believe in the Bible? I swear the whole damned thing makes me sick every time I allow myself to think of it. . . . I give you my word that if I thought that I should never be able to run a successful newspaper without that class of stuff, I'd say To Hell with Journalism. What are your views? I wish to God I held your job. Why don't you do something about it? It's bound to come sooner or later anyway. And forgetting for a moment the moral side of it, what a hell of a nice fix we'd be in . . . if Hearst should come out tomorrow with a full page announcement that the Hearst papers will hereafter reject all doubtful medical and financial clairvoyant fake ads.[20]

But Ralph could see no reason for such intense concern. "I think it ridiculous to maintain that a paper should pander to paternalism by constituting itself the protector of its readers against their own foolishness as you would have it do," he replied. He then suggested that the only way to protect readers would be to hire "a tremendous and prohibitively costly staff of experts in innumerable different lines of business from mines through medicine to metaphysics" in order to screen out the deceptive claims. And then, he predicted, "about the only advertisements which would get into the paper, according to your standard, would be the death notices." He did think it justified to refuse ads offering cures for venereal diseases, because they could "shock the casual reader," and for abortions, because they were illegal. Otherwise, he thought it unnecessary for newspapers to look out for consumers to any greater extent than did postal or other federal and state regulations.[21]

A few weeks after this exchange, *Collier's* magazine published an article describing some of the most dangerous patent medicines, especially those formulated with addiction-producing cocaine, opium, and morphine and for which the recently enacted Pure Food and Drug Act now required ingredient labeling but not honest advertising. Joseph preserved it and Ralph's letter in a scrapbook he had begun. He also compiled some figures showing that the paper had taken in approximately $150,000 for medical advertising in 1906.[22]

Even if he couldn't agree with his brother, perhaps Ralph could appreciate the irony in this situation. He knew as well as Joseph that their father's call for "drastic independence" of his newspapers did not extend to the thought processes of his sons, which he tried to keep totally in his control. This, no doubt, was the most troublesome factor in the lives of both the elder sons, and their ways of dealing with it the critical point of difference between them. During these important formative years, Joseph's ability to appreciate his father's wisdom and at the same time disassociate himself on certain points was what suited him best for the role he was preparing to play. Curiously, his combative streak is what made him both independent of and also very much like his father. At Bar Harbor later that year, Pulitzer dictated to Joseph a memo to Ralph complaining that Ralph's diaries dwelt too much on "trouble, vexation and annoyance" that "I am impotent to deal with." To the memo Joseph appended this:

> Dear Ralph, One cold day and one rainy day have kept the great mogul indoors most of the time. Hence this belly-aching tone! He apparently doesn't want to be told anything unless it is that Hearst, Brisbane, Carvalho and Goddard [all of the *Journal*] have all jumped into the river, that no one in N.Y. is reading anything except the morning, Sunday and evening *World,* and that the price of white paper has dropped to nothing. Anything else he considers unnecessary and as indicating a particular desire on everyone's part to hound him down. J.P. Jr.[23]

— 8 —

Hopes and Hazards

When Joseph returned to St. Louis in the fall of what would have been his senior year had he stayed at Harvard, he was approaching a commencement of sorts that was for him fully as significant as receiving a college degree. Still more interested in the news operation than anything else about the *Post-Dispatch,* he concentrated his attention on city editor Oliver K. Bovard, of whom he had commented earlier in the year, "His self-confidence and positiveness are certainly sublime."[1] He had had the opportunity in May to compare Bovard's and Chapin's methods when Chapin came to St. Louis to "wake up the office." He found Chapin "much less tyrannical here than in New York. Here he is actually kindly. . . . That is where he beats Bovard, who hardly knows the meaning of the word receptiveness, and who by his surly unappreciative manner probably makes for the *Post-Dispatch* as many enemies of the people who come into contact with him as he does friends. But in his sacred regard for the principle which he calls 'privilege of publication' Bovard beats Chapin."[2]

Nine months later he wrote: "Bovard is doing *very well*. He shows not the slightest disposition to jump the traces, is polite and considerate and not the martinette he was last year and is working like a dog. I don't believe you've got a better newsman on the World but hesitate to say this for fear you will steal him from us."[3] He even went so far as to say that if Bovard "does not eventually develop into one of *the* newspaper men of the country, I shall be disappointed."[4] He wasn't. Bovard shortly became the paper's managing editor, a post he held for nearly three decades under the second Joseph Pulitzer, leaving a record for which he is still singled out.[5]

The association between the young Pulitzer and Bovard was one of those that are in a sense forced by fate upon individuals and could easily have been stressful, difficult, and unpleasant for both. Instead, it was largely harmonious because it was based on a mutual respect that had to have been instigated by Bovard, thirteen years Joseph's senior and by all accounts a man who said only what he thought and believed and never temporized. After Joseph's father, Bovard certainly was the young man's most important teacher — and to some extent, he seems always to have thought of theirs as a teacher-pupil relationship, even after Joseph inherited full authority as editor and publisher. For his part, Joseph never ceased to have the highest respect for Bovard as an editor and surely considered him the paper's most valuable employee. But at the same time, he had a sufficient sense of his own ability and special position to be able to learn from Bovard without being dominated by him. He was was neither hesitant nor fearful about mentioning, in writing to his father, points of news judgment on which he and Bovard had differed. Nor was he afraid to admit his own mistakes, as when the *Times* beat the midday edition on a fire story because he had lost track of the copy in the last-minute rush before deadline. "It made me infernally sore and taught me a lesson," he confessed.[6]

From the beginning of 1908, there were indications that Pulitzer and his son were on perhaps the best terms ever. In February, Joseph was named a director of the Pulitzer Publishing Company, publisher of the *Post-Dispatch,* an "indication of confidence" he greatly appreciated.[7] He admitted, however, that he had "never attached much importance to titles after observing the veritable 'brain storms' you have brought on yourself so often in your frantic efforts to manufacture titles that would soothe the injured feelings of your great journalists, such as Second Assistant Vice Pres (wasn't that one of your concoctions?). . . . I don't care much about titles; responsibility and authority are what I want."[8]

He was gradually getting more of both. Frank O'Neil died suddenly in January, and B. E. Bradley, who had been managing editor of the Chicago *Inter Ocean,* was hired to replace him. About the same time, managing editor Harry L. Dunlap resigned and Bovard was designated acting managing editor. Dunlap and Bovard had not gotten along—in part, at least, because the city editor was the more capable man. Shortly after these changes took place, Pulitzer asked Joseph to report "how those new stars are doing in their respective planetary systems."[9] Joseph rated both highly, especially Bovard, who, he said, "has developed amazingly in a year":

> O'Neil last year used to say of him that he could only appreciate police news. He has entirely outgrown this narrow view and shows excellent judgment in determining the relative value of news, be it police, political, financial or any other kind. He is conscientious, very fair, and insistent on keeping the news columns strictly accurate and clean. He is a real worker and has his mind concentrated from the time he arrives at 7 until he leaves at 5. He is a good judge of men and a good executive. As firm as Chapin in giving orders, he is less arbitrary. He has unusual talent for illustrations, diagrams, effective type display and pleasing make-up. . . . He is getting out a fine, bright, snappy, amusing, reliable and sane newspaper.[10]

In the same letter, he described his visit to the St. Louis House of Delegates, the city's lower legislative body: "Ye Gods and Little Fishes, I can't possibly describe the motley crew of half drunken thugs that we looked down upon from the visitors' gallery." He was surprised that the city "should allow itself to be represented by such a gang. . . . About 75% of them are saloon keepers. And I must say that my confidence in popular, representative government has been greatly shaken." Witnessing this led him to think, he said, that the *Post-Dispatch* had been wrong the previous year in denouncing State Representative Theron Catlin for voting against putting public utilities "at the mercy of just such thugs among the City House of Delegates. . . . I must say I would have voted just as he did."

When Joseph suggested that his father let him sit in as managing editor during Bovard's vacation in late August, Pulitzer professed alarm in a letter to Bovard marked "STRICTLY and most ABSOLUTELY CONFIDENTIAL":

> My dear Mr. Bovard:
>
> Joe startles me by suggesting that he wants to take your place during your vacation. I told him that he was utterly unfit and that it was ridiculous. I wish to show no favoritism of any sort. Yet although I have spoken so sharply and honestly believe in merit only, I think it fair to ask you to actually name the person who is to take your place . . . and incidentally express your impartial, unprejudiced, fearless opinion about Joe's news instinct, his exact degree of unfitness and actually name the person who in your honest judgment is fittest.
>
> I know that this is an embarrassing question and I give you my word that I will never hear what you say and will regard it as a personal favor if you will give me your opinion exactly as if he were in no wise related to me.[11]

Bovard's response was that he thought Joseph could handle the job, calling his news instinct "keen and broad" and "unusually well developed," though "naturally his judgment is immature."[12] He said more experienced men would be nearby should Joseph need help.

Joseph thoroughly enjoyed the assignment. "This one week has been a wonderful experience for me, for it has given me self-confidence, and after all, you have got to have self-confidence to do anything," he wrote midway through his tour of duty. "I told you I had a good time during my vacation, but that good time didn't compare with the one I'm having now," he continued. "I have been in heaven for the past week, and I shall indeed be sorry when Bovard returns."[13]

He wrote a long letter on the day his "reign" ended, reporting that he had gotten compliments from editors in both New York and St. Louis, "but being the proprietor's son and in danger of having my head turned by all these fawning sycophants, I must of course assume that they were not sincere. But whether they were sincere or not, I care little for their opinions. It is yours I want more than anything else, so won't you write and tell me what you think . . . of what I accomplished?"[14] He then proceeded to take credit for meeting deadlines, "playing up the best news we had every day on the first page and for beating the town on several stories, and for stirring up the whole staff and encouraging men to make as many suggestions as possible. As you see, I have claimed credit for almost everything in sight." He was proudest of getting out an extra edition on Labor Day morning, giving the result of a morning baseball game: "We made a big sale on that extra (for 10,000 papers, I believe) for the other papers waited until their regular home edition before going to press." He also said he would immediately begin a regular routine of spending an hour and a half each day talking with the various business department heads, reading his father's correspondence to them, and studying daily, weekly, and monthly advertising, circulation, and financial reports. Under that regime, he predicted, "I shall accomplish as much as I used to accomplish in a day's aimless wandering from one department to another."[15]

Pulitzer was pleased. "I am only too glad to express immense satisfaction and surprise about your general success," he wrote from Wiesbaden, where he was taking a cure. He said he had received highly favorable reports on Joseph's editorship from Ralph and several other executives, "and only Bovard is cold-bloodedly critical. I personally think altogether too much so." He said he liked most "the enthusiasm, ambition and *love of work* you showed. No man can do much without the latter no matter what his talent and no man can help doing something and perhaps considerable with it." He cautioned his son not to aspire to the managing editorship himself, but "you do want to know whether you have a competent managing editor and staff and the more you watch the individual members of the staff, the more you dare to change, the more you develop knowledge of men, their exact work and value, the more fit you will be as the head of a great news machine and newspaper." He was especially pleased that Joseph showed a talent for making the paper attractive and "talked about," saying that this would "lift it above the commonplace" and "raise the question among people in the cars and everywhere — 'Did you see that?' with the answer: 'No! Where did you see it?' and the reply: 'I saw it in the P–D.' "[16]

Actually, Bovard's comments were largely positive, stressing only the fact that Joseph had "limited actual experience in news handling that may have led him to make some decisions Bovard would not have made. Their biggest difference was over the front-page prominence Joseph gave the Labor Day ball game. "He stood his ground where he thought he was right and I wrong," Bovard wrote the publisher, explaining that he would have put the story on the first page of the sports section.[17] But that view hadn't influenced Joseph at all. Neither Bovard, White, Ralph, "nor anyone else under the sun except you can ever convince me that I overplayed the baseball story," Joseph wrote his father. "The town had gone temporarily insane on the subject. It was in the air. . . . I know I was right."[18]

All that year Joseph had grown surer of something else as well: his deepening affection for Elinor Wickham. Back in February, his father had proposed another foreign trip for him — this time to Cuba — because "travel abroad is education as much as pleasure, and you need it."[19] But he had made no issue of it when Joseph replied that he thought it better to stay in St. Louis until summer, when he would like to sail his boat from New York to Bar Harbor, "stopping off here and there to see my friends at New London, Narragansett, Newport, Jamestown, mostly Jamestown!!"[20] Pulitzer agreed to this, "*especially if this young lady should like it.*"[21] He knew Elinor's family summered at Jamestown, and he had decided the relationship had become so important that the young lady should have a code name, "The Divinity," which began to show up often in the letters between father and son.

There was nothing unusual about Pulitzer's wanting to guard

the identity of Miss Wickham in the correspondence between Joseph and himself. His use of code served not only as a means of protecting sensitive business information, but also helped establish a measure of privacy among the members of his far-flung family, who kept in touch via letters and telegrams. The fact that he decided to codify the young lady suggested that she stood a chance of becoming a member of the family, a matter of the highest interest to Pulitzer. That he liked her from the time of his son's first descriptions of her seems certain, for he encouraged the relationship and wanted frequent information about it. "He has noticed you have not mentioned your divinity in the last two or three letters," a secretary pointedly nudged Joseph in April.[22] He replied that he had purposely delayed writing until he had bought a car—a 1906 Packard runabout—with his father's $1,200 birthday gift and an additional $860 from his bank account. He explained, "After looking into all the cheaper cars I discovered that they don't last and that I could do better buying a secondhand high class car, paying more for it." He described the machine as "good as new . . . newly painted, very good looking, can make 50 miles an hour, now seats three people and after I get an extra rumble seat made . . . will seat four." He considered the $2,060 price a bargain, for the car had been used only a year and had originally cost between $4,000 and $5,000. He called it "the best present you've ever given me with the possible exception of the boat." Among "the greatest advantages of owning a machine is that it gives you something to talk about," he observed, explaining that he and a young lawyer friend had dinner the previous night "and we talked autos for three hours, steadily."[23]

The car was, of course, a great social asset. "I note your remark about my not having mentioned the Divinity in my last letters," he wrote. "If not, it was an oversight. I still find her most attractive and incidentally, in this connection, I find the automobile most useful. We take spins together quite often, and next Sunday four of us, she included, are going out into the country on a picnic."[24] He still rode the streetcar to work, he explained, because the half-hour ride gave him time to read the morning papers, "and anyway I wouldn't care to have the men in the office seeing it every day."[25] One of his most detailed letters was written in mid-April, when he described a Sunday afternoon outing with three friends:

> After congratulating each other on the weather, we started
> off . . . ran out to the Valley Park Hotel on the Manchester
> Road, 18 miles out, where we had lunch. Thence we went
> on out . . . 20 miles further, when bang went the lefthand
> front tire. We had no extra one, and were up against it, as
> they say on the Bowery, when along came another machine.
> Seeing the dejected expression on our faces, the driver
> stopped and hopped out, introduced himself as Scudder of
> the Scudder Sail Processing Company, his friend as Mr.
> Bader, an automobile dealer who had just sold a car to
> Scudder and was just giving him his first lesson, and a
> Miss Hill, a chemical blonde, who retired to the side of the
> road and began picking violets.

Scudder lent them his spare tire, and "after that nothing happened
except that as we neared town we were nearly choked to death by
the dust raised by the many machines ahead of us, all turned
homeward."[26]

In the same letter, he described a dinner he'd attended given to
launch the campaign for circuit attorney of Billy Connett, a young
lawyer with whom he had played tennis:

> On one occasion, Harry Hawes, who is a fine orator, was
> urging Connett's friends in a most serious, impressive
> way, to stand by him after his election, as well as before it.
> "How many of you, my friends, after the smoke of battle
> and the joy of victory have passed by will remember this
> young man Connett, whom you have just put into political
> office," he asked, in a very serious and dignified tone. Up
> on the table in a far corner of the room jumped a very
> much intoxicated individual waving his napkin over his
> head and shouting: "I will, Harry! I will! I'll stand up for
> Billy! You bet your life I will!" Incidentally, he was the only
> man in the 300 who was at all spiritually involved, which
> surprised me. This outburst of his provoked much laugh-
> ter and no resentment, but when, during the mayor's speech
> he jumped up again and shouted some incoherent remarks
> to the mayor . . . he was finally picked up and thrown out
> bodily. Altogether, I enjoyed the evening immensely.

He saw Elinor regularly, and almost exclusively. The names of other young ladies appeared in his letters, but seldom were mentioned a second time. Aware that the couple was contemplating marriage, in late summer Elinor's family sent her on a six-month trip around the world; there was some doubt about whether an alliance between this old St. Louis family and the lately arrived, newly rich, and New York–based Pulitzers was advisable. Perhaps a separation would cool the relationship. Elinor's mother was a Catlin, a family that had made its money in tobacco manufacturing in St. Louis. Her lineage through her father, Edmund Wickham, who died in 1907, went back to the preeminent Carter family of Virginia.[27]

"The Divinity must be just about arriving in Japan," Joseph wrote his father in mid-September. "I have had three letters from her, òne written from the train, one from Seattle, and one from the steamer mailed at Victoria." He said he had "not changed a particle" in his desire to marry her, "nor shall I change during these next six months. I fear they will be long in passing, but I find that a great consolation lies in work. I guess I'll survive."[28]

In October, he sent copies of some of the reports on his temporary managing editorship to Elinor in Japan — including his father's congratulatory letter on his performance — and reported to his father that he had received four more letters from Elinor. "In spite of the lady's prolonged absence, I like St. Louis more than ever," he emphasized. "I feel that in this town I have a wonderful opportunity to make something of myself, to help the community, and to please you. As a community, I far prefer St. Louis to New York, and I prefer the P–D organization to the *World*. . . . For a long time to come I shall be satisfied to become a prominent St. Louisan. And if Providence has destined me ever to become a prominent American, that can come later on."[29]

This relative contentment was soon shattered. Pulitzer recalled Joseph to New York that winter. Ralph had been ill again, and Pulitzer feared that he never would be strong enough to assume full responsibility as publisher, so he turned to Joseph as his only alternative. Once again the young man had no specific duties; he was just to observe and ask questions. During dinner one evening at the Seventy-third Street mansion when Pulitzer happened to be at home, he exploded at Edith for making too much noise in carving her squab. She broke down in tears. Joseph angrily came to her defense. "This is just too much," he exclaimed. "I won't allow you to speak to my sister in this way. I'm not going to stand any more of your bullying. I'm through. I'm pulling out."[30]

He left the table and the house and returned to St. Louis, where he made the rounds of competing newspapers, asking for a job as a reporter, but none would hire him. The exact chain of subsequent events is unclear, but it appears that he returned to New York and had a session with his father, the upshot of which was that Joseph was ordered to leave home. He wrote a letter accepting this, which he showed to his mother and Edith.[31]

Pulitzer responded in a telegram suggesting a compromise. Joseph replied that he appreciated the gesture but frankly didn't think it was possible for them to get along. "For years I have resented the realization that I was nothing but a rich man's son of no market value in this world and dependent for everything I had on you," he began. "I am so selfishly constituted that I am unable to make allowances for your many afflictions," he continued, adding that "being thus nearly always dissatisfied, I feel that I was acting the part of a hypocrite in swallowing my resentment and simulating demonstrations of affection." Furthermore—"probably the most important of all"—was that he wanted to get married but didn't want to do so, once his father consented, "on an allowance that I might be deprived of any day. And there is one more reason . . . my profound detestation for life in New York and my horror at the prospect of it, no matter how remote." He conceded, "Perhaps I am ruining my life by writing this letter . . . but I am young and foolish and optimistic and I prefer to believe that instead of ruining it I am beginning it. . . . I shall not go to hell as you may fear."[32] He credited himself with having the health, ambition, and persistence to make something of himself, and predicted that in the process his affection for his father would not diminish but grow—a prophecy that eventually came true.

Pulitzer's next gesture was to assure his son that he regretted ordering him out and to offer him a choice of three alternatives, evidently presuming that Joseph's attraction to Elinor Wickham made all but the first quite unappealing. It was, essentially, the status quo: Joseph's staying at the morning *World* until Ralph's return, and then going back to the *Post-Dispatch*. The second choice, as recorded by Joseph, was his going to Paris "to shift for myself, study French journalism and rub up my French." The third was going to work on an American newspaper, "preferably in Denver or on the Pacific coast" but not in either St. Louis or New York. Joseph's first reaction was to reject all three, but after sleeping on it he agreed to return to the morning *World* for "10 days or 2 weeks at the longest," after which he would ask to be assigned to the Sunday *World* as assistant to the Sunday editor "with or without title." There he would cultivate "my only real aptitude," working up Sunday feature ideas. In addition, "I shall expect to spend one week out of every month in St. Louis until Ralph's return, when I shall go back to St. Louis for good." He called his most recent assignment at the *World* "absolutely unprofitable to me" and a waste of "4 valuable months that I can never regain," adding, "I must get started at something I can do well." He said he felt he owed it to his father, Ralph, and himself "to make one more attempt to get along with you on your newspapers."[33]

Apparently unbeknown to Joseph—although there had been threats off and on for several years—Pulitzer drastically revised his will, which had been drawn in 1904, during the contretemps of March 1909. The consequences were the most severe for Joseph. The original will made him the recipient of the income from three-fifths of the stock in both the *World* and the *Post-Dispatch,* with Ralph and Herbert each to receive one-fifth shares. Those provisions were revoked in a codicil dated March 23, 1909. Pulitzer changed the distribution to six-tenths to Herbert, two-tenths to Ralph, one-tenth to the principal editors and managers of the newspapers, and only one-tenth to Joseph, cutting him from a 60 percent share to a 10 percent share. Further, in a move most likely influenced to some extent by Joseph's preference for the *Post-Dispatch* and St. Louis over New York and the *World,* the codicil authorized the sale of the *Post-Dispatch* if the trustees eventually so desired, but forbade them to sell the *World.* "I particularly enjoin my sons and my descendants," Pulitzer directed, "the duty of preserving, perfecting and perpetuating 'The World' newspaper (to the maintenance and upbuilding of which I have sacrificed my health and strength) in the same spirit in which I have striven to create and conduct it as a public institution, from motives higher than mere gain."[34]

Pulitzer seems never to have recorded anything indicating his reasons for dividing the newspaper assets unequally among his sons, though his assessment in 1904 of their relative capacities for work would be a plausible explanation, given Ralph's fragile health and Herbert's youth. Joseph's fall from first to last five years later so closely parallels the clashes between them as to account for that change. Untested Herbert's move into first place could be explained as hope for his potential, while the verdict on Ralph remained the same. Pulitzer's concern about Ralph's health came through in a rather backhanded way in a June 1909 letter: "I have just finished a conversation with [secretary Norman G.] Thwaites, cross-examining him as to how you stood the heat last summer. He said very well. This encourages me especially as I assume that like thousands and thousands of professional and business men you will live in the country or at the sea shore; will not exceed the four hours [of work per day] limit; will not even do that much if you are not feeling well; will stay away any day you like. . . . Incidentally if you go to the city it may do you some good to observe sympathetically and appreciatingly the work real journalists have to do during the heated term — who are not proprietors nor proprietor's sons."[35]

Whatever his motivations, for the sons their father's erratic temperament seems to have been explanation enough for his changing the will. It still gave them equal votes in the newspaper trust it created. After their father's death, they agreeably arranged more equitable incomes without, technically speaking, altering the dividend distribution. But time would show that Pulitzer's initial assessment of Joseph as the best suited to carry the torch in the next generation had been right.

New Responsibilities

A
s unsettling as the events of March 1909 had been, Joseph came out of them a more pragmatic man. Realistically speaking, marriage to Elinor Wickham was highly unlikely unless he achieved some sort of peace with his father — and largely on his father's terms, whatever they might be. No one yet had found a better way to deal with so moody and mercurial a temperament than the course Joseph now chose: respectful obedience, even if it meant long periods of less agreeable duty at the *World* and away from Elinor.

He had her full understanding. That summer she wrote a friendly note to Pulitzer that pleased him and brought a generally encouraging response. He sent his reply to Joseph, telling him that he could withhold the letter "if you think it will do harm to your suit" and simply tell Elinor that he thanked her but had been too ill to respond. "I should not like to feel that I have done anything in the matter but good, not only to you but to the girl, whose happiness singularly enough I seem even more called upon to respect than yours," he wrote.[1] The response itself, which Elinor may never have read, was vintage J.P.: "I probably think as much of you as the person you so truly describe as my lazy 'and good for nothing son'—many a truth is spoken in jest." He complimented her "for the good influence you have exercised over him," concluding that "he already owes you a great deal, although it has not been sufficient to remove his growing disaffection and disrespect toward me." And finally: "Try your moral sense and get him to tell you the truth what his conduct toward me has been for the last ten years, and see whether you cannot influence him toward a father who is already old and broken, totally blind, cannot sleep, has an infinite variety of infirmities with one foot and a half in his grave, and expects nothing from his children except a little less intense selfishness and some sympathy."[2]

Now resolved to show his father nothing but courtesy and cooperation, Joseph did not let this ruffle him. During the spring and summer, he had described his work at the *World* and a trip of several weeks to Europe—where he saw his father at Aix-les-Bains—in bright, agreeable detail. At the *World,* he spent most of his time in the news department, observing how the assistant city editor orchestrated coverage of "the ordinary routine news." He knew his father wanted him to spend two hours a day in the business office and pledged to do that as soon as he returned from a trip to St. Louis. His eagerness to see Elinor, even though he didn't mention her name, came through when he wrote that he knew he would enjoy the trip, "and I am sincerely grateful for it." He pledged to report his observations of the *Post-Dispatch* on his return and described the major *World* men as "all well and happy, as we are printing the news and making money."[3] Joseph was himself the subject of a piece of routine news in August, when he was stopped in Jamaica, Queens, for speeding at thirty miles an hour and was fined $10. His guilty plea "was received with a satisfied sigh by the court," the *Times* reported.[4]

Joseph seldom heard from his father, but was patient and uncomplaining. Finally, he got two letters in early October from

Berlin written by secretary Norman G. Thwaites. Both were generally upbeat. Thwaites said the publisher liked two of Joseph's suggestions to exploit interest in the new field of aviation. One was that the *World* drop an imitation bomb—a bundle of *World*s—on a battleship soon to enter New York harbor and thus show its vulnerability to air attack; the other was to commission a flight from New York to St. Louis for a prize of $20,000. He didn't like a proposal that the *World* reprint the editorial comments of the leading midwestern papers while President William Taft toured that section seeking support for a tariff. "Let politics alone, particularly printing mere editorial utterances and opinions in an off year, and other academic things, theories, speculations, conjectures," Joseph's father advised. "They are not of universal interest but mere class interest. Always think of what would interest everybody."5

A month later, accompanied by daughters Edith and Constance aboard his luxurious 269-foot steam yacht *Liberty*, which was specially built for him in 1907 at a cost of $1.5 million to operate as noiselessly as possible,6 the senior Pulitzer was nevertheless in a dark mood. A new ailment—sharp rheumatic pains in his shoulder—was annoying him. While walking on the deck with Edith one morning, Pulitzer talked about "Joe, his future and his present situation," she recorded. "Father clearly stated that he was only too willing to set the date for Joe's wedding if only Joe would settle in New York and work steadily for six months." This was "not so much for Joe's sake as for Nell's," because Pulitzer felt "that he must protect her just as he felt some years ago about Frederica, when he exacted a six-month delay from Ralph." He had absolutely no reservations about Nell, but [underscored three times] "if Joe cannot buckle down and work he is not fit to marry." He complained about Joseph's having told people at the *World* of his dislike for New York—"the worst thing he could do." As for St. Louis, Pulitzer considered it "a provincial town" that "affords far less scope than New York for a man ambitious for honor, importance, power and prestige." It was the same old story: Pulitzer was distressed by the young man's independent streak and was annoyed because his son didn't share what had been his own goals at that age. "Joe would be married now," Edith was told, "had it not been for his own arbitrary unwillingness to respect and obey

Father's judgment with sincerity and zeal." Pulitzer did make a significant concession, though: "Joe has good news instinct but lacks soundness of judgment which . . . he can acquire through experience."[7]

As he had for eight months now, Joseph took this stoically. If his father wanted obedience, he would get it. "Will devote every moment to your assignment. Am very grateful," he cabled to London at one point. When Pulitzer wrote cryptically from Naples in late November that he was thinking of having Joseph come over so that they could discuss "the personal matter in which you are so greatly involved,"[8] Joseph replied that he would "be only too glad" to make the trip, but when it didn't materialize he did not complain. He produced a lengthy response to a list of questions from his father concerning the young man's assessments of various news and business executives, his opinion on whether pages two and three of the *World* should carry advertising (he voted no), and the extent of Joseph's criticisms of the work of writers and artists. One criticism was of a cartoonist "for caricaturing J. P. Morgan's diseased nose on the ground that it was unfair." He said it was a struggle "to get over my natural instinctive horror of hurting a man's feelings." He respectfully disagreed with his father's opposition to building American embassies in Europe, calling it "undignified, to say the least, for ambassadors to have to operate out of hotels."[9]

He spent Christmas in St. Louis but was ordered back to New York as soon as the new year opened. "I have returned from St. Louis with a fresh mind and full of enthusiasm and a desire to do what I can to improve the Morning World," he wrote. He thought he had the answer, one that would have been a great sacrifice for the *Post-Dispatch*: "Make Bovard absolute, complete, actual, official managing editor of the Morning World." He considered Bovard, who had been working in New York since late November as one of four candidates for the *World*'s managing editorship, "the strongest newsman in this shop today" because he consistently produced bright story ideas and was an effective critic and leader of the news staff. Remarking on a critique Bovard had written describing the organization of the *World,* he said he was "amazed that this man, who only a few years ago was taking want ads over the counter on the St. Louis Star should today be able to write a letter so closely reflecting many of your ideas, sometimes apparently in your very words." If he were in his father's place, he would give Bovard the top news job with absolute authority to run the *World* for a month to suit himself, after which Bovard would either get the job or return to St. Louis.[10]

As it turned out, Bovard stayed for several months rotating in the managing editor's job with the three other candidates, *World* men Charles M. Lincoln, J. J. Spurgeon, and Robert Lyman. In the end, Pulitzer gave the job to Lincoln and offered Bovard the assistant managing editorship, which he declined, saying he would rather be concertmaster in St. Louis than "play second fiddle" in New York.[11] It was a fateful decision, one might speculate, given the *World*'s eventual demise against the *Post-Dispatch*'s growth and prosperity. Even more intriguing is the question of what might have happened had Joseph not resisted New York so firmly and become editor and publisher of the *World,* with Bovard as his managing editor. But the tangible significance in the matter is what it suggests about the second Joseph Pulitzer's ability to size up men and situations. "I have an instinctive, firm, absolutely positive conviction that he is the man we need and are looking for," he wrote of Bovard. Pulitzer wasn't impressed. "Repress your foolish enthusiasm for Gushless," he advised, using Bovard's code name. "He has not done a single big thing although having more time than anybody to think."[12]

On January 4, 1910, for the first time since May, Joseph raised the issue of his wish to marry in a letter to his father: "We are both anxious to end the demoralizing suspense of this long three years of waiting *this spring,* and I beg you to end it by giving your consent," he pleaded, because "our minds are and have been for a long time made up."[13] In a note the next day, he apologized again for the things he had said the previous March about their not being able to get along and admitted that marriage "without your assistance . . . is out of the question."[14]

Apparently satisfied at last, Pulitzer summoned Joseph to join him at his villa at Cap Martin in March, a week before his son's twenty-fifth birthday. During that visit, he consented to the marriage and told Joseph he was giving him $1,000 for his birthday. "As I sat by the window of the train yesterday as we skirted the edge of the Mediterranean as I looked back toward Cap Martin and saw the villa," the young man wrote the day after they parted,

> it made me realize more keenly than I have realized in all my life under what deep obligation I am to you and how very much at fault I have been in the past in not feeling this obligation. . . . In a way I hated to leave you back there and even now with the happy prospect that I have before me I feel very selfish in going away. The thought of that letter I wrote you a year ago has haunted me and at this moment I can't forget it. It fills me with shame. Your generosity to Nell and me has floored me. . . . I intend to prove my appreciation by doing all that lies in my power, little as it may be, to help you. I will gladly forfeit any pleasure, even my contemplated visit to St. Louis, if it will please you. I ask only that you put me to the test.[15]

He celebrated his birthday aboard the *Lusitania* on the return trip by giving a dinner complete with "special little menus with our names engraved on them and the dates March 21, 1885–1910" for himself and two Englishmen he had befriended.[16] He also interviewed British explorer Sir Ernest Shackleton on the voyage and sent his story to the *World* by wireless.

In April it was announced that Miss Wickham, "a debutante of last season, when she was maid of honor at the Queen of the Veiled Prophet's ball, the annual social event of St. Louis," and who was related on her mother's side to "the Catlins, one of the oldest families of this city," would marry Joseph Pulitzer Jr. on June 1.[17] Pulitzer apparently had yielded on another issue as well, for the announcement revealed that after a wedding trip abroad the couple would live in St. Louis.

Once the marriage was announced, Pulitzer became a most enthusiastic backer. In May, he instructed the *Post-Dispatch* treasurer to give Joseph $3,000 from Pulitzer's personal account, and sometime before June 1 another $5,000, as the first installment of a $20,000-a-year personal allowance his son was to receive in addition to his salary. He authorized the payment of any bill of $10,000 "or thereabouts for the purchase of any wedding present Miss Wickham may make," cautioning the treasurer to "treat the thing strictly confidentially even in the office."[18] He also modified his will to include a $250,000 bequest to Elinor.[19]

The elder Pulitzer did not feel well enough to attend the wedding, which was held at the Wickham home on exclusive Vandeventer Place — then the best address in St. Louis — but, always extravagant with gifts, he sent a $50,000 solid-gold dinner service as his wedding present. "I hope there will be as little as possible in the papers about the wedding and no publicity of presents," he had written a few weeks before.[20] However, his gift and that of the bridegroom were reported in the non-Pulitzer newspapers.[21] Joseph gave his bride a cluster of diamonds, which she wore on her wedding gown. Edith Pulitzer was a bridesmaid, and Ralph was his brother's best man.[22] The bride was given in marriage by her Uncle Daniel Catlin, one of the earliest St. Louis friends of the first Joseph Pulitzer some forty years before.

—— 10 ——

On Trial

On their return to New York following a three-month European honeymoon, during which Elinor finally met her father-in-law, Pulitzer cabled them that they could go on to St. Louis, "but permanency impossible yet." That made it impractical to buy a home, so the newlyweds rented an unfurnished three-story brick house at 3836 Lindell Boulevard for $100 a month. It was on the edge of the city's best neighborhood, where most of the economic and social elite—including nearly all the members of the most exclusive St. Louis Country Club, of which the young Pulitzers eventually became members—had their homes at that time.[1] Joseph considered the rental "the best house in town for the money," estimating its selling price at $3,000. It had a generous lawn, large living and dining rooms downstairs, and four large bedrooms and a sitting room on the upper floors. They bought some furnishings and borrowed some items from Elinor's family.[2]

Had Pulitzer been certain that Joseph's career would be at the *Post-Dispatch,* he probably would have given the couple a house, as he had Ralph and his wife in New York in 1905—right next door to his own mansion on Seventy-third Street. Joseph made it clear to his father that he understood the situation: his future hinged on his father's decision as to whether Ralph had the physical stamina to become eventually the *World*'s editor and publisher. But Joseph could not resist commenting that he was "looking forward to going to work on a paper which I regard as superior in most respects to the World. Its only inferiority, as I see it, is that its influence is confined to St. Louis and Mo. and is not international as is the World. On the other hand its influence in St. Louis far exceeds the World's influence in New York City."[3]

Ten days later he described his enthusiasm for his routine as assistant managing editor, a position he had created for himself and that kept him constantly busy in the newsroom and the composing room. The work involved "the really active duties and responsibilities which I like and which somehow I have never had in New York."[4] Pulitzer said he would try to decide after the elections whether Joseph could stay in St. Louis, but protested: "Don't blame me, blame circumstances, circumstances! They are fate, destiny, anything you please, although not always everything. . . . My advice to you is to make the best and not worry or trouble me. Even if you don't write disagreeable letters you don't want to feel that you have lodged a disagreeable thought like the misery you endured the last two years of your deep love, because I brought you to New York." He said Joseph would help himself if he made "a strong record in St. Louis," not only as the "unessential" assistant to Bovard but also by getting more experience on the business side: "Yes! The wretched and much despised business . . . of which you know *nothing* and of which, after all, you ought to know something if you have the ambition to be the head even of the P-D. You ought to spend half your time in concentrating on that, and that is not enough." In a postscript, Pulitzer added another reason for delaying on the house: "Incidentally, further, although strictly private, a baby is needed for a house and vice versa!"[5]

At that point, he had only one grandchild, Ralph Pulitzer Jr., born August 28, 1906.

During October and November, Bovard prepared as requested detailed summaries of *Post-Dispatch* news performance for Pulitzer, who had now been "retired" for more than three years and even before that had professed only slight interest in the St. Louis paper "because I do not read the paper and do not consider myself one-tenth as much interested in or responsible for it as the editorial page of the *World.* "[6] Bovard's reports credited J.P. Jr. with a number of news suggestions that were successfully followed through, and with writing an editorial recommending that public golf links be built in Forest Park, the major park in St. Louis, which local officials pledged to do. A "Special Report on J.P. Jr." began: "He is thinking all the time."[7] Joseph continued his diary, though at weekly intervals, when he was to give "the pith, point and essentials of the specially interesting things."[8] When he noted his disagreement with Bovard's plan to send a reporter to sound out Senator Robert La Follette of Wisconsin and *Louisville Courier-Journal* editor Henry Watterson on Theodore Roosevelt's prospects in 1912 and other speculative political topics, Pulitzer ruled that his son was "quite right." But it was a delicate matter, he pointed out, "as to how you will deliver the message to Bovard." He wanted it clearly understood that "Bovard is responsible and you, Joe, are absolutely his subordinate." There was to be "No Nepotism! No Nepotism! No Nepotism!" Just how Joseph conveyed the message is unknown, but this is what it was:

> Mr. Bovard must stop playing politics. . . . Mere opinions, dissertations and not news. Space is too valuable. I would kill a man in New York who did that sort of thing. Be very chary of all speculative, conjectural politics; stop statesmanship, La Follette especially, who is a blatherskite. Very bad judgment indeed. Stick to local news and human interest features.[9]

The elder Pulitzer revealed how fully in charge he considered himself by directing Joseph to make it clear to all the *Post-Dispatch* executives that the son did not speak for his father: They should not consider anything "Andes' wish because they had consulted you. This is dangerous!"[10] But to make the matter more complicated, Pulitzer encouraged his son to nag the advertising and general managers about clearing pages two and three of ads if he was "*sure to tell both that you have no authority whatsoever* but are only practicing moral, friendly suggestiveness and exercising perseverance. I believe that if you were to nag these gentlemen as much as you nag me on some subjects and remind them fifty times, the pages will be cleared and you will have achieved reform without responsibility."[11] How closely Joseph's work was being followed came through in this: "Your diary states: 'Corrected grammatical error on the editorial page.' Andes would like you to send him this instance of error with your correction."[12]

His father's gentler side revealed itself in an occasional personal letter: "Delighted to hear of your house and home—appetizing description. . . . I am interested in every detail, not, of course, on account of the d——d money but because the money is simply an indication of the kind and character. Any particularly handsome furniture you would like to have or need?" He was sending along some books, including Lord Acton on the French Revolution, "but don't think for a moment that I would be surprised to hear that you cannot stand them. If so don't read them. You can't change nature or force taste." He closed "With love to Nell or Elinor, as I prefer. It sounds so much more literary and stately."[13]

Shortly before Christmas, Joseph responded, describing their domestic life as "a quiet one": "I get home usually about 6, and am glad to stay home for dinner, read and chat afterwards and go to bed early." They had a French lesson—something they knew Pulitzer would like—at the house two afternoons a week from 5:00 to 6:30. A former governess of Nell's would talk with them and listen while they read aloud. "She corrects our mistakes in grammar and pronunciation," Joseph explained. They took drives once or twice a week, and on Sundays slept late and then read the Sunday papers, lunched with Elinor's mother, attended a park concert, and usually had a few young people in for five o'clock tea.[14]

This routine was broken at year's end when Joseph received instructions through Ralph to stay in New York after he and Elinor joined their mother at Christmas while Ralph endured a month of close scrutiny and advice while cruising to Athens aboard the *Liberty*. In recent years, the entire family had been celebrating the holiday aboard the yacht, running between the Virginia coast and New York, but Pulitzer was not up to it for what would be his last Christmas. Joseph's gift to his father was a framed photograph of Elinor, which of course its recipient couldn't see but which he could have a secretary describe to him as he sometimes had one of them describe scenery or great works of art he had seen in brighter days. The gift pleased him.

The instructions he had Ralph pass along directed Joseph to work primarily as *World* managing editor Albert Lincoln's assistant, in the hope, it seems likely, that he would be as enthusiastic about that role in New York as he had been in St. Louis. He was specifically instructed not to spend more than an hour a day in the business department, a reversal of what he'd been told to do in St. Louis. Ralph said their father considered this a fine opportunity for Joseph to "remove the bad impression which your past reluctance to stay in New York on several occasions left on his mind." Two other reasons for this assignment, Ralph added, were that Joseph could observe "a crusade Father is just starting for an extra session of congress to lower the tariff" in which the *Post-Dispatch* would be expected to take "a very active part" and could help plan a $100,000 promotional campaign Pulitzer had authorized for each of the newspapers.[15]

Joseph accepted the assignment cheerfully, writing that both he and Elinor were "very well satisfied to be here." And, not surprisingly now that she was with him, "New York seems far less unattractive to me now than it used to." Their absence also meant they would miss the busy social activity of St. Louis in January, which neither regretted.[16] They "telegraphed refusals to several large formal balls," he wrote, "such as that of the Imperial Club, which you may remember and which are very stupid affairs, which otherwise I suppose we should have had unwillingly to attend."[17]

As that indicated, when they were in St. Louis, they were a part of what *Post-Dispatch* women's feature writer Marguerite Martyn described as "The Charmed Circle" of St. Louis society. In fact, after a dinner party back in December at which Joseph met Theophile ("Toto") Papin, the man from whom all the best families sought advice when presenting their daughters to society, he suggested that Miss Martyn interview Papin for a Sunday feature on "What Is Society?" Papin responded that St. Louis society was on a par with that of New York, Baltimore, New Orleans, and several European cities and that the "best social phase in St. Louis is dining, with now and then a ball." He described a dinner "in a house which is at the very heart of things socially . . . in conservative old Vandeventer place [where Elinor's family lived]. There were twelve of us — three married pairs, three young women a year or so past the debutante stage, and three bachelors. The women were beautifully gowned. One wore a Liberty long trained velvet effect. Another a frock just brought from Paris. The men were served with cocktails in the palm room. The women drank nothing." The dinner conversation dealt with such topics as the new city charter, one of the city's periodic crusades to deal with smoke pollution, and a debate on whether to attend the rather risqué "Salome," which a touring opera company was to perform soon. Papin conceded that women, by the standards of the times, were growing more "mannish" by taking part in outdoor activities. "Yet that is no fault. The average young woman is improved by her golf playing, her walking, riding, motoring. Of course everything can be carried to extremes." One extremist, he suggested, was the daughter of Former President Roosevelt, Mrs. Alice Roosevelt Longworth of Washington, who nevertheless was "an awfully nice person. Awfully nice, and she does not smoke cigarettes."[18] (The *World* made it front-page news accompanied by a two-column photograph of the daring lady the next year when Mrs. Craig Biddle of Philadelphia lighted up in the dining room of the Bellevue-Stratford Hotel there. "Now any woman in Philadelphia society who wishes to smoke a cigarette publicly will be doing the proper thing," the paper commented.[19])

Joseph and Elinor's next trip to St. Louis was in February 1911, just long enough to attend the "wedding (at last)" of Daniel Catlin's daughter Irene, to whom, Joseph suggested, his father might want to send a gift in view of his long friendship with Catlin. "Of course the Catlin family are very much excited," he wrote, "as Irene is getting along in years." On their return to New York, Joseph resumed his routine of eight or more hours a day at the *World*, broken by an occasional outing, as when he and Elinor visited the Metropolitan Museum of Art. "The paintings which pleased me most," he wrote, "were two by Henner and several of the French army in battle by Detaille and Meissonier." His favorite sculpture was by Rodin, who had done a bronze and marble bust of the elder Pulitzer in 1907. The piece Joseph liked was *Hand of God,* which he described as a "strange work showing a strong powerful wrist and hand rising up out of the base of the marble holding in its grasp two nude figures." He thought his selections "may reveal a peculiar taste, but they are all things which any man like myself without any artistic education can understand and appreciate."[20]

As it happened, Joseph was at the *World* just at the point of what was perhaps Pulitzer's greatest journalistic victory: the dismissal by the U.S. Supreme Court of a criminal libel suit against the publisher and the *World* brought by Former President Theodore Roosevelt. During the last year of Roosevelt's second term, the *World* had accused him of complicity and lying to cover up the activities of financier William Nelson Cromwell, a Roosevelt crony, who appeared to have raked off for himself most of the $40 million paid for U.S. rights to build the Panama Canal. Pulitzer had suspected corrupt dealing in the matter after learning that Cromwell was a large donor to the 1908 Republican campaign, and he launched a *World* investigation.[21] Roosevelt was outraged beyond reason in ordering the suit. Since there was no federal law on which it could be based, the Sedition Act of 1798 having expired two years after its adoption, the action was grounded on an English measure adopted in 1662 that President Grant had unsuccessfully invoked some years earlier against Charles A. Dana of the *New York Sun.* As soon as Roosevelt's effort failed likewise, the old Rough Rider ordered a second suit filed. The only possible basis his harried legal advisers could find this time was that several copies of the *World* containing the "libels" had been circulated at West Point, a federal military reservation. Could this be enough for a federal prosecution? The federal district court did not think so and quashed the indictments. Roosevelt appealed, but a unanimous Supreme Court ruled that the indictments were properly quashed. There was jubilation about this in the *World* office, Joseph wrote his father the next day, but "personally I am not in entire sympathy with this enthusiasm, for, as far as I can see, the question of whether we have grossly libeled several citizens remains quite unanswered, and the only thing that is proved is that Roosevelt in attempting to correct a supposed evil in so doing committed a greater one."[22] He was referring to the fact that several others besides Roosevelt and Cromwell had been mentioned in the course of the paper's discussion of the matter. Curiously, the question of what had become of the $40 million was lost sight of in the battle over freedom of the press and was never definitively answered. Though Joseph's dissent of sorts could have caused a parental outburst, it apparently didn't.

That did not signal, though, that the elder Pulitzer was softening, for his son shortly received a sharp rebuke for something he had written back in mid-December, when he was was working at the *Post-Dispatch*. He had written his father that there were "several matters of some importance pending" which he was not reporting "as they are not pleasant and it would do you no good to know them."[23] Came the reply: "Then why mention them at all? This is worse than saying what they are as I shall probably exaggerate their importance. Please omit these Cassandra-like statements because it gives me palpitations of the heart."[24] In the same letter Pulitzer answered Joseph's comment that *Post-Dispatch* advertising manager William Steigers thought a 20 or 25 percent raise in advertising rates was advisable in order to decrease the volume of advertising with no loss in receipts and a resulting increase in the news space. Assuming that this was a request for his approval, Pulitzer answered: "Why not do it himself? I would give him a second gramophone or a flute or a guitar." But, on being warned by general manager Florence D. White that Pulitzer had "unequiv-ocally prohibited" any rate increase without his specific consent, Joseph took the precaution of writing his father that "under these circumstances, I assume that Steigers will have to wait for his second gramophone unless you reverse this order."[25]

But it was impossible for him to check his intense dislike of false and deceptive advertising. He had touched upon the subject again during his recent stint in St. Louis by relating that Bovard had ordered a story on "get rich quick" schemes. The postmaster general had told reporter Carlos F. Hurd that people had been bilked of $100 million by such schemes in the past five years. "I fear the average reader must have doubted the paper's sincerity in printing such a broadside when the columns of the same paper contain numerous Get Rich Quick ads," Joseph had commented.[26] From New York he reported that the *World* was the only paper there carrying the advertising of "unscrupulous" moneylenders who "suck the very life out of the ignorant poor. We should kill these ads before we are exposed."[27] Then, in a longer memo, he described a "distinctly high class" Sunday feature on the six new Democratic governors "which would have lent the paper tone" were it not surrounded by garish medical ads for everything from reconstructive surgery for the nose to hemorrhoid cures. He quoted the openings of several, including, "When the stomach stops working properly because there is wind in it use Stuart's Dyspepsia Tablets" and "New Vitality for Men," the language of which "would give you an immediate attack of nervous prostration." Another such ad then running regularly in the *World* under the heading "$3.50 Recipe Free for Weak Men" began: "I have in my possession a prescription for nervous debility, lack of vigor, weakened manhood, failing memory and lame back, brought on by excesses, unnatural drains, or the follies of youth . . . "[28] Thus armed with what he considered ample damning evidence, Joseph again made his case: "In view of the fact that all the reputable high class magazines and newspapers no longer print such ads, I respectfully submit the suggestion that both as a matter of ethical policy and as a matter of business policy, ads of this nature should be thrown out of the paper, not so much because they are fraudulent and disgusting as because they tend to undermine whatever elevating influence the paper derives from the tone of its undoubtedly high-class editorial page, and from the much improved tone of its news columns."[29] The reference to tone meant the gradual shift away from sensationalism which Pulitzer had ordered in turning the morning *World* particularly away from circulation competition with Hearst's *Journal* after the Spanish-American War of 1898.[30]

Pulitzer, then at Cap Martin, never heard this proposition and heard almost none of the evidence. As soon as secretary Thwaites read the few words necessary for the publisher to sense what was coming he cut Thwaites off and dictated a cable to Joseph: "For tenth time I forbid your sending annoyances like potash [advertising]. . . . Offense tactless, stupid, cruel. You should realize my condition and need of repose." Then he dictated a letter:

> I wish you would turn your attention to the news and you might learn something, and not bother with ads. . . . The

first thing any God-damned fool can do is to criticize
something he could not possibly correct if he tried and
which I certainly cannot. I again forbid you to refer to any
disagreeable subject under the sun which you ought to
know I am impotent to correct without still greater trouble
and annoyance. You of all men in the world ought to
respect my afflictions, age, insomnia and what not. If my
sons cannot help me, cannot relieve me and are satisfied
that I should carry on the burden at a distance under the
most melancholy circumstances they at least ought not to
aggravate my lot. . . . Ordinary employees respect my need
but not you. I should like you to read this thing to your
wife. Talk it over remembering many, many years ago at
Bar Harbor you almost broke me up by one tactless, gross
letter and that I have told you ten times at least not to send
me any disagreeable things. What on earth is the matter
with you? Now don't answer, don't refer to this subject. I
don't want to receive one word raking it up, but remember
the injunction.[31]

— 11 —

The Founder's Last Year

The pain Joseph experienced for having again upset his father was soothed somewhat by a letter from Thwaites accompanying his father's. It explained that Pulitzer was near exhaustion from overwork. He had been straining himself since the beginning of the year, when he had held long sessions with Ralph during the trip to Greece. Now back in France, "except [for] his ride, which never lasts more than three quarters of an hour, he does not cease to busy himself with newspapers and office matters, doing practically no reading of the kind he likes," Thwaites explained. "I am so sorry there was an explosion before I had said half a dozen words as to what your memo contained, although I had selected what appeared to be a good moment after keeping your communication 24 hours awaiting a propitious moment. . . .

His health is bad and his mind occupied with ... candidates of various kinds who irritate him." Making matters worse, Thwaites added, secretary Harold Stanley Pollard, "the soother, is in Paris and J.P. misses him."[1]

Still, Joseph was remorseful and apologized. "I shall not be guilty of the offense again," he pledged.[2] Now back in St. Louis, he was sitting in for Bovard while the managing editor took a week's trip to see Washington, D.C.; he had never been there, and Pulitzer thought he should visit the capital to "improve his mind." Joseph thought this opportunity was benefiting him too, "for it puts me in a position of having to create, pass upon and handle news and to command men." He said he had long thought he would be "sadly deficient" when it came to commanding, "but the experience, brief as it is, is helpful."

And, speaking of brief experiences, he hoped his father would settle the question of whether he and Elinor were to be New Yorkers or St. Louisans when he returned to the United States in April. Both were prepared to accept the elder Pulitzer's decision, he emphasized, and if they were to become New Yorkers, he was sure they would "grow to like both the town and the office. But when I am there only for a month I see their bad features more clearly than their good." He said he found being shifted back and forth "demoralizing and destructive of ambition and enterprise."[3]

Sometime during the previous year, Joseph's sister Constance had contracted tuberculosis, the prescription for which was complete rest in a tranquil environment. Accompanied by Edith, she had gone to live in Colorado Springs, and Pulitzer had suggested that Joseph and Elinor visit them. They were glad to oblige. Neither had been farther west than St. Louis. Joseph arranged in advance to visit on the way out the offices of William Rockhill Nelson's *Kansas City Star* and the raucous and garish *Denver Post* under entrepreneurs Harry H. Tammen and Fred G. Bonfils. They reached Kansas City on March 23, and Joseph spent most of the day at the *Star,* where he asked Nelson about his policy of always "boosting" Kansas City. "His paper fairly bristles with civic pride," he reported, "in strong contrast (as has often been pointed out to me) with the sharply critical and dissatisfied tone of the P-D." Still, Nelson told him that his paper often did crusade and expose wrongdoing, although "we don't stick our nose into every corner

dog fight." He also reported that the *Star* had found that manufacturing its own paper—which Ralph was considering for the *World*
—was uneconomical. Kansas City's parks and spacious residential
districts so impressed the visitors that Joseph could not resist this
remark containing a barely subliminal message: "Poor New Yorkers!
Whenever I think of the way they are penned in as compared with
the western houses, surrounded as they are nowadays by grass,
trees, flowers, fresh air and light, I pity them."

The outdoor splendor of Denver and its surroundings impressed
him even more powerfully, and he wrote a vivid description of it,
concluding: "The scenery was simply magnificent and to my mind
far more majestic, primitive, and inspiring than that of Switzerland."
Against this backdrop, the *Post* offered its own visual spectacle:

> On the outside of the building is this sign painted in large
> gold letters, "Oh Justice! When thou hast been expelled
> from all other habitations, make this thy temple!" . . . Inside,
> the walls of the business office are painted to represent
> icicles hanging from the ceiling and meeting flames rising
> from the floor. Every want advertiser gets a present. On
> that day they were giving cut glass to the women and
> carnation boutonnieres to the men. In the back the "Coal
> Man" was busy selling Denver Post coal at $3.50 a ton
> compared to the coal trust's $5 and more a ton. Outside a
> steam calliope was shrieking its unmelodious tones and
> attracting persons out for lunch within a radius of 10 city
> blocks to the office to see what it was that could make so
> much noise. On top of the calliope was a negro 8 ft. 6 in.
> tall, a freak out of the Sells Floto circus. In the basement in
> view of the street the presses were busy grinding out
> 90,000 Posts written in the worst slang in America, printed
> mostly in red ink, full of Hearst comics and features,
> without an editorial page, with a back page bearing a title
> line and looking exactly like the first page, and filled inside
> with ads paid for at the flat rates of 9 cents a line daily and
> 12 cents Sunday. . . . The paper is hated, abused, despised
> and yet it takes in over a million dollars a year.[4]

They spent the next day and a half in Colorado Springs with

Constance and Edith, visiting and taking in more scenery before turning homeward. Joseph thought Constance would need at least another year there and remarked on Edith's selflessness in taking care of her sister.

On returning to St. Louis they found that Elinor's eighty-year-old paternal grandmother had died. Joseph served as a pallbearer at the funeral. He sent his father several marked pages from *Post-Dispatch* midday and Saturday editions he had supervised, hoping to show his skill at getting and presenting news. One page reported a fire that had broken out just forty-five minutes before deadline. "I cautioned all hands to be scrupulously accurate and moderate and in consequence we had the only accurate statement of the number killed (three at that time)," he related. He also supervised the handling of a feature story about an East St. Louis divorce proceeding which took a lighthearted look at spouse abuse, as Joseph explained it, by raising "the grave question of whether or not a man has a right to spank his wife" if she keeps him awake until two o'clock in the morning with her chattering. He ordered that the transcript of testimony be printed. No doubt reflecting prevailing attitudes, the jury took the man's side and refused to grant the divorce. Recognizing the intense interest in the recently discovered disease infantile paralysis, Joseph arranged for the publication in full of a Washington, D.C., physician's paper on prevention of the illness. He also suggested several stories to *World* managing editor Lincoln, including one about the hazards of overexertion in college athletics in light of the recent deaths of several of the best college athletes within a few years after graduation.

As for the paper's business operations, Joseph reported that Sunday circulation was up 8,000 in the city and 3,000 in the country over the previous year and likely to reach 300,000 in 1912. The daily was doing better than holding its own, even though the *St. Louis Times,* its newest competitor, had reached an estimated 50,000 circulation and was beginning to make money. He thought the *Post-Dispatch* had several of the "best feature specialists in the country outside of the Hearst force," particularly in women's feature writer-artist Marguerite Martyn, humorist Clark McAdams, and a comic artist, Jean Knott. That team, he predicted, if transferred to the *Evening World,* "would compare favorably with Hearst's circus staff, for if they can find ideas in St. Louis, how many more ideas they could find in New York!" Then, again letting his preference for the *Post-Dispatch* show, he added: "I have always contended that it is a far greater and more severe test to turn out a bright paper here than in New York because here the material is so limited, and incidentally, too, the money to be spent."[5]

There was less money for the arts in St. Louis too. No doubt encouraged by his father's strong interests in music and art, he had begun to give some attention to helping to raise the cultural tone of St. Louis. In late 1910 he asked his father to make a substantial contribution to the St. Louis Symphony Orchestra and Pulitzer obliged, pledging $2,000 a year for five years *if* a total pledge of $50,000 were achieved. When that goal appeared unreachable, Joseph suggested that he reduce the contingency to $30,000 — which he did, as well as increasing his annual pledge for five years to $3,000.[6] In May, Joseph canvassed wealthy St. Louis owners of fine paintings to loan them to an exhibit at the Art Museum for the summer, when the owners would be away from the city anyway. Within a week he had commitments from fourteen owners. "Anything that will tend towards giving recreation to the poor devils who must inhabit that sun-baked city in the summertime is to my mind worth trying," he concluded.

Even in mid-May, temperatures were in the upper eighties, providing the opportunity for Sunday picnics in the country with other young couples. During one of these, at a place called Musick's Ferry on the Missouri River about twenty miles outside of town, the four men "hired a skiff and rowed down the river about a mile and then went in swimming as God made us."[7] Two days before his first wedding anniversary, Joseph wrote that the past year had been "far and away the happiest year of my life and one that I shall, I hope, always remember that I have you to thank for. . . . [W]e very, very often get together and agree that it is to you that we should be grateful for our happiness."[8]

Despite his own frequent, newsy letters, Joseph heard little from his father during the first five months of the year. He assumed he was still out of favor for resurrecting the subject of dishonest ads. In fact, the reason was that Pulitzer's health had remained poor. Instead of returning to New York in early April as planned, he had stayed abroad, going in May to Wiesbaden for a cure and then crossing, going directly to Bar Harbor. On June 21, he telegraphed Joseph and Elinor to join him in about a week, "and be sure to call her Elinor and not Nell." In the meantime, he instructed his son to get reports from all *Post-Dispatch* department heads for the "minute effects in every respect" of starting a morning edition of the *Post-Dispatch.*[9] Then he was to make notes during the train trip to Maine so that his presentation to his father would be "most condensed and direct."[10] The main reason for considering this was the rumor that Hearst was planning either to start or buy a St. Louis morning newspaper.

Joseph prepared a report giving both the pros and cons of such a move. He came out cautiously in favor, confessing "grave doubts about its paying for many years"[11] but a willingness to take that risk in the face of the evening's solid circulation and advertising superiority among the city's newspapers. He also sensed that Pulitzer might have an ulterior motive. "Pardon my curiosity," he wrote, "but are you really seriously considering this step or is this inquiry . . . largely a bluff for W.R.H.'s benefit and to keep him out of the field?" He confessed that it made him "feel very much like a mother must feel when she must cut off her child's curls" to contemplate cheapening the evening paper by shifting most of its serious news and editorials to a morning edition, thus leaving its character like that of the *Evening World.*[12] Probably unbeknownst to him, general overseer Florence White thought along similar lines. "St. Louis does not need another morning paper any more than it needs a new Bible," he wrote Pulitzer, adding, "There is as much virtue in the threat as in the execution, and it is far less expensive."[13]

At Chatwold during July and August, Pulitzer was able to spend only short periods at a time with various family members because he tired quickly. His best energy, as always, went to thinking about and dispatching instructions to his newspapers. He did some of this through Ralph and Joseph, who, after their mother, probably got more time with him than anyone else. Joseph's last working session with him seems to have been in August, when he took notes while White reported to Pulitzer on a variety of things, including his view that Hearst had no current plan to move into St. Louis but probably would eventually. "If this proves true,"

Joseph inserted in his notes, "now is the time to start our morning edition. If not now, we never will, and he will."[14]

But there the subject languished. Too restless to stay without interruption at Chatwold, Pulitzer sometimes cruised on the *Liberty* that summer and fall along the East Coast. In September he wired Joseph and Elinor that they could take a fortnight's holiday and said he wished his wife would let Herbert join him for that length of time to cruise south. "I am hungry for him or somebody," he concluded. "I am dreadfully tired and unfit. Miss you. Love to all, Father."[15]

Herbert, with a tutor, did join him, and was aboard the yacht when it put in at Charleston at the end of October so that the ship's physician could consult with a Charleston doctor about an ailment that had kept Pulitzer in bed. The medical conclusion was that it was indigestion, but when he seemed to worsen, Mrs. Pulitzer was summoned from New York. Her husband was in a coma by the time she reached his bedside, and he died twenty minutes later, at 1:40 P.M. on Sunday, October 29, 1911, at the age of sixty-four. Heart failure was given as the cause of death.

Pulitzer's body was taken from Charleston to New York by a special train. It lay in state in the library of his Seventy-third Street residence from late Monday afternoon until shortly before the funeral at 2:00 P.M. Wednesday. Several hundred *World* employees and others came to the house to pay their respects. A crowd of 600 filled St. Thomas Protestant Episcopal Church at Fifth Avenue and Fifty-third Street for the service, and 2,000 persons gathered outside. The proceedings nearly lost their solemnity because of the behavior of a large group of former *World* editors— now employed in various places around the country—who had been invited to attend the funeral. Together, they made a large group, and their pleasure at being reunited with so many of their former co-workers made it nearly impossible for the funeral procession's organizers to whip them into line by twos just behind the family and the current *World* staff. As one who was there described it:

> No game of hide-and-seek could have been more fascinating than the discovery of favorite individuals in that throng. Joyously and heartily, the ex-editors lent themselves to this

diversion. Every man had the most gratifying success in his efforts. Whoops of delighted recognition filled the air.

"Jim, you towheaded fraud, put it there!"

"Hi, Dick, wait for your old sidekick!"

Happy pairs, reunited after decades, danced together on the pavement. The orderly line, held for a moment, broke up in confusion. Reminiscences were yelped from one ex-editor to another. Men ran up and down the line, seeking someone they hadn't yet found.

Newspaper photographers assigned to cover the event were dazed momentarily by this spectacle. Posed to record the somber expressions of the group as it approached the church, "they took one look at the bright faces . . . and their nerveless hands dropped to their sides. . . . Very literally, the photographers fell back." Some took pictures to have as souvenirs, one of which, "without its Fifth Avenue background, would have served nicely as a snapshot of Old Home Week in Haynesville Centre." A combination of physical force by the procession's organizers, the sight of the coffin, and the sound of the great organ as they reached the entrance of the church halted the merriment. "Something like an electric shock" went through the former editors, and "the line formed as if by magic. Reverently, two by two, with bent heads and lowered eyes, and hearts full of memories, the editors who had helped Joseph Pulitzer to build his *World* followed their dead chief into the crowded church."[16]

As the funeral began, all the machinery at the *World* and *Post-Dispatch* — more than five hundred engines — was turned off, and all activity ceased for five minutes. There were 116 floral pieces dominated by lilies of the valley, Pulitzer's favorite flower. The captain and crew of the yacht sent a life buoy of white carnations with "Liberty" lettered on it in violets. The services, both at the church and at the family plot at Woodlawn Cemetery, were the prescribed rites of the Episcopal church. There was no eulogy, but tributes flowed from near and far, many of which were printed in the Pulitzer and other newspapers. "I have always classed Joseph Pulitzer as one of the greatest men of this time. He was a genius in newspaper making, but most of all a patriot," said *New York Times* publisher Adolph S. Ochs. "His death is a national loss, and his place will be hard to fill."[17]

— 12 —

St. Louis for Good

A week following the death of the founding Pulitzer, the *World* ran an editorial signed by Ralph and Joseph reprinting Pulitzer's 1907 "retirement" message as "The World's Platform" and pledging fidelity to those ideals.[1] In St. Louis, Joseph ordered the platform to be run daily on the editorial page. Organizationally, Ralph was elected president of the Press Publishing Company, and Joseph was reelected secretary. Ralph became editor and publisher of the *World*, and Joseph assumed those titles at the *Post-Dispatch* after being elected president of the Pulitzer Publishing Company at that company's annual meeting the following February. Because their father had not resolved the matter, the sons were able to decide their respective assignments—and, not unexpectedly, for Joseph it was St. Louis for good.

Both newspapers were in sound financial shape and capably managed. Joseph was naturally pleased to have his news machine under Bovard's direction. He had continued to praise Bovard to his father even after Pulitzer had declared that he had overrated the man's ability. Joseph couldn't agree. "Given his own organization and almost absolute authority . . . such as he has here and never had in New York, he would be very hard to beat," he had written in May. "The men that he has made out here work like dogs for him. For he's the boss and they know it. In New York there was no boss and they knew it. It's the old story of needing a head, which you have so often complained about—and that I know explains his failure in N.Y."[2]

As that comment shows, he was glad to give Bovard virtually a free hand in forming and carrying out news policy. The ambitious managing editor eagerly took this opportunity. Foremost, Bovard wanted *his* newspaper to have its own personality and not be thought of as the *World*'s western adjunct. To that end, during the decade following the elder Pulitzer's death, he stopped much of the *Post-Dispatch*'s use of *World* wire and syndicated material for coverage of events outside St. Louis. He considered the output of those shared services superficial, pitched as it was to a large, general audience. He wanted to offer his readers deeper understanding and consequently began sending reporters far afield. He sent reporter Claire Kenamore to cover unrest along the Texas-Mexico border and in 1916 to accompany General John J. Pershing's troops in pursuit of the murderous General "Pancho" Villa. Two years later he established the paper's Washington bureau, which he used to get better coverage of Missouri affairs and to develop investigations of national scope. One of these dealt with federal oil leasing arrangements that led to the U.S. Senate's Teapot Dome investigation, and another revealed malpractices that resulted in the impeachment of U.S. District Judge George W. English.

Reporters who delivered more than the surface of the news for Bovard got recognition and salary increases; those who didn't were out. His manner among his subordinates was aloof. He was always to be addressed as "Mister Bovard," not as "Jack," as some had known him in earlier days. He never socialized with co-workers after hours and usually took a table by himself at the restaurant where many *Post-Dispatch* employees ate lunch.[3] The managing editor never sought recognition for himself except in the matter of salary, which went to $10,000 the year Joseph Pulitzer II became editor and publisher. His pay peaked at $75,000 in 1932, and then dropped back as the paper's profits declined during the Depression to $60,000 in 1938, the year he retired.[4] Some years he probably was the highest-paid managing editor in the nation. The second J.P. was "astonished" to learn that the *New York Times* and *Herald Tribune* managing editors were paid only $34,000 and $16,000 respectively in 1938.[5]

The main reason the elder Pulitzer had given for not making Bovard managing editor of the *World* was that he saw in him an "excessive, premature, dangerous love of power."[6] He didn't want a man in charge who would challenge the publisher's ultimate authority. His son, however, both liked Bovard's bold leadership and did not feel threatened by it. He therefore watched willingly as Bovard took charge of every segment of the paper's news operations "until all news, feature, critical, photographic and artistic content of the paper was being produced under his direction, with all departmental editors responsible to him."[7] The only content Bovard did not control was advertising and the editorial page — and he could throw out advertising if he needed space for an important news development.

The editorial page was under George S. Johns. He had joined the paper in 1883 as a reporter, rising to hold various responsible positions, including overseer of everything but the business office, as had suited the elder Pulitzer's shifting assessments of his key men. For most of his career, Johns was in charge of editorial policy, leading campaigns during the 1890s and into the new century for improvement of the city's disgracefully inadequate schools, streets, water and sewerage systems, police, night lighting, and public transportation. His frequent targets were corrupt, do-nothing politicians and judges who were putting money appropriated for these things into their own pockets. Their civic attitude — not to mention ignorance — was well typified by Mayor Henry Ziegenhein's answer to a *Post-Dispatch* reporter's question about the poor street lighting: "Vell, ve got a moon yet, ain't it?"[8] During the early years of his editorship, Johns admitted, "my ideal of an editor was a pungent writer who could put the greatest amount of poison into the fewest lines — who could quickest reach the vitals of his adversary with the point of his pen." As a result, he recalled, "my daily mail was bedecked with skulls and crossbones. But the miracle was wrought" as reforms were achieved.[9]

Even though many a politician and wealthy St. Louis business-man detested the *Post-Dispatch,* Johns became well-known and highly respected in the city, most of all for his organization of the annual *Post-Dispatch* Christmas Festival, which for many years provided a holiday meal for thousands of the city's poor as well as gifts for their children. Nevertheless, in 1907, Pulitzer decided that the editorial page under Johns had gotten into a rut and was losing vigor. He sent the editor on a trip abroad, and while he was away replaced him with Horatio W. Seymour, a younger man with a good record on three Chicago newspapers. When he returned, Johns was given the title of news editor, a position in which the apprentice Joseph Pulitzer Jr. observed of him: "I think highly of him as a critic, but little or nothing of him as a creator."[10] Seymour wasn't happy as Johns' successor with Johns still hovering around, so when an opportunity came to transfer to the *World,* he took it, and Johns was reinstated as chief of the editorial page until he stepped down, but did not fully retire, in 1929. Judging by the small number of memorandums he wrote Bovard and Johns, J.P. Jr. (as he signed himself) infrequently criticized their day-by-day execution of their responsibilities during the first several years of his tenure. After all, the paper was getting along quite well, particularly as a news medium, and broader concerns demanded the young publisher's attention.

One of these was to plan for new quarters for the thirty-eight-year-old newspaper. It had outgrown its fourth location, at 210 North Broadway, where it had been since 1902. The new plant was an eight-story structure at the northeast corner of Twelfth Boulevard and Olive Street on land owned by Elinor's Uncle Daniel Catlin, who had accumulated some $3 million worth of downtown real estate.[11] For the remaining thirty-eight years of the second Joseph Pulitzer's career, this building was his headquarters. The *Post-Dispatch* had grown steadily, from a circulation of 987 in 1878 to 181,717 daily and 260,193 Sunday in 1916, ahead of all four of its competitors: the morning *Globe-Democrat* and *Republic* and the evening *Star* and *Times.* The paper was doing so well, he wrote his mother, that he felt "safe in saying that you will not feel the new building expenses in your dividends."[12] The cornerstone was laid on October 9, 1916, with three-and-a-half-year-old Joseph Pulitzer III handling the same trowel his father had used in the *World* cornerstone ceremony in 1889. St. Louis Mayor Henry Kiel and U.S. Senator James A. Reed of Missouri made short addresses, after which the publisher remarked that the "vote of confidence" represented by the paper's circulation growth "would not have been so liberally cast, had it not been deserved. That we may continue to deserve it by further improving the *Post-Dispatch* as a newspaper and as a medium for the use of the power of publicity in the public interest, is our purpose in erecting this building."[13]

The young cornerstone-layer, Joseph Pulitzer III, was the first of the three children of Joseph and Elinor. He was born on May 13, 1913, followed by Kate Davis, named for her maternal grandmother, on October 13, 1916, and Elinor, named after her mother, on March 31, 1922. Starting in 1914, the twenty-nine-year-old editor-publisher began acquiring land in St. Louis County, in what became the suburb of Ladue, where he and Elinor planned and supervised the building in stages of a twenty-room house that was the centerpiece of 100-acre "Lone Tree Farm," named for the large oak a short distance from the house beneath which were swings and other playthings for the children. It was a working farm, with orchards, pastures, barn, stable, and other outbuildings. Its vegetable garden, chickens, and cows produced much of the food for the family and large staff. Just off the back of the house was a large square flower garden that supplied the house with arrangements for much of the year. For most of its existence, Edward L. Dwyer, a large, congenial man who could be firm when necessary, oversaw the operation of Lone Tree Farm. He also was Pulitzer's chauffeur, a position that became essential when his employer's eyesight began to diminish.[14]

As early as 1903, when he was in St. Louis for the first time, Joseph had experienced transient episodes of diminished vision. This eventually was diagnosed as a form of chorioditis, or inflammation of the choroid, the middle layer of the surface of the eye to which the third layer, the retina, is attached. As is usual, the retina was affected as well. The disorder usually is chronic, and can be (as it was in his case) progressive.[15] There probably was a hereditary factor, via his father. Herbert too suffered from impaired vision and eventually had to have an eye removed. In Joseph's case, the most rapid deterioration was in his left eye, in which he became virtually blind by the time he reached his mid-thirties. He gradually lost all but about 20 percent of the sight in his right eye as the result of scarring of the retina close to the center of vision. Only the lower part of the retina remained clear — the part that produces the upper sight, accounting for his ability to shoot ducks. In order to see another person clearly, he said, the person had to be close and in a good light.[16] He consulted frequently over the years with the highly regarded ophthalmologist Dr. William H. Wilmer of the Johns Hopkins University Medical School in Baltimore.[17] While a variety of treatments were tried, the avoidance of strain by reading, which by midlife became nearly impossible except for large headlines, and plenty of outdoor exercise and fresh air seemed the most beneficial. As severe as this handicap was, particularly for a newspaper editor, he let it affect him minimally, no doubt recalling the example of his blind father. He lost the ability to drive a car quite early, and before long secretaries had to read to him, as with his father. Fortunately, the prescription for outdoor life fit perfectly with his passions for sailing, bird-shooting, and salmon-fishing, all of which he could do with little assistance from others.

He could still see well enough when the United States entered World War I in 1917 to get Dr. Wilmer's permission to volunteer for military service. He had enrolled in a naval training course in 1916 with hopes of entering the naval aviation corps as an officer. Two years later, however, he could not pass the vision examination for flying, but he was accepted into the ground service. He entered training for that duty in September 1918, at the Great Lakes Naval Training Station near Chicago and enjoyed the experience of being one of three student officers appointed to enforce discipline among the ninety others. Fellow St. Louisan Theron Catlin, Elinor's cousin, was appointed detachment commander. Joseph made light of this in a letter to his mother: "He has an easy job as all he does is to stand up to his full height of 6 ft 4 inches and look handsome and review the rest of us at inspection."[18] As it turned out, his group was barely through its training when the armistice was signed on November 11.[19]

The reporting of that historic event provided an example of

Bovard's steely attention to detail in evaluating news. Word had reached St. Louis on November 7 via United Press that the armistice had been signed and hostilities were to cease at 2:00 P.M. that day. The *St. Louis Star* immediately issued an extra edition, touching off a victory parade that wove its way past the new *Post-Dispatch* building. As Bovard's biographer related it: "In the third floor newsroom, the managing editor scanned an Associated Press dispatch stating that such a report, not officially verified, had been picked up in a cable message by the Navy's intelligence service. The Washington bureau, in response to Bovard's telephone call, could furnish no confirmation. Bovard then studied the latest official news from the front. Up to eleven o'clock the German armistice commissioners had not even entered the French lines, and Pershing's army was heavily engaged in front of Sedan as late as 1:45 P.M. It seemed obvious that the signing could not possibly have taken place."[20] Accordingly, Bovard ignored the flash as well as the jeers from the crowd outside the building when the regular noon edition came out with no mention of it. The next day he was proven right, and he sent the following telegram to United Press head Roy Howard, who had signed the erroneous dispatch and had been trying for years to sell the United Press service to the *Post-Dispatch*:[21]

> ROY HOWARD, BREST, FRANCE
> UNITED PRESS, NO. HA HA.
> O.K. BOVARD

The previous year, Pulitzer himself had stirred up a little community turmoil in delivering the welcoming address to a convention in St. Louis of the Associated Advertising Clubs of the World. Perhaps emulating fellow publisher William Rockhill Nelson of Kansas City, he commended the virtues of St. Louis and her citizens—from the city's record of military enlistments to its parks, playgrounds, and fine symphony and art museum—all showing it to be "a most progressive city, an enlightened city, and above all, an American city. . . . In short, don't accept the view of the man who never gets off Manhattan Island and who, likely as not, thinks of a St. Louisan as a suspicious gentleman who is always waiting to be shown, who lives in the shade of the Anheuser-Busch [brewery] and reads nothing but the *Westliche Post.*"22

The German-language daily was offended, charging in an editorial that "the second generation of Pulitzer is wanting in the high quality of sentiment and gratitude" and adding: "This young upstart forgets that his father was once city editor of the Westliche Post. In his haste to prove he is an American and not a Hungarian (a great race of people, by the way), he forgets that his father was once of the type he is now assaulting. There is a popular song entitled 'Don't Bite the Hand That's Feeding You.' If young Pulitzer had known this song and shared the sentiment thereof, he would not have made his disgraceful attack on a large part of our citizenship and an implied attack on the memory of his great father."23

Joseph undoubtedly regretted having given offense, but at about the same time, his wife was the subject of more favorable stories reporting that she was among fifteen members "of the fashionable St. Louis County colony" who had founded the St. Louis County Welfare Association. "These women, whose husbands' aggregate wealth would make a staggering figure, will devote their efforts toward bettering conditions for the less fortunate 'other half,'" said a story in an unidentified newspaper almost certainly *not* the *Post-Dispatch*.24 A few years before, Elinor had been described as "one of the most accomplished amateur dancers in St. Louis," particularly of the "tango Argentino."25 In 1918, when she lost a $2,000 bowknot pin containing about a hundred diamonds somewhere in downtown St. Louis, she advertised in the morning *Globe-Democrat,* which had gained a circulation advantage about which it could not resist editorializing in its news columns: "With the large circulation of this paper—greater than the daily circulation of any other St. Louis paper—good results may be expected. When Joseph Pulitzer Jr. lost his dog, he promptly placed an ad in the *Globe-Democrat,* and the dog was returned. The *Globe-Democrat* hopes to be able to give equally efficient returns to Mrs. Pulitzer."26 But it apparently didn't, for there was no story to that effect.

There were some uncomfortable times for Elinor when her husband's crusading, liberal, and usually Democratic newspaper angered the wealthy and usually Republican St. Louis establishment, to which her own family had long belonged. But, Pulitzer recalled, "she'd stand right by me even though her family and those families had been quite close."[27] There was a particularly unpleasant period about two years after their marriage, when the paper began to question the dealings of many in the business community in railroad freight franchises. Elinor's Uncle Daniel Catlin, through his connection with the St. Louis Union Trust Company, was among those involved in financial arrangements to establish a direct link between St. Louis and the West Coast via the Frisco Railroad. After Interstate Commerce Commission investigators concluded that these arrangements "could be interpreted as manipulations . . . to create outrageous profits for a few insiders," the *Post-Dispatch* sharply criticized the financiers' practices, especially their being both buyers and sellers of certain franchises.[28] As a result, members of several important families would not speak to the young publisher "for a good many years."[29] Ultimately, the Frisco Railroad scheme failed and a number of its promoters lost money.[30]

In hopes of promoting efficiency and innovation in his own newspaper, in the spring of 1918, J.P. Jr. announced establishment of "The Joseph Pulitzer Prize" of $100 to be awarded annually on Christmas Day for "the best acceptable constructive criticism or suggestion on the subject 'How Can the Post-Dispatch Be Made a Greater Newspaper?'" Everyone in the organization—editorial, business, and mechanical personnel—was encouraged to take part. He invited criticism about anything the paper printed or failed to print and urged employees to submit their ideas for news and public service opportunities as well as for new departments, columns, or features.[31] Although this competition failed to produce any important reforms and was dropped within four years,[32] it reflected the son's intention to follow the same dissatisfied course that had marked his father's administration. He also continued one of his father's intermittent practices—the "Blow Your Own Horn" report, in which he asked various department heads to frankly brag about their accomplishments. These were confidential, for the publisher only. Like his father, he drove the organization by a combination of praise and criticism, accepting without apology an autocratic role. But unlike his father, he was more open to dissent and thoughtful counterargument, provided the dissenters had a sound basis. He did not like excuse-makers, as is evident in a comment to business manager Albert G. Lincoln: "Suggestions are welcome, alibis not."[33]

While he did not step into the job with all of this philosophy definitively worked out, his was not a tentative personality, as his readiness as a youth to challenge some of his father's judgments had shown. Norman E. Isaacs, who watched the operation of the *Post-Dispatch* closely when he was managing editor of the *St. Louis Star-Times* in the 1940s, put it this way: "There was an extraordinary degree of confidence to him. You get confidence out of a lot of people, but attached to it is a touch of braggadocio. There wasn't any such thing in him. It was almost as if he knew who the hell he was; he knew what his name meant, and he was perfectly prepared to assert himself when he felt it was necessary."[34]

Isaacs's observation about the power of the name is especially pertinent. By 1922 an apparent metamorphosis in which the son concluded that he had reached the administrative stature of his father became complete. That January, Joseph Pulitzer Jr. sent out cards announcing that he would "henceforth drop the suffix 'Jr.'" and sign his name "Joseph Pulitzer."[35]

Triumphs and Tragedies

T his Joseph Pulitzer's stature as a most important St. Louisan was evident in his December 1922 selection as host during a two-day visit to the city by eighty-one-year-old former French Premier Georges Clemenceau, who was on an unofficial speaking tour of several U.S. cities. Clemenceau, himself a publisher of reform-minded newspapers for many years, felt a professional kinship with the Pulitzers. His main themes during the tour were that the world had not seen the end of German milita-rism and that the League of Nations would have little success as a peacemaker.

In preparation for the visit of "the Tiger," as the tenacious premier had been known during the war, a large upstairs bedroom of the Pulitzer home was redecorated. For many years afterward it was known as the Clemenceau Room. As a memento, the old statesman planted a small cedar tree in the Pulitzers' front lawn, an act that had to be done by candlelight and moonlight because of a one-hour power outage at the home. The only other mishaps involved Clemenceau's valet, who managed to get lost in St. Louis three times during the two days.[1] More than once during his busy schedule, Clemenceau brushed aside expressions of concern that at his age he might be overtiring himself. At one point he remarked to Mrs. Pulitzer: "Write me in 56 years [the interval since his last visit to the United States] and I will see you again."[2] By ironic fate, he came closer to that goal than she, outliving the young woman by four years.

Probably the greatest shock of Pulitzer's life came in 1925, the fifteenth year of his marriage. On March 16, while he was deep-sea fishing with friends off the Florida coast, Elinor was in New York for a week's shopping. On her first evening there, she went dining and dancing with several of their New York friends. About midnight, George McMurtry, one of the friends, was driving her to the apartment where she was staying. An oncoming car forced McMurtry to swerve his, hitting a pillar supporting tracks of the elevated train along Third Avenue. The windshield shattered, showering both passengers with glass. Both suffered cuts of the face and neck, but a doctor who examined them found these to be superficial, and Elinor went on to spend the night at the apartment of Mrs. Julius Walsh in the Plaza Hotel. By morning, she was barely conscious and was taken to the Manhattan Eye, Ear, and Throat Hospital, where she fell into a coma. Ralph and Herbert Pulitzer were at her bedside when she died at 5:30 P.M. An autopsy revealed that a blood clot that had formed in an artery had been carried to her brain, causing a cerebral embolism.

Because Pulitzer's whereabouts were only generally known, a number of boats and planes were pressed into a search. An express boat carrying the message that Mrs. Pulitzer had been injured found the fishing craft about one hundred miles below Miami in the Florida Keys. By the time the party reached the mainland, word had come that Elinor was dead. She was thirty-seven years old. Her children were eleven, eight, and two.[3]

Clark McAdams, author of the popular "Just a Minute" editorial page column in the *Post-Dispatch,* was in the fishing party.

McAdams read to Pulitzer during much of the train trip from
Florida to St. Louis. "He loved his wife, and it was a terrible blow
to him," McAdams recorded shortly afterward. "He said she had
always been good to him through his blindness, and he seemed to
feel that he could hardly take her place with little Joe, who was
very close to her."[4] The body, accompanied by Ralph and Herbert,
was taken to St. Louis by train. A day later, a special train chartered
by the McMurtrys and other New York friends made the run to St.
Louis in a record 22 hours and 10 minutes.

The funeral, the Episcopal service read by a Presbyterian minister,
was at the Pulitzer home, which was filled to overflowing with
flowers. A blanket of roses from her husband covered Elinor's
coffin. Young Kate Davis was sternly instructed by her Aunt
Frances (Mrs. Charles W. Moore) not to cry: "Whenever you get to
feeling funny, just count the roses!"[5] A brief private burial service
followed at Bellefontaine Cemetery. In his wife's memory, Pulitzer
gave a "period room" to the St. Louis Art Museum furnished and
decorated with items Elinor had especially liked. In a letter of
condolence, Clemenceau recalled his "delightful memory of this
happy family, and of the dignity of the wife, of the sensitivity of the
young mother, expressing a touching sincerity in her gestures, in
her smile, in her attentiveness, and in her voice."[6] Ralph Pulitzer
wrote this poem, titled "E.W.P.," as a tribute:

> Gracious and gay and glad and quite unspoiled
> By all her luxury of loveliness,
> Worn without thought like some familiar dress,
> Or like the pearls her careless fingers coiled;
> A mellow wit that, laughing, flicked and foiled
> All fustian pomp; a smile like a caress
> For those she loved, swift tears for their distress,
> And gentle pity for the sad and soiled;
> Subtle her spirit, simple her whole heart,
> Zestful for life, its wonders and its wiles,
> She met its duties and she paid their toll;
> And thus she played her unpretentious part,
> Decking self-sacrifice with gallant smiles,
> A mirthful ministrant, a saintly soul![7]

Pulitzer's first concern was to find a governess for the children. The "essential qualifications," as he listed them to Mrs. Fred W. Allen (Elinor's cousin, the former Irene Catlin), whom he asked to help him find candidates, were "private character, Protestant religion, cheerful temperament, ability to control children and as great cultural and educational background as possible including especially English literature and history."[8] He took several weeks to check the backgrounds of several candidates, the children being looked after in the meantime by the French nurse already employed in the household. (With her, young Joe and Kate Davis were to speak French.) At the end of April, Miss Sedric Williams—about thirty years old, the daughter of a Cambridge, Massachusetts, lawyer—was hired as governess. She had served during the war as a volunteer nurse and most recently had been working as a head salesperson in Saks Department Store in New York City. Kate Davis liked her immediately, but her brother took an instantaneous dislike—so much so that he once resorted to lighting slips of paper and slipping them under Miss Williams's door.[9]

In June, Pulitzer took his son and two other guests on a trout- and salmon-fishing trip to Nova Scotia, traveling there from Bar Harbor on the new yacht, *Discoverer,* built under his direction the previous summer. In order to set sail before daybreak, the party decided to sleep the night before aboard the yacht. At about 10:00 P.M. they were hailed by a man in a rowboat—Ernest, the butler: "You have forgotten the salad dressing, Sir," he called. "Having narrowly escaped this disaster, owner, guests and crew turned in," Pulitzer recorded.[10]

His sense of humor intact, he gradually recovered from his loss and was able to enjoy life again. The following February, he asked editorial page editor Johns: "Wouldn't there be some fun in a light, breezy, good-natured editorial on 'flaming middle age?' Why blame the kids for enjoying the excesses that their parents so greatly enjoy? Flaming youth is not responsible for the increased divorce rate, the short skirt, open violation of the prohibition law ... for 'red hot' mammas, movies and tabloids and other signs of the times. Why blame the kids?"[11]

In April, Pulitzer remarried. His bride was Miss Elizabeth Edgar, whom he had known for a number of years. She was the daughter of William Boyce Edgar, secretary of the Edgar Zinc

Company, and a granddaughter of Timothy Bloomfield Edgar, a banker and railroad director. During the war, she had been a nurse in a hospital near Paris where victims of gas warfare were treated. Later, in St. Louis, she and several other young women had run a fashionable dress shop on Maryland Avenue called the Suzanne Shop. She was skilled at embroidery and other fine needlework, but also especially enjoyed riding and other outdoor activities. She rapidly became her husband's most enthusiastic shooting and fishing companion, sports she had not tried before they were married. Perhaps her most remarkable accomplishment was her relationship with her stepchildren. The children were told to call her "Mommie," and the term was both given and accepted with affectionate sincerity. For young Elinor, of course, Elizabeth was the only mother she ever knew. After young Joe followed his father and uncles and entered St. Mark's, in 1926, his stepmother wrote him a letter every day. In later life, he thought this might have been too much of a good thing, but at the time he greatly appreciated it.

Shortly after the marriage, Pulitzer wrote his mother, who was living in France, that he was "very, very happy not only on my own account, but because of the really wonderful devotion the children feel for Elizabeth, who is with them constantly and who makes so many sacrifices on my account that it makes me feel ashamed of myself." He also described recent improvements to the family's home, which included some additions to the house, a new driveway, "more than half a mile long, and a new white fence, an old Southern type of fence by the way, around the outside and with the flowers and blossoms that are always here in May, it is lovely and is often admired."[12] Pulitzer's mother, who died in 1927, apparently never met his second wife, but a niece recalled that after his remarriage she and her sister were taken by their mother, Mrs. William Gray Elmslie, the former Constance Pulitzer, from their home in Colorado Springs to St. Louis to "inspect" the new wife. "Mother took an instant dislike for her," the niece recalled, "because she smoked, talked loudly and swore. I, on the other hand, took to her right away. In fact, whenever she was in the room I would gravitate to her immediately and stay near her. *She* knew who I was, which I don't think Uncle Joe ever did."[13]

Although a fourth child, Michael Edgar Pulitzer, was born in

1930, the stepchildren had no sense of being displaced in Mommie's affections. "She was the least intellectual person that ever walked the face of the earth, and I think also at the same time one of the wisest about people because she was very, very intuitive. . . . This was one of the things that Daddy adored about her," Elinor recalled. "She did an extraordinary job, I think, in retrospect, of bringing up three totally new, different children, and fairly . . . there was no favoritism with Michael or any of that business, ever."[14] A family friend once complimented "Liz," as most friends called her, as "the best vitamin-without-complex I know and I wish you were available at my corner druggist."[15] Her transition into the family also went smoothly because, in Kate Davis's opinion, "Daddy just assumed it was all going to work" and conveyed that confidence to the children more by his matter-of-fact manner than by anything he said. One of his most distinctive attributes, in her view, was that he never brooded. That, certainly, was in striking contrast to his father's nearly perpetual gloominess during the years his children grew up.

There was, however, another somber time for the family when Pulitzer received word on July 29, 1927, that his mother had died suddenly at her chateau at Deauville on the northern coast of France. She was seventy-four. He had remained close to her, seeing her usually during the summer at Chatwold in Bar Harbor and sometimes at the house in New York City. During one visit to New York, young Joseph Pulitzer III, about four years old, had found the small pistol "Granny" kept in a bedside table. He picked it up and it discharged, the bullet passing through the bed's headboard and into the wall. Hearing the shot, his father rushed to the room and instructed his son calmly but firmly to point the weapon away from himself and others and to drop it.[16]

The day following Kate Davis Pulitzer's death, a *Post-Dispatch* editorial full of meaning for her children called her "a beautiful and inspiring woman" whose "stout heart and a fine humor bravely balanced the fears and misgivings of her husband." It gave the much-published example of how she had helped her husband overcome his doubts about buying the *World* in 1883, thus giving "New York the greatest free newspaper it has ever had."[17] For the children, of course, there were memories of many other unpublicized incidents of intervention on their behalf with their mercurial father.

The senior Mrs. Pulitzer had run Chatwold nearly every summer after her husband's death until 1924, when she decided it was too burdensome. Under terms of her husband's will, Ralph was the next in line to take charge of the place, if he wanted to. He did not, so the option passed to Joseph, who became the new lord of Chatwold, with Elinor and then Elizabeth as its lady. Each season after her death, the memory of Kate Davis Pulitzer was visible at Chatwold, in her striking full-length portrait by John Singer Sargent. The remainder of the year it, and Sargent's portrait of her husband,[18] hung in the dining room of the St. Louis home along with one by Goldbeck of Elinor Wickham Pulitzer. But each spring, her namesake granddaughter recalled, Granny's portrait was shipped to Bar Harbor to be with the family, and returned with them in the fall. Grandfather's stayed in St. Louis.

Days of the Summer Palace

With just a few exceptions, from the time he was eight years old in 1893, Joseph Pulitzer II spent some part of every summer at Bar Harbor, Maine. That year his father had leased Chatwold, one of the grandest summer "cottages" to have been built on Mount Desert Island on the shores of Frenchman Bay by various wealthy families. He bought the estate the following year. The sprawling frame, stucco, and stone structure had some twenty-six rooms and seven bathrooms, red-curtained windows, and a large veranda on the ocean side. The spacious entrance hallway was paneled in rich black walnut. Most of the bedrooms and several guest suites were on the second floor, and on the third floor were quarters for some of the twenty or so servants. Also on the 15-acre site was a separate servants' dwelling, a caretaker-gardener's cottage, a large stable (which was replaced by a garage when automobiles were permitted on the island), and two greenhouses. The driveway was lined at intervals by huge hydrangeas growing in pots and kept alive over the winter in a heated greenhouse.

Chatwold was only ten years old when the Pulitzers took it over, but its fussy new owner thought it needed extensive renovations, especially the addition of soundproof quarters for himself. Accordingly, he had built at a cost of $100,000 a three-story stone tower of 1,920 square feet containing the master's bedroom and those of his secretaries, a huge dining room and library that opened onto a veranda facing the sea, and in the basement a swimming pool filled from the ocean. The secretaries immediately named this edifice the "Tower of Silence," although it proved otherwise. On cloudy days, Pulitzer could still hear the foghorn on Egg Rock, a short distance out in the bay. He asked authorities to silence the horn out of sympathy for his condition, but they refused.[1]

The first season the second Joseph Pulitzer took charge of Chatwold, he leased it from his mother for $2,500 and took over the expense of staffing and provisions. When the deed passed into his hands within a year, he became responsible for paying the local tax on the estate, which came to $4,169 in 1924. Only a few other properties, on larger acreage, were assessed more. He thought this was unfair and appealed to the Bar Harbor town fathers for relief—to little immediate avail, possibly because he had nearly $22,000 in improvements made to the house shortly after taking it over. These included the installation of wallpaper hand-painted with Swiss landscape scenes across 51 feet of the dining room walls. The tax levy eventually was reduced somewhat after he had the tower removed in 1936, but he continued to believe he was unfairly taxed. In 1935 a building contractor said the house had a market value of $165,000.

The operating expense of the huge estate was correspondingly high. At the peak of its use in the 1920s and 1930s, it cost between $20,000 and $32,000 annually to occupy it for a four-month season from June 15 to October 15. Even if the place went unoccupied for a season—as it did in 1932, when the family vacationed in California—there were fixed costs of between $7,000 and $11,000 a year. In 1931, more than $5,500 was spent on greenhouse and other plants in order to give the main house a constant supply of fresh flowers, vegetables, and melons. Perhaps the most prized employee for several seasons was the exceptional Swiss chef, Fred Burkhard, who worked for Pulitzer's mother — and later for Herbert — during the remainder of the year. Two daughters of Ralph Field, the gardener and year-round caretaker, remembered Chatwold dinner parties in those years as large, elegant affairs that they were fascinated to watch from hidden vantage points. The food, which they were occasionally allowed to sample, always tasted special. Freshly made peach ice cream was served at the July Fourth fireworks display put on each year for the residents and staff. "Life there was like living in a fairy tale," the former Betsy Field recalled.[2]

As much as he enjoyed these things, Pulitzer became concerned about the outlay for it all when his dividends followed the business decline in the early 1930s. He had a secretary prepare a careful analysis of his personal income and costs, and for a time considered leasing or selling Chatwold, but his realtor found no one who was interested. In fact, the secretary calculated that, with a $170,000 surplus from 1931, Pulitzer would have more than $544,000 available for 1932, but then there would be a drop to $368,000 for 1933. Rather than adding to the unemployment rolls, he ordered a 10 percent across-the-board cut in the salaries of the domestic help in January 1933 and reopened Chatwold. Before making the cuts, he had a secretary determine the current rates for the various domestic help positions. This showed that, even with the reduction, nearly all his employees would be paid above the norm. For example, his butler, Albert Gould, was paid $162 a month when $150 was typical. The lower rate for the two chambermaids was $69, $19 more than most. Otherwise, he saved a few thousand dollars by trimming here and there. One small economy was to tell Field to raise fewer of the gardenias that were used on breakfast trays: "The children can very well get along without them, and if we had only just enough for Mrs. Pulitzer's use and for an occasional gift, that would suffice." The tower came down in 1936 at a cost (including some remodeling of the cottage itself) of $33,000. And there were ever-present maintenance costs. Pulitzer gradually concluded that the family could be just as comfortable in a smaller place, especially after the two older children were away most of the time and began spending their summers in Europe.

From 1930 on, Pulitzer usually arrived later in Bar Harbor than most of the summer cottagers because June was the month he and "Liza," as he always called her, fished for Atlantic salmon on the Restigouche River near Matapédia, Quebec. There Pulitzer leased fishing rights to a stretch of the river each June. They stayed at one of two "camps" along the river: Brandy Brook, which he leased, or Grog Island Camp, which he owned. Brandy Brook was his favorite. Both places were rustic but very comfortable and offered spectacular natural beauty and, most years, huge catches for the privileged few. During the three or four weeks they spent there, the Pulitzers would have a number of guests, a few at a time for a few days each. Among these were John M. Olin, a St. Louis industrialist whose conservative political views did not mesh at all with his host's but didn't get in the way of their recreation, and Dr. James F. Mitchell, a prominent Washington, D.C., surgeon. "This fishing week with you is my great holiday of the year and does me more good than any vacation I could have," Mitchell wrote Pulitzer in 1935. It was not unusual for a season's catch to run to 225 or more fish weighing from 20 to 45 pounds each, with Pulitzer himself taking more than one hundred. Friends in St. Louis and elsewhere and *Post-Dispatch* executives came to expect the arrival of a large fresh salmon packed in crushed ice, compliments of J.P., during June or early July. The fish were shipped by train, but they spoiled unless repacked with ice at regular intervals. "Many a claim was filed for negligence in proper handling," recalled Arch R. King, Pulitzer's financial secretary.[3]

The salmon-fishing trip was Pulitzer's main vacation of the year. He had the least contact with the office during that time, though the *Post-Dispatch* was sent to him in Canada and he sometimes took a reader-secretary with him. When he returned to Bar Harbor, his office files would be waiting, having been packed and sent from St. Louis. He would have only one reader-secretary at a time with him at Bar Harbor, where several copies of the *Post-Dispatch* and one copy of each competing paper were sent daily. His morning routine at Bar Harbor was a quick dip in the frigid ocean before breakfast, his devoted Liza right beside him. After breakfast, newspapers and correspondence would be read to him and he would dictate replies, memos, and telegrams. He often telephoned St. Louis as well, so his editors and managers always knew, as had those under his father, that he was in charge and aware of what was going on whether he was physically present or not. In late morning, he and Liza would take a walk up Newport, one of the so-called "mountains" of Mount Desert Island.

Except for inclement days, most afternoons were spent on the yacht, which from 1924 until the war was the 75-foot schooner *Discoverer* he had built at a cost of $53,000. Captain William I. Conary of Deer Isle, Maine, was her skipper, with a crew of four. Pulitzer had employed Conary for a number of years to run and care for his smaller boats. In fact, Conary had taught him how to sail. Pulitzer regarded the man as a friend as much as an employee, and as something of a practical political philosopher who could help him stay in touch with the attitudes of working-class Americans. His daughter Kate Davis remembered the two men often having long talks out on the water, her father asking questions and listening intently to Conary's views on issues of the day. After Conary retired on a pension provided by his employer, Pulitzer hired his nephew, Maynard Conary, to run the yachts *Troubador* and *Victoria, Discoverer*'s smaller successors. Pulitzer turned over *Discoverer* to the Coast Guard in 1942 for use as a patrol boat against possible submarine attacks on the coast. She was returned after the war, stripped of her luxurious appointments and damaged by fire. Pulitzer accepted a $12,000 settlement from the government and sold the boat for $4,900.

The yacht, which cost between $8,000 and $12,000 a year to operate, was enjoyed mainly by the family and their friends but occasionally by Pulitzer employees. Once or twice each season, *Discoverer* was turned over for a day to some of the permanent help—such as the Dwyers and the Goulds, who moved their families to Bar Harbor for the summers. Mrs. Dwyer, whom everyone knew as Tillie, was told to invite anyone she wanted and that the ship's cook would prepare whatever she ordered. Often on these days the crew would anchor off one of the islands in the bay and row the passengers ashore for a clambake.[4] Pulitzer also was generous when an employee became seriously ill. After Field suffered a heart attack in 1937, he paid all the medical expenses and offered him a six-week vacation in a warmer climate. When

Maynard Conary's wife was told she needed a second major operation within two years, Pulitzer arranged and paid for a thorough examination and second opinion. She was found to be in no danger and the surgery was not done.

In the evenings, life at Bar Harbor was largely a round of cocktail and dinner parties at the various cottages or at the Bar Harbor Club. Chatwold was the scene of many of these, as the order for eighteen Virginia hams in 1927 and a liquor bill of $1,622 in 1933 suggest. Pulitzer genuinely enjoyed the parties, especially the society of the attractive women—this occasionally to Liza's anger and dismay. In a forgiving mood at other times, she would say, "Joe just loves to kiss!"[5] In the usual course of events, by mid-August he had enough of parties and wanted to vary the routine. It was time for the annual cruise aboard *Discoverer* along the northeastern seaboard, stopping here and there for shopping, dining, and parties with friends. The Pulitzers usually took along one or two other couples, the yacht comfortably sleeping seven passengers in addition to the crew. Sumptuous spreads were prepared in the yacht's well-stocked galley, and guests from ashore often joined the cruisers for meals. The log Pulitzer kept of the 1927 cruise of twelve days between Bar Harbor and Stonington, Connecticut, describes among other things a variety of parties on shore and off, stops at Cape Cod and Martha's Vineyard, and a visit to a bookstore where a copy of *The Ten Pleasures of Marriage,* published in 1682, was purchased. In the book, Pulitzer noted, "the 'pleasures' are frankly discussed in the open style of Tom Jones and contemporaries." One evening following a large dinner of duck and other delicacies from Bar Harbor, the ship's party read aloud from the book.

The Pulitzers' cruising companions for at least fifteen years were St. Louis investment banker Eugene F. Williams and his wife, Marie. Williams wrote an account of the 1945 cruise. As usual, there was J.P.'s prescribed pre-breakfast plunge into the ocean for himself and the guests, but within a few days Williams could say, "The ocean is getting colder and colder, but as we are getting tougher and tougher we just shake off the icicles and keep laughing." That evening, with Pulitzer and Williams dressed in white flannels, the party attended a dance at the Isleborough Yacht Club. Among the other guests was Chicago publisher-merchandiser-philanthropist Marshall Field, who had put up most of the money for *PM*, the liberal (some said Communist) ad-less New York newspaper that had been the brainchild of Ralph Ingersoll, former general manager of Time Inc. Williams recounted that as Field waltzed by the dance band, its "very neurotic, slightly intoxicated" drummer grabbed Field "by the forelock, which by the way is as perfect as Gabriel Heater says 'Kreml' can make it, and cries, 'At last I've got you. You are the —— capitalist who has started all these wars.' Field gives him an uppercut and then quite a nice little fight ensues with other musicians and guests joining in. One of the onlookers was heard to remark, 'All Field had to do was raise his hand and say, "Stop, I am the editor of P.M." and the drummer would have taken his dirty words back and embraced the editor.'" Not explaining whether it was because of that incident or for some other reason, Williams continued: "Joe very nasty, treating strange ladies to champagne but not a drop for his sailing gals. We leave in high dudgeon and open some on boat and J.P. comes aboard hours later in wonderful humor. Then more fun and laughter."[6]

Champagne and other alcoholic potables were always abundant on land and on sea, as much so during the Prohibition years of 1919 to 1933 as afterward. Among his other duties, Pulitzer's Bar Harbor caretaker, Ralph Field, kept an inventory of the stock at Chatwold. In view of the need for secrecy, Pulitzer wrote Field in 1927 to "overhaul the liquors I left at Chatwold and wire me, in code, the number of bottles of whatever you find, using the words: Red for Scotch, White for champagne, Blue for gin and Black for Vermouth." The reply was: "Eighteen red, twenty-eight white, two blue, two black."[7] His stock was augmented by more than a thousand quarts the following year when the contents of his mother's wine cellar in New York were divided among the three sons. Joseph's share included about 190 quarts of champagne, 140 of gin, 68 of rye, 30 of Scotch, and several hundred of various wines. The daughters' husbands apparently were thought to be responsible for supplying their households. William Moore, Edith's husband, did at one point offer his brother-in-law the services of his bootlegger. The hired help at Chatwold had other resources. Basil Rudd, one of Pulitzer's secretaries, made home brew in the basement of caretaker Field's cottage. Enforcement of prohibition became a concern at Bar Harbor when "enforcement crank" Howe

Higgins was nearly elected sheriff in 1930 and entered the Republican primary in 1932. That year, Bar Harbor Club secretary Cecil Barret asked Pulitzer for a contribution to the campaign of "our candidate," young Bar Harbor businessman and military veteran Harold Hodgkins, saying, "The coming season is likely to be a 'poor' one anyhow, so let us hope it won't be dreary also." Pulitzer gave $50.

In 1938, Pulitzer did not open Chatwold, leasing a smaller cottage instead but saving only $2,000 by doing so. He had again authorized a realtor to seek a buyer—asking price $225,000—but none was found. The family occupied Chatwold for the next three seasons, operating on a reduced scale with the third floor and the tennis courts he had added closed. The final big occasion for the Pulitzers at Chatwold was twenty-four-year-old Kate Davis's wedding reception there on August 30, 1941, near the end of the last season they occupied the place. This followed her marriage in Bar Harbor's Church of Saint Sauveur to Army Air Corps Lieutenant Henry W. Putnam. The bride and groom and their families received congratulations on the lawn overlooking the ocean while strolling musicians played. Dinner was served in the dining room, which was decorated entirely in white flowers, and at tables throughout the main floor, each table having a different arrangement of white lilies, seashells, and coral. Putnam was killed in action May 25, 1945, during an air raid over Tokyo, leaving his wife and small daughter, also named Kate Davis. Their second daughter, Hope, was born after his death. His widow remarried on October 12, 1946, to Army Air Force Major General Elwood R. Quesada. They had two sons, Thomas and Peter.[8]

The Pulitzers stayed in leased houses from 1942 to 1946. All the buildings but the garage at Chatwold were torn down in 1945–46, and for a time Pulitzer considered constructing a new, smaller house on the site and obtained one estimate of $38,000. Some of the lumber and bricks, certain windows and doors, and choice furniture, paintings, and fixtures from Chatwold were saved and stored in the garage with that in mind. But when Mrs. C. Morton Smith, who owned a small cottage (by Chatwold standards) died in 1946, her place, Beechcroft, went up for sale and Pulitzer bought it, paying $19,000 for the land, house, caretaker's house, garage, and greenhouse. For $14,000 he enlarged the house considerably, especially its kitchen, using some of the Chatwold materials. But most of the valuable salvage went up in smoke when a fire swept most of Mount Desert Island in October 1947, destroying three hundred homes of permanent residents and forty summer homes, including that of Edith Pulitzer Moore. The only thing salvaged from Edith's three-story cottage was a white statuette of an angel which had been stored in the attic. She immediately bought another home. Beechcroft wasn't touched.[9] Had Chatwold still been standing, it almost certainly would have burned and there would have been a substantial insurance settlement, but even with that Pulitzer would not have been interested in recreating the place. As he had written to Boston architect and salmon-fishing companion J. Hampden Robb in 1942, "the day of the summer palace is over."[10]

— 15 —

Editor and Censor

F or years it was the conventional wisdom that the "shadows" of managing editor Oliver K. Bovard and editorial page editor George S. Johns "obscured Joseph Pulitzer 2d as he grew up on the *Post-Dispatch.*"[1] Pulitzer, never a seeker of publicity, did nothing to dispel that view, but as already noted, he liked an active role too much to retire into the background and leave the work to others. Bovard himself, responding to a request from Pulitzer in 1924 for his assessment of the paper's development during the past decade, had written:

> When you came out the editors acquired for the first time, at least in my experience as an executive, a powerful ally with influence if not authority in the Business Office.

Your instinct was for the editorial end and you gave a sympathetic ear to our complaints.

The beginning of the improvement dates here and it continued progressively with the increase of your authority and the business growth of the paper. You had ideas for improvements of your own and you welcomed and solicited what the rest of us had. Out of these two conditions, your great desire to make the paper better and still better and your power to commandeer the things needed . . . the Post-Dispatch of today was developed.[2]

That probably was as close to apple-polishing as Bovard ever came in his career. But the facts were there. Looking into the record, he dated Pulitzer's contributions back to 1912, when he had instructed advertising manager William Steigers to cut down the number of ads on certain pages in order to make more room for news, a step obviously to Bovard's liking. Other early memorandums to news, editorial, advertising, circulation, and business executives show Pulitzer as an active, committed, and independent thinker about all the newspaper's departments. His model, obviously, was his father, who was at best a halfhearted delegator of authority. As he matured in the job, the son also leaned definitely in the autocratic direction, but much less so with Bovard, whose talent so impressed him, than any other subordinate. Once a business executive, such as the advertising manager or business manager, had proven capable, he paid less attention on a day-by-day basis to that man's performance than he did to what the various editors were doing. This, too, paralleled his father's priorities. The suggestion that he tended to defer to the older hands probably stems from the fact that, while he could be forceful, he usually stopped short of insisting on having the last word. He quite likely came as close to perfection as any American newspaper editor has in the matters of courtesy and civility. Under the second Joseph Pulitzer, the *Post-Dispatch* was "a 'Mister' newspaper,"[3] an admiring former competitor observed. That did not mean he was aloof or unapproachable. Editorial writer Irving Dilliard, who eventually became editor of the editorial page, once estimated that Pulitzer "must be as warm, generous and human a metropolitan newspaper proprietor as there is in the country."[4]

However, George Sibley Johns, the editorial page editor when the younger J.P. took charge, saw the publisher from a different perspective. Johns, a Princeton graduate twenty-eight years the publisher's senior with the reputation as "Mr. Post-Dispatch" around St. Louis, had known Pulitzer since the younger man was seventeen, and thought of him more as his pupil than as his boss. He addressed him as "Joe." After all, his eldest son, George Jr., had been born in 1885, the same year as Joseph Pulitzer Jr. Nevertheless the younger man tried to be assertive. There was a typical exchange when Pulitzer objected to the use of the phrase "these two Jews" in an editorial headed "Izzy and Moe" as "inexcusable. Bad writing; bad editing." Johns responded: "My dear Joe: I feel sure if you had in mind the definition of the word 'Jew,' you would not find in it any reflection on race or religion. It is a highly honorable designation of a man who belongs to the Hebrew race and is an Israelite in religion."[5]

Accordingly, Johns often did just as he wished, even after receiving instructions to do otherwise. In March 1921, for example, Pulitzer, who did not ordinarily review editorials before they were printed but reacted afterward, was annoyed by two favoring unilateral naval disarmament, saying these put the paper "in the so-called pacifist class." He instructed Johns to "make it an unwritten rule never to write a disarmament editorial which shall not contain an equally strong plea in favor of keeping up our naval preparedness and spending the money that is necessary to do it pending . . . disarmament by agreement."[6] But three months later an editorial applauded congressional interest in discontinuing the naval construction program. Again Pulitzer protested, saying he would regard any representative who voted for that "as a visionary and impractical pacifist" for failing to recognize "that we must continue to build so long as our naval competitors continue to build." He instructed Johns to "take particular pains" to see that all on the editorial page staff "get this point."[7]

He tried to reserve decisions on presidential endorsements for himself. When Johns in early 1920 editorially raised some questions about Herbert Hoover's qualifications as a statesman, Pulitzer cautioned him "to go no further than this in questioning his availability" because "he is likely to prove satisfactory in this as in other respects and . . . it is not at all unlikely that we will find ourselves supporting him. Please be guided accordingly."[8] Eight years later, he found it necessary to remind Johns that he was "not to commit the paper even inferentially to any presidential nominee . . . until I have been consulted."[9]

However authoritarian that may have been, he followed his father's practice of never requiring a writer to write against his own conscience, whether it be in endorsing candidates or some thing else. "I'll be hanged if I can swallow compulsory military training at Missouri University so long as we don't adopt compulsory military training as a national policy," he wrote Johns in 1926.[10] He asked the editor to assign someone on the staff who agreed to write an editorial to that effect. One of his sharpest memos to the editorial editor was this objection to the use of trite expressions: "I protest against YOUR passing editorials of this kind. 'The interest of the people are vitally at stake'; ' . . . have ridden rough shod over the rights of the people.' Hell's bells!"[11] Pulitzer succeeded in gaining much more control of the editorial page after Johns's retirement in 1929 brought an end to what Pulitzer later described as "the old-fashioned, cock-sure, know-it-all attitude of . . . the Johns era."[12]

A certain degree of tension was inevitable, and that between Pulitzer and Bovard was more complicated. This was in part because the domain Bovard had carved out for himself with little interference from the publisher was much larger than Johns's. It also had to do with the unusually confident and dominating personalities of the two men. Each had a genuine respect for the other, though probably not in equal proportions. From the first year he had known Bovard, Pulitzer had regarded him as an extremely capable leader. In Bovard's behavior toward Pulitzer there was an element of compulsory obedience, as suggested when he wrote in 1935, "As in everything . . . your authority has been, of course, absolute."[13]

Even so, theirs was not an abrasive relationship. Year after year during his long tenure as managing editor, Bovard demonstrated the extraordinary ability the younger Joseph Pulitzer had so emphatically commended to his doubting father. By the time Bovard retired at the age of sixty-six in 1938, the *Post-Dispatch* had to its credit a long list of investigatory achievements—a number of which had won Pulitzer Prizes or other recognition—all largely attributable to the managing editor's skillful direction of the capable news staff he had assembled. As one of his pupils expressed it, he ran "a one-man school of journalism."[14] He preferred reporters trained in history, politics, and economics, and considered college courses in journalism "worse than useless, a waste of the student's time."[15] In his opinion, those worthy of the craft would be able — as he had been, with only a fifth-grade education — to pick it up in a disciplined newsroom.

A recital of a few of Bovard's achievements will reveal his methods. He was chiefly responsible for establishing the paper's Washington bureau in 1918, first as a means of covering Missourians in Washington, but shortly becoming the operations center where important national investigative campaigns were launched and pursued. The most outstanding of these was the at times single-handed pursuit by the *Post-Dispatch* of the facts that became the Teapot Dome scandal of the 1920s involving U.S. Navy oilfield leases in western states. Washington bureau reporter Paul Y. Anderson, with important behind-the-scenes direction and support from Bovard in St. Louis, was chiefly responsible for the exposures of bribery, collusion, and fraud which brought the downfall of those involved. For this he won a 1928 Pulitzer Prize.[16]

On the local scene, Bovard's persistence resolved a complicated maze of kidnapping and blackmail in the mid-1930s which put several wrongdoers in jail. To begin with, *Post-Dispatch* crime reporter John T. Rogers, despite considerable personal risk, became the intermediary in gaining the release of a kidnapped physician without the payment of ransom. Rogers received a bonus of $7,280 — a year's salary — and other staff members who assisted on the story also got bonuses.[17] Then, to net the cleverest of the suspects, Bovard ordered the publication of potentially libelous statements in order to test what he felt sure was a false claim. This defeated the attempt of Mrs. Nellie Tipton Muench, who had helped plan the kidnapping, to win the sympathy of jurors and the public by pretending that she had just given birth to a child.

Mrs. Muench was a colorful character. She was the wife of a prominent physician, the daughter of a minister, and the sister of a Missouri Supreme Court judge. During the 1920s she ran one of the city's most expensive dress shops, many of whose customers, she claimed, were married men of means and position who were

clothing mistresses in her finery. She was no stranger to court-
room proceedings, having been implicated in several shadowy
thefts of jewels and extortion attempts but never convicted. Shortly
after being charged in the kidnapping, and to the surprise of
virtually everyone (for there had been no hint of her being preg-
nant after twenty-two childless years of marriage) Dr. and Mrs.
Muench announced the birth of a son. A friend testified that
Mrs. Muench was "just crazy" about her son, whom she lovingly
called "Pudgy," "little hog on a log," and "little fat pig on a lard
bucket."[18] Bovard was suspicious, and directed an investigation in
which the *Post-Dispatch* found a wealthy bachelor physician from
whom Mrs. Muench had blackmailed $18,000 after convincing
him that he had fathered her child.[19] Then the child's real mother,
an unwed Pennsylvania girl, came forward and convinced the jury
that the infant had been taken from her and given to the Muenches.
Following revelation of the "baby hoax," they were convicted in
federal court in the kidnapping, fined, and sent to prison.

As that case showed, Bovard's main tactic was persistent investigation. This sometimes meant detaching a reporter from all other
assignments for weeks or months in order to follow all possible
leads. The physician's kidnappers were caught almost four years
after the crime, thanks largely to the paper's continuing interest.
In another case, after closely reexamining the facts and careful
deduction, the managing editor solved a murder eight years after
it happened. In shorter order, under his direction the paper pursued
racketeers and dishonest politicians into jail, defeated an attempt
to saddle St. Louis with a perpetual streetcar franchise, and proved
election fraud involving vote-stealing, dishonest counting, ballot-
box stuffing, and the carrying of 40,000 "ghost" voters on registration rolls. The vote fraud series won the paper a Pulitzer Prize for
meritorious public service in 1937.[20]

Of course, some investigations proved to be dead ends, and
even Bovard's news sense was fallible. He sacrificed a great beat for
the paper in rejecting the exclusive rights to the story of Charles A.
Lindbergh's historic transatlantic flight in 1927. Lindbergh was
working as a mail pilot out of St. Louis when he decided to attempt
what no one had done before. He asked the *Post-Dispatch* to
finance and sponsor his flight, but Bovard refused. "If anything
happened it would always be on my conscience," he told Lindbergh.

"To gamble on a man's life for a piece of newspaper promotion is something for which I will not take the responsibility." After Lindbergh got other backing, Bovard turned down the rights to the pilot's first-person account of the flight—which he could have had for $500 and for which Lindbergh ultimately got $85,000 through the *New York Times* news service[21]—saying he was certain the young adventurer would fail. When that proved wrong, he had no regrets. "If the decision were to be made again, it would be the same," he maintained.[22] The *Globe-Democrat,* which took the *Times* service, presented the account to St. Louis.

Pulitzer later said he was sorry he hadn't tried harder to persuade Bovard to change his mind about the Lindbergh story, but this had not been a major dispute. The basis for several of their early differences was the fact that Pulitzer didn't share Bovard's chilly attitude toward the *World,* whose material Bovard could have done without. When the *World* came out in September 1921 with a twenty-one-day exposé-style series on the revival of the Ku Klux Klan—for which it won a Pulitzer Prize the following year— Bovard sharply abbreviated it and ran it inside the paper. Pulitzer thought he had underplayed it, but he conceded that he might have done the same since the *World* had given Bovard no advance notice of the scope of the series. That made no difference, Bovard replied. "My presentation of that story was my deliberate judgment at that time, and, with all respect to your own, it remains unchanged," he explained. "Although had you been here," he continued, emphasizing Pulitzer's residence in Bar Harbor at the time, "I would have deferred to your views, if my own did not change them. Adopting the candor of your letter—the World's handling of that story was the most striking example of overplaying and exaggeration that I have seen. And worse than that, it violated one of the elementary principles to which these newspapers are consecrated, that is, fairness." In sum, he concluded, the *World*'s story "was an exposé of a perfectly legal organization of probably less than one hundred thousand persons instead of eight hundred thousand, as the World said, which was ridiculous in its composition and secrecy and undoubtedly un-American and a possible danger to public welfare in spots."[23] Years later, Herbert Bayard Swope, who as *World* executive editor had superintended the series, incorrectly recalled that the *Post-Dispatch* had rejected it, but captured something of Bovard's attitude in reminding Pulitzer: "When we made the vast, deep and important exposure of the K.K.K., which led to jail sentences for some, and broke up the organization, Bovard didn't take it. It was pure snottiness on his part."[24]

His alleged pettiness aside, Bovard's comments suggest that racism had a part in influencing his judgment. Racism showed up again when Pulitzer criticized the managing editor for not printing a photograph of a lynching in 1925. Bovard's rationale was that the photo "would have been shocking to a great many people. Even among those who sympathize with lynching upon occasion, there are comparatively few who will take a hand in the job and fewer still who will look at it, except the roughneck element."[25] Pulitzer's opinion was that the photo should have been printed for precisely the reason Bovard withheld it—its shock value. He did not, however, press the question of news policy toward racial injustice during Bovard's tenure as managing editor, even though the paper had editorially called for the prosecution of lynchers.[26] After Bovard retired, the paper gradually stepped up its coverage of the black civil rights cause and stayed ahead of its competition in promoting awareness of racial issues.[27]

A more persistent difference between the two men had to do with the balance between serious news and entertainment in the paper. Recalling his father's injunction to "always print that which interests everybody," Pulitzer objected that "the paper is drifting too much towards looking out for subjects of purely intellectual interest, and . . . may be overlooking opportunities to develop . . . subjects that are of emotional rather than purely intellectual appeal. In other words, the very old fashioned and well named Human Interest story." He advised Bovard to select "the story that everyone will read" over "the story that the managing editor feels he ought to print though it may be of limited interest because it is part of the history of the day."[28] He also thought the paper should have more humor in it, particularly a frequent short amusing item on page one, such as the *World* often printed. In early 1920 he related some recent examples: "A good one about Jack Barrymore interrupting the lines of his play to call a man in the audience a damned fool. Another . . . about a ten-thousand dollar city official who wanted a secret telephone number, and who, when he discovered that the telephone company knew the number, was much annoyed and promptly cancelled it."[29]

They went back and forth on this over the years, neither yielding much to the other, while probably achieving a certain balance by unspoken compromise in the process. Bovard's view was that if he, with limited space to fill, printed only what everyone would read instead of what he judged significant, he would end up omitting important news: "I have for many years felt that given the space and the staff a newspaper might be made as popular as the genius of editors permitted and at the same time be as highly esteemed as, say, the New York Times, for completeness of news and intelligence of editing. Few, if any, papers today enjoy, I believe, both popularity for their entertaining qualities and prestige among . . . two story thinkers. Perhaps this is because publishers do not agree with the view that this dual role is practicable. I realize of course the foundation for the kind of paper I have in mind would have to be laid in the business office. Advertising would have to be considerably reduced in volume and at the same time made to yield greater revenues to meet added costs."[30]

The reference to "the kind of paper I have in mind" is a telling expression. It both revealed the reluctant subordinate in Bovard and showed that he had definite ideas about what a newspaper should be. At the same time, he was cynical about the likelihood of change in the desired direction. Some years later, Pulitzer objected to the publication of an article in a planned series containing poetry by Gertrude Stein on the grounds that "there are many illiterate and ignorant readers like myself who must strongly object to having this stuff thrown in their faces and who must be humiliated at their inability to understand it. If I may give you my opinion as to this series, I would throw the remaining five articles in the waste-paper basket." Bovard replied: "In they go! *But* — other readers object to having Walter Winchell, Horoscopes, race horse tips, inane comics thrown at them; the answer to these critics always is that the features they dislike are not for them and they don't have to read them. In respect of *features,* the paper is a cafeteria — something to flatter the taste of every customer. One view of G.S. is that she is a *novel* type of crossword puzzle."[31] Pulitzer liked the cafeteria analogy, but thought "it ought to be a cafeteria whose menu is printed in English rather than French or

Italian and whose dishes are of the kind that would generally appeal to the great majority of people." He said he drew "a sharp distinction" between providing features "which appeal to the average or below average and our news policy, which should continue on its present plane of, may I say, higher intelligence—especially insofar as the significant news is concerned."[32]

Despite that standoff, Bovard's implication that publishers are overly beholden to balance-sheet considerations did not fit the metropolitan newspaper publisher he was addressing as well as it did most others. Probably the best evidence of this was a step Bovard could only have applauded but apparently didn't. In 1929, Pulitzer established at the *Post-Dispatch* what may well have been the most comprehensive, formalized system of advertising censorship in American newspaper history.[33] In doing so, he finally accomplished what he had failed to persuade his father to do: rid the paper of false, misleading, and distasteful medical, financial, and other advertising content. The cost was substantial. An average of $63,220 in unacceptable advertising was turned away each year during the Depression decade of 1929–39, during which the paper's total advertising linage declined by 40 percent. There was an additional substantial cost in the numerous man-hours devoted to evaluating advertising claims. Some advertisers, angered by the rejection of part of their schedules, withdrew all their advertising from the paper. In 1938, the annual cost of the censorship operation was estimated at $200,000. But Pulitzer remained firm. He had hired Leslic E. Prichard, an analytical research chemist who could determine the true properties of various quack cures and nostrums, as the full-time head of the paper's three-member Advertising Censorship Board at a starting salary of $10,000 a year. He gave him this mandate: "When in doubt, leave out."

Joseph Pulitzer had come to doing this gradually, as he observed over the years after becoming publisher that both governmental and voluntary efforts by advertisers were doing too little to protect those who are most vulnerable to deceptive patent medicine advertising. A letter he received from a Nebraska reader in 1913 urged him to ban patent medicine ads in language much like his own to his father: "By getting rid of such dope humbug you will confer a favor and a lasting service to all mankind, one far better than all your other, worthy as they are, activities."[34] But at first he had let the advertising department rely on the advice of the National Vigilance Committee of the Associated Advertising Clubs of the World, which acted as a clearinghouse for information on ineffectual or dangerous products but did not employ a testing staff of its own. The committee provided information on products at the request of member newspapers, making it easy for papers that did not care to know to remain ignorant and continue selling space. In 1916, the committee issued a confidential "special bulletin" to its members listing thirty-three medical and cosmetic products for which "a leading newspaper of the central west with a circulation of over 100,000" (presumably the *Post-Dispatch*) was refusing to accept advertising.[35] But as late as 1925 the paper was running ads for "Snake Oil," the popular name for Miller's Antiseptic Oil, touted as relieving rheumatism, neuralgia, colds, "and kindred aches and pains," and Lane's Pills, which "don't cure disease" but "prevent it by keeping your liver active and your bowels clean. Take one tonight."[36]

Once Pulitzer insisted on careful screening, he watched the process closely. At first, there was reluctance among the paper's advertising executives. "I didn't like the idea of keeping advertising out of the paper," former national advertising manager and censorship board member Ben L. Brockman recalled. "I couldn't conceive of going to Pulitzer at the end of the year and saying, 'Hey, Mr. Pulitzer, do you think I ought to have a raise? I lost a million lines of advertising!' It was contrary to my nature."[37] In 1931, advertising manager George M. Burbach got nowhere when he tried to get Pulitzer to relax the censorship board's bans on a number of "borderline" products, such as Mountain Valley Water, which was harmless though advertised as a remedy "that aids in the treatment" of the kidneys. After looking over a list of such accounts, worth about $40,000 a year to the paper, Pulitzer wrote Burbach: "I should say that they are all, including Mountain Valley Water, glaring examples of fake, misleading advertising almost certain to lead to injury to the public health, and as such definitely unacceptable."

In the second year of its existence — despite the deepening Depression and accompanying decline in advertising revenue — the censorship operation was expanded to include "any advertising of a doubtful nature" including that deemed offensive to the prevailing

standards of taste and decency. As a result, the trade publication
Editor and Publisher reported, the *Post-Dispatch* "barred . . . some
outstanding campaigns that were accepted by most other metropolitan newspapers," among them "the kissing campaign of White
Owl Cigars," which Prichard described as "showing a man and a
woman in a tight embrace kissing each other, with the question,
'How does she kiss you?' " Explaining the board's rejection of the
campaign, Prichard wrote: "Can you imagine anything more distasteful than associating intimate kissing with breath odors derived
from the use of cigars? There was also the thought that pictures of
this sort may have an effect upon the morals of youths, encouraging them to be less concerned about kissing, petting, etc." The
campaign would have brought in $10,200 to the *Post-Dispatch*,
which was the only newspaper in the nation to reject it. It was
also the only newspaper to reject an ad for the movie *Bird of
Paradise*, illustrated, in the words of *Editor and Publisher*, with "a
huge silhouette of a naked caveman, bearing in his arms a white
girl wearing a couple of ostrich plumes and a smirk."

The newspaper far outdistanced government regulation of advertising, in effect pointing the way toward some eventual reforms. The
board's scrutiny included policing of classified advertising, taking
into account the harsh realities of the Depression. Prichard reported
to Pulitzer, "Realizing that many of the working class were hard
pressed by economic conditions, the Classified Department has
checked each and every help wanted ad to verify its authenticity,
so as to avoid waste in time, car-fare, etc. to our readers." He said
it was not unusual to find that such ads were false, apparently
taken out "by some disgruntled or discharged employee to cause
embarrassment to their former employer." When it came to national
advertising, the Federal Trade Commission, which had existed
since 1914, had concerned itself almost exclusively with unfair
competitive practices among advertisers instead of with consumer
protection. The Food and Drug Administration policed labeling
but not advertising claims. In 1935, the FTC made what the
Post-Dispatch considered a weak gesture toward the consumer in
ruling that Father John's Medicine could not be advertised as a
"remedy" but could be described as a "treatment" for colds. The
Post-Dispatch found the distinction meaningless and continued to
reject the copy. It preceded by six years a 1937 FTC ban of a baby

food advertisement that claimed the product enabled the body to store more calcium than drinking three to four times the amount of milk would provide. One of the biggest losses was the half-page color Fleischmann's Yeast ads in the comic section, which were dropped because the company could not substantiate its nutrition claims for the product. Those ads, Brockman pointed out, were "pure profit": "If we got an ad for the comic section we'd just reduce the other things in the section to make room for it." He eventually enticed Fleischmann's back into the paper—without the health claim—by pointing out that the company wouldn't get far with its stockholders by saying, "No, we didn't sell much yeast in St. Louis, but we sure spanked the *Post-Dispatch.*" Increasingly, as it became plain that the paper was not going to relax its standards, advertisers modified their copy to make it acceptable to the *Post-Dispatch* and used the same copy in other newspapers. But others, such as Lifebuoy soap, whose term "body odor" offended Pulitzer, refused to change and stayed out of the paper.

All this took place quietly. On Pulitzer's orders, there was to be no self-congratulatory trumpeting about the advertising standards. "No paper should publicize its good acts because a good newspaper is expected to do those things," he told Brockman. It is interesting that even though the founding Pulitzer had rejected this means of public service, his statements in the paper's platform that the *Post-Dispatch* would "always fight for progress and reform" and "always be devoted to the public welfare" were cited by Prichard as his philosophical touchstones.

Although it felt the effects of the hard times, the *Post-Dispatch* was never in serious financial trouble during the Depression decade. It began and finished the 1929–39 period with 47 percent of the total newspaper advertising linage in St. Louis. Its nearest competitor, with 30 percent of the linage, was the morning *Globe-Democrat.* The *Post-Dispatch* net profit slipped downward from 18.5 percent in 1929 to 9.6 percent in 1939.[38] That would probably have been sufficient justification for most publishers to trust advertising credibility to "caveat emptor" and accept whatever came in. In 1929, the *Post-Dispatch* sold 23,760,760 lines of advertising; in 1939, it sold 14,166,098 lines, a decline of slightly more than 40 percent. The censorship policy undoubtedly was a factor, but Pulitzer had meant what he said when he had summoned Brockman to Bar Harbor in June 1929 to outline the policy: "I'm not interested in how much this will cost."

—— 16 ——

The *World* in Decline

Just what caused the *World* newspapers to come apart financially and go out of business in the second year of the Depression has been a matter of some speculation and debate ever since. The general conclusion has been, however, as Richard Kluger expressed it in 1986, that "Pulitzer's three sons milked the operation of its profits and declined to make the sort of investment in staff and white space . . . needed to achieve the solidity of its quality competitors."[1]

Kluger's generalization is far too broad, but it is not, in fairness, entirely wrong. It is most misleading in suggesting that the three Pulitzer sons were equally inept at or uninterested in newspaper management and that the *World*'s failure lay essentially in the newspaper's journalistic shortcomings, for among the others who doubted almost to the very end that the *World* had to be sold was Joseph Pulitzer of St. Louis. Material from his papers reveals more fully than has previously been published the chain of events and judgments—good and bad—that led to the sale. This shows that, starting in 1925, Joseph unsuccessfully encouraged his brothers to take steps that might have kept a Pulitzer voice alive in New York.

This was to him a most delicate, private matter. By 1930, word was fairly widespread in newspaper circles that the *World* — morning, evening, and Sunday collectively—was in serious financial trouble. The papers had not followed the *Post-Dispatch*'s example in censoring advertising, so that was not a factor. In fact, the *World* accepted some ads, such as those for the then extremely dangerous practice of surgical face-lifting, which most other New York papers were turning away.[2] Yet the New York Pulitzer newspapers simply were not making it against their competition. Morning *World* circulation had been essentially stagnant for twenty years, and for most of the 1920s its advertising linage lagged that of the *Times, Herald Tribune,* and *American,* its main New York rivals. The merger of the once independently powerful *Herald* and *Tribune* in 1924 was evidence that daily journalism in the city was changing, and other consolidations were in the offing. And by the mid-1920s there were three new tabloids, Joseph Medill Patterson's *Daily News,* Hearst's *Mirror,* and Bernarr McFadden's sleazy *Graphic.*

It occurred to some who were aware of all this that the Pulitzer in charge of the prospering *Post-Dispatch* might be able to reverse the *World*'s fortunes, and a rumor that he was going to try began circulating. When it reached Frank McCabe, an official of the New York classified advertising managers' organization and former *World* classified advertising manager, he wrote to J.P.: "I hope the reports are true. The name of Joseph Pulitzer is inspiration enough in itself. How we could work for your father."[3] He then applied for his old position, noting that "the *World* led the country in classified advertising" when he had been in charge. The response, though technically honest, covered up more than it revealed: "I can only say that the report that I am going to New York to be actively associated with the management of the World is not true."[4] Pulitzer had been downright deceptive two years earlier in responding to an inquiry about the *World:* "My entire time being spent in directing the publication of the St. Louis Post-Dispatch and having only remote contact with the publication of the New York World, I referred your letter of December 12th to the editor of the World, my brother, Ralph Pulitzer."[5]

The fact was that he had kept much more closely in touch with the operation of the *World* newspapers than he cared to disclose. As secretary of the *World*'s parent, the Press Publishing Company, he drew a weekly salary: $80 in 1930. In a letter to Ralph in 1925 (reminding his brother of "the great importance of keeping the news columns free of political bias"), he referred to himself as "a constant reader of the World."[6] From the mid-1920s on, he had been troubled by what seemed to him mismanagement of the New York properties, and he was disappointed that Ralph and Herbert had not exercised more hardheaded business leadership. In his own mind, though, there was a limit to how emphatically he was entitled to advise or criticize because of the understanding among the brothers that St. Louis was his domain and New York was theirs.

Actually, the *World* had been mainly in Ralph's care, Herbert being underage and totally inexperienced when their father died. Further, even though his father had expected Herbert to have a career in journalism, the youngster had escaped the intense parental tutoring and criticism his older brothers had endured. He had, in contrast, been pampered by his father, who in his later years had kept Herbert with him more than any other member of the family. For most of his adult life, Herbert's interest did not extend much beyond collecting his six-tenths of the dividends. He was seldom seen in New York or St. Louis, spending much of his time in the leisure pursuits of bird-shooting and fishing, enthusiasms that formed a lifelong bond between him and Joseph. There is little evidence to suggest, though, that either Ralph or Joseph harbored any resentment toward Herbert because of his carefree ways. In fact, there was among the three a remarkable degree of acceptance of one another as each was—a reaction, perhaps, against their father's excessively judgmental personality. Although impossible to quantify, this familial warmth and gentlemanly reserve among the brothers toward one another might itself have contributed to the *World*'s

FIG. 21.   Oliver K. Bovard, managing editor of the *Post-Dispatch* from 1910 to 1938. A member of the news staff for 40 years, starting in 1898. Young J.P. II was fascinated by Bovard and learned much from him.

FIG. 22.   Benjamin H. Reese, managing editor of the *Post-Dispatch* from 1938 to
1951. A member of the news staff for 38 years, starting in 1913.

FIG. 23. Raymond L. Crowley, managing editor of the *Post-Dispatch* from 1951 to 1963. A member of the news staff for 41 years, starting in 1922.

FIG. 24.   George S. Johns, editor of the *Post-Dispatch* editorial page from 1897 to 1929.

FIG. 25.   Clark McAdams, editor of the *Post-Dispatch* editorial page from 1929 to 1934.

FIG. 26. Charles G. Ross, editor of the *Post-Dispatch* editorial page from 1934 to 1939.

FIG. 27. Ralph Coghlan, editor of the *Post-Dispatch* editorial page from 1939 to 1949.

FIG. 28.   Irving Dilliard, editor of the *Post-Dispatch* editorial page from 1949 to 1957.

FIG. 29.   Daniel R. Fitzpatrick, *Post-Dispatch* editorial cartoonist from 1913 to 1958.

FIG. 30. Florence D. White, over-seer for Joseph Pulitzer (I) of both the New York and St. Louis news-papers. One of J.P. II's mentors.

FIG. 31. Frank R. O'Neil, general manager of the *Post-Dispatch* when J.P. II first went to St. Louis in 1903. O'Neil saw great poten-tial in the young man.

FIG. 32.   Julius H. Klyman,
editor of the *Post-Dispatch*
"Pictures"; Newspaper Guild
official; resident radical, 1922–58.

FIG. 33.   Raymond P. Brandt,
Post-Dispatch chief Washington
correspondent from 1934 to 1962.

FIG. 34. Marquis W. Childs, *Post-Dispatch* Washington correspondent, syndicated columnist, and author. With the newspaper for 47 years.

Fig. 35. Virginia Irwin, *Post-Dispatch* star European correspondent during World War II but assigned to women's news and features afterward. At the newspaper for 30 years.

FIG. 36. Sam J. Shelton, assistant to the editor and publisher of the *Post-Dispatch* from 1945 to 1955.

FIG. 37. George M. Burbach, *Post-Dispatch* advertising manager, then general manager of KSD and KSD–TV from 1913 to 1955.

FIG. 38.   Charles J. Hentschell, *Post-Dispatch* production manager, then business manager, from 1941–1955.

Fɪɢ. 39.   James T. Keller, treasurer of the Pulitzer Publishing Company from 1906 to 1945.

FIG. 40.   Ben L. Brockman,
Post-Dispatch national
advertising manager from 1929
to 1955.

FIG. 41.   Harold O. Grams,
program manager of KSD
and KSD–TV under J.P. II.
With the broadcasting
operations for 40 years.

FIG. 42.   Fred F. Rowden, *Post-Dispatch* advertising manager from 1945 to 1955, later business manager.

FIG. 43.   Stuart M. Chambers, treasurer of the Pulitzer Publishing Company from 1945 to 1955.

FIG. 44.   Arch R. King, chief secretary/reader to J.P. II from 1936 to 1955.

decline and fall. There is at least some circumstantial evidence to that effect.

To begin with, if Herbert was detached, it must be said of Ralph that since inheriting proprietorship of the *World* he had been a less active editor-publisher than Joseph, much more inclined than his brother in St. Louis to leave decisions to editors and managers. In the first years after their father's death, this may not have mattered much. The *World* newspapers were solid properties, particularly the founder's beloved morning *World,* which under the old man's handpicked editor, Frank I. Cobb, had enjoyed its longest period of public service importance between 1904 and 1923 with circulation in the 290,000 to 380,000 range. However, having discarded its frankly sensational tone of the Spanish-American War period, morning *World* circulation advanced only slightly during that time span. Cobb died of cancer at the age of fifty-four in 1923. The more sedate and cerebral Walter Lippmann succeeded Cobb as editorial page editor, and the flamboyant Herbert Bayard Swope became the paper's executive editor, a new title he created for himself. Swope's main innovation was the widely copied "opposite editorial" or "op-ed" page, where the work of the paper's two best columnists — its book reviewer and dramatic critic — were displayed.[7]

In large measure, Ralph Pulitzer deferred to the judgments of these men on news and editorial policy. Similarly, he only loosely directed the advertising and circulation departments, whose overall supervision was under men his father had hired. For example, by 1920 Ralph knew that business manager Don C. Seitz, though one of his father's most trusted lieutenants, had become a liability. Many of Seitz's responsibilities had been parceled out to subordinates, among whom there was insufficient coordination. The reason for his poor performance appeared to be Seitz's entanglement in a variety of bad personal investments, which became embarrassments to his employer. Ralph's solution to this, after Seitz refused the publisher's offer to make him the *World*'s roving correspondent in Europe, was to have the company eradicate Seitz's $30,000 of debt and demote him from the morning *World* to the *Evening World.* His salary stayed at $20,000 a year, but he lost the commission based on profits that had been worth at least another $5,000 a year.[8] Before leaving the company in 1926, Seitz

completed, largely on company time and with the cooperation of
the heirs, the first biography of the founding Pulitzer, *Joseph
Pulitzer: Liberator of Journalism.*[9]

Though also unhappy with Seitz's performance, Joseph was not
at all sure that he was the man to blame. "I write you this, not in a
spirit of criticism, but for whatever it is worth," he began a letter
to Ralph in early 1925, and then raised this question: "Does not
the record of the past few years suggest that . . . the entire business
administration of the paper under [Florence D.] White's General
Management is open to question?"[10] It appeared to him that because
White had "had a free hand" the *Evening World* had been "permitted
to reach an almost dying position," the Sunday *World* was "showing
steady signs of slipping," and the morning *World,* "splendid newspaper as it is," had by raising its price from two to three cents
surrendered first place to the *New York Times* when only a few
years ago it had a lead of over 100,000. He concluded: "I want the
World to set the pace. As it is, I see it getting badly licked." Several
weeks later he asked *World* circulation manager N. R. Hoover to
project what the circulations of the morning *Times, American,*
and *World* would have been on April 1, 1925, if the *World* had not
raised its price from two to three cents. Hoover calculated that the
World would have been first, 22,000 ahead of the *Times* and
24,000 ahead of the *American.* Instead, it was 6,400 behind the
Times and only 1,500 ahead of the *American.*[11]

"Those figures, in my judgment, contain a severe reflection on
the Business Management of the World," Joseph wrote Ralph in
one of two letters on the same day.[12] In turn, this revived "my old
thought that three-cornered publication of a Morning, Evening
and Sunday issue is fundamentally unsound." (The usual objection,
which he didn't specify, was that advertisers would not regard
each paper as a separate entity but would consider all three as one
medium.) When he might have first raised this with Ralph is not
recorded, but by the spring of 1925 he believed "it is this condition that is probably at the bottom of most of our troubles. It
suggests the possibility of selling the Evening to Munsey, and of
buying the American from Hearst. It seems like a ruthless move,
but I believe that if it could be done the paper would be a stronger,
sounder and far more secure instrument of public service with all
of its resources, financial and intellectual, concentrated in one

great edition, rather than as at present divided between two issues, both of which are slipping."[13]

Near the end of the year, Frank A. Munsey, who had megalomaniac ambitions of assembling an empire of five hundred newspapers and in New York already owned the *Telegram* and the *Sun,* offered $5 million for the *Evening World.* Joseph urged Ralph to have "the best brains in The World office" determine the effects the sale would have on circulation and advertising for the morning *World* and again suggested finding out if Hearst would sell them the *American,* possibly in exchange for the *Evening World.* He was highly enthusiastic about getting rid of the evening paper, which specialized mainly in crime news and gossipy, lightweight entertainment. It "still strikes me as just as colorless, purposeless and inconsequential as the Morning is vivid, powerful and important," he wrote. "I believe that the surprise that would be caused by the move would be forgotten in a week, and that the public would soon come to sense that in the Morning and Sunday World it had Pulitzer Journalism at its best, with all of its courage, all of its intelligence, all of its initiative and all of its resources concentrated in this one publication, the Morning and Sunday World." Sounding as if *he* were the man in charge, he continued: "In considering the financial result of the move, I should like you to figure the possibilities of our being able to go back to two cents. At three cents you may before long stop losing, but you cannot possibly grow as fast as your two cent competition; you will, therefore, continue to fall behind." Full of confidence, he concluded: "In the meantime I would not worry about Munsey's offer. I don't think he is likely to withdraw it, and if he does, I believe you can do as well, or better, elsewhere."[14]

That closing comment matched the unhurried mood in New York. Ralph did ask Florence White and business manager John F. Breshnahan what they thought of selling the evening paper, and both opposed it. "Continuing Junior [code for the *Evening World*] in the family spells safety," Breshnahan argued. "I cannot help but think that Junior yoked with Senior [the morning *World*], background, tradition and future, makes the institution more powerful financially and otherwise." He was confident that $5 million "and more could be gotten any time we were sure that it would be wise to divorce Junior from the family and center all of our efforts in

Senior and Seniority [the Sunday *World*]," a prediction that proved profoundly wrong. He also thought time was on their side, with Munsey over seventy, Ochs nearly that age, and Hearst sixty-four: "Within five or ten years it is fair to assume that two or three of them will be gone. . . . The Times, in my opinion will not be as ably conducted when Ochs goes. The American may be merged with the Mirror, and if Munsey's present hope does not materialize, the Telegram may be merged with the Sun." Therefore, he found Munsey's offer "far from exciting."[15] White was even cooler toward it. He believed that Junior could readily earn $500,000 a year, a sum that for ten years "could be devoted to Senior up-building, and at the end of that time you would have the Junior property. If the same use were made of Uncle Frank's proposition, the difference would be that at the end of that period you would *not* have the property." He thought the public would see the sale "as a sign of disintegration" and "a reflection on the commercial success of the retained Senior."[16] (This all became irrelevant when Munsey died a month later of peritonitis following an appendectomy.[17])

Ralph agreed that it would be a mistake to sell the evening paper, he wrote Joseph, unless they could simultaneously buy another morning paper to combine with Senior, thus offsetting "the demoralizing effects of the sale on the public mind." But the *American* was the only such prospect, and he saw no point in approaching Hearst. He was convinced that Hearst would not include his comics in such a deal, but would shift them into his tabloid *Mirror,* thus keeping the bulk of the former *American* readership for himself and leaving the *World* "a very small proportion."[18]

What both Ralph and White seemed to ignore was the fact that *all three World* newspapers combined had failed to earn $500,000 in 1921, 1923, and 1924, averaging earnings of $403,400, or slightly more than 3 percent of gross revenues averaging $15,091,000 in each of those years. With earnings in excess of $1 million in 1922 and 1925 on similar revenue, the average earnings for the five years was $688,562, an average 4.8 percent return.[19]

To Joseph, this was alarming. Seen in light of the papers' weak competitive positions in both circulation and advertising, it seemed to him, he wrote Ralph in early 1926, that "recent earnings have been too high and . . . we have been forcing golden eggs out of a really sick goose." At the end of the letter, he showed some testiness in asking if Herbert was in Palm Beach, as he had been led to believe: "I wired him there, but, as usual, have had no reply."[20] Ralph confirmed that Herbert was in Florida and had invited Ralph down for a visit. He agreed that Joseph's conclusions about earnings "are probably quite right," and in line with a proposition he had raised in a letter to Joseph just two days earlier: to enlarge the Sunday comics by four pages at a cost of $150,000 a year in hopes of gaining circulation. He suggested that the added cost could be taken out of *World* dividends, if Joseph agreed. Ralph said he could "get along perfectly well on my salary plus P-D dividends" and without any *World* dividends,[21] which had averaged $250,000 for each of the last five years. Joseph replied that he would "gladly agree to anything that will bring World circulation out of the doldrums," but he thought it should be done at no additional cost, by cutting four pages from elsewhere in the Sunday *World* to compensate for the expanded comic section. "I personally feel it would be downright stupid and wasteful simply to add four pages at an additional cost of $150,000 without offsetting it by economies in other parts of the paper," he wrote.[22] He said he favored the expansion of the comics as a "defensive measure" to keep from losing more circulation, but doubted that the move would result in much gain.

At midyear he complained with "brutal frankness" to White about the slipshod way in which the weekly "blanket reports" on the *World*'s business operations were being put together. "I submit that such erratic performances are intolerable, disquieting and suggestive of utterly unbusinesslike management," he wrote. "These blanket reports are my principal reliance and I must ask that henceforth they be made letter perfect."[23] There may have been some improvement, but the following May he complained to Ralph about a "hopelessly balled up report" put together by a business office lieutenant named Botsford. He urged Ralph to fire him, but he didn't, and in October he got another strongly worded complaint from his brother having to do with a misleading report on the cost of paper. "Botsford shows that as usual he has been bulling around with the figures trying to make the weekly report jibe with the monthly report," he complained. "Why not can Botsford?"[24]

He had not "canned" Botsford, Ralph replied in a remarkable

revelation of the *World*'s deficient fiscal management, because lately Botsford had caught "several quite definite mistakes in auditing" by *World* treasurer Alvin S. Van Benthuysen. Ralph thought Botsford should be kept on "as a check in these matters. . . . It would be very dangerous if we relied on Van Benthuysen (who, with all his merits, has a distinct weakness in often not knowing the practical meaning of the figures he works with) and substituted a new man for Botsford who would know nothing of the ins and outs of the office."[25] Ralph's implication that somehow two incompetents were better than one could only have intensified Joseph's concern. In December he again urged Ralph to drop back to the two-cent price, after which, he predicted, "you will find yourself in an honest to God situation of having to 'strip for action' and, to mix the metaphor, in a situation where you must discard every ounce of extra weight that you may be carrying. That means getting the dead wood out of the office, not only to reduce the pay roll but to improve operation." Trying to be understanding and diplomatic, he conceded "the fact that we have been fortunate enough not to have to face as uncertain a situation as that which now confronts the World." However, he added, the *Post-Dispatch* had always had "a much more compact" management than the *World,* "especially as to the executive heads and assistants." And when it came to paring down news-gathering costs, "when we give the word to Bovard, he passes it on to [city editor Ben H.] Reese and men are dropped to a point where the payroll is cut to the bone."[26] That hadn't been happening in New York. As James W. Barrett, the *World*'s last city editor, observed, "economy put a crimp in Swope's style as executive editor." He singled out particularly Swope's "never-to-be-sufficiently-goddamned habit of giving his office absent treatment or administering it from the race track."[27] Swope later became the New York State racing commissioner.

The *World*'s Fall

During early 1927, probably with the help of *Post-Dispatch* treasurer James T. Keller, a renowned penny-pincher, J.P. got together a report comparing *World* and *Post-Dispatch* operations. The *World* came off poorly in virtually every respect; it was as frail as the *Post-Dispatch* was robust. The single most sobering finding was that for the five years between 1922 and 1926, *World* expenses had increased about 20 percent while revenues had grown only 9 percent. In one year, 1926, the *World* had a gross income of $16,413,686 and almost identical expenses of $16,389,444, leaving a profit of only $24,242 — less than two-tenths of one percent. In the same year, the *Post-Dispatch* took in $9,795,499 and had expenses of $8,044,727, for a 22 percent profit of $1,750,772.[1] Another way of looking at this, as a chart showed, was that the

World spent $8.4 million more than the *Post-Dispatch* for virtu-
ally no gain, while the St. Louis paper earned $1.75 million on less
than half the *World*'s outlay. Although the report says nothing to
this effect, it is fair to conclude that people on the business side in
St. Louis had begun to look at the situation defensively. Unless
something was done immediately about *World* costs, it was a
virtual certainty that the *Post-Dispatch* would be asked for a
transfusion to save its ailing sister. In such an event, might it too
be drained of its vitality?

Accordingly, the report provided a detailed examination of the
production costs of the two businesses. For the five-year period,
the morning *World*'s news and editorial department costs alone —
Swope's domain — were up $390,000. And, "while the editorial
department was being allowed to spend $390,000 more, the reve-
nue producing advertising department was being allowed to spend
only $129,999," the report noted. Furthermore, the numbers
revealed that White's prediction of the previous year that the
Evening World would produce $500,000 a year was way off. It had
earned only $181,000 in 1926, and over the previous five years the
gap between expenses and revenue had grown smaller, although
this seemed justified "to help stagnant circulation." It also appeared,
the report said, that the *Evening World*'s advertising department
"was probably starved, its increase having been $111,000 in five
years as compared with substantially large increases in all other
departments."

To get at the heart of the matter, comparisons were made
between the *Post-Dispatch* and the most sorely troubled morning
and Sunday *World,* which had earned $392,000 in 1922 but lost
$85,000 in 1926. There were telling disparities in news depart-
ment payroll costs of the New York and St. Louis newspapers.
Taking into account the need for a larger staff and the higher pay
scale in New York, the analysis found a difference in payroll
between the two operations of $5,438 a week or $283,000 a year,
at least $73,000 of which "might very well be saved" without
cutting back on local coverage. "It should not cost more than twice
as much to cover local news in New York with the aid of the City
News Association as it costs to cover the local news of St. Louis
without such aid," the report observed. It noted that the *World*
used twelve editors to fill 120 columns of news space, where the

Post-Dispatch used seven editors, at a difference in cost of almost $32,000. Disparities in the numbers of news executives, editorial page and reference department employees, artists, photographers, gravure technicians, and copy boys suggested that savings of another $100,000 were possible. And, the report wondered, couldn't the writings of popular *World* columnists Frank Sullivan, Franklin P. Adams, and Heywood Broun "be modified so as to make them syndicatable," thus reducing their $52,000 cost to the *World?*

It also observed that the downward slide was continuing. In the first three months of 1927, the analysis showed, the *Post-Dispatch* had retained nearly 17 percent of its gross income while the *World* had overspent its income by 1.5 percent. In view of this, a harsh prospect (somewhat gingerly expressed) deserved consideration: "One solution to your problem might be in the discontinuance of the Morning Edition." The report projected net savings to the company in this event of $1.8 million if the suspension cut advertising revenue by half; $779,000 if it declined by three-quarters. Also, "in consideration of the World dropping its morning edition, the Times and Herald Tribune undoubtedly would be willing to go to 10 cents Sunday. It is estimated that 10 cents Sunday would add at least $650,000 to World revenue. It would also seem that the Evening World would get at least 75,000 of the morning circulation, which would make it possible to increase advertising rates. A 2 cents a line increase would add at least $200,000 to revenue."[2]

The receipt of this analysis seems not to have been acknowledged in writing, and it may never have been recognized orally. There is a revealing story about it, assuming this report—which was unsigned but contained things known only to J.P. and his top business executives—was the one being referred to: Some years later, J.P. told his sons that a few days after it was mailed, he and Keller followed their report to New York since Pulitzer needed to go east to consult with his ophthalmologist. But when they saw Ralph, they didn't mention the report, believing the rules of courtesy gave him the privilege of bringing up the subject, which he simply did not do. After exchanging a few pleasantries with his brother, J.P. turned to his treasurer and said, "Well, Mr. Keller, let's go see Dr. Wilmer," and they departed for Baltimore.[3]

Starting in 1927, however, the *World* did begin—haltingly in

Joseph's view — to respond to the economic realities. The morning *World*'s price was dropped back to two cents, but, coming two years after the price increase, this was too late to recapture lost readers. It also printed fewer pages, another economy reaping very little benefit; for two cents, readers could get a 60- or 70-page *New York Times* or *Herald Tribune* or a 30-page *World*. Joseph informed Ralph in February that on the advice of advertising consultant Walter G. Bryan the *Post-Dispatch* had cut its column width from 12.5 to 12 ems, which would mean a savings in paper amounting to $80,000 a year, and that "another tip he gave us saved a very large sum in income taxes." (He didn't elaborate.) Bryan and J.P. also discussed the *World*'s situation, Bryan pointing out that while *World* competitors had been gaining advertising at the rate of a million lines a year, the morning and evening *World*s had lost nearly half a million lines. Joseph urged Ralph to see the man "and encourage him to talk freely."[4] Ralph did so, but decided against hiring Bryan, whose fee would have been $100,000.[5] Nor did the *World* decrease its column width until 1930, announcing the change, expected to save $200,000 a year, in the trade publication *Editor and Publisher*.[6] The announcement was an unwise move in Joseph's opinion: "Mention of this saving . . . might be used by World competitors to stir up resentment among World advertisers," he pointed out. "In this office it is the rarest exception when we give out an interview to trade papers."[7]

He was addressing Herbert, who was now in charge in New York. He had come back into the picture in 1928, taking over while Ralph took a European honeymoon with his second wife, novelist and historian Margaret Leech, and staying on after Ralph's return. (Ralph and the former Frederica Vanderbilt Webb had been divorced in 1924.) By the time Herbert arrived the outlook was grim. At the end of 1928, Swope, discouraged by the necessity of cost-cutting and believing "the paper is slipping fast and I don't want responsibility charged against me," resigned.[8] Ralph liked Swope very much, but agreed it was just as well that he step down as executive editor. He would have been willing to keep him on in some kind of advisory capacity, but Swope declined. Evidence that the contrasts between the New York and St. Louis Pulitzer papers were apparent to others showed up in a letter from *New York Evening Post* editor Oswald Garrison Villard to *Post-Dispatch* editorial writer Clark McAdams: "You are getting out a wonderful paper, and I wish to heaven we could have you and Mr. Bovard running the *World* — God knows you are needed here!"[9]

Moreover, there was what can be read as recognition of the growing gravity of the situation in the correspondence between Joseph and his brothers. This began with a highly unusual flare-up between Joseph and Ralph in 1928 which involved the *Post-Dispatch* but also revealed a certain general uneasiness. After the *Post-Dispatch* announced a planned one-cent per agate line advertising rate increase, the seven largest St. Louis department stores canceled their *Post-Dispatch* advertising. Joseph wrote Ralph about this — even though it wasn't the first time the department stores had boycotted the paper for the same reason — and was annoyed when Ralph responded that he had "talked to Herbert about the potash [code for 'advertising'] situation, and we think, without the slightest intention of butting into your conduct of the fight, we should, as trustees, keep ourselves acquainted in greater detail with the situation."[10] "Don't think me finicky," Joseph wrote back,

> but while I welcome your interesting yourself in this situation and do not regard it as butting in so long as you act as brothers of mine, or as interested stockholders, or as newspapermen devoted to the best interests of the Post-Dispatch and determined to do everything in your power to perpetuate it — this is always my attitude toward you and the World — I, frankly, don't like to have you say that you and Herbert "should, as Trustees" do anything about it. If, except in some matter of supreme importance, we get to working with one another or against one another "as Trustees," I think we will all be in the soup.[11]

Ralph couldn't agree: "As brothers we accord each other the privilege, which confidence and affection give, of advising each other, etc., but as trustees under certain circumstances this is not a privilege but an obligation and a duty which we cannot get away from." He probably had the *World*'s plight in mind when he continued: "As a matter of fact, I am the lad who is most likely to get stepped on by my fellow trustees under the dictates of this

duty, but I consider their reserve rights unquestionable, and I
have such complete confidence in their affection and integrity
that I am not disturbed by the possibility of a majority position
over-riding my position in some future possible emergency."
However, he concluded, "this is at present wholly academic, and I
hope will always remain entirely theoretical."[12]

In the fall, Joseph raised a subject that others would point to
after the sale of the newspapers as the reason for their inability
to compete: the lack of sound news policy.[13] He wrote to Ralph
that he found the *World* account of Republican presidential candidate Herbert Hoover's first campaign speech "so hopelessly infected
with pro-[Democrat Al] Smith enthusiasm, if not actual animus
against Hoover as to make me feel, once and for all, I cannot rely
on the World for news of the coming campaign." He called this a
"fatal tendency, so painfully in evidence four years ago and about
which I have spoken repeatedly." Sounding as angry as his father
had on past occasions of this kind, he criticized the story on four
specific points, one of which was this: "What in thunder right has
the World to answer Hoover's remarks as to prosperity by injecting
its opinion or the opinion of its reporter or of its Managing Editor,
or of someone around the office, that this prosperity has been due
to the Democratic Federal Reserve Act? Again, obviously, if the
World thinks that (and I agree it is probably very largely true), the
editorial page was the place to say it." He finished with a flourish:
"If this sort of political writing is being done deliberately it is a
crime, and if it is not being done inadvertently and through
ignorance of how to print news impartially it is, if anything, even
worse."[14] His annoyance seems justified, for as *World* city editor
James W. Barrett wrote later, "Instead of printing all the news we
printed only some of the more interesting stories and called ourselves a 'selective newspaper.' To cover up the lack of accurate
information we took to dressing up the stories and unloaded on
our readers such substitutes for news as 'This World We Live In'
'All in the Day's Work' 'Along the Way' (for God's sake!) and—
catch this one—'Interesting Thoughts on Interesting Topics.' "[15]

There was, unavoidably, a sharp reflection on management in
what Joseph had written, and though he had begun "Forgive
me, old man, for greeting you with a kick, but I am bound to
do it," Ralph surely felt the sting. As the decline continued, the

strain upon him became severe. At the end of January 1930, a physician advised Ralph—and also telephoned Joseph to report his findings—to stop working and get out of the country because he was on the verge of a nervous breakdown. Joseph insisted that he follow the doctor's advice, and on February 10, with the approval of the directors, Ralph turned over the presidency of the Press Publishing Company to Herbert and shortly thereafter departed for Africa.[16]

The day before the doctor advised Ralph to step down, Joseph wrote a letter to both his brothers, suggesting several possible eliminations from the *World*'s executive line. He then proposed a division of duties between them that would put Herbert in charge of business operations and Ralph in charge of "the purely intellectual activities of the paper," including crusades, editorials, columnists, and reviews but not news, "which, because it so often involves questions of how to spend money," should be a part of Herbert's domain.

He urged Herbert to "get over your misgivings resulting from your lack of business experience and be prepared to take over responsibility for executive decision as to business matters. . . . Most of the World's difficulties are due, I am convinced, not so much to errors in managerial judgment, but to the chaos, delays, contradictions and lack of decision resulting from too many cooks working at cross purposes at the bottom and no one at the top saying promptly and finally 'Yes' or 'No.' If you will assume the responsibility which you are physically and temperamentally already qualified to do, of saying 'Yes' or 'No,' and then sticking to your decision, and if you will eliminate the supernumeraries below you and concentrate departmental responsibility . . . I believe the result would be a vastly improved condition over that now in existence and that you could get away with it." After all, even some prosperous papers were cutting corners by trimming their staffs and eliminating some of their comics and the *World* should do the same—"and if talk results, it cannot add much to the talk that is already going on."[17] On the same day, Joseph notified the *World* business manager to stop his $80-a-week salary, saying he would return what had already been paid him that month.[18]

An even harsher reading of current competitive realities by *World* circulation manager N. R. Hoover drew attention to distressing implications for the sons of Joseph Pulitzer. The continuation of the paper's no-holds-barred editorial liberalism was dragging down both circulation and advertising, he argued in a memo to Herbert. The brothers failed to realize, he said, that they faced a different environment than their father had. "The stimulus the city got from the crusading attitude he assumed toward the political problems of his time was right. The public, conscious of the appalling political corruption of the time, looked upon him as the Moses that would lead it up out of the political morass of the eighties and nineties. . . . But times have changed." The evidence was in the kinds of papers that were succeeding. Evidently not rating the *Post-Dispatch* as one that was succeeding, he doubted "if one outstanding crusading newspaper success today can be called to mind. It's the middle-of-the-road plodder, busy giving all the news in an attractive manner, keeping away from controversial arguments, that is the outstanding success." He listed several such, including the *Times* and the *Sun* in New York and the *Bulletin* in Philadelphia, calling the editorial page of the latter "so insipid it might not be there at all for the influence it exerts, yet the *Bulletin* is an advertising mint and its circulation is past a half million. It has absolutely no editorial backbone but it has the news and *it has the ads.*" Similarly, the *Times* "has hedged on editorial opinion and it has thrived on it."

But year after year, going back at least as far as the anti-Klan series, and including its endorsement the previous fall of Socialist Norman Thomas for mayor and its ongoing ridicule of prohibition, the *World* had made many more enemies than friends. It didn't matter that the paper's policy was less radical than it seemed — subscriptions were stopped following the endorsement of Thomas by people who believed the *World* had become a socialist paper. In exposing Klan activities as "unAmerican and cancerous," the paper had won praise, but it also "tended to alienate that certain large class of alleged Nordics who . . . subconsciously sympathized with the Klan's aspirations, a big factor in the hinterland of the country districts around New York City." And in its caricature of the Anti-Saloon League it had offended "thousands of simple-minded rustics, and many of them are also here in the city, who resent the bow-tie, the bulbous nose, the high silk hat take-off on the old-time Evangelical clergyman." This was different from cartoonist Thomas Nast's popular attacks on Tammany boss William Tweed two generations earlier because "crooked or vulnerable politicians aren't numerous" while the followers of Protestant clergymen are. His recommendation: Gradually abandon ("a policy that has been in existence for forty-eight years couldn't be kicked away at once") this editorial policy that was alienating so many readers and advertisers. "Why should your paper take up the cudgels in defense of the liberties of the plain people when you hurt your property in your fight in their defense and those same people do not even give you the support they could?" he asked. Instead, adopt "a policy of constructive, cheerful optimism. I know how silly that reads but it's the best way I can put what I have in mind. Make it a rule to discuss things that are constructive, forward-looking. . . . Cease whining and complaining."

The success two years later of Franklin D. Roosevelt and "Happy Days Are Here Again" is proof enough of the truth in what Hoover had said in his memo to Herbert. But to have accepted his advice would have meant breaching the tradition of which all three brothers considered themselves trustees. Still, as events played themselves out, they may well have reflected on the perils of unceasingly swimming upstream. Like the foreboding chant of a Greek chorus from offstage came this near the end of Hoover's plea: "I can't forget what a representative of the Scripps-Howard organization once said to me . . . : 'It's the policy of our people as much as possible to say nice things about men and things, and when rough things have to be said, get it over with as soon as possible and then forget it. Sticking to nasty things in a newspaper gives a bad impression of the paper.' "19

Concurrent with all this, Joseph was having lawyers explore the legal possibilities of having the *Post-Dispatch* loan money to the *World* newspapers or of selling or discontinuing the morning and Sunday *World*s. Of the first possibility, St. Louis attorney John F. Green advised that a loan was possible since "the stockholders of the two corporations are practically the same persons" and "there is no one in position to call the directors to account even if they overstep the line of prudence." But, he cautioned, it would be unwise to make a loan that "would embarrass or hinder the development of the Pulitzer Publishing Company."20 That, apparently, was sufficient to kill the idea of a loan, for the subject didn't come up again. The second question was trickier, and two lawyers disagreed on it. John G. Jackson in New York argued that because the will of the founder enjoined his descendants from selling "the World newspaper," they could not sell "an integral part of the business . . . unless expressly authorized by an order of court to do so."[21] Green, however, said that as his firm construed the will it did not prohibit the sale because the policies the elder Pulitzer "enjoins upon his sons and descendants can be carried forward . . . by the publication of one paper instead of two." They advised, though, that a new owner should not be permitted to use the *World* name because this probably would harm "the prestige and continued success of the Evening World."[22]

Of course, there was still the question whether anyone would be interested in buying the papers. The most desirable buyer from the standpoint of prestige would have been the *New York Times*. A few days before leaving town in February 1930, Ralph took Herbert to the office of *Times* publisher Adolph S. Ochs, where he introduced his brother to Ochs and Ochs's son-in-law and eventual successor, Arthur Hays Sulzberger. Ralph told Ochs that because of his health he was resigning and being replaced by Herbert. There was no specific discussion of the *World*'s troubles, Herbert reported in a letter to Joseph, but Ochs expressed pessimism about near-term improvement in the economy, adding that "he was a great optimist as far as America went and its extraordinary recuperative powers." After Ralph and Sulzberger had left the room, Herbert told Ochs he would like to have the benefit of his advice from time to time "to help me in my new duties" and also mentioned that he believed his brothers had told Ochs "that we had a difficult situation to face here and that this prospective move would go a long way towards ironing it out." Ochs responded that "he would be glad to see me any time and saw no reason why [the] World and Times should not cooperate, [and] broke off to say that he would discuss that with me at length some other time and explain fully what he meant."[23]

"This prospective move" referred to the likelihood of an agreement to raise the price of their Sunday papers to ten cents, but the matter had wider implications. During a luncheon with Ochs in New York in January, Joseph had made it clear that the price increase would help the *World*. Ochs had responded that with a

$10 million surplus in government bonds, he didn't need the extra revenue. Joseph then asked: "Might it not be possible for you to so crowd your competition that a change in that field might occur?"[24] This was apparently intended to suggest that the *World* could be forced out of business. Ochs professed to have no such prospect in mind, but suggested that they meet again soon to discuss the entire situation. They met two days later, but all Ochs had to offer was a promise of "some sort of cooperation" to their "mutual advantage."[25] Sometime in April, *Times* business manager Louis Wiley visited Herbert at his home to inquire—on Ochs's behalf, Herbert thought, though Ochs later denied this—whether the morning and Sunday *World*s were for sale. Herbert said Ochs would be the first to know if such a decision were reached. By late August it had been reached, and Herbert, *World* general manager White, and business manager John F. Breshnahan met with Ochs.

Afterward, White concluded that Ochs was "anxious to buy," although not at the $8 million asking price (gross less plant and equipment) they had named. Instead, Ochs had devised a formula valuing the worth of the *World*'s Associated Press franchise, its advertising and circulation at a total (White estimated) of $6.6 million. He thought, however, that if the Pulitzers resisted such an offer, Ochs probably "would buy on the basis of the projected gross for the current year, $7,500,000, against the advice of his people."[26] Breshnahan was somewhat less assured. To him Ochs seemed more interested in acquiring the morning paper only, rather than it and the Sunday *World*. He also had said, Breshnahan reported, that "he would prefer a melding of [the] American and World because Hearst competition has no fear for him." But Breshnahan seemed to discount the mention of Hearst as a bluff—White had ignored it in his memo—because he concluded, "I doubt [Ochs's] courage not to make an offer."[27] Both men noted Ochs emphasized that he did not consider their having met as a commitment and that they were free to negotiate with other potential buyers. Although not saying so directly, neither seemed to think this diminished what they interpreted as his eagerness to make a deal.

As soon as he had read those memos, J.P. asked White to write him a more detailed report, probably to get an idea of Herbert's role. Herbert was not mentioned in either of the other memos. White reported that the meeting had been held in a suite at the

Ritz-Carleton Hotel in early evening and that Ochs "had moved a straight-back chair directly in front of Herbert and from the time the real business opened up, nervously crossed and recrossed his legs and palmed his thighs and knee-caps—all the while listening intently" as Herbert proposed a merger of the morning papers. This and some occasional "fidgeting" by the *Times* publisher was read by White as a strong inclination to buy. Eventually, Ochs observed that, because the *Times* was considered ultraconservative "in the minds of many," such people were likely to resent its merger with the "fighting" *World*. White countered that "such a union would be the greatest in newspaper history" and that Ochs personally ought to appreciate "the succession to the mantle of J.P." Ochs agreed with that and, as the meeting broke up, embraced White "with a speech as to how long we had been acquainted. I thought he was going to kiss me."[28]

Meyer Berger's official history of the *New York Times,* published in 1951, says that as the meeting broke up it was agreed to meet again at the same place two days later. At that next session, Ochs told Herbert and White that on reflection he had concluded that consolidation with the *World* would be unwise, but that he thought the *World* could be preserved if it were reorganized as a corporation and sold or leased to its employees. He said he wanted the newspaper to survive and was prepared to contribute substantially if this were done, but he did not mention a figure. White reportedly liked the idea, but Herbert Pulitzer "turned from it."[29] No record of this second meeting seems to have been preserved by the Pulitzers. The subject of lease or sale to employees shows up nowhere in their memorandums. Also, Berger's account that Ochs was "flabbergasted" by the Pulitzers' proposal to sell him two of their newspapers, calling it "a startling and totally unexpected proposition,"[30] is contradicted in White's second memorandum to J.P., which says Ochs admitted "that of course the subject had often been discussed at the office."[31]

With these ambiguities clouding the picture, just how Ochs's reaction may have struck the brothers is an open question. In any event, they put out other feelers. Those to Cyrus H. K. Curtis, who had purchased the *Philadelphia Public Ledger* from Ochs in 1913, and to Ogden Reid of the *Herald Tribune* were rebuffed.[32] One proposition did come forward on the initiative of others. A month after the meeting with Ochs, Alexander Troup, who had run newspapers in New Haven and Hartford, Connecticut, and was then publishing marine hardware catalogs in Lewiston, Maine, visited J.P. in St. Louis. Troup said he represented a group "interested in Democratic politics" which had authorized him to offer $30 million in cash for all three *World*s and the *Post-Dispatch.* He said they would not be interested in acquiring just the morning and Sunday *World,* but probably would make a deal for the whole property in either New York or St. Louis. They had learned through "newspaper grapevine channels" that the *Post-Dispatch* was netting between $750,000 and $1 million annually. J.P. believed the offer was genuine, and in early October Troup wrote him that his backers remained interested in dealing whenever the situation seemed right.[33] This was not to be, however, because as the brothers assessed the situation at this point, they should be able to turn a fair profit on the *Evening World* if they could get rid of the morning and Sunday *World*s. A report prepared jointly by James Keller and *World* treasurer Alvin S. Van Benthuysen encouraged this belief. They projected that, standing alone, the *Evening World* would get something better than the 17 percent of New York evening newspaper advertising linage it had in 1929, remaining in third place behind the *Sun* and the *Journal,* but narrowing the 7 percent gap between it and the *Journal.* This showing, plus salary savings economies of $200,000, could produce a profit of nearly $600,000 in the first year, they predicted.[34]

In the last months of the year, almost all hope vanished. As the Depression deepened, the morning and Sunday papers careened toward a record annual loss of nearly $1.7 million, and no firm and acceptable offer for them materialized. Swope had been maneuvering behind the scenes since February to find sufficient backing to add to the $2 million he could put up, and he had some encouragement from Hearst when he proposed a *World-American* merger.[35] But in October, Hearst told White that the sale as proposed, with no plant or equipment, only temporary use of the name, and only part of the features, was worth no more than $5 million to him. That he was prepared to offer—in bonds on the combined *World* and *American* properties, not cash—and he would want the name of the *World* "for a sufficient length of time to make the amalgamation successful."[36] This resulted in some informal negotiation that ultimately got nowhere.[37] Swope kept up his search for partners almost until the very end, but found none.

Almost as early as Swope had expressed interest to Ralph and Herbert, Joseph had heard from Peter Grieg, a former reader-secretary, that an unnamed "newspaper friend" had told him that Roy W. Howard of the Scripps-Howard chain was trying to come up with an offer to buy all three *World*s and then sell the morning and Sunday *World*s to Hearst, keeping the *Evening World*.[38] Howard had met Ralph Pulitzer aboard ship in 1928, when Ralph was returning from his European honeymoon. In Swope's opinion, Howard, who finally got the newspapers, had the "inside track" from that point.[39] A more plausible explanation, unsatisfactory though it seemed to many at the time and since, is that by the end of 1930, with the Depression getting deeper, the brothers concluded that the *World* newspapers were lost but that the *Post-Dispatch* could—and must—be saved. When Howard offered $5 million for all three papers, with the intention of killing the morning and Sunday papers—not selling them to Hearst—and combining the evening paper with the *Telegram,* they concluded that they must act. Financially, Hearst's October proposition might have been better, but that was water over the dam. In any case, accepting it would have meant a distasteful compromise with an old foe for whom they had little respect.[40] In contrast, the principles of the forebearers of the new combination—Joseph Pulitzer and Edward Wyllis Scripps, who were contemporaries but never met—had been virtually identical. As the first *World-Telegram* expressed it, "They saw that the duty of a newspaper ran to its readers only—to all its readers: not to any single group, social, political or financial."[41] The importance of that philosophical kinship to the Pulitzers, however illusory it might have been in current conditions, is strengthened by J.P.'s disclosure to Howard after the sale that a $5.5 million bid by Paul Block, publisher of the Brooklyn *Standard Union,* had been rejected as "probably not made in good faith" because he most likely was representing Hearst, "as he has done in many deals, and as indicated by the fact that he could hardly print the World with his Brooklyn . . . plant and yet [was] not bidding for any tangibles."[42] As for the other possibilities, they had good reason to believe that a *World* with Swope again playing a major role would be no more sound now than it had been a few years before; in any event, there was no specific offer. Similarly, the interests represented by Troup apparently evaporated.

There was one final, short-lived burst of hope before the very end. In order to sell all the newspapers, the brothers had to seek approval of the Surrogates Court to break their father's will. As soon as they learned that this was under way, *World* employees, led by city editor Barrett, launched an effort to raise enough money to buy the papers themselves. A majority of the 3,000 people pledged, some offering their life savings. It was an exhilarating twelve hours, between noon and midnight on February 25, 1931, at the end of which employees had pledged $750,000 and outside interests a like amount, but still far short of what was needed. Surrogate James A. Foley agreed that the losses were so great as to justify authorizing the sale in the interests of conserving something for the heirs and that the Scripps-Howard offer was the only prospect the heirs had.[43] Of the employees' plan, Heywood Broun wrote afterward: "I'll readily admit that 1,000 to 1 would be a generous price against any such undertaking."[44] Yet Ochs, who was in Hawaii at the time of the sale, was according to one interpretation so demoralized by the realization that what had happened to the *World* under second-generation management could happen not too many years hence when the *Times* passed to his heirs that he persisted in believing that a successful employee takeover could have been arranged.[45] The *Evening World* ceased publication on February 26, and Scripps-Howard's consolidated *World-Telegram* appeared the next day. The final issue of the morning *World* was published on Friday, February 27, 1931. As it went to press, the editorial staff gathered around the city desk and sang an improvised farewell to the tune of "Good Night, Ladies": "Good-bye *World*, we're going to leave you now."[46] The financial calamity had an ironic finish, for when the final edition hit the streets the demand was so great that newsstand dealers hiked their prices by ten or fifteen cents, and a dealer near Grand Central Station asked a dollar a copy. But the *World* was history. It had been a Pulitzer paper for forty-eight years.

Why did it turn out as it did? Following the sale, Barrett wrote an angry little book entitled *The World, the Flesh, and Messrs. Pulitzer* in which he said:

> What happened was this: For ten years the *World* went
> ahead under the momentum that the original Joseph
> Pulitzer gave to it. After that it needed a strong guiding
> hand. As before noted, Ralph was idealistic, Joseph was
> fierce and Herbert was stubborn, but none of them was
> strong. The strong hand lacking, the *World* declined; the
> Pulitzers got tired of it and found a way to get rid of it.[47]

So it appeared, at the time, to someone without access to all the
details related here. Those details, though, make Barrett's indictment seem unfair to all three of the brothers — and, even without
the added information, especially unfair to Joseph, whose success
in St. Louis was no secret. But Barrett did not know that J.P. had
(1) urged consideration of trimming the *World* to a daily and
Sunday operation as early as 1925, viewing the publication of
three newspapers by one management as unfeasible under current conditions in New York; (2) advised against the *World* price
increase from two to three cents; (3) called attention to the lack of
a sound news policy; and (4) pointed the way toward more eco-
nomical operation and effective management, drawing upon his
Post-Dispatch experience. Whether more timely action on some
or all of these matters would have made it possible for the family
to stay in business in New York is impossible to know, but it is
clear that Joseph Pulitzer II had comprehended the problems as
accurately as anyone who gave them serious thought. More than a
decade later, he remembered the sale of the *World* as "one of the
most tragic moments of my life."[48]

How painful an ordeal it had been is shown by his reaction in
1954 when Louis M. Starr of the Columbia University Oral History Research Office asked about the episode: "I don't think I want
to discuss this," he replied. Then he offered to talk about it if Starr
would turn off the tape recorder. Saying he saw no point in that,
Starr offered to skip the subject altogether. That started Pulitzer to
reflecting. "Well, the point is, to have it known that a newspaper is
for sale is just about the worst wound you can give it," he began.
"If we had gone around to the Barretts and those people, they like
to think a big offer could have been made — a lot of money could
have been raised. Old *World* men would have backed it to the
hilt. . . . I think if there had been any great possibility of that the

offer would have materialized because the fact that the *World* was in trouble was no secret. I think in fairness to them they were prevented from being more active than they were by the prohibition in the will against the sale. . . . If we had gone around peddling it to ex-*World* men and the *World-Telegram* offer which was pending at the time had failed to materialize, it would have been a death blow to the thing. It would have folded almost overnight, I would say." He favored the sale, he said: because

> I felt it was beyond my meager ability to see how the thing could be saved. . . . Looking back on it, it was a case of being bucked by the class circulation and advertising of the *Times* and the *Herald Tribune* on top and the mass newspapers, particularly the *News,* at the bottom. We discussed the possibility of killing the morning and going ahead with the evening. Well, if we had done that, we would have killed the only character and prestige, the only edition having any great reputation. It was the morning *World.* Then, we'd lose it. If we killed the *Evening World,* we would kill the only thing that kept things going as long as it had. That had a certain amount of advertising. My feeling was that if we kept going at the rate we were going, the *World* was bound to collapse and would probably take the *Post-Dispatch* down with it.[49]

A day or two after the founding Joseph Pulitzer died in 1911, *World* editor Frank Cobb looked the namesake son in the eye and said, "Now you two boys have got to decide which one of you is going to run this newspaper. I know from my previous experiences that two men can't run one newspaper."[50] Joseph agreed with that, and had of course been pleased to be able to choose St. Louis. Nobody will ever know if he would have been a bigger success than he was by somehow taking charge in New York as well as in St. Louis, or by forsaking the latter for the former, but he was content and possibly very wise to think he had enough to occupy his abilities where he was. The *Post-Dispatch* was solvent and had a solid cushion of reserve as the second year of the Depression decade opened, but like most other newspapers it was losing advertising linage and circulation and it was anyone's guess how long and steep the decline might eventually be. And also being forged in the fires of the Depression was a new challenge for the forty-six-year-old editor-publisher: a collision with the newspaperman who, after his father, he admired above all, Oliver K. Bovard.

— 18 —

Exit Bovard

Oliver Kirby Bovard did not mourn the *World*'s passing. In fact, he was gleeful—so much so that he couldn't resist writing a letter the next day to the editor of the *Post-Dispatch,* marked "not for publication" and signed, coldly, "Observer." In it, he delivered a sharp kick to the deceased's corpse and, by implication, to Ralph, Joseph II, and Herbert Pulitzer. He almost certainly believed that had *he* been picked as the *World*'s managing editor in 1910 rather than Charles Lincoln, and been given extensive authority, this wouldn't have happened. The letter was extraordinarily arrogant and mean-spirited, particularly since Pulitzer had consulted closely with Bovard during the final days of the ordeal and had asked for his editorial counsel on the "valedictory" message signed by the three brothers which ran in the *World*'s final edition.[1] Bovard knew how painful this had been for his boss, yet he wrote:

> The World fell sick when J.P. died in 1911. The paper really died when Frank Cobb died in 1923. What the World has done since has been merely ghost-walking, and finally the ghost has been laid. . . .
>
> Among the many injunctions which Pulitzer laid upon his editors the most sapient was "always keep burning the twin lights of common sense and judgment." The World doused those beacons when Cobb's body was carried over the side. He was the last man on the bridge to steer by the chart which the founder left to his successors.
>
> Business conditions and changing competition had no terrors for Pulitzer. He believed and proved that editorial success was followed by business success, as certainly as the wake follows the ship. Indeed, he once said he neither needed nor had a business manager; all he required in the counting room was a good bookkeeper. . . . But Pulitzer was great—one of the few great editors America has produced.
>
> The voice of his World and Cobb's thundered across the country, and in time of public excitement it was awaited with expectancy. In the days of the ghost World that voice was succeeded by the clatter of the typewriters of the dilettanti of politics and the wise-cracking columnist. . . .
>
> I shed my tear when the World died. Now I can only laugh.[2]

This surely rankled Pulitzer, but he let it pass. It was, after all, quite in character for Bovard, whose self-assurance could only have been reinforced by the fact that while the *World* declined the *Post-Dispatch* had moved forward as one of the nation's premier newspapers—some thought even its best. "The *Post-Dispatch* stands second to no other newspaper in this country as a liberal news-daily, free and unfettered, able to say what it thinks without fear or favor," said *The Nation* in marking the paper's fiftieth anniversary in 1928. "We wish it were possible to speak with similar enthusiasm and hopefulness of the other Pulitzer daily, the New

York *World* . . . but it is so far inferior to the *Post-Dispatch* and its chief rivals as a gatherer of news as to cause great alarm to its friends." It credited Pulitzer with "extraordinary wisdom" for having kept the St. Louis paper "true to his father's finest traditions," but saved its greatest praise for Bovard: "He is not only a born journalist, a rarely able news-gatherer, an inspirer and leader of his fellow workers, but also a thoroughgoing old-fashioned American liberal. We place him first in the list of newspaper executives in this country. . . . Best of all, he is as ready to espouse an unpopular cause as a popular one."[3]

Not quite a decade later, Bovard's espousal of a sharp shift to state socialism through the nationalization of utilities and other public services as the way out of the Great Depression led to a break with Pulitzer and Bovard's retirement. There was genuine regret on both sides that it had to come to this, but the same single-minded devotion to his conception of journalistic duty which made Bovard so extraordinary an editor may also have made it inevitable. This man who had coolly responded "Not necessarily" to an anguished reporter's plea that he not be fired because "I've got to live!" seemed toward the end to be on the verge of hysteria himself. Because it was not generally understood that an insatiable thirst for complete command of news and editorial policy by Bovard was at the bottom of this, and because of Bovard's reputation as a man of imposing calm and rationality—a "surgeon of facts," reporter/columnist Marquis W. Childs called him[4]—it was outwardly a puzzling turn.

It was not so puzzling to Pulitzer, who had observed Bovard's cocksureness at close range for more than thirty years and had long since accepted it as part of the man's exceptional ability. The managing editor had shown an interest in socialism as a way out of the nation's economic difficulties starting in 1930, when he observed the socialistic arrangements in Sweden during a visit there. He subsequently encouraged Childs, then a Washington correspondent, to study the Scandanavian countries, with the result that Childs wrote two approving books, the second dedicated to Bovard.[5] In 1931, Bovard worked closely with Charles G. Ross, the paper's chief Washington correspondent, on an 18,000-word interpretative article entitled "The Country's Plight—What Can Be Done About It?" It covered three full pages of the paper on

November 29, 1931, and won Ross the Pulitzer Prize for correspondence the following year. The popular response was so
huge that the paper distributed more than 20,000 free pamphlet
reprints.[6]

The article reflected Bovard's views as much as Ross's. Several
passages and virtually all the major conclusions appear in an
undated memo from Bovard to Pulitzer entitled "Communism,
Capitalism, and the Middle Ground," probably written in the summer of 1931.[7] Much of the supporting argument came from essays
and commentaries by government and academic authorities whose
ideas had appeared either on the paper's interpretative "dignity
page" — a Bovard creation over which *he* had control — or elsewhere in its news content. The article blamed the Depression on
unrestrained profit-driven capitalism and widespread laborsaving
mechanization, both of which were squeezing the laborer/consumer
to the breaking point and, unreformed, would ultimately destroy
capitalism itself. Industry, not government, it concluded, should
adjust the imbalance of industrial profit and consumer buying
power by redistributing profits to provide full employment and
better pay. Government couldn't order this without first removing
the property-protecting clauses from the Constitution, an unlikely
prospect, Ross believed. Government could, however, significantly
aid in the redistribution of wealth by levying higher income,
estate, and gift taxes on the wealthy and by lowering tariffs. It also
could nationalize public utilities and the railroads, using the profits
earned either to decrease rates or to cut the taxes of wage earners.
As for the charge that this was tantamount to establishing Soviet
communism in the United States, Ross noted that the Soviets, like
the British, were seeking a middle ground between capitalism and
communism and that in the United States the "real threat" to
political stability "comes not from the handful of Communists in
our midst but from the conservative extremists who are not willing
to yield an inch."[8]

Nor was Bovard willing to yield any possibility of error in this
interpretation of the situation. "I have thought of these things
constantly from all points of view for a long time and the opinions
I have expressed are fixed," he informed Pulitzer several weeks
before the article appeared.[9] Shortly after that, in his negative
response to a memo from Pulitzer asking whether Bovard thought

Walter Lippmann's column would be worth $50 a week, there was evidence of what became his great discontent. "The daily press, as a whole, in my opinion, is failing lamentably to aid the public to understand what is really going on in the world and what a pass this country has come to," he wrote. "Instead of enlightening readers, editorial pages rather misinform or add to the general mental confusion through half-baked opinions based on ignorance of fundamentals. . . . As a result, most newspaper readers have been confirmed in the ignorant idea that government can do anything; therefore, government should step in and wash out the great depression."[10]

He considered Lippmann to be one of those responsible. When Pulitzer subsequently suggested that Bovard meet with Lippmann when the columnist passed through St. Louis, because "at least you will agree he is thinking and trying to find out what it is all about," he got this reply: "I must dissent from the proposition . . . that I would agree Walter Lippmann is 'thinking and trying to find out what it's all about.' I think Lippmann is a writer employing an exceptional opportunity to propagandize a theory. This theory, briefly stated, is that the Government can cure the country's economic ills by arbitrarily changing the value of money. My own view . . . is that [this] is as fallacious as would be the proposition that the Government could control the weather by monkeying with the barometer." He would "be glad to say hello to Lippmann . . . but as for exchanging views, I don't think it worthwhile. He is, of course, familiar with the reasons which influence those who reject his inflationist ideas."[11]

After Lippmann, whom Pulitzer knew from *World* days and saw at Bar Harbor, began appearing in the *Post-Dispatch,* Bovard wrote a critical memo headed "More Misinformation from an Authoritative Source," which Pulitzer asked if he could send on to Lippmann. Bovard consented, but he supplied a copy without the heading. "I do not wish to offend him or any of the other purveyors of misinformation who have access to the paper's columns," he explained. "I do not blame them. As long as they can sell anything they write without further responsibility, it is not surprising that they should write what they think is true, or think ought to be true, without going to the trouble of finding out whether their views square with the facts. This is especially noticeable in the case of men who have not had the benefit of the discipline of a strict news room."12

What he saw as a lack of discipline in others seems to have been the root of Bovard's discontent. If any place the answers were to be found, he thought, it was where he had been for so long: superintending the flow of factual information on which the life of the democracy depended. He was dissatisfied, not with himself but with the failures of others—including the President of the United States and his publisher—to recognize "the facts" that produced the Depression and "the facts" that would end the crisis.

In the year following the publication of "The Country's Plight," Franklin D. Roosevelt was elected President in a landslide of 472 electoral votes to Herbert Hoover's 59, and the era of the New Deal began. Bovard was not impressed. To him, it was politics as usual and Franklin Roosevelt's ambitious legislative program was nothing more than political blather geared to mollify the gullible public. For one thing—a point on which he was correct in the short run but ultimately wrong—most of the President's economic proposals were unconstitutional infringements of property rights sure to be struck down by the U.S. Supreme Court. But that did not mean he believed the Republicans could have done better. "There is no important difference between the parties," he had advised Pulitzer before the election, suggesting that the paper endorse no one.13 Nevertheless, J.P. threw the paper's support to Roosevelt, considering him a traditional Democrat, the party with which the *Post-Dispatch* usually sympathized. By the end of the President's first term, however, Pulitzer was disenchanted and shifted the paper's support to Republican Alfred M. Landon. Believing Roosevelt wanted to go too far in government supervision of the marketplace, the publisher thought Ross's recommendations in 1931 that industry reform itself were sufficient. "You will doubtless think that there is some 'dynamite' in [the article's] reference to the maldistribution of wealth," he had written his brother Ralph. "That it is maldistributed, I am certain. That it will ever be altogether fairly distributed, I am equally uncertain, but that the country can and must make progress towards the goal of fairer distribution . . . I am most certain." He predicted that, "when driven to the wall," industry would give in, "just as it was finally driven to the eight hour day."14

But Bovard grew increasingly skeptical. As Roosevelt entered his second term, the managing editor saw no progress at all and called for more radical measures. Revising his "fixed" views of four years earlier, he had decided that industry would not voluntarily cut profits in order to create more jobs and pay higher wages; the answer lay in amending the Constitution to permit nationalization of all natural resource, public utility, and public service industries, producing jobs for an army of 10 million government workers. When he suggested that the paper print a memorandum he had written to this effect, Pulitzer balked, writing from his fishing camp in Canada:

> My reason for objecting to publication of the memorandum was that I believed that it showed a strong leaning on the part of the paper in favor of not only the elimination of the property clauses [from the Constitution] but also in favor of empowering the federal government to fix wages, hours and conditions of labor. Now, as a matter of fact, while I was always opposed to eliminating the property guarantees, I was disposed to favor the proposition that a government should have the power to regulate, when it found that to be vital and necessary, hours, wages and conditions of labor. Today, I have just about reached the conclusion that not only should the property clauses be retained, but that the additional power should not be given either the federal or state government except within the narrowest limitations, child labor for instance, and that, if we are to have capitalism, it must be just as free of governmental interference as we can possibly make it. That being my opinion, and not wanting to have it supposed that the paper favors that sort of an amendment and its consequences, I hope that you can so phrase the article as to make it purely expository in tone.[15]

Bovard reworked the article to remove, in his view, "all possible suggestion of leaning toward amendment" and suggested that if Pulitzer still feared that readers might think the paper favored amendment an editorial disclaimer could be run in the same issue. "With some reluctance" Pulitzer approved publication of the article, to be accompanied by an editorial disclaimer. "In a nutshell, I would rather trust the Supreme Court than Congress," he explained.[16]

On October 4, 1936, the editorial title page carried, unsigned, Bovard's presentation. The accompanying editorial ended on a dubious note, leaving open only a small chance that the paper would support Bovard's view: "We must . . . recognize [constitutional amendment] for what it is—a proposed solution that violates the cardinal principles of our present system."[17] Two weeks later Pulitzer told Ross he could not agree with Bovard that Roosevelt was a coward for not making constitutional amendment an issue during the current election campaign, "for politics must be regarded realistically, and there is much in the argument that if he were to come out now for radical revision it would be misunderstood as confirmation of his desire for dictatorship." It could develop, he thought, that Roosevelt favors amendment and believes "that he as a re-elected president with no third term ahead of him is the man to bring it about." The paper should stay neutral, he concluded, "until we know what sort of amendment is proposed."[18]

Pulitzer's hesitancy undoubtedly fed Bovard's frustration. Another contributing factor was the managing editor's interest in the emerging—and to his mind prudently changing—economic arrangements of the Soviet Union. He viewed the communist experiment optimistically and, after sending Washington correspondent Raymond P. Brandt to Russia in 1931 to do a series of articles, visited the country himself in 1934 and 1935. Although he did not write anything about his findings, he came back impressed with much that he had seen in that state-controlled economy. It had seemed to both Brandt and Bovard that the Soviets were gradually moving toward the right, away from pure communism. Similarly, Bovard thought, the United States was leaning toward the left, away from pure capitalism. Both countries were seeking a middle ground. These impressions led him to conclude that some form of socialism, based on the nationalization of all business activities associated with basic human needs, was the only way out of the Depression. He did not favor dictatorship, but believed instead in a highly centralized economy to equalize the distribution of wealth coupled with democratic processes to preserve and protect civil liberties. He did not identify himself with any particular socialist thinker. When Pulitzer suggested an "extensive interview" with American Socialist party leader Norman Thomas, who was *not* impressed with the Soviet experiment, Bovard flatly rejected the idea: "He is prejudiced. He is as much anti-Communist as he is anti-Capitalist. He thinks his particular blueprint is the only safe guide to Heaven on earth."[19] Similarly, after the publisher recommended that he consider a point of view contrary to his own in a book by constitutional historian Charles Warren, Bovard found it flawed because Warren had used the undistinguished Calvin Coolidge, "whose only remembered sayings are, 'I do not choose to run' and 'That's a lot of ham,' " as an authority.[20]

He continued to press his version of socialism on Pulitzer piecemeal in conversation and in memorandums through the mid-1930s, but, it seemed to him, to little avail. He showed increasing annoyance with the editorial page, which had remained largely supportive of Roosevelt's initiatives even after Pulitzer shifted the paper's support to Landon in 1936, an exercise from which editorial writers who disagreed were excused. In late July he had asked Pulitzer for full control of the newspaper as general manager. He was told that he was "too radical for editorial control and too contemptuous of business for business office control."[21]

The managing editor also, in Pulitzer's view, began to editorialize in the news columns. This showed up when Roosevelt attempted in 1937 to "pack" the Supreme Court by seeking congressional authority to appoint additional justices likely to support New Deal measures. The *Post-Dispatch* opposed this editorially, and so, Pulitzer thought, did Bovard in what should have been straight news accounts of presidential activities, including a story about a "fireside chat" and another about a dinner speech. "Sorry, but I feel that it is my duty to question the extent to which we have been editorializing against the Court scheme in our Washington dispatches," he wrote Bovard. "I believe I am as anxious to beat the Court scheme as you are but am frankly fearful that readers, especially pro-Roosevelt and neutral readers, will lose confidence in our news columns if we continue the present policy."[22] He suggested that Bovard could write a signed column, if he thought that would help readers get the truth, but the managing editor rejected it: "The paper has too many now, and, furthermore, correction never fully compensates for error." Yet he had tried to do precisely that in editing the material in question. "The paragraphs to which you take exception as editorializing in the news columns are, in my considered opinion, interpretative news reporting," he explained. This was a "defensive mechanism" to protect readers from one of the paper's columns which he thought had falsified the issue. "The mere recording without regard to harmful effects is much easier on the editor, and I shall cheerfully return to that simple life," he averred. He also noted that because editorial cartoonist Daniel R. Fitzpatrick had developed a "habit of distorting my ideas," he had quit making suggestions to him.[23]

There was another flare-up when Pulitzer asked him to stop printing "reports of the war in Spain or of any Communistic conflicts anywhere which are written by a partisan sympathizer of either side, Communist or Fascist." He particularly thought that a piece by Soviet partisan Mikhail Koltsov in which references to "the workers" and "the proletariat" appeared frequently "gives ground to the very natural suspicion that the paper has, as the Catholic letter writers might say, gone 'pink' in its news reporting of the Spanish Civil War. I, for one, distrust the accuracy of such reports. Let us substitute straight away American news reporting." But as Bovard saw it, there was no logic in any group's thinking the paper "had gone 'pink' in its news reporting because of the publication of a brilliant reporter's accounts of one side of the war." He'd much prefer to use Koltsov, who "at least has witnessed what he wrote about," than Associated Press dispatches by reporters who "have had to be content in the main with handouts." And "to taboo 'the workers' and 'the proletariat' is to proscribe realistic terms now in general use in writing about the Spanish war." Sounding as if he believed that the aristocratic Pulitzer didn't really understand the Spanish conflict, he explained: "This is because the war actually is between the workers, or the proletariat, on the one side, and the other classes of society on the other. . . . [T]o identify causes or their adherents by other names than the true ones would be, in my opinion, anything but good American news reporting. The paper picks up the terminology of other activities, some of them comparatively petty, sports, amusements, politics, economics, etc. Why bar the nomenclature peculiar to a historical epoch, of which the paper is one of the living historians?"[24]

Maybe the difficulty was, as Bovard recalled Pulitzer having remarked to him a few years earlier, that the managing editor took the paper "far more seriously than people on the outside do." He was aware, he noted, of "the implications of that observation." The one he almost certainly held was that the publisher didn't take the paper seriously enough. "I dislike criticizing other sections of the outfit with which I am associated," he explained, "and I am afraid the frequency with which I do this may suggest to others a chronic state of mind." But in view of the continuing misrepresentation on the editorial page, he felt he had to protest. One recent editorial had attributed directly to Adolf Hitler the line "Austria will fall to us as a ripe apple." In fact, Bovard pointed out, the *Manchester Guardian* had reported that a third party had "alleged" that those words were Hitler's. Another editorial was guilty of "selective and not fair reporting" in its explanation of Senator Harry S Truman's 1934 primary victory over U.S. Representative John J. Cochran. The vote totals were correct, but he believed the editorial unfairly diminished Cochran's popularity. It had reported that Truman had won because of the influence of Boss Thomas J. Pendergast's machine in Truman's home Jackson County, but ignored its lack of influence in his failure to carry the city of St. Louis and St. Louis County, both Cochran strongholds. The omission amounted to inaccuracy in Bovard's view, and such carelessness on the editorial page,

> where the writer has ample time for deliberation . . . is in my opinion inexcusable and, I confess, personally aggravating. Here in the newsroom, where we are in competition and have to work fast and think fast and are exposed to error in many ways because of the nature of our work, we make few mistakes and rarely are guilty of prejudicial writing, and since the paper stands or falls, progresses or slips as a result of the cumulative effect of the work of all divisions, and since our record is clean in this regard, I feel justified in pointing out, even complaining of the seeming lack of appreciation of this fundamental on the editorial page — where the high ideology of the paper's platform should be a daily reminder of it.[25]

The inference to be drawn was clear. The sections of the paper under his command were all but faultless; given the chance, he would bring the editorial page up to that standard. In the current crisis, the most annoying shortcoming of the editorial page was its "lack of understanding of the fundamentals of economics." This, Bovard suggested to Pulitzer, "may be causing other informed persons to shun it or not take it seriously." He then took apart an editorial on the plight of cotton farmers, using such phrases as "the old bunk about . . . " and "as every school boy should know" to point out the writer's ignorance. "What the mumbo-jumbo of the final paragraph means is beyond my capacity for mind reading," he concluded.

> But this is true: the United States is unique economically among nations. It is potentially self-sufficient. Its inhabitants are able to produce at home everything necessary to their physical comfort and well being.
>
> Until this fortunate situation is in some way rationalized for the general welfare, our national economy, which began to go haywire with the advent of overproduction some years ago, will continue that way. In the meantime, such editorials . . . contribute greatly to the confusion in the public mind about these vital matters.[26]

By early 1938, Bovard had reached the boiling point. He had put together a "thesis" of sixty-two double-spaced typewritten pages based upon what he called "practical economics." Its title was "Forward with Socialism and Democracy," and it contained, he told Pulitzer, the outline of his views on "the malady which afflicts the country . . . all in one place, for your convenience."[27] In a foreword, which began "I sit at my desk in the newsroom, where I have sat for twenty years," he described the work of the editors and reporters as he surveyed the scene: "Investigate and verify are their watchwords. Their work is to sift facts from rumor and report before they begin to write the news. They are the historians of their time." In one way and another, he continued, whether dealing with war, crime, politics, or business, they were working on "the greatest news story of modern times, the progressive rising of the masses of all peoples against economic oppression, lately become acute through rapid development of labor saving machinery."

In most ways, the thesis developed the same line of argument as "The Country's Plight" of seven years earlier, but in a tone of greater urgency. The conclusions reached, Bovard wrote, were "inescapable in the author's opinion." There were two major differences from the earlier treatise. The first, already noted, was Bovard's belief that the Constitution would have to be amended to permit large-scale nationalization of public service industries. He had discarded his earlier belief in self-reform by industry in favor of a governmentally centralized economy. The second difference was the article's manner of presentation. Where Ross's article was developed by drawing widely upon various sources of authority in its presentation, Bovard presented his "facts" almost entirely as self-evident truths or as conclusions that were valid because he held them. This was typical: "In the first half of Roosevelt's first term (1933–34) it became apparent to discerning readers of the newspapers and students of our political system . . . that Roosevelt's proposed political remedies, all temporary, all emergency measures, were both unworkable and unconstitutional."

Bovard had nothing good to say about Roosevelt, whom he described as "a man of inherited wealth, one who had never worked for wages or salary," and who had no intention of dismantling property rights in order to protect the human rights about which he professed great concern in speeches. He portrayed the President as a poor sport who blamed his critics, from the Supreme Court to "most of the daily press," for his administration's failure to improve economic conditions. The failure, Bovard contended, was because of Roosevelt's "utter lack of comprehension of the capitalistic system," in which industries are "always fighting among themselves for supremacy or survival." What the President didn't see was "the simple fact that the mechanical productive power of the country is so great . . . that all of the goods needed or desired by the 'consuming public' can be produced without the aid of all the human labor power of the country." That, he said, was the "fundamental first and continuing cause of the plight of the country" and why "no amount of pump-priming of any character, lending money to industry, increasing available credit, etc." would rescue the existing system. In his analysis, it was in a downward spiral toward doom created by the inability of consumers to support industry. The end would be hastened by confiscatory tax increases upon industry to pay welfare benefits to the unemployed. The only way out was for government to "go into business" and make money in a nationalized economy freed "of the blight of competition and profit motive." As a result, "the government could repeal tax after tax," probably keeping only the personal income and inheritance taxes, which foster "desirable social ends." Yet even with all this, there would still be "a vast field for 'private initiative' and all of that. Fortunes, reasonable but not swollen ones, could still be made, but the million-dollar-a-year income would become a thing of the past."

Only the economy would be controlled, Bovard emphasized. The constitutional guarantees of civil liberties "would be sacred and secure with the Supreme Court." He brushed aside the predictable "epithets" of "Bolshevism" and "radical" sure to be directed against his proposal: "There is no inconsistency between Socialism and Democracy. . . . It is a common trick of the professional opponents of any change in American economics to mislead the uninformed into believing that no alteration is possible without eventual and inevitable substitution of Communism. . . . Economics bear no necessary relation to politics or religion. There can be democracy as the political form and complete or partial Socialism or Communism as the economic system." He said that under socialism the worker is paid according to the value of his services to society, but under communism according to his need. Bovard did not get into how, under socialism, the relative values of services would be determined, but he suggested that "the red-baiters in this country" who predict "the murder of the rich, the destruction of the churches, the 'nationalization of women' etc., etc.," under any form of socialism might be reminded of Sweden, where "none of these dire calamities have befallen" and democratic institutions exist.

Bovard was no doubt best qualified to comment on matters in the final section of the thesis, titled "Politics, the Press, and the People." It was a scathing critique of relationships he had observed closely through all his working life. The reason the general populace had trouble understanding the facts he was laying out, he argued, was that they had not been explained to them "in a way they can understand. It is only the fortunate few who have had the benefit of sound guidance in their reading and thinking to whom the thing is plain." He continued, noting that bossism—the exchange of favors for votes, mainly—has dominated the operation of both major parties to the point that meaningful distinctions between them are nonexistent. Politicians are in the business of getting themselves reelected or reappointed and spend most of their energy trying to keep themselves on the public payroll and recipients of what they term "honest graft." To reach these goals, they engage in sloganeering geared to mislead the public into believing that if elected they will bring "vast improvement in the state of the masses of people." With only a few "notable exceptions," which Bovard did not name, the newspaper press had abetted these politicians rather than informing the public about what was really going on. He called the presidential press conference a "strange proceeding, a phenomenon without a counterpart in any other country" which gave Franklin Roosevelt "something of the character of an oracle speaking in parables." The long reports of the conferences "as a rule contain no news," though many newsmen "attempt to interpret the oracle" in "a semi-weekly riot of speculation . . . as to what the President is going to pursue in vital public matters. Just the reverse of what a meeting of a public official with the press should produce."

Bovard took a swipe at "the American phenomenon of newspaper 'columnists,' writers who discuss over their signatures all manner of public questions, both foreign and domestic, in a tone of familiarity and assurance. . . . Like the politicians, they deal largely in generalities, since the important thing is to be popular in order to sell their 'columns' to more papers . . . but it is to be feared their combined effect is to confuse issues rather than clarify them. . . . The political boss finds this state of affairs made to order for his purposes." And then came a passage that left no doubt as to where in all of this Bovard placed Pulitzer:

> It must be admitted that there is a large measure of truth in what some of the smug, economically secure people in the upper income tax brackets say of the common people, that they are too much occupied with the movies, the radio, baseball, newspaper "comics" and "features" and, above all, in the rushing about in their "used" automobiles, to have any time for public questions. But can the common

people be blamed for this? After all, their leaders, the important people, those who belong to the country clubs, the chambers of commerce, those whose names appear on the committees of 100, those who control our complex system of production and distribution, those in public office and running for office, in short, all of the upper strata of American life, assure the common people that there is absolutely nothing wrong with our American institutions. Just a few people who refuse to "cooperate" are interfering with the perfect functioning of these institutions.

In sum, the press "has so far failed in its peculiar function of keeping the people interested in and informed about public affairs as to be open to the charge of having defaulted. . . . This is due, of course, to the progressive commercialization of the press. . . . As American politics bear little likeness to statesmanship, so the average American city newspaper bears little relationship to journalism." As for newspaper proprietors, "he is a rare owner that can separate his attitudes to public questions from his personal interests as a business man."

A few months before unveiling his thesis, Bovard had renewed his complaint to Pulitzer that news was getting short shrift in the *Post-Dispatch*. "Too frequently," he said, advertising was crowding the main news section, making it impossible for him "to display the news to advantage. It is a chronic imperfection in the paper." He considered it Pulitzer's responsibility to put a stop to this. "Space is lavished on every special department of the paper, but the news department is generally cramped. . . . To the analytical mind it shows a predominant interest upon the part of management in the froth of newspaper content. The daily magazine and sports departments are never crowded." Pulitzer instructed the advertising manager to work cooperatively with Bovard and provide more space if at all possible, but Bovard said he lacked "confidence in the integrity of the advertising department" and had hoped he "would not have to deal with them."[28]

Similarly, in the course of writing his thesis, his dislike of having to deal as a subordinate with Pulitzer intensified. While he did not name any names, his language made clear that he saw the publisher for the most part as just another businessman and lumped him with the others in the press and politics who refused to understand the causes and cures of the Depression. Self-interest, he contended, kept these people from acknowledging facts readily apparent. "Only a political party with leaders who base themselves on economics and recognize the realities of the day can solve the problem for the United States, simple as it is in this land of abundance," he declared. "They will do the duty of the defaulted press and explain the problem in its extreme simplicity to the people." It was as simple as "the idea that all men are born 'free and equal,' as the Declaration of Independence says. Equally deserving, that is, of an opportunity to make a decent living if they are willing to work for it. That is all Socialism contends for." He concluded his treatise with a sweeping historical generalization: "What a spectacle of misery and hopelessness the world presents today after 2000 years of dependence upon voluntary compliance with the injunction: 'Do unto others as ye would have them do unto you.' Socialism seeks to enforce that rule through reasonable application of the power of government."

Pulitzer did not find the analysis either compelling or complete. He was diplomatic in expressing his doubt that Bovard had found *the* answer. "Won't you be good enough to add a chapter to your thesis which might be headed, 'How and when should the campaign be launched, and how should it be conducted and how should it not be conducted'?" he asked after reading it.

> In other words, having reached the conclusion that your type of socialism is a possible or probable way out, how should the paper proceed to spread the doctrine? . . . Your arguments have so clearly the ring of sincerity that they are persuasive, and yet when I get to thinking what they would look like and sound like in cold black type I cannot help wondering how much good they would do, and I cannot help thinking that probably we can do as much or more good by continuing our present policy of making haste slowly. After all, there is such a thing as jumping from the frying pan into the fire. Be that as it may, I should like to know how you would put the philosophy into type.[29]

Bovard replied that he didn't expect the paper to adopt his

philosophy until the "pressure of events" forced it to. Then, the attack "would, of course, be double-barreled — news columns and editorial page — and one man necessarily would have control and direction of the whole. Borrowing a practice from the thoughtful magazines, a new form of special article would be employed which would be factual, expository, interpretative and argumentative." This would "show up the crackpots and irresponsible but influential people who get their fantasies into the press and on the air. The same weapon would be turned on the kept economists of the big banks and industries." Roosevelt "eventually would emerge from the flow of fact and analysis in plain view as the incapable demagogue that he is." There should be no despair because new leadership had yet to emerge to bring in the new order, he continued, because "historic advances usually bring to the [surface] men capable of taking charge and there is no telling where a forceful leader may be hidden today." In view of Bovard's dislike of the President, it is strange that he suggested there might be some leaders among Roosevelt's underlings, though he wasn't sure. Still, the editor who pointed the way could make his case "with confidence because of his faith in the alternate triumph of common sense over nonsense in a free country."[30]

It was more than Pulitzer could take on faith. In a telegram from Bar Harbor he asked Bovard to expand the thesis to explain how his plan would reduce unemployment and the federal deficit. "Sorry, not inclined to add to thesis," Bovard replied. "Answers to your questions are implicit in the philosophy expounded."[31] Six days later he resigned.

Bovard had submitted a resignation letter more than two months earlier, prompted, he said, because of "my inability to sympathize with much of the paper's general course. . . . As you know, I feel that the paper lacks a philosophy of its own and merely marks time in this stirring period."[32] After trying unsuccessfully to dissuade him, Pulitzer had agreed to accept the resignation effective May 13, 1939, one year from the date of the letter. This understanding was not made public, and Pulitzer's effort to get Bovard to refine and delineate his thesis continued. It is likely that the resignation would have been withdrawn had Pulitzer consented to publish the thesis, and quite possible that Bovard had submitted the resignation to be "effective at your convenience," hoping it would force Pulitzer to give in to him. As Bovard biographer James Markham expressed it, his "desire to run the whole show" was probably Bovard's outstanding characteristic.[33]

By late July it was clear that Pulitzer was not going to relent. When, faced with sharply declining revenues,[34] Pulitzer said he planned some economy measures, including a few dismissals from the news staff, Bovard disagreed. He used the opportunity to ask that his resignation be accepted in two weeks. Pulitzer consented, and Bovard posted a notice to the staff, written in blue pencil on copy paper on a newsroom bulletin board:

> With regret I have to tell you that I have resigned because of irreconcilable differences of opinion with Mr. Pulitzer as to the conduct of the paper and am leaving the office August 13. I recognize the rights and responsibilities of ownership and make no complaint.
>
> I salute you, a splendid body of men and an exceptional newspaper staff. I shall always be proud of my association with you, and my best wishes remain with you, collectively and individually.[35]

Three days later, this notice, printed in large headline type, appeared on the bulletin board:[36]

> The Post-Dispatch platform, which I placed at the masthead 27 years ago, shall continue to be this newspaper's guide and its only guide.
>
> JOSEPH PULITZER
> August 2, 1938

Shortly thereafter, Bovard's successor, Benjamin H. Reese, had the statement framed and hung on a wall near his desk.[37]

There was the predictable speculation about what really lay behind this development. Paul Y. Anderson, formerly a top *Post-Dispatch* reporter who idolized Bovard even though the managing editor had fired him earlier in the year because of his alcoholism,[38] wrote a long and sometimes bitter and mistaken account for the *St. Louis Star-Times,* for which he had become a correspondent. The article's emotional tone, however, probably fairly represented the feelings of most who had served under Bovard. "Among newspapermen everywhere, to think of the Post-Dispatch without Bovard is like trying to think of the New Deal without Roosevelt," Anderson wrote. The managing editor had quit, he contended, because the paper had abandoned "its position as a great liberal newspaper" by deciding "to desert the New Deal." Had he seen Bovard's thesis, he would have known Bovard had hoped Pulitzer would do precisely that and that he was discouraged because, in large measure, Pulitzer hadn't. Anderson suggested that Ralph and Herbert Pulitzer probably had more say in *Post-Dispatch* policy-making than Joseph because they were the majority stockholders, though they rarely appeared in St. Louis. Men who had been on the staff more than twenty-five years had never seen Herbert, he remarked, and Ralph "hunts lions in Africa." In fact, as previously noted, under their father's will Ralph and Herbert were the recipients of larger shares of the paper's earnings, but they had agreed from the outset that Joseph had full control of the St. Louis paper and that his compensation and bonus would be adjusted to make up for his shortfall in dividends. After the demise of the *World* in 1931, Joseph was the only brother who continued to work. Bovard, who as one of the "principal editors and managers" of the paper also shared in the dividends, surely knew all of this.

No one, including J.P., would have disagreed with what Anderson said about Bovard's competence as a newsman: "He was the best friend of every competent man who ever worked for him. . . . Honor where honor is due: For most of the distinctions which have come to Post-Dispatch men, Bovard is entitled to a large share of the credit. He would show a reporter how to pull off a terrific story — and then insist that the reporter be given a salary increase for pulling it."[39] He credited the managing editor with the ideas that won Pulitzer Prizes for reporter John T. Rogers in 1926 for the investigation leading to the impeachment of U.S. District Judge George W. English, and for himself in 1928 for disclosures of irregularities in naval oil leases which led to the Teapot Dome investigation.

The managing editor put his own explanation of the break into a rambling, inconsistent memo to Pulitzer which was sharply critical in some places and kind in others. He dated his dissatisfaction from 1932, when he had returned from vacation to find that the paper had taken on columnists Arthur Brisbane and Walter

Winchell and from that point increasingly used "the frothier and more banal type of features." He thought that these and "the rest of the quack stimulants to circulation" were "wholly irreconcilable with the spirit of the paper's platform." Yet, "while the news department has not been what I should have made it had I been untrammeled, I freely acquit you of any harmful interference. I take pleasure in telling you that many of your criticisms have been helpful and I confess that . . . I have not on the whole liked criticism from you. Obviously, I regarded your criticism of fundamentals as unsound, otherwise I would not be writing this letter." The paragraph Pulitzer liked best was this:

> Now if anything I have written sounds severe, I want you to know that one of the things that Clark McAdams and I most often said about you to each other was that it was to your everlasting credit that the things the paper has done to earn the fine reputation it bears were done under your administration and could not have been done without your full and cheerful approval. That is true today and I am glad to repeat it.[40]

Pulitzer wrote to Bovard:

> I cannot tell you what a wrench this gives me. Perhaps I can express it best by telling you that for many years your name has stood, as it now stands, in my will as a trustee and guardian . . . until he came of age, of Joe, Jr. [Joseph Pulitzer III] and now of Michael, for the stated reason that you were above all others familiar with the traditional principles and policies of the Post-Dispatch and that I could, therefore, rely on you after my death with every confidence in your judgment and integrity.[41]

Bovard had long known his value to the *Post-Dispatch*. His salary when he became managing editor in 1910 was $4,500.[42] It jumped from $20,000 in 1926 to $50,000 in 1927, second only to Pulitzer's $100,000, probably to make sure he wouldn't take a job elsewhere. "My judgment is emphatically in favor of holding on to Bovard," Pulitzer had told Florence White in 1922, "not because he is invaluable to us, but because he would be infernally valuable to a competitor."[43] His salary peaked at $75,000 in 1932 and moved between $50,000 and $60,000 during the remaining six years of his career. The next highest paid executive, treasurer James T. Keller, received $26,000 in 1938. In addition, as an executive eligible under the founder's will to share part of one-tenth of the paper's annual profit, Bovard received the largest slice — $12,340 in 1937.[44] In his later years, he was not the highest-paid managing editor in the United States, as some thought, but he may have been second highest. F. J. Hause of the *New York Daily News* received $120,716 in 1935, but Edwin L. James of the *New York Times* earned only $32,500 that year.[45] Bovard had several job offers after he left the *Post-Dispatch*, but he turned down all of them. The most tempting was full control of *PM*, the liberal, adless New York daily conceived by Ralph Ingersoll which appeared in 1940.

Despite his interest in socialism, Bovard and his wife, Suzanne, enjoyed his income on a luxurious 92-acre estate, Windridge Farm, near Clayton, in St. Louis County. Their only child, a son, died in infancy. At his estate, Bovard personally supervised the care of large apple and pear orchards and the couple entertained small groups of friends. His other recreation, which in earlier days he had sometimes enjoyed with Pulitzer, was bird-shooting. During a hunting trip to Saskatchewan in the fall of 1945, he developed viral pneumonia and died on November 3 at the age of seventy-three. His funeral was attended by some three hundred persons, including a *Post-Dispatch* contingent led by Pulitzer which formed an honor guard flanking the casket following the Episcopal service.[46]

Shortly after Bovard's resignation, Pulitzer had asked Charles Ross, author of "The Country's Plight" and who had been recalled from Washington in mid-1934 to take charge of the editorial page, to make a careful study of Bovard's thesis. Pulitzer wanted to know if Ross agreed that the managing editor's arguments were "not always dispassionate." Ross did agree, saying that he found the work "shot through at times with a very perceptible malice; it sets up — against the writer's advice to you in telling how the Post-Dispatch should campaign for P E ["practical economics"] — personal devils." He said that although Bovard seemed to think

"The Country's Plight" charted a course toward socialism, in his own view it clearly argued "for reform within the existing system." He found both Bovard's brief for constitutional amendment and his "whole attitude toward politics and public men" totally unrealistic. "We can expect no politician-less Utopia under Socialism or any other form of government. . . . I decidedly do not believe that the Post-Dispatch should nail to its masthead, as Mr. Bovard would have us do . . . the program which he urges. . . . To propose such an assault, no matter how we might qualify our words, would inevitably label us in the public mind as 'red.' It would destroy such power as we may now possess to bring about needed reform." Instead, he recommended that the paper should continue "on a thoroughly liberal course . . . as I believe we have always, according to our lights, tried to do."[47]

A measure of the devotion of many of Bovard's subordinates became evident nine years after his death, when a biography of the managing editor by James W. Markham, then an assistant professor of journalism at the Pennsylvania State College, was published. A letter to the editor of the *Post-Dispatch* signed by thirty-four men and women who had worked under Bovard said the book "left a decidedly wrong impression" of the man as "a cold, hard overlord who had no personal feeling for his staff. On the contrary . . . he was a fine, fair, appreciative human being who thought of others as human beings and so respected them."[48] They did not take issue with Markham's more substantial criticism that without benefit of much reading beyond newspapers and magazines, and without a college degree, Bovard was relatively shallow as a political philosopher. "He often discovered late in life various ideas with which a university education would have equipped him in his twenties," Markham concluded. "When he developed what was to him a new idea, he did not realize that Aristotle, or Locke, or Jefferson, had worked out its designs better than he had. The idea was original to him; therefore he thought it was original to the world."[49]

And not everyone saw him as socially sensitive. Sometime after Bovard retired, *Post-Dispatch* national advertising manager Ben Brockman and Bovard both happened to be staying at the Biltmore Hotel in New York. When Bovard saw Brockman in the lobby, he started to walk toward him, obviously eager to greet him. But

Brockman, recalling how Bovard never had spoken to him when they happened to meet on the *Post-Dispatch* elevator but instead simply held one finger aloft in response to Brockman's greeting, decided to turn the tables. "I saw a smile break over his face," Brockman recalled some forty-five years later at the age of ninety-two, "and I said to myself, 'Why you dirty son of a bitch. When you worked on the paper, you treated me like a goddam dog.' I passed him up like the coldest piece of ice you ever saw. . . . It was one of the meanest things I ever did, and I never regretted doing it."[50]

— 19 —

Life After O.K.B.

While Bovard's resignation was a genuine disappointment for Pulitzer, it gave him the opportunity to manage the news department more completely, just as the Johns retirement had provided the chance to take fuller charge of the editorial page. His having done that had, among other things, signaled Bovard that Pulitzer had no intention of being a figurehead. In turn, this probably helped generate in Bovard the anxiety that led him to ask for full control as general manager. Disappointed though he ultimately was, it is a measure of Bovard's domination of *Post-Dispatch* newshandling that for the twenty-six years of his service under the second Joseph Pulitzer the memorandums between them occupy only five folders in Pulitzer's papers in the Library of Congress. By contrast, the memorandums between Pulitzer and Bovard's successor, Benjamin Harrison Reese, fill twenty-two folders, all but part of one covering the thirteen years of Reese's managing editorship. This correspondence, dealing with virtually every aspect of the internal workings of the news department and including a steady stream of news and feature ideas, shows Pulitzer as more deeply involved in the paper's news apparatus than ever before. Perhaps in part because Pulitzer was taking a more active role, he did not think Reese's pay should equal Bovard's. The new managing editor started at $20,000, one-third of what Bovard had been making, and ended his career at the *Post-Dispatch* in 1951 with a salary plus a share of dividends of $33,301.[1]

Reese, forty-nine when he was promoted, had worked under Bovard for twenty-five years, four years as assistant city editor and twenty-one as city editor. Like Bovard, he was a big man—6 feet, 4 inches tall—with a booming voice and a no-nonsense manner with subordinates. He was better educated than his predecessor. Bovard's schooling had ended with the fifth grade, but Reese was a high school graduate who had finished at the top of his class of six in 1906 at Hobart, Oklahoma. He had been fullback on the school's football team and first baseman on its baseball team and had written about his athletic exploits in sports reports for the Hobart *Republican.* "I saw to it that Reese got a good account of his 'achievements,' " he recalled.[2]

After promoting him, Pulitzer's first instruction to Reese was to visit Bovard at his desk, so the staff would see them talking together. In one of those conversations Bovard told Reese that he had expected to be there another year, breaking in his successor; Reese took this to mean that Bovard believed an outsider should have been brought in because no one on the staff was qualified. "I had been on the city desk 25 years, slaving my heart out for 'dear old Pulitzer'—sorta like 'dear old Yale,' " Reese recalled. "Dwight Perrin, former city editor of the *New York Herald Tribune,* had been assistant managing editor about 12 years. Had Bovard been unmindful of a duty to train a successor to take over in the emergency of death, or resignation?" (In fact, in a private conversation with Pulitzer in 1936, Bovard had said that in the event of his death, "by all means" his successor should come from the staff because no outsider could possibly have as much knowledge of the paper's traditions as an insider. In that same conversation, Bovard told Pulitzer that in the event of the publisher's death, he thought it best "to put the paper in my control until the other owners could pull themselves together."[3])

Great as he once had been, in Reese's estimate Bovard at the end became "too possessed, too egotistic, too know-it-all, too settled into a pattern. Being human, he made mistakes of judgment — news and otherwise." Reese thought Bovard came to view himself and the paper as one and the same, even to the point of secretly hoping "the PD would fold (as had the N.Y. World) so that it could be said that Bovard WAS the PD."[4] Although he professed not to believe that, he was confident, Reese reflected in 1954, that when Bovard quit "Mr. Pulitzer at that time didn't know whether Bovard *was* the *Post-Dispatch*. . . . He was so doubtful about it that after he had accepted Bovard's resignation, and after I sat in Bovard's old chair, he came to my desk and said, 'Don't you think we ought to have Bovard around here for around ten thousand dollars a year for consultation and advice?' "

Reese dissuaded him. "If you want Bovard here," he replied, "you better bring him back and put him at this desk, because either I've got to have the opportunity to do this job, or you want Bovard to do it." He related to Pulitzer that once when Bovard had returned from vacation he had remarked to Reese that during his absence assistant managing editor Joe Adams had attempted to lay out the paper as Bovard would have done it, with the result, Bovard thought, that "it's neither Bovard nor Adams — it's nothing." Reese predicted that "it would be the same thing with Bovard around here again. It's got to be Reese or Bovard." He did *not* tell Pulitzer of another incident that took place just after Bovard's resignation had been accepted and Reese had been named his successor. "Do you see this hook, with all these yellow memoranda from the publisher?" Bovard asked Reese. "I get these things and put them on a hook. Every six weeks or so, I just empty the hook into the waste basket." Those words, Reese recalled, were spoken "with utter contempt for Mr. Pulitzer."[5]

As it turned out, the transition was relatively smooth despite the belief of some staff members, Reese thought, that "they were getting a police court managing editor."[6] In a memo to the staff, Pulitzer said he looked "with every confidence to a distinguished career for Mr. Reese in his new post."[7] As a precaution, though, his understanding with Reese was that the first year would be a trial period.[8] James Lawrence, who for most of his forty-eight-year career was a *Post-Dispatch* editorial writer, got to know Reese when Lawrence was news director for KSD radio. Reese "was not an intellectual giant," Lawrence recalled. "I always suspected that J.P. named him because he was an able administrator who, unlike Bovard, would carry out orders."[9]

To be sure, Pulitzer was confident in himself, even though he did reveal in a letter to his brothers that during late 1938 "we ran an extra liberal paper in order to smother the whispers that the paper had been hurt by Bovard's resignation."[10] At about the same time — presumably for the historical record — he dictated a memorandum for his files disputing published assertions such as one by former reporter Paul Y. Anderson in *The Nation* that the newspaper had Bovard to thank for whatever reputation for distinction it had achieved.[11] "I believe that as publisher of the *Post-Dispatch* I should be credited with the following," he began. He first mentioned placing the founder's platform in the masthead on November 7, 1911, a few days after his father's death, "and seeing to it that this platform is lived up to." He took credit for the creation of separate sports, editorial, and daily magazine sections, "starting the first roto section west of New York," and "clearing important pages of advertising . . . despite protests of advertisers." He noted that he had assembled and held "one of the highest paid newspaper staffs in the country" and listed the salaries of Bovard ($55,500), treasurer James T. Keller ($26,115), editorial page editor Charles G. Ross ($25,480), advertising manager George M. Burbach ($25,096), editorial cartoonist Daniel R. Fitzpatrick ($23,432), and reporter Anderson ($16,548), among others. As for editorial outlook, he had held "to an editorial policy which might be described in its efforts to conserve our American form of government and in particular our civil liberties, as conservative; and which might be described in its support of the application of the power of government to remedy evils as they arise, financial, political and social, as progressive." He came as close as he ever would to criticizing Bovard's nationalization idea by saying that the paper "has been and is politically anti-Nazi, anti-Fascist, anti-Communist, and, economically, anti-totalitarian. As I see it, it is better to suffer the ills we have than to fly to others we know nothing of." Dropping his usual modesty, he said he had been "publishing a newspaper which has been described by Franklin D. Roosevelt as 'a great journal,'" and followed that with quoted compliments of eleven additional notables.[12]

In the spring following Bovard's departure, Pulitzer wrote to his brothers: "I do believe the paper is a better paper than it ever has been and that the community so regards it. . . . It isn't easy going but all we can do is to keep plugging away. As a friend of mine likes to say, 'I'm doing the best I can with my shaped head.'"[13] Perhaps the main reason for his positive outlook was that Pulitzer had it made clear, through Reese, that Bovard's recent excesses were a thing of the past. This understanding was reflected in a memorandum from Washington bureau chief Brandt: "No member of this bureau has a desire to propagandize any political philosophy or to build up any political person through the columns of the Post-Dispatch. . . . The bureau . . . welcomes this policy of 'no editorializing,' and no more writing 'from a point of view.'" Thanking Brandt, Pulitzer wrote: "Let us concern ourselves with telling the reader what has really happened rather than what you or I or someone else thinks of the happening."[14]

With that matter rectified, Pulitzer proceeded along the paper's well-established lines. One of his first memorandums to the new managing editor was this reminder: "Again let me warn you against permitting the business office to press you too hard in favor of this, that or the other economy."[15] He gave Reese the authority, as he had Bovard, to exclude advertising to make more space for news if in his judgment news developments warranted.[16] And, as always, advertisers were neither to get promotional favors nor to be shielded from embarrassment in the news columns. Practically, those principles were traceable to the paper's desirability as an advertising medium. Philosophically, they came from the founding Pulitzer and were pursued by the son with a zeal that seemed constantly renewable. As were his memos to the editorial page, those to Reese were sprinkled with references to "the founder of this newspaper" and "my father." He liked to characterize himself as just another "constant reader," whose service and satisfaction should be the paper's first concern.

There was both similarity and difference between the first Joseph Pulitzer and the second when it came to getting articles of

wide popular appeal into the paper. The father could be positively
ghoulish: "$500 reward with the utmost pleasure to the reporter
who will discover beyond peradventure the author of the recent
murder — the woman cut up. Please keep this very secret or THE
JOURNAL will have it."[17] His son was more reserved: "Here, it
would seem, is a murder case with all the elements of a Rudyard
Kipling or Somerset Maugham fiction story: titles, tropics, love
and mystery. I urge that we follow it closely for possible development in the news columns, in Pictures and in the Everyday
Magazine."[18] Yet when the *Globe-Democrat* carried on the front
page of its society section an account of how a sixteen-year-old boy
had been "kidnapped" by an older woman, quoting her as saying,
"I love him more than I do my husband. He's more of a man at 16
than most men are at 35," Pulitzer wrote Reese: "Let me point to
the enclosed feature . . . as a most clinical example of journalistic
filth which should not appear on the first page of the Post-Dispatch.
I cannot imagine any circumstances that would justify its appearance anywhere in the P–D. In my judgment it is the kind of thing
which tends to destroy the reputation and prestige of the American newspaper."[19] Instead, he never tired of reminding Reese that
the proper way to gain circulation was to run as often as possible
"talk making" items about the "odd, unusual, quaint or curious"
which would, as his father often had said, make people ask, "Did
you see thus and so in the *Post-Dispatch?*"[20] This fit with his
assumption that the paper's thoughtful and detailed news presenta-
tions served relatively few readers. Noting that *New York Times*
Sunday editor Lester Markel had reported that 80 percent of the
population range between "definitely moronic" and "ignorant but
willing to learn," leaving only 20 percent who are well informed,
he commented that such a breakdown "suggests that while we are
doing a highly useful job with our type of news presentation we do
need more space for magazine features and sports."[21]

Reese had overall charge of the budget for news operations and
such a free hand in its use and distribution that he could say,
"There's no story in the world too expensive for us if we really
want it."[22] That of course reflected the attitude of the publisher,
who only occasionally nudged the managing editor in the direction of economy, to the despair of his business managers. He once
wrote a long-lost prep school friend that they regarded him "as a

'pushover' and a spendthrift" because "my interests have always been in the news and editorial phases of our work."[23] Still, he was not oblivious to costs. A few months after Reese took over, Pulitzer expressed surprise that of the 135 newsroom employees only 31 were producing local news. To him, that demonstrated the "relatively high" payroll expense of the "Everyday Magazine," "Pictures," the Washington Bureau, and the sports staff.[24] When it seemed to him that the Washington bureau was getting extravagant in buying stories for the Sunday paper from outsiders rather than getting them from its own staff, he asked Reese to "watch this item of expense."[25]

The paper's willingness to spend considerable sums of money in the pursuit of news continuously frustrated the competition. It once drove *Star-Times* managing editor Norman Isaacs to do something "slightly unethical." Both papers were interested in accusations of election fraud in Kansas City, where some ballots had been impounded. As usual, the *Post-Dispatch* "sent up a crew and we had only a few [reporters]," Isaacs recalled. But Harry Bowles, one of the few, was prolific, producing three or four stories. Isaacs decided to invent bylines for some of Bowles's stories to make it appear that his paper had a larger contingent in Kansas City than it did. But his inspiration backfired. To Isaacs's dismay, the *Post-Dispatch* "just counted the number of *Star* bylines and immediately sent in more troops. . . . They weren't going to have the *Star-Times* send six, seven people in there. I imagine they sent in fifteen instead of what they had to start with. . . . But that was the way they operated, and I'm sure it was Pulitzer's direct instructions. He wanted what they got." When it was all over, Isaacs turned to Aaron Benesch, his city editor, who had been unenthusiastic about inventing the bylines: "Aaron, that one sure bit us on the ass. Let's not do that again!"[26]

Isaacs's point is well illustrated in the way Pulitzer reacted to the March 25, 1947, Centralia, Illinois, coal mine explosion in which 111 miners were killed. The *Post-Dispatch* immediately set up a bureau there composed of a bureau chief and seventeen reporters and photographers. Three days later Pulitzer sent this to Reese:

The Post-Dispatch, having so often had to damn the miners

and their leader, John L. Lewis, I somehow feel it is our peculiar duty to turn ourselves inside out to get to the bottom of what clearly appears to have been faulty inspection of the Centralia mine, to the end that safer conditions can be assured for the future, those responsible for failure to do their duty be brought to justice . . . and that we undertake to do whatever we can do to help the prospects of the bereaved families. . . .

. . . My general thought is that we might bring all ends of the story together — the law, the seeming failure to enforce it, with photographs of all principals. . . . In other words make a presentation of all the facts which might be useful to the [U.S. Senate investigative] committee and which might very well anticipate the committee report.

This may take a full page or for all I know a dozen full pages. It may take a staff of a dozen men.[27]

The result was a special twenty-four-page rotogravure section published a month later and distributed free in the Central Illinois mine area. Subsequent investigations supported the paper's findings and resulted in stronger state and federal mine safety laws. For this the *Post-Dispatch* won its third Pulitzer Prize "for disinterested and meritorious service."[28]

To avoid undercutting the managing editor's authority, Pulitzer ordinarily communicated on news matters — meaning everything but the editorial page — only with Reese. That left Reese the option of disclosing Pulitzer's interest, which he often did, especially in the effort to rid the paper of one or another of the publisher's "pet hates." Two of the most intense were paraphrasing rather than quoting directly and overwriting. Whenever either showed up, as they did inevitably, Reese got a memo. After a short Associated Press story in early 1939 quoted U.S. Senator George W. Norris of Nebraska as predicting that a congressional investigation of the Tennessee Valley Authority would ultimately uncover no wrongdoing, Pulitzer wrote: "Here is an example of a space-eating so-called Washington news story which in my judgment contains no real news. My father once taught me to beware of opinions on opinions. . . . The prophecy may be correct but what of it? Isn't the average reader content to await the committee's report?"[29] Because

Washington bureau stories so often seemed overblown to Pulitzer, he said he was "strongly tempted" to put up signs there saying "Write your story for what you think it is worth and then chop it in half."[30] On another occasion he became so annoyed by Associated Press paraphrasing of a speech by President Roosevelt, using, in his opinion, two hundred extra unnecessary words in the process, that he told Reese reading it made him "sick at his stomach." Reese related that to AP executive director Kent Cooper. "The question in Mr. Pulitzer's mind," he explained, "is whether we have to buy the United Press to get . . . first person quotations?"[31]

Similarly, echoing one of his father's most persistent themes, he periodically declared "Intelligent Condensation Week," directing Reese to "ask every man on the [newsroom] floor to apply his mind to this subject when planning, writing and editing copy. I am convinced that as a general rule, all P–D stories run too long."[32] A few days into such a campaign, Reese forwarded a memorandum from the city desk to Pulitzer reporting that a human-interest story by reporter Arthur Hepner had "required little boiling down since the necessity and desirability of such treatment has been dinned into the ears of the staff recently."[33]

Some in the newsroom thought Pulitzer's directives were followed to extremes. When, in 1943, he asked several subeditors to submit directly to him confidential and completely candid "Blow Your Own Horn" reports—something his father had done on occasion—one replied:

> Whenever you express an interest in some situation that expression is at once translated into a sort of inferential command to publish everything that bears on the subject, however remotely. The effect is to set up for the time being a sort of "Pulitzer must" department in the paper. If it's a big day for these departments and the war is in an active phase, just try to blast something else into a 26-page paper. Sometimes I think our discrimination ends at the J.P. line.[34]

That observation was on the mark, even though Pulitzer emphasized from time to time that he was making suggestions, not "must" rules, and said Reese could ignore him "if my ideas don't stand up."[35] He sometimes simply left Reese no choice, as when he wrote: "I don't like 'must' rules, but I do urge that you issue a 'directive' banning all double negatives, not to mention triple and quadruple negatives."[36] Those memos, dubbed the "yellow peril" by staff members because they were typed on yellow paper used by no one but Pulitzer, never were casually regarded. They were so closely identified with Pulitzer that his portrait by painter Wayman Adams, commissioned by the staff in observance of his sixtieth birthday in 1945, shows him holding some of the yellow sheets.

When it came to the substance of the news, Pulitzer saw it as the paper's main duty to mobilize the usually apathetic electorate. In suggesting a story on State Senator Joseph H. Brogan, who was running for his ninth term and whom the *Post-Dispatch* thought was part of a triumvirate in control of the Senate responsible for sidetracking a number of popular reform measures, he wrote: "Let's throw the spotlight of publicity on this bird and his record from the very inception of his campaign and give the people of St. Louis every possible opportunity to think about him and decide whether he is really the type of man that they deserve to have represent them. Between ourselves, as I see it, this makes a pretty good test case to indicate how badly at times American democracy works. Of course, the story should not say this, but we CAN say it editorially."[37]

Particularly after the Depression and his difference with Bovard, the question of the distribution of wealth keenly interested Pulitzer. The attention the paper gave to this was, in the view of several of Pulitzer's well-off social friends, one reason the moneyed of St. Louis preferred the *Globe-Democrat* to the *Post-Dispatch*.[38] When President Roosevelt proposed in 1942 that incomes be limited to $25,000 a year, Pulitzer suggested that Reese try for interviews with about a dozen of the richest men in St. Louis for their reactions to the idea. Pulitzer, who knew most of these people, said his "guess would be that those who are against it would have nothing to say but that those who favor it or those who have accepted it as sound might say so." He advised against printing the incomes of those interviewed, but would say that they varied "between $50,000 and $—00,000." Further, "should any one of them come out with a blast against it I should not print it but would say in effect that only one or two of those interviewed opposed it." In a remarkable postscript, coming from a man whose income in lean Depression years had exceeded $300,000, he added: "Incidentally, without having had any opportunity to study the case against it, I have come around to favoring it and accepting it as unavoidable." His more considered opinion two years later was that the idea represented Roosevelt's "tendency occasionally to go off the deep end."[39] To adjust to such an eventuality would have meant a revolution in the publisher's lifestyle.[40]

If hardly a commoner in economic terms, Pulitzer's taste in entertainment was essentially Everyman's. "Probably I am eccentric on the subject of dramatic criticism which, even when written by the Alex Woollcotts, has always been one of my pet abominations," he wrote in reaction to a negative *Post-Dispatch* review of a play he had enjoyed. "On Thursday night the packed audience was certainly responsive," he reported, "so much so, indeed, that the guffaws of a man sitting right behind me got to be a nuisance." He recommended that "henceforth, we satisfy ourselves with dramatic reporting and forget dramatic criticism" because "my hunch is that what the St. Louis playgoers want to know is not whether the critic thinks it's lousy or brilliant, but rather what kind of a reputation this play has made for itself; how the public has received it elsewhere; how well the St. Louis cast is performing it, and only very incidentally and in general, what supposedly expert critics have had to say about it." In a postscript he said it would be all right "as a concession to the pride of the author" to let him express his opinion "in two or three lines."[41]

Only occasionally, and in minor matters, did Pulitzer use his position to exercise control over stories with a personal connection. In ordering coverage for a golf tournament at the St. Louis Country Club, to which he belonged, he commented, "Club members, naturally, do not like to see photographs of their wives and daughters in which drinking is over emphasized."[42] And he took pains to avoid or sidestep personal or family publicity. For example, he asked that his son-in-law, physician Louis H. Hempelmann Jr., not be referred to in the paper as the son-in-law of the publisher: "Louis is getting along very well under his own steam and his wife objects, and I think rightly, to this form of identification."[43] He also advised Reese to "go a little slow" in the use of photographs of his other son-in-law, Air Force Lieutenant General Elwood R.

Quesada, to avoid the impression that Pulitzer was "using the paper to plug for a family connection."[44] When a suit was being contemplated in an estate matter against Herbert Pulitzer, his brother told Reese he was "glad to leave entirely to you the decision as to how and where to display the item. My offhand guess is that the New York papers will print it on an inside page."[45]

But there were times when he could not resist arranging some newspaper exposure for his friends. When Mrs. Joseph L. Werner, a frequent duck-hunting companion of the Pulitzers, killed her limit of seven ducks with just four shots in the fall of 1946, Pulitzer drafted a suggested story and headline and sent them to Reese, calling the item "perhaps good for page one."[46] There, with few changes, it appeared. When family friend Maggie Porter, who had taken over Porter Paint Company following her husband's death, had the top of her hardtop convertible covered with flowered wallpaper and the seats done in matching chintz, she drove over to her friend Joe Pulitzer's and asked him to buy her a drink. He did, and also had a photo of Mrs. Porter and car run in the *Post-Dispatch*.[47]

Yet if these same people found themselves in unpleasantly newsworthy circumstances, they could expect no favors from their editor-publisher friend. "Am asked and as usual have refused to show special consideration in the divorce case of Mr. and Mrs. Francis Niedringhaus which I understand has been or is about to be filed," he once wired Reese. He asked only that the managing editor "take pains to see that our report is accurate and fair to both sides."[48] What went for friends went for Pulitzer himself, who in the fall of 1943 pleaded guilty to having too many ducks in his possession—he had shot thirty-six during one day's outing—and paid a fine of $500. As he related in a letter to his eldest son, then in the Navy: "We ran the . . . story on the first page and that attracted favorable attention coming so soon after our printing there the story that Dr. MacIver, the minister, had been arrested while driving for being stewed. Seemingly, few papers around the country paid much attention to it, but this neighborhood, including Illinois, knew all about it, especially by radio."[49]

Another rather dramatic example shows how seriously he saw the paper's obligation when it came to publishing sensitive information. On being read a short story printed on page three on June 24,

1941, reporting the death by suicide of socially prominent Mrs. Catherine Dameron Weakley, wife of state representative William B. Weakley of Pike County, the vacationing Pulitzer wondered: "Why in THUNDER didn't the story tell how she committed suicide?" Within a few hours he found the missing fact in a letter from a friend thanking him for a salmon: "The whole city is stunned by Mrs. Weakley's hanging herself." Off went a memo to Reese asking why the story was not on page one and why the method of suicide was omitted. The answer was that Reese had reluctantly agreed to omit that detail at the request of J.P. Jr., who had been asked by a friend of the Weakley family to "handle the story with restraint."[50] Now twenty-eight and preparing for his future role, the third Joseph Pulitzer had been exercising some editorial authority while his father was out of town. He took responsibility for the decision in a memorandum to his father and got this response:

> I hate to say this to you but you were guilty of an unforgivable journalistic sin when you asked B.H.R. to suppress a salient fact—the fact that she [Mrs. Weakley] hanged herself. . . . I cannot overemphasize this point. It is at the very heart of what I regard as journalistic honesty—honesty with the readers and honesty with the staff. Showing reasonable consideration for families is one thing. . . . It was not necessary to state all the gruesome details and to say that she hanged herself in her cellar or her bathroom . . . or . . . what she was wearing, etc. . . . but the reader was definitely entitled to know how she ended her life. I would not suppress such a fact in a case of a member of my own family and I hope and feel sure that you never again will do so, no matter how much anguish it may cause them and you.
>
> Forgive me for this blunt criticism but I do want to bring home to you the fact that under the Pulitzer philosophy of journalism the reader must be given the facts which he is entitled to find in the Post-Dispatch irrespective of how strong the appeal or how strong the pressure that may be brought from those interested in requesting or demanding suppression.[51]

Pressure of a more stubbornly persistent kind kept the *Post-Dispatch* from reporting about racial discrimination as vigorously as it might have during Pulitzer's lifetime. Nevertheless, the paper's record in handling the topic was exemplary overall in the context of the times. In line with his commitment to helping the poor and disadvantaged, the first Joseph Pulitzer had shown his dislike of racial prejudice by having Booker T. Washington as a guest at Chatwold, supporting several black students at Tuskegee Institute, and ordering a *World* editorial scolding President William Howard Taft for not appointing some blacks to federal posts in Southern states. When the editorial came out, he found it too mild. "I really admire the amazing moderation and toning down to the uttermost minimum of my convictions—life-long convictions, if you please," he sarcastically wrote Frank Cobb.[52] Even so, that ended it. The issue was not as pressing during his editorship as it became during his son's. It may have been the most perplexing single issue the second Joseph Pulitzer faced as editor, involving as it did deep-seated and thinly disguised racism on the part of many in his employ, including, successively, all three of his managing editors.

Yet despite this, the paper's attitude toward blacks was far more supportive over the years than that of its competition and many other metropolitan dailies. In 1951 it was singled out on that account by Florence R. Beatty-Brown, mainly because its special features and editorials had been unusually attentive and fair-minded. The features described the achievements of blacks positively, and the editorials criticized such manifest examples of racism as lynching, poll taxes, discrimination by trade unions and political organizations, and the exclusion of black artists from concert halls, among other things. The paper quoted singer Lena Horne's statement that blacks of her generation "are having a hell of a time" and commented: "Lena Horne has both money and fame, but they are tarnished by old prejudices." Yet as supportive as such stories were, Beatty-Brown observed, "it would have taken a careful and most detailed reader . . . to piece the picture together from the infrequent segments . . . that appeared. It is evident that most [whites] do not comprehend the problem in its many facets." The problem was bigger than inadequate press coverage, she concluded, calling it "doubtful if the design woven by the *Post* in regard to the Negro can change much more until the local and world fabric changes. The newspaper, though most important, cannot fight the battle for intergroup understanding alone."[53]

Pulitzer agreed. His attitudes about reform were strongly tempered by his reading of the readiness of whites to support change, and thus his memorandums show a mixture of activism and resignation. The latter he expressed a number of times by concluding that publicity of one kind or another "might do more harm than good." By current standards that may seem evasive, but at that time and in a city identified in many ways with the South, it seemed to him pragmatic. He had grown up amid segregation practices so commonplace as to appear the norm. Such were the realities that while he had had no objection to attending classes with blacks at Harvard,[54] he never identified any as his social friends. A black servant in his home for several years, Walter Wanzer, performed the more menial tasks and ate his meals at a separate table from the white servants.[55] But at the same time, he recognized the moral issue. Responding to an appeal in 1941 from his nephew, William S. Moore Jr., one of his sister Edith's sons, to help the boy overcome his parents' objection to letting "three outstanding colored boys" attend the summer camp at which William was a counselor, he wrote: "I am sorry but I must agree with your family as to what is unquestionably one of this world's greatest problems."[56] It was, he believed at that time, an issue that was not likely ever to be fully resolved. "I can't see that there is anything to be done about the Negro problem," he said the following year, "except to treat them with the utmost consideration and sympathy and by all means inviting the [soprano Marian] Andersons and [actor/bass-baritone Paul] Robesons and Booker Washingtons to lunch at the White House and to sing before the D.A.R. BUT— not attempting and especially not pretending to give them racial equality. It is too bad that cats don't like dogs and vice versa but they don't, never have, and, so far as I can see, never will. The same is true of blacks and whites. As I see it, this is one of nature's dirty tricks. There is actually little anyone can do about it."[57]

Less than two years later, however, he found himself in agreement with a U.S. Supreme Court order mandating higher education for blacks. "I favor taking this position," he told editorial page editor Ralph Coghlan, "but in doing so let me say that we should express ourselves with the utmost restraint and in the full realization that many good people will be hurt and others infuriated. Clearly, this is not a subject for eloquence, but rather [calls] for that kind of restrained writing which, by its very restraint, reveals between the lines a sense of serious journalistic responsibility. Furthermore, I do not believe we should go into the entire field of social equality of the negro at this time, but should limit our arguments to education." He candidly explained the reason behind his call for restraint:

> I must admit that I would dislike sitting next to a negro or a negress at a movie theater or at a lunch counter or occupying a hotel room next to a family of them, and that I did not enjoy a recent experience in a railroad club car when a stout, overdressed and over-retiring negro couple sat smoking opposite me, and that to this considerable extent I am prejudiced against social recognition of the negro — while I must admit all this I cannot see any justification for a state-supported or a privately-supported university denying the negro the opportunity for education.[58]

Over the next several years Pulitzer developed a broader and somewhat militant outlook. This showed up in his continuing interest in the issue and his willingness at times to go against the tide. For example, at the newspaper itself blacks have served as receptionist on the news-editorial floor for most of the *Post-Dispatch*'s history. Although such employment could be seen as tokenism, in the opinion of longtime national advertising manager Ben Brockman, keeping a black in such a visible position more often than not "rubbed [white] people the wrong way."[59] In any case, Pulitzer's instructions to Charles Crawford, who held the position for more than two decades, were: "A baby or a bum can have a news story, and at any cost don't let a news story out of the office. Treat citizens with courtesy but don't let them bully you."[60] Accordingly, Crawford was a significant gatekeeper. If anyone tried to evade dealing with him, other employees usually saw to it that the person was steered back to the receptionist's desk. Crawford also had the instruction, apparently from Pulitzer himself, that even if a black seemed not to have a story, he or she should be allowed to see the city editor, in order to go away satisfied.[61]

That probably was not always the outcome, for as Pulitzer knew, blacks had reason to be dissatisfied with the paper's treatment of them in news stories. Prejudice had long prevailed in the newsroom. As city editor under Bovard, Reese had sent reporter Richard G. Baumhoff to cover the court of a black justice of the peace who handled cases involving blacks, "hoping," Baumhoff recalled, "that I could pick up some funny stories." Routinely for some years, Baumhoff added, "a female Negro was not 'Mrs. Smith' but 'the Smith woman.' "[62] For years blacks complained, to no avail, about their identification by race in crime stories.[63] In such a climate, Pulitzer was restrained in writing Reese in 1941: "Please don't misunderstand, I am not pressing the point, but I have often wondered whether a Negro reporter might not be worth while.... Of course, I can see the objections." Reese's response was curt: "I vote NO as to news department." He added that there was one black *Post-Dispatch* employee "whose services are used on certain occasions."[64] It was nearly a decade before the paper hired its first black reporter. He was John Hicks, a University of Illinois journalism school graduate who was assigned to work almost exclusively among blacks. Some whites refused to be interviewed by him, leading Beatty-Brown to conclude: "The *Post* is moving more rapidly than the public is ready to accept." As of 1950 the paper had "around 47" blacks among some 2,000 employees, all but five in "common labor jobs."[65]

These statistics could not have surprised Pulitzer. Three years earlier, he had asked for a survey of the paper's eight major department heads on their willingness to employ black copy boys or office boys. Six were opposed. One thought "it would not look proper to have Negroes in a department to which the public has occasion to visit." Another "expressed considerable concern as to having a Negro boy from 16 to 19 years old among the women in his department." City editor Crowley "most emphatically said, 'No, it would lead to all sorts of trouble. We have enough trouble with the white ones.' " In relating this to Coghlan, who with production manager Charles J. Hentschell had no objection to hiring blacks, Pulitzer remarked, "Under these circumstances, what is the unfortunate publisher supposed to do? I am stumped."[66] But a few days later he stated: "I should like to see Negroes employed whenever there is an opportunity to do so with the least possible friction."[67]

This changed little, even after the paper was picketed by Communists in 1948 for hiring so few blacks, an event the paper covered with both a story and a two-column photograph.[68] Nor did the march of events, the publisher's concern, and the paper's editorial policy combine to eliminate racial prejudice in news judgments generally, though they probably made some inroads. Pulitzer's suggestions to Reese for coverage of blacks and black concerns usually were phrased tentatively, leaving the way open for a negative response. This was typical: "In these days of Negro prejudices, this may be debatable, but Ed Wilkinson, my Negro barber, tells me that Roland Hayes owns and operates a farm in Georgia which contains nothing less than 600 acres. That's quite a farm. If true, it might make a Pictures feature."[69] In 1945, he asked Reese to keep Coghlan informed about the operation of a recently adopted New York state law guaranteeing blacks equality in employment. This would help, he said, in formulating a decision on whether to support enactment of such a law at the federal level editorially. He and Coghlan were "in doubt on the theory that the bill might precipitate trouble in the South and elsewhere and do more harm than good," he explained, but one editorial writer, Ferdinand Gottlieb, "is strongly for it."[70]

Yet despite Pulitzer's continuing concern, Reese stuck to his practice of downplaying events involving blacks. Pulitzer came as close as he ever would to a showdown with the managing editor in 1947, when he drafted a memo to Reese suggesting a search for a black columnist who could "express the legitimate feelings, hopes and aspirations of the American Negro." It concluded: "How, may I ask, without the rankest hypocrisy can we preach tolerance on the editorial page and then deny a qualified Negro . . . an opportunity to speak for the Negro? Sooner or later we must face this issue, why not now?"[71] But he never sent it, evidently deciding against such a direct confrontation.

The next year, Reese complained during the annual convention of the Associated Press Managing Editors organization because the AP was not routinely identifying blacks in stories it transmitted so that member papers could discriminate if they wished. The *Post-Dispatch* "subordinates Negroes," he said, "but sometimes we are out on page one with a story about black people, assuming they are white." The Associated Press declined to change its practice.[72] Pulitzer may not have heard about that, but in another instance a reporter had complained to Coghlan that the news department was deliberately playing down the story of sit-in demonstrations by black women who were refused lunch counter service at three St. Louis department stores. Coghlan routed the memo to Pulitzer, seeing no point in consulting Reese. The paper had printed a three-paragraph story, and the city's two other dailies printed nothing at all. "We have been generally friendly to Negroes," Coghlan wrote, "but if we go too far we will arouse deep antagonisms and perhaps do more harm than good. What puzzles me is just how far is too far. I would be pleased to have any suggestion from you that you might care to give."[73]

Pulitzer had no answer; it was a dilemma with which he continued to struggle. In 1950, after reading a letter to the editor from a black St. Louisan, Henry Winfield Wheeler, that struck him "as an almost perfect statement of the Negro cause," he asked reporter Donald Grant to interview the man with a view toward publishing the story on the Sunday editorial title page. Again he was apprehensive, beginning the memo to Grant: "There is dynamite in this suggestion."[74] Grant sought the interview, and Wheeler, who preferred to write rather than speak his thoughts, wrote a letter to the reporter identifying grievances of the type that in a few years became the text of the black civil rights movement. He began by saying blacks want "the same treatment under our Constitution as every other American citizen," including the right to marry whom they choose, regardless of color. He continued:

> The persons, be they Black or White, who object to this right are Fascist in their thinking. I want my daughter to have the right to go to a Public School, not as a Colored girl, but as an American girl enjoying the same opportunity as her White playmate. I want my boy and my girl to be given the same job opportunity according to their ability and efficiency as any other individual. I want the right to eat and sleep in any hotel that I can pay the price. I want the right to live anywhere that I choose in any neighborhood so long as I am a law-abiding citizen. I want the right

to go into any Theater or Public Place just like all other
Folks. I want the right to enjoy peace and prosperity under
the stars and stripes, which rights have been bought by all
of us by blood and tears and toil. I want Human Dignity.

"I am sorry to report," Grant wrote in submitting this to Pulitzer,
"that in my opinion an interview with Mr. Wheeler would not be
suitable for publication." Pulitzer agreed, saying, "I fear I made a
mistake" in suggesting the interview. "I agree that publication of
his views would do the Negro cause more harm than good."[75]

While that exchange was taking place, the paper was in the
midst of printing a hard-hitting thirteen-week series that Pulitzer
helped plan, entitled "Progress or Decay? St. Louis Must Choose."
Eight of the segments included information about the needs and
problems of blacks, and one was devoted entirely to that topic.
Blacks, among others, benefited directly from the urban redevelop-
ment projects that the series spawned. The newspaper began the
fund-raising effort with a $250,000 pledge.[76]

This answered a call beyond what most editors of the day would
have considered their duty. Even without it, Pulitzer might have
concluded that the paper's efforts toward improved race relations
had been more than adequate. He could have pointed to John
Gunther's conclusion in *Inside U.S.A.,* published in 1947, that the
Post-Dispatch "is probably the most effective liberal newspaper in
the United States." Gunther credited the paper with helping to
make St. Louis "a great town for civil liberties" whose "intellectual
climate is almost all that a civilized person can ask. The city is 13
percent Negro; yet in spite of this fact, the Negro problem is
nowhere near the preoccupation that it is in [neighboring] Kansas
City."[77]

Coming seven years before the landmark Supreme Court school
desegregation decision,[78] this was high praise, but it also obscured
some harsh realities the newspaper did not ignore. "There is more
than tolerance and democracy to be considered," the "Progress or
Decay" series pointed out, when the facts were that blacks in St.
Louis were on the "short end" of education, jobs, pay, housing,
and recreational and health facilities. Among other specifics, it
noted that neither the city nor the county had a single nursing or
convalescent home open to blacks, that schools were only partially

integrated, and that just weeks before the city's board of aldermen had voted 21 to 6 against desegregating theaters, restaurants, hotels, and other public places.[79] With so much unfinished business, Pulitzer had no illusions about being able to swiftly overcome white resistance but stayed with his gradualist approach, a version of the Court's eventually battered "all deliberate speed" formula for school desegregation. "I advise going slow in pressing the subject of non-segregation in hotels and restaurants," Pulitzer cautioned the editorial page in late 1954, a few months before his death, "lest we do the cause of non-segregation more harm than good."[80]

World War II

Events leading to the Second World War were well under way as Pulitzer entered the most active period of his editorship. Other than a brief *World* campaign in 1895 which helped avert war with England over a disputed Venezuelan boundary,[1] and the jingoistic example of the *World* during the Spanish-American conflict, there was nothing he could draw on in the experience of his father in fashioning the paper's response to the threat and then the reality of the ordeal of a second world war. Bovard, who had largely superintended coverage of World War I, was gone. The question of how to respond to the rival authoritarian ideologies of fascism and communism was both complex and new.

His early memorandums give the impression of a man reluctant to enter this unfamiliar terrain. At first, he shared the widespread hope that a second war in Europe could be averted, even though the editorial page, of which Charles G. Ross had become editor in 1934, had been skeptical of British Prime Minister Neville Chamberlain's appeasement efforts. "I must confess that as much as I despise totalitarianism, I have thought from the first that Chamberlain was right in trying for an understanding with Italy and Germany and that it ill-becomes us Americans who conceived of and then gave a death blow to the League of Nations to criticize Chamberlain and his present policy," he wrote Ross in March 1938. "As long as England is unprepared and unwilling to fight, what on earth can she do but attempt to negotiate as best she can?" He wondered whether writer Ferd Gottlieb's editorials had been "tinged by his particularly violent hatred of Hitler."[2]

Two months later he leaned definitely toward isolationism as he wrote, "Instead of making faces at and giving lectures to European fascists, we should concern ourselves with our own failures to live up to the duties imposed on us by the democratic process here in the United States." It seemed to him that, in Germany, "fascism was a natural development resulting from the natural inability of the Germans to govern themselves. Why not tell our readers so and tell them that if they want to do something to prevent fascism in this country, the place to do it is at the polls? Meanwhile, much as I despise fascism, let us not overlook the popular support which put Hitler and Mussolini into office."[3] He was more emphatic by fall, telegramming editorial writer Ralph Coghlan, "However much you and I may despise Hitler, our people are certainly and rightly so not in favor of our going to war to help in another remaking of Europe. As I see it, we can only hope that the British efforts toward conciliation will at least temporarily be successful."[4]

Most of all, he hoped that the United States could remain neutral. Two years after opposing Franklin Roosevelt's reelection, Pulitzer drafted an editorial that in effect retracted his earlier doubts about the man. He now believed that with Roosevelt committed to neutrality, the United States could "escape some of the worst effects of the present world madness." The shift in favor of the President was "unimportant," he argued, against the greater need for a government "that will preserve our liberties and help our people to withstand the attacks that have staggered most of the civilized world. . . . Whenever Roosevelt is helping to preserve

American democracy . . . we are pro-Roosevelt." He left a small
space for a retreat from total isolation by noting that the *Post-
Dispatch* should strive to present "a realistic understanding of
what is happening" and interpret those events "to the end that
there may be preserved, as far as possible, the kind of country, the
kind of civilization, that we all love."[5]

Following the declarations of war against Germany by Great
Britain and France in September 1939, the paper began carrying a
daily war summary in addition to separate stories on individual
developments. When a survey showed that among *Post-Dispatch*
readers, 74 percent of the men and 64 percent of the women read
the war summary, it seemed to Pulitzer that the paper should
present more summaries of all the news. Armed with the support
of four others, including Coghlan, who was now in charge of the
editorial page, and cartoonist Daniel R. Fitzpatrick, Reese replied
to Pulitzer, "Frankly, I think your plan would cheapen your paper."
Preparing additional summaries, Reese argued, would require
more staff at increased cost, consume too much space, and require
alteration of the conservative typographical display to which
readers—Pulitzer himself included, Reese pointed out—had grown
accustomed. He also expressed a concern that one cannot imagine
coming from Bovard, his predecessor: that additional summariz-
ing might "reduce our pulling power for advertisers" because
readers might settle for the summaries and not read inside pages
carrying ads.[6] Obliquely evoking one of the first J.P.'s misdeeds,
editorial writer Irving Dilliard contended that an expansion of
war bulletins "would throw us right into the machinery of whip-
ping up a war psychology. The *Post-Dispatch* would be doing the
very thing which certain newspapers are criticized in history for
having done in the Spanish-American war." He thought the paper
had already given the war "more attention than it deserves,"
pointing to the leading editorial of the previous day, "which was
meant to remind our readers that an overwhelming number of
problems remain to be worked out in the United States regardless
of war in Europe."[7]

Pulitzer put the expansion of summaries "on ice,"[8] but remained
more intensely interested in war coverage than anything else. He
suggested a page one editorial to "explain in part at least the
hopeless contradictions that are occurring nearly every day in 'it

is reported' stories never subsequently verified and censored news reports from the opposing sides." He thought the paper would benefit if "it takes its readers into its confidence and admits that it is not omniscient."[9] Both Reese and Coghlan disagreed, arguing, in Coghlan's words, that such an admission "would have the psychological effect of impairing" rather than improving reader confidence. "After all," he reasoned, "the function of a newspaper is to present the news in true detail and perspective at all times — in war and peace. This is much more difficult in war time, but we dare not admit it is *too* difficult; otherwise we in effect confess ourselves incompetent in a crisis. I think the contrary is true."[10] Again, Pulitzer was dissuaded.

There was a family factor in his concern over the flow and reliability of news from Europe. His eldest son, Joseph Pulitzer III (known then and now as Joseph Pulitzer Jr.), and his bride of three months, the former Louise Vauclain of Philadelphia, were completing a summer-long European wedding trip in Italy as Hitler's expansionism continued. They had been joined in August by Kate Davis Pulitzer, the publisher's eldest daughter, and were staying at a house they had rented for the month from close American friends Charles H. (Buddie) and Brooke Marshall[11] at Porto Fino when Germany and the Soviet Union signed the nonaggression pact — causing many, Pulitzer included, to believe war was imminent. The young people were not particularly concerned because the Italians they knew did not seem worried. At the end of August, they began making their way by car back to France, reaching the northern coast on August 30. They saw military preparations all along their route in France. On August 31, thanks to Pulitzer's efforts through ambassadorial channels, they got the last available places on the British liner *Andora Star* out of Cherbourg. They abandoned their car, which would never be recovered.[12] German troops invaded Poland within hours, followed by the British and French declarations of war. Throughout this time, civilian communications across the Atlantic were virtually impossible. Pulitzer's last word from his children had been on August 29, and he became desperately fearful for their safety. After an anxious week, during which he sent a flurry of cables and sought U.S. State Department assistance through the paper's Washington bureau, Pulitzer got word that they would reach New York on September 13. The crossing took longer than usual because the ship followed a zigzag course as a precaution against submarine attack. That precaution was well justified. On September 3, a German submarine sank the British liner *Athenia.* There were twenty-eight Americans among those who died.[13]

Although both Reese and Coghlan remained strongly for neutrality, Pulitzer gradually moved during 1940 from opposition to ambivalence to a firm belief that the United States must aid the Allied nations. In May, he suggested that the Washington bureau do an article on the President's use of the Rev. George Endicott Peabody, headmaster of FDR's prep school, Groton, for support and guidance. "As I see it, there is something genuinely sentimental in Roosevelt's dependence on . . . 'the Rector,' as Grotties call him," he wrote Ross, who had left the editorial page to return to the Washington bureau. "Evidently it is a case of a religious man who believes he can bring religious forces to bear to win and end the war."[14] At about the same time, however, Reese informed Washington correspondent Childs that after consulting Pulitzer, Coghlan, and Brandt he had decided not to print an article Childs had written about the diminishing British fleet. "We do not want to publish anything . . . that might be construed as propaganda intended to push us into war," he explained.[15] Two days later, Pulitzer told Coghlan that he didn't think even the severing of U.S. Atlantic and Pacific trade routes by the Germans and Japanese would justify entering the war. However, should the Germans "steam up the St. Lawrence and bomb hell out of the Chateau Frontenac Hotel in Quebec, which is just the distance of a long home run from the American shore," or land in Cuba, Nassau, or Bermuda, "I am convinced we would have to resist with force."[16] He also sympathized with listener complaints that National Broadcasting Company commentator H. V. Kaltenborn was encouraging intervention in broadcasts heard over *Post-Dispatch* radio station KSD. "I will not permit a hired hand like Kaltenborn to foment war hysteria over our station," he declared, adding that the commentator would be dropped if this continued.[17]

Events moved swiftly. On June 3, the War Department agreed to sell surplus and outdated war materials to Great Britain; on June 5, Germany invaded France. In a speech at the University of Virginia on June 10, Roosevelt shifted U.S. policy from "neutrality" to "nonbelligerency." Commenting on this—without consulting Pulitzer, who had just started his annual salmon-fishing vacation on the Restigouche River in Quebec—Coghlan charged in an angry lead editorial headed "To the Brink" that "President Roosevelt all but declared war yesterday."[18] Roosevelt had recklessly ignored a number of important facts, he asserted. Among these were that there had been no overt acts by Germany against the United States; that polls showed public opinion strongly against entering the war, and that the U.S. Army "is microscopic compared with the great legions of Germany, Italy and France." He described the European hostilities as the outgrowth of "age-old hatreds" in which the United States had no part. It was too much to ask this country to "police the world"; it should be asked only to keep others "from transporting their wars to this hemisphere."

Calls and letters of agreement poured into the *Post-Dispatch.* Staff members were greeted with congratulations wherever they went. A woman from suburban Webster Groves told Coghlan that Roosevelt "reminded her of a drunken man out in a street looking for a fight." Members of the board trustees of the public library in nearby Collinsville, Illinois, told fellow trustee Irving Dilliard how fully the editorial "stated their own sentiments." Advertising manager George M. Burbach brought word that the directors of the St. Louis Municipal Opera were "highly enthusiastic about our editorial." U.S. Senator Bennett Champ Clark of Missouri, who had not been treated kindly by the *Post-Dispatch,* found the piece "so excellent" that it overpowered his dislike of the newspaper. He had the editorial read into the *Congressional Record.* [19]

Coghlan was "absolutely dazed" by the response. "I thought Roosevelt had a powerful following for his foreign policy and that our editorial position would be unpopular," he wrote Pulitzer. But, now reassured to the contrary, "I am convinced we have something really big here and we ought to make the most of it."[20] It took a few days for Pulitzer to respond. Reader-secretary Lincoln Hockaday had not yet arrived at the fishing camp, and the editorial had been garbled by the French-speaking telegraph operator who received it, and further mutilated by the cockney accent of the chauffeur/factotum who read it to J.P. The man was "distinctly a better hand at making cocktails and toddies than he is at reading a garbled editorial. Besides I was suffering from hysteria at the time, not war hysteria but fish hysteria," Pulitzer confessed. His initial reaction was almost totally supportive. "Sympathizing with and helping the Allies by selling them war materials is one thing, but burning up the country with bellicose statements that are certain to lead us into war very soon and in an utterly unprepared condition is a very different thing," he wrote Coghlan.[21] He suggested that Reese devote the next editorial title page to excerpts from the recent U.S. Senate Naval Committee report detailing the country's unpreparedness. Print it in "freak body type," he advised, "so that it will catch the eye and be generally read, in other words print it as Hearst might print it."[22]

But within the week he became more temperate. Because events had moved so fast, he wrote Coghlan, he now believed that the United States must immediately extend its zone of defense to the Caribbean and, "as soon as we are prepared to do so," to the entire Western Hemisphere. He wanted the editor to understand "that at heart I am not a so-called isolationist." Despite the "past sins" of the British and French empires, it might now be "America's destiny" to lead a crusade "to keep the flame of Democracy burning in the United States and to rekindle that flame in England and France" and their possessions "now that they have been purified by their ordeal of fire."[23] On the question of conscription, he considered it a "patriotic necessity" for the *Post-Dispatch* to support a general draft vigorously. "I for one am convinced that a liberal dose of sacrifice, discipline and goose-stepping would be good for all of us," he telegraphed from Canada.[24] This rather striking shift of viewpoint in only a few days suggested that Pulitzer's commitment to isolation had from the start been considerably weaker than that of members of his news and editorial staffs.

It was, in fact, a decisive turning point for the editor-publisher, and he wanted the news as well as the editorial pages to reflect his new sense of reality. In his memorandums to Reese, his thinking turned increasingly toward subjects that would foster patriotism and loyalty to American socioeconomic arrangements. He suggested that the managing editor assign reporters to do interviews with as many as one hundred St. Louisans of German, Austrian, or Czechoslovakian origin who had recently visited Germany to find out whether they were "beginning to think that the Hitler way of life, with all its 'efficiency' is probably better for the average or below-

average income group than the American scheme." He said he had
heard that some of these people who worked as domestic servants
in St. Louis "went back to the homeland and came back disgusted,
and there are doubtless many stories on the other side and a good
many in between." But he was not in favor of publishing the story
regardless of what the interviewers found: "If the preponderant
view should turn out to be that conditions in America, bad as they
are, are a damn sight better than conditions in Germany it would,
I believe, make an exceedingly interesting and useful Sunday
story—the kind of story, by the way, that the Saturday Evening
Post might print."[25]

In the fall, when both were at Bar Harbor, he called on Walter
Lippmann to get his off-the-record views on intervention. The
columnist told him that he was opposed, but at the same time
considered it imperative that the United States keep the British
Navy afloat and from falling into German hands. For that reason
Lippmann approved of the recent exchange of fifty aged American
destroyers for rights to construct naval bases at several British
possessions, the beginning of the so-called lend-lease policy. He
was less than candid with Pulitzer about this, for by this time
Lippmann was committed to intervention on Britain's behalf and
had even helped behind the scenes to arrange the destroyer deal.[26]
"He gambles on the belief that Hitler will do everything in his
power to keep us out of war," Pulitzer recorded in a memorandum
of their talk.[27] Lippmann also told him that the realities of the
rapidly developing situation meant that President Roosevelt had
close to absolute power in deciding how to deal with the Allies,
including the power to commit the nation to war without a congressional declaration.

Many years later, Lippmann told his biographer, Ronald Steel,
that he had found it necessary to influence Pulitzer to "rein in his
staff" in order to keep the *Post-Dispatch* from demanding a congressional investigation, which would have revealed the columnist's
role in escalating U.S. involvement in the war.[28] Though Pulitzer
put nothing in writing about Lippmann's having asked him to do
this, it is plausible, given the emerging difference between the
publisher and his top editors on isolation versus intervention.
Three days before the publisher saw Lippmann, Coghlan had
written a memo to Pulitzer in which he said he was certain that

Lippmann favored U.S. intervention and "was one of those who cooked up the destroyer deal."[29] Whether this reached Pulitzer at Bar Harbor before he saw the columnist is unknown.

In any case, the day after he saw Lippmann, Pulitzer dictated some "Notes on U.S. and War," which began: "Let's get away from the appearance of pacifism and holding out the too-confident hope that we can avoid war. Let us rather tell the people that they should get ready for war." The realities, he continued, resolved into the "question of how long can we postpone war and by postponing it get ready for it. . . . If we must throw the dice with death may it not be, after all, that the Roosevelt gamble may in the long run be the best gamble? To accept this thesis one must believe, as I do, that although Roosevelt has been dangerously impulsive and emotional and irregular in many of his acts and utterances, he is not deliberately planning to lead us into war."[30]

This put Coghlan in a most uncomfortable spot. Scarcely two weeks earlier, he had written an angry lead editorial, sharply critical of the destroyer deal, under the headline "Dictator Roosevelt Commits an Act of War."[31] It concluded:

> If Roosevelt gets away with this, we may as well say good-by to our liberties and make up our minds that henceforth we live under a dictatorship.
>
> If Congress and the people do not rise in solemn wrath to stop Roosevelt now—at this moment—then the country deserves the stupendous tragedy that looms right around the corner.

Pulitzer had been with him then. In fact, they had agreed that the *Post-Dispatch* should buy a full page in the *New York Times* to reprint the editorial.[32] But now Pulitzer wanted him to stop attacking Roosevelt: "I hope we can for the present at least cease charging the President with jingoism and dictatorship. . . . Let us make our position crystal clear . . . that we are not blind isolationists, that we are not for peace at any price, that we see all too clearly the menace of Hitler and Hitlerism and that our one and only objective is WE MUST GET READY FOR WAR."[33]

He then drafted a long memorandum outlining the paper's editorial position on the war. "I know, my dear Ralph, that you have agonized over this problem to a point that brought you close to a nervous collapse," he wrote toward the end. He said he realized that he and Coghlan disagreed about the President's intentions, but that he had concluded after "a very close and studied re-reading" of Roosevelt's July speech accepting the Democratic nomination for a third term "that he is not deliberately or with calculated recklessness leading us into war."[34] Instead, he argued—much as Lippmann had, though he did not mention having consulted the columnist—the President was only being realistic and pragmatic.

Shortly thereafter the paper editorially endorsed Roosevelt for a third term. This generated several rumors among disappointed readers. One was that powerful advertisers had dictated the choice. Another was that the paper had exchanged its endorsement for Federal Communications Commission permission to operate radio station KSD full-time. Yet another claimed that Herbert Pulitzer controlled *Post-Dispatch* purse strings and had forced his brother into making the endorsement.[35] The *New York Times* ran two short items about the endorsement, one headed "Supports President It Called Dictator," the other reproducing *New York Herald Tribune* editor Ogden Reid's wire to Pulitzer: "Say it ain't so, Joe."[36]

Although Coghlan tried to constrain his isolationist beliefs, by 1941 he decided he could compromise no further. He asked for a leave of absence without pay or a transfer to another part of the paper. "I think it is a monumental error for the United States to enter the European war," he told Pulitzer. He believed the nation had "a separate destiny," which it would sacrifice by entering the war, and that Pulitzer's policy required him to soft-pedal or ignore his strong convictions. "I feel I have been in a strait-jacket and no man can work well in a strait-jacket," he explained. "I have felt that I was engaged on two fronts, the journalistic front and the front-office front."[37]

Pulitzer did not respond directly in writing. However, his memorandums over the next several weeks indicate that he managed to keep Coghlan on the page by becoming more conciliatory toward the editor and more reserved than previously in his expressions of support for Roosevelt. For example, calling it "purely a suggestion," he thought the President might be reminded editorially: "You were elected largely on your promises not to take us into war, but since election you have said little or nothing to confirm your pre-election pledges. . . . If you think the country should go to war or that it inevitably will be drawn into the war, has not the country a right to know your opinion?" At the same time, though, he stressed "that if we say this it should be so phrased as to make it impossible for anyone to say that we are trying to cast a slur on the honesty of the President's pre-election promises."[38]

Just the week before writing that, Pulitzer had met with Roosevelt in Washington, D.C., to ask the President to use his influence to get Herbert Pulitzer accepted into the Navy as a pilot. His younger brother had been a Navy flier and flying instructor during World War I but was a questionable candidate for reenlistment because his right eye had been removed in 1934. One-eyed pilots were not unheard of, but despite his brother's efforts Herbert was rejected and so joined the Royal Air Force. He spent the war years in England. In thanking Roosevelt for seeing him about this matter, Pulitzer wrote: "I thought your Inaugural Address was magnificent."[39]

For the balance of the year, Pulitzer held to his belief in the inevitability of U.S. involvement. In late May, he drew a rather drastic picture in resisting pressure from Coghlan and others on the editorial staff to make a firm commitment to isolation. The situation was so grave, he contended, that he supported "our present policy of taking more and more risks of war" even though that could mean that "much of our present so-called 'civilization' " and "our recent conception of capitalism, the profit system and free enterprise" are gone forever. He would concede that Germany might win and admit to readers "the hideous possibility and even probability" that this war, like the last, would not make the world safe for democracy. It would be necessary to fight "solely and simply because we think that Hitler is likely, sooner or later, to menace our American liberties. Trade is not worth fighting for; the American standard of living is not worth fighting for; world power is not worth fighting for. American liberty is worth fighting for."[40]

The memo was to Coghlan, but Reese read it first and objected forcefully. He saw no need to "flop over to intervention," shocking readers and giving the *Star-Times* the opportunity to "take full page one advantage of this, probably with some . . . copy on previous jumping beans." Instead, he counseled restraint, arguing, "It will not be long before the administration will lead to the way outlined in your memorandum."[41] Apparently accepting this, Pulitzer relaxed his pressure on the editorial page, but he grumbled that a mechanics' strike in California which was delaying shipbuilding "seems unpatriotic." He showed impatience in saying he agreed when Joseph P. Kennedy, former U.S. Ambassador to Great Britain, told Yale graduates it would be proper to criticize the President if one conscientiously believed presidential inaction was endangering the country.[42] By midsummer—after the Nazis had attacked the Soviet Union and as U.S. lend-lease support and convoying of goods had been stepped up—Pulitzer found himself "disturbed over the people's seeming lethargy, indifference, tendency to be fatalistic, lack of 'unity,' or however you want to describe it" and wanting "to change the tone of our page from its more or less passive . . . acquiescence in the Roosevelt policy to a very much more positive tone." This would "bring home to the people the need for the ultimate elimination of Hitlerism from this world even though that should involve landing another A.E.F. [American Expeditionary Force] in Europe to do it."[43]

Back in the office in late August after two months of treatment for tuberculosis at a Colorado sanitarium, Coghlan, like Reese, argued for letting events guide a gradual pro-war shift: "Since the Post-Dispatch has been accused of leftist tendencies because of our liberal views, and because we are not afraid to attack wrong . . . I can easily imagine critics saying: 'Oh, yes, the Post-Dispatch was against the war until Russia got into it, but now it is all in favor of going in and saving the Bolsheviks.' We would be accused of following the party line. Such word-of-mouth advertising in a Catholic city like St. Louis would not do us any good."[44] Pulitzer responded that Coghlan had made a "beautifully reasoned argument. . . . I hasten to say that I do trust you completely to put into execution the policy of 'gradualness' which you describe." His said his views in May had been "badly expressed and could very easily be misunderstood as indicating that I want the paper to do pronto another Mexican jumping bean act. I did not have that in mind or if I did I stand corrected."

As conciliatory as that sounded, however, Pulitzer made it quite

clear that he expected the staff to move clearly away from isolationism and criticism of the President, adding:

> What I do deplore is evidence I seem to find from time to
> time and not infrequently in Fitz's cartoons of a deep—
> forgive me for saying so but at times it seems almost
> hysterical—distrust of Roosevelt's purpose. Parenthetically,
> let me say that you personally have not written a line
> of this kind. Although I was, I admit, very distrustful of
> Roosevelt when he pulled his secret destroyer deal I'm
> bound to tell you I've gotten over it. . . . I do think that the
> man deserves our confidence and the confidence of the
> country. . . . I must say that I sympathize with FDR deeply
> when he likens himself to Lincoln in the desperate days of
> the Civil War.[45]

He shortly ordered the preparation of articles describing "progress
and delay" in the nation's defense readiness, believing that the
public had been subjected to a campaign "of positive misinformation": "It was being deluged with a great hullabaloo about the
industrial might of America with all kinds of headlines about all
kinds of production worth all kinds of billions to a point where the
average reader, myself included, could not help thinking that everything was fine. It was Baruch who woke me up and he fairly
sickened me with the picture he gave me of confusion, of lost
time, guns without ammunition, tanks without guns, etc., etc.,
etc."[46]

Bernard Mannes Baruch, then seventy-one, the wealthy, retired
financier who had become an adviser to presidents (Woodrow
Wilson had called him "Dr. Facts") was to Pulitzer both a friend
and a seer. The so-called "elder statesman," who had served as
chairman of the War Industries Board during World War I, declined
a similar post under Roosevelt but served unofficially without pay
as a close critic-adviser to the administration as the second world
crisis developed. At the same time, as one of his biographers put
it, he "carefully cultivated his friendships with the top moguls of
journalism." In turn, he was highly regarded by most newspapers,
and one, the *Illinois State Journal,* called him "the most useful
citizen of America."[47]

Usually through Washington correspondents Raymond Brandt or Marquis Childs, but sometimes personally, Pulitzer frequently sought Baruch's counsel to aid his editorial decision-making. "You are a good man to talk to," Baruch wrote J.P. in mid-1941, "because you listen, absorb and then have something to give back."[48] The two men stayed in close touch as the United States moved toward active combat in 1941 and throughout the war. In 1943, Baruch's influence got Childs a rare, private, off-the-record meeting with Prime Minister Churchill in London.[49] (When Pulitzer ran afoul of the game laws that year while duck-hunting, Baruch offered to speak to Interior Secretary Harold Ickes about it, but Childs, certain the publisher would not want this, politely declined.[50])

Despite the deterioration throughout 1941 of relations between the United States and Japan, which had signed a mutual defense pact with Germany and Italy in September 1940, Pulitzer and his editors focused nearly all their attention on Europe. In May, Reese had raised the question of whether Japan would declare war on the United States if the Navy, in convoying goods to Great Britain, began shooting to deter German submarine threats to the American ships. He was concerned about how the United States could handle "a two-ocean war with a one-ocean Navy."[51] The attack on Pearl Harbor made that worry a reality. Among measures taken to protect the U.S. coastline from attack, Pulitzer's yacht *Discoverer* and a number of other pleasure craft were taken over by the Coast Guard and used as patrol boats.

Still, the defeat of Hitler remained the primary concern in 1942. Pulitzer wanted *Post-Dispatch* readers to understand the limitations and personal sacrifices the war would impose on all of them. He also wanted them to unite strongly behind the President. He had a "tremendous feeling of sympathy," he wrote Childs, "which I am sure nearly everyone feels, for the dreadfully, almost sickeningly, over-burdened man in the White House." He said that after his daughter Elinor, who was county chairman of the infantile paralysis drive, had reminded him that the President would be sixty on January 30, he had decided to devote a full page of the Sunday magazine to full-length photographs of Roosevelt "as Secretary of the Navy running through France in his riding breeches, and Roosevelt today, letting the pictures tell their own tragic story." He asked Childs to write "a deeply sympathetic human interest story — of course, without slopping over — " to accompany the photos.[52]

At the end of the month, Childs reported that Baruch had told him, in response to a question, that if he were running a newspaper he would "make a decided distinction between facts that might give harmful information to the enemy and facts that the country should know in the interest of its own safety." He believed that no man, "even the President," was above considerations of the public welfare and warned that public complacency and overconfidence were great dangers. Childs also reported on Baruch's attitude toward the newly created War Production Board (WPB) under the chairmanship of Donald M. Nelson, a production executive with Sears Roebuck Company, saying that Baruch's candidate to head the effort had been Supreme Court Justice James F. Byrnes. Childs said he interpreted "this to mean, in view of Byrnes' obvious unfitness, that Mr. Baruch wanted to run the show himself from behind the scenes." As it had turned out, Childs continued, Baruch, "who is not without his own vanities, [is] pleased that Nelson constantly consults him and has even invited him to sit in on sessions of WPB."[53] The following year, Roosevelt created the Office of War Mobilization to coordinate the work of all the domestic war agencies and named Baruch's man Byrnes, whom he dubbed "Assistant President," as its head.[54]

Pulitzer had a sense of mission similar to Baruch's. As an editorial idea, he wrote to Coghlan in early February that "before 6 American welders or 60 or 600 go on strike, they should think to themselves that in a sense they are in direct hand-to-hand combat just as much so as if they were in a bayonet charge against 6 or 60 or 600 German or Japanese welders. . . . In truth this philosophy applies to every last one of us, however obscure or inconspicuous may be my part or your part or their parts in helping to win this war."[55] After Nelson was named to head the War Production Board, he wanted the editorial page to support him: "The business man in this country has been denounced from hell to breakfast and usually he has had it coming to him. But even a penny-pinching note-shaving dealer in pots and pans, when he delivers . . . in good quality and at a fair price, is performing, let us not forget, a highly useful function."[56]

Newspapers — more than any other medium — were important

too, he contended, suggesting that "we throw bouquets at our competitor the Globe-Democrat—and possibly the Star, although I seldom read it—and ourselves" for helping St. Louisans understand the war. He would, naturally, emphasize *Post-Dispatch* contributions, "but almost EQUALLY" the *Globe-Democrat*'s, because it provided some news services and commentators not available in the *Post-Dispatch*. "I DO think that in these days of lazy, casual listening to the radio (although I would not say this for we don't have to say it) we might well, by implication, remind the reader of what a hell of a fix he would be in without his American newspaper."[57]

From this point forward, there was no question about how firmly Pulitzer stood behind the Allied war effort. This was dramatically evidenced in a short leading editorial he wrote in early March 1942 and had printed in bastard measure and type almost twice the usual size:

WAR PROGRAM FOR THE HOME FRONT

> To win this war,
> We must keep production up—
> And we must keep inflation down.
> This means:
> Everybody working,
> No strikes,
> Every machine running 24 hours a day;
> And it also means:
> Ceilings on profits, prices and wages.[58]

The statement about inflation followed Baruch. Pulitzer wired Childs to "give Bernie my best and ask him how he likes our 'War Program for the Home Front,' which we are repeating editorially from time to time."[59]

In addition to watching the domestic front, Pulitzer felt he needed a better grasp of events in Europe. In early summer, he asked the British ambassador to the United States to recommend an Englishman, preferably a graduate of Oxford or Cambridge University, who knew and understood the European war theater. He wanted such a man to be one of his secretaries. The ambassador suggested A. Mervyn Davies, a 1923 Oxford graduate who specialized in history, had served with the British air force in World War I, and was currently with the British Information Service in New York. Davies was hired and taken immediately to Bar Harbor. He mainly summarized and read from leading British newspapers and periodicals for Pulitzer, but because Pulitzer had only one secretary at a time with him at Bar Harbor, Davies had to attend to all the mail and personal matters as well. Back in St. Louis, he was more the specialist. When it appeared that Winston Churchill was to be the main architect of British war policy, Davies spent an entire day describing Churchill's life and career to Pulitzer. On another occasion, he gave the publisher a detailed description of the Balkan invasion. Pulitzer kept a huge globe in his office, mounted in a movable floor stand. Because J.P. could see its markings with relative ease, Davies often used it to explain troop and ship movements.

Davies sometimes contributed editorials about the war to the newspaper. He had become a U.S. citizen and, because of his training and background, was interviewed by a military official as a candidate for what was described as a "strategic and very dangerous mission" with about twelve others in Europe. Pleased to have been "tapped on the shoulder by Uncle Sam," Davies was disappointed when he wasn't selected. He later learned that Pulitzer had intervened, arguing that Davies was already in a strategic position and should stay at the *Post-Dispatch*.[60] Pulitzer also tried to keep editorial writer Dilliard out of the Army, going as far as to seek Roosevelt's intervention.[61] But Dilliard felt he should serve, dissuaded Pulitzer, and was granted a leave of absence. He rose to the rank of lieutenant colonel in military government work.[62]

The paper's support of the war did not eliminate every difference between Pulitzer and the editorial page. Another clash developed in September 1942 after Coghlan ran several editorials critical of the United States and Great Britain for failing to establish a so-called "second front." The purpose would be to cause a division of the German forces and thus weaken the Nazi advance into the Soviet Union, which had been under way since Germany had violated a nonaggression pact and invaded Russia in June 1941. Pulitzer believed the two countries were unprepared to take on this new task and ordered the editorials stopped. "I especially object to spreading the suspicion that Roosevelt and Churchill are deliberately letting Russia bleed to death in order to save Tory capitalism," he explained. "I will not, and positively do not, believe it of Roosevelt and Churchill. I really think it is wrong to spread the idea."[63] He was particularly critical of the "loose thinking and looser writing" in an editorial by Ernest Kirschten and suggested that Coghlan let Kirschten go whenever he could find a replacement. But Coghlan came to Kirschten's defense, saying he thought the editorial "was a good one" and that its reference to the bleeding of Russia had been "sufficiently qualified" as a "terrible suspicion" so that "no one could possibly accuse us of harboring such an idea."[64] However, he pledged to print nothing more on the subject.

Pulitzer's confidence in Roosevelt and Churchill proved justified when the British and the Americans launched their North African campaign in late October and over the next several months reduced the German forces by fifteen divisions and more than 2,000 airplanes.[65] In mid-November he drafted an editorial memorandum to Coghlan in which he said the *Post-Dispatch* now had "only two choices," either to ignore the fact that a second front had been established or, "preferably, come out flatly and plainly and say, in effect":

> Mr. President, we salute you. When we were arguing for a second front last summer to relieve Russia, you were planning such a second front, and quite obviously and quite properly we knew nothing whatsoever of your plans. Those were dark days in June and July. We had to have a second front. We along with everyone else knew that and said so. You knew it too. But you couldn't say so. Now you have given us a second front, and in doing so you have magnificently and brilliantly lived up to your title as Commander-in-Chief. If our urgings and our criticisms seemed to you at the time to be unjustified we regret them.

After dictating the memo, however, he apparently decided silence would be the better choice and didn't send it to Coghlan.[66]

On the home front, Pulitzer was pleased by the extent of labor and management cooperation in keeping production up and inflation down. One example was Emerson Electric Company in St. Louis, headed by his friend Stuart Symington (later Secretary of

the Air Force, a U.S. senator, and a Democratic presidential hopeful),
whom he described as "an unusually liberal, honest and patriotic
young business man with a good labor record and a personal
record of working day and night to turn out government orders at
a very modest profit."[67]

Further evidence of his hawkishness showed up in Pulitzer's
occasional use of the pseudonym "Stephen Decatur," after a U.S.
Navy hero of the War of 1812, to sign letters he wanted printed on
the editorial page. In one published in early 1942, he dealt with the
question "What are we fighting for this time?" which he presented
as having arisen in a discussion between a World War I veteran
and a young soldier. The best answer the veteran could have
given, "Decatur" concluded, was: "If you want to know what
you're fighting for, why don't you take a trip over to Berchtesgaden
and ask Hitler for the answer...? He would probably turn a
couple of handsprings and then sing you a verse from the German
battle song, 'Today Europe is ours; tomorrow the whole world.' "[68]

At the beginning of 1943, as the Allies' outlook improved, Pulitzer
decided that the question "What are we fighting for?" deserved
deeper consideration in order to "stimulate and clarify public
thinking" about world cooperation after the war. Pulitzer, Ross,
Reese, Coghlan, and Julius H. Klyman, editor of the paper's rotogravure "Pictures" section, agreed to invite a list of prominent
people representing various shades of economic, political, and
social concern to contribute articles to a "symposium" on the
question. The focus would be on "general principles" in the belief
that "specific blueprints on highly controversial questions such as
independence for Poland, Finland or India, Japanese immigration
or the Negro problem might cause disunity. Agreement on general
principles is important; details can and must come later."[69]

The twenty articles were published between February 21 and
May 2, 1943, and later made available in booklet form. Both
President Roosevelt and Vice President Henry A. Wallace provided
statements, Roosevelt observing, "There is an important job of
education to be done so that the tragedy of war will not come
again."[70] Pulitzer told Reese that he liked "Wallace's vision of a
middle class world with a strongly competitive economy, with
government giving employment when private enterprise fails to do
so, and I like, also, his clear statement of the fact that where more

than one-half of the people cannot read and write democracy is impossible and force has to be employed."[71]

Among the contributors were George W. Norris, former U.S. senator from Nebraska; Virginius Dabney, editor of the *Richmond (Va.) Times-Dispatch;* Robert Moses, New York City park commissioner; Harold G. Moulton, president of the Brookings Institution; Philip Murray, president of the Congress of Industrial Organizations; Wayne L. Morse, a member of the National War Labor Board; Robert Minor, assistant general secretary of the Communist party in the United States; Mrs. George Gelhorn, St. Louis leader of the National League of Women Voters; the Right Rev. William Scarlett, Episcopal bishop of Missouri; and James P. Whiteside, a "common man" from Missouri.

Despite their differing perspectives and points of particular emphasis, there was among the contributors a thread of agreement about war aims which was reflective of the popular consensus on the correctness of the Allied cause. The first objective, it was agreed, was to win the war; the second was to achieve international cooperation and understanding sufficient to maintain peace. There was little disposition to go lightly with the Axis powers. "Victory cannot come by appeasement," wrote Senator Norris. "It cannot come by a negotiated peace. There must be an absolute and unconditional surrender."[72] There is no question that Pulitzer fully agreed.

After the series started, Edgar Monsanto Queeny, chairman of the Monsanto Chemical Company, with headquarters in St. Louis, and a social friend of Pulitzer's, complained that he didn't think "the industrialists' point of view" had been presented. Pulitzer invited him to do so. The piece was, predictably, a spirited exposition of "free enterprise." In submitting it, Queeny told Pulitzer: "And we can do all that is promised if your old sheet will keep *That Man* out of the White House for the fourth term!"[73] That advice was not followed. When the time came, Pulitzer instructed Coghlan to come out for Franklin Roosevelt: "In a nutshell—this is not intended for editorial use—'with all his faults we love him still.'" He thought that after the election, though, it would be well to "tell Roosevelt that were it not for the war he would not have been re-elected, that under ordinary circumstances no one has any use for a fourth term."[74]

Pulitzer's eldest son read the "What Are We Fighting For?" series in Hawaii, where he had been sent after taking Navy officer training in 1942. Because he had for several years been working in a news-editorial apprenticeship similar to that his father had served—absent, notably, the extremes of paternal temperament—he was first assigned to shore duty in a public relations office. Among other things, he wrote his father, the unit reviewed press reports for breaches of "the Navy's conception of military security— frequently violated by Time and Life, incidentally." It was not particularly hazardous duty as he described it, and although he missed his wife, Louise (Lulu to her friends), and disliked the curfew, blackouts, and wartime shortages, he found the assignment "very pleasant."[75] He gave this up, however, by requesting sea duty, and he spent twenty-seven months on a destroyer, earning five battle stars in various engagements in the central and south Pacific. An art collector since his Harvard days in the mid-1930s, he noted in a letter to his father's business secretary, Arch R. King, who had helped him arrange insurance for his growing collection, that he had picked up a couple of native spears in the Solomon Islands "which are not quite good enough to put on my fine arts policy."[76] His most profound wartime experience came during an assignment to inspect Japanese ground installations after the U.S. Marines captured Iwo Jima. He found a book on the art of Vincent Van Gogh in a foxhole. "I thought of some desperate Japanese soldier trying to escape the horrors of fighting," he recalled. "It made me reflect on the futility of war. . . . It sobered me up."[77]

Two of his cousins, also grandsons of the first Joseph Pulitzer, died in combat. Army Private First Class William S. Moore Jr. was killed in France on November 11, 1944, at the age of twenty-four, and his brother, Marine Private First Class Richard W. Moore, died on Okinawa on June 19, 1945, at twenty-three. Richard, who had survived the Iwo Jima campaign, had volunteered, despite family protests, for the second Pacific assignment. The brothers were sons of the former Edith Louise Pulitzer and William S. Moore. Two other of their five sons, Lieutenant David E. Moore and Flight Officer Adrian P. Moore, served during the war.[78] As previously noted, a son-in-law, Army Air Force Captain Henry W. Putnam, husband of the former

Kate Davis Pulitzer, died in an air raid over Tokyo on May 25, 1945.

Back in St. Louis, Pulitzer's younger daughter, Elinor, worked as a volunteer at Barnes Hospital, and Mrs. Pulitzer worked five afternoons a week in the surgical ward at Children's Hospital.[79] At Barnes, Elinor did some secretarial work for a young radiologist, Dr. Louis H. Hempelmann Jr., who had graduated at the head of his class at Washington University in St. Louis and served a year's internship at Phillips Brooks House in the Harvard Medical School. They were married June 5, 1943, and shortly thereafter went to Los Alamos, New Mexico, where he worked on medical aspects of the top-secret Manhattan Project, which developed the atomic bomb. Shortly before the marriage, Pulitzer wrote to his son, Joe, that at first he had not liked Hempelmann's "German parentage, but I soon concluded that he is not the Prussian type but, on the contrary, is the good type of German." He thought the young man showed "great promise of developing into an important and highly useful scientist."[80] Dr. Hempelmann became an authority on the biological effects of radiation as a researcher with the United States Public Health Service and the University of Rochester School of Medicine and Dentistry in New York.[81] Joseph Jr.'s wife, Lulu, lived in Washington, D.C., during the war. She was one of the organizers and a co-director of the Stage Door Canteen, which arranged performances for military personnel by major artists and entertainers.[82]

At the end of 1943, Pulitzer began to think that the *Post-Dispatch* should be doing some of its own European coverage rather than relying on wire service and syndicate dispatches—as it had until now, except for the month Childs spent in England that summer.[83] He first tried to get permission to go himself to North Africa, Italy, and England, but the Army Public Relations Bureau had a flat ban against editors and publishers visiting the front. Baruch had tried without success for a year and a half to pull strings to get Henry R. Luce of Time Inc. into those areas.[84]

But for reporters, it was different. Just before the D-day landings in France on June 6, 1944, Richard L. Stokes of the Washington bureau and Virginia Irwin, formerly a "woman's angle" and feature article writer for the paper, were accredited as correspondents. Both were enthusiastic about the work. "I should tell you how grateful I am for this assignment," Stokes wrote Pulitzer. "I have never felt so alive in my life."[85] He recounted being bombed and shelled and living the same hard life as the troops.

Irwin had it no easier and, if anything, relished the challenge even more than Stokes. She had contrived to get such an assignment for at least a year, with no success. Finally, Reese had agreed to grant her a leave of absence in mid-1943 to join the Red Cross and encouraged her to submit articles while she was away. The Red Cross sent her to England, and the articles she wrote so impressed the Washington bureau chief Brandt that he requested she be accredited. Irwin provided the paper's first report on D-day, getting her information from the first of the wounded to reach a marshaling port on England's southern coast. On July 11, she managed to get into France, and from then on she spent as much time as she could with troops in battle zones. Most of her pieces were about fighting servicemen — many of them from Missouri — written much like those of Pulitzer Prize winner Ernie Pyle, who died while covering the war in the Pacific. In one of these she wrote: "I missed eternity by a matter of yards when a German 88 shell, aimed at a bridge we had to go over, landed off to our left."[86] Yet she worried less about such hazards than about the efforts of friendly military authorities to keep her out of danger. To avoid protection, she became elusive; at times even the paper didn't know her whereabouts. Pulitzer cautioned her, "[Don't take] too many chances and don't hesitate to ask to be relieved whenever you decide you want to come home."[87] There was little chance of that.

Her greatest achievement was reaching Berlin on April 27, 1945, ten days before the German surrender on May 7, while the city was under Russian attack. Irwin and *Boston Traveler* correspondent Andrew Tully made the hazardous trip without military authorization. Displeased by this, military censors held their dispatches for release until May 8, by which time many more correspondents were in Berlin. Still, Irwin's eyewitness accounts of Berlin's fall got first-page play in copyrighted articles in the *Post-Dispatch* and, via Associated Press, were carried in many other papers. Brandt called her feat "the greatest newsbeat of the war." Pulitzer granted her a bonus of one year's salary, $4,680. Stokes, who had been handicapped by illness and problems with military censors, was not as productive as Irwin. He got a bonus of a half year's salary, $5,186.[88] Had the dollar amounts awarded been disclosed, the sharp differential between the valuation of male and female employees surely would have caused talk. Actually, allowing Irwin to become a news correspondent represented a sharp break with the past at the *Post-Dispatch,* and it did not usher in a new era of sexual equality in news-editorial employment practices. After her shining hour, the news operation returned to the Bovardian mold in which women were considered qualified only for society and feature section assignments. After the war, Irwin got some of the better such assignments, but she also got what she considered one of the worst, the paper's "Martha Carr" advice column. Stokes, in contrast, was selected to cover the Nuremberg Trials. Irwin continued to work for a number of years, but took early retirement at age fifty-five. "When I retire," she had remarked, "my memories will be of war, of sitting around at some battalion command post, huddled over an old pot-bellied stove and fanning the breeze with the lads who are doing the fighting."[89]

Between March 5 and June 4, 1944, as events continued to turn in favor of an Allied victory in Europe, the *Post-Dispatch* began to look ahead in a twenty-two-article series by Charles Ross entitled "Men and Jobs After the War." Its concern, as the title indicated, was measures needed to establish a workable postwar economy. Ross's subjects included "The Case for Speed in Reconversion," "For Low Profits on a Great Turnover," "Industrial Employment and the Farm Problem," "Competition Versus Monopoly," "Effects of Women's New Role in Industry," and "Views from the Right on Government Regulation." Reprints of the series were made available in booklet form.

Yet another series, written mostly by Pulitzer himself, came out the next year. During the final days of the European war, he was among eighteen American editors and publishers invited by General Dwight D. Eisenhower, Supreme Commander of the Allied Expeditionary Forces in Europe, to visit sites of the Nazi atrocities and the decisive Allied landings. Among his companions were Julius Ochs Adler of the *New York Times,* Ben Hibbs of the *Saturday Evening Post,* Walter Stone of the Scripps-Howard chain, Stanley High of *Reader's Digest,* John Randolph Hearst of Hearst Publications, and Norman Chandler of the *Los Angeles Times.* Their tour included the concentration camps at Dachau and

Buchenwald just days after their liberation and a confidential, background interview with Eisenhower at Allied Expeditionary Forces headquarters.

Pulitzer found the grim evidence at the camps so shocking that it was difficult to capture in words alone. In London, a cabdriver told him that the *London Express* had put together a photograph exhibit on the camps. As soon as he returned to the United States after his fifteen-day trip, he urged the release of Army Signal Corps motion pictures taken at the camps and commissioned a display of twenty-five life-size photo-murals to illustrate the extent of the Nazi atrocities. In Washington, Brandt secured AAA-1 priority for the paper on which the prints were made. They were displayed for twenty-five days in a recently completed but not yet occupied annex to the *Post-Dispatch* building. More than 80,000 people viewed the exhibit, and an even larger number attended the forty-four showings of the Army film in the city's Kiel Auditorium. The exhibit then went to Washington, D.C., where more than 88,000 saw it at the Library of Congress, then to Boston, Cleveland, New York, and other cities. In most places, newspapers of the host cities met or shared the cost of exhibition with the *Post-Dispatch*. The demand for showings was so great that the *Post-Dispatch* made a duplicate set of murals to tour through its Missouri and Illinois circulation area. The Detroit *News* was so eager for the exhibit that it got *Post-Dispatch* permission to make a third set of prints.[90]

During the trip to Europe itself, Pulitzer made notes in a stenographer's notebook, written large with a heavy pencil so he could read them. From these, he dictated a series of diary-like accounts of the experience, written in the first person and reminiscent of his letters of many years before to his father in some of their visual detail. They were published between April 29 and May 27. Beforehand, he had pictured Eisenhower's office "as a drab, barn-like bare room," but found it instead to be "a charming room that might have been a small study in a New England country house":

> At the end was a fireplace, before which the General stood in that most characteristic pose of his with his hands on his hips and his feet rather wide apart. The

plaster walls were painted a robin's-egg blue, relieved by a few water colors. His desk, in front of the high French windows on the left, was not an office desk, but a handsome mahogany piece that might easily have come out of some old English house. Floors were carpeted and you could have sworn you were in the room of an old friend.

When the editors were introduced to General Eisenhower, Pulitzer, having learned that fellow editor Amon Carter of the *Fort Worth Star-Telegram* planned to give the general a case of bourbon, beat Carter to the punch by presenting him with a bottle of seventeen-year-old Wilkens bourbon. "I am told that General 'Ike,' unlike Gen. Bradley, is not averse to an occasional snort," he reported. A longer segment from his account of that session conveys more of Pulitzer's style, but the first sentences may astonish latter-day reporters who recall *President* Eisenhower's frequently tangled press conference syntax:

> I was struck by his masterful command of English. I recall the English of President Lowell of Harvard. Eisenhower's was even better. . . .
>
> I was struck by the kindliness of the man—a kindliness that is combined with tremendous force. . . . He was wearing the short, cocky army jacket which barely reaches down to the waist. As he talked he revealed a little mannerism, which, to my mind, is a certain indication of a man in good condition.
>
> As he talked he would frequently and quite unconsciously raise his weight and stand on his tiptoes. I recall that in the old days this was a peculiar characteristic of that great light-heavyweight, Kid McCoy, the man who probably in all the history of the ring packed the hardest punch for a man of his weight.
>
> Later I inquired of one of his aides as to how the General keeps in such good condition. He replied: "Well, he has a punching bag and about once a week he walks by it, gives it a slap with the palm of his hand and goes on about his business."[91]

After reading the articles, J. Roy Stockton, the paper's sports editor, suggested to Pulitzer: "When you get a chance, why don't you have a chat with Mr. Reese about joining the Post-Dispatch staff as a regular? You are a damn good reporter."[92] Pulitzer's work and several Fitzpatrick cartoons it inspired, plus articles about the photo exhibit, some photographs, and maps, were issued in a booklet entitled "A Report to the American People."

He made three public appearances following the trip. On May 18, at the invitation of the Missouri House of Representatives, he addressed the Missouri legislature in Jefferson City. Four days later he was one of several who spoke at Carnegie Hall in New York City at a rally sponsored by the Society for the Prevention of World War III. On May 30, he spoke briefly to open the paper's atrocity mural exhibit in St. Louis. At each appearance, his message was blunt and direct: those responsible for the atrocities should be speedily tried, and shot if found guilty. His remarks produced these headlines in the *New York Times:* "Urges Executions of 1,500,000 Nazis / Pulitzer Tells Rally Here That General Staff, Gestapo, SS and Industrialists Should Be Shot." He said his figures were only estimates, because "the War Department for some reason has been reluctant to release information on the subject. But I estimate that somewhere between 1,000,000 and 2,000,000 is a reasonable figure. Possibly 1,500,000 may be the final total."[93] Even before his trip, he had urged Coghlan to take "the strongest, toughest most remorseless attitude towards all Germans until the day arrives when they have had their German bestiality educated and whipped out of them. Economic opportunity for Germans in our own self-interest after the war, yes; but gentle, sentimental consideration in the meantime, no." Even earlier, he had said he was convinced that it would be necessary to execute large numbers of Germans "and then put the German people on parole and keep them on parole for at least one or probably two generations."[94]

Pulitzer was disturbed when only a relative handful of German militarists were charged with war crimes. He had understood Eisenhower to say when he met with the editors that he favored the course of action Pulitzer had been advocating. "I am still trying to carry out the purpose of the assignment that you gave us editors at that time," he wired the general. He asked for Eisenhower's "views on or off the record" as to why so few had been indicted, but apparently received no answer. He speculated to Brandt that the widely reported belief that military officers "regard their opponents as honorable soldiers and not as criminals" was the probable explanation.[95]

In any case, the publisher's harsh line was widely applauded by, among others, many St. Louisans of German descent. "One thing that has astonished me," he wrote in response to a congratulatory letter from *Milwaukee Journal* editor Lindsay Hoben, "has been the absolutely complete absence of resentment of our position by what used to be called our German-American South side. Indeed, we have had only a very few letters of opposition, and they came from screwballs with very fine Anglo-Saxon names." He said he had received "numbers of letters from German families, one of the best having come, by way of example, from Adolphus Busch III," president of Anheuser-Busch. "When we find that a dog has hydrophobia or a rat has bubonic plague," Pulitzer concluded, "we protect society by eliminating them. That in my opinion is what we must do with German militarism. . . . Hitler after all was merely a symptom of an old, old disease. I do hope that the Milwaukee Journal may see fit to follow this approach."[96] When Gottlieb told Pulitzer that some ministers opposed showing the atrocity films, he responded: "If some of these conscientious objector pastors try to make a real issue of the films, I would crack them over the head without mercy."[97]

Gottlieb knew why. Just the day before, on June 4, 1945, Pulitzer had dictated a memo to the editorial writer which fairly summarized the evolution of his thinking through this war and his conception of geopolitical realities:

> Of course, we favor liberty and independence as a principle for all people everywhere, BUT—until the Golden Age and Brave New World arrive—is it not the ugly fact that liberty can be gained and preserved only by force of arms? How did we gain and preserve our American independence? Was it not by licking the British in 1778 and 1812? What will produce and preserve Philippine independence? Is it not the American Navy and Air Force? What degree of "independence," if any, can Poland look

forward to? In the last analysis will not the Russian army settle that question? What about independence for the unfortunate Syrians? Sooner or later . . . will they not have to look either to British arms, Russian arms or French arms for their so-called "independence"?

This is by no means to say that we should not continue to do our damndest to bring about a world peace organization. But are we not kidding ourselves when we think that under that peace structure "enlightened self-interest" will not continue to be the first motive of the Big Four? Are we going to let Russia tell us what kind of government Colombia or Panama or Mexico should have? I doubt it. I don't see how we can get away from "zones of influence" and in the last analysis, I cannot escape the conclusion that independence for the Porto Ricans or the Newfoundlanders or the Hottentots must depend on force somehow, somewhere and that the best we can hope for is that the abuse of that force will be restrained by the peace organization. How about it?[98]

Pulitzer had come, in short, from his belief in neutrality and isolation in 1938 to what seemed to him in 1945 to be a need to recognize new realities in the search for global order. His reading of events in Europe had swiftly extinguished his hope that the United States could stay out of the war. As the horror played itself out, he was convinced that the nation now had no luxury of choice but must continue to be a major international player.

After two cruiseless summers, the Pulitzers and their usual August cruising companions, Eugene and Marie Williams of St. Louis, were back on the water in 1945. They were sailing aboard the *Troubador*, a used yacht Pulitzer had purchased to replace *Discoverer*, which had been damaged beyond rehabilitation during her Coast Guard service. They heard the news of the Japanese surrender and the war's end on August 14 while ashore at a cocktail party. Two days earlier, while eating dinner aboard the yacht, they had heard what proved to be a premature radio announcement of the war's end from United Press, which had also jumped the gun in 1918. The women leapt to the deck with a megaphone to signal the news, only to be greeted by calls from other boats: "Shut up, false alarm." They retreated below "to find Joe in a towering newspaper rage" because of the error.[99]

Joys and Sorrows

March 21, 1945, was a doubly significant day for Pulitzer. He had reached both his sixtieth birthday and the age at which his father had it announced, at simultaneous dinners attended by sixty guests each in New York and St. Louis, that he was retiring from active supervision of his newspapers. The namesake son had no more intention of retiring than his father had had, and said so. But, like the first J.P., he wanted to mark the occasion well, and he outdid the affair of thirty-eight years earlier by giving himself a dinner in the Gold Room of the Jefferson Hotel attended by 1,060 guests. Most of these were current *Post-Dispatch* employees, plus fifty-seven of the paper's "alumni," people who had either retired or moved to other jobs. For the forty from out of town, Pulitzer secretary Arch R. King managed the complicated wartime transportation and housing arrangements. Pulitzer Publishing Company paid everyone's expenses. A printed and bound transcription of the evening's proceedings, and a souvenir menu in which their names were printed, were sent to all *Post-Dispatch* employees then away on military duty.[1]

The dinner was preceded by manhattan cocktails and accompanied at appropriate intervals by Harvey's Gold Cup sherry, Cook's Brut champagne, and Benedictine. Russ David and the KSD orchestra provided music, while host and guests, most seated at tables of ten, enjoyed filet of lemon sole sauté amandine, breast of guinea hen in port wine sauce, and trimmings. After a few manhattans, one guest, a stringer for the paper from outside the city, was seen picking up the bowl of French dressing at his table and drinking it all. A more glaring mishap, in the recollection of Harold O. Grams, then a KSD announcer and later head of all the Pulitzer broadcasting operations, was that the hired entertainer, comedian Zero Mostel, "kind of laid a bomb."

Even so, following a somewhat formal start, there was plenty of laughter during the after-dinner remarks of the nonprofessionals. These began with Pulitzer announcing a pension plan, as had his father at the earlier dinner. It expanded and modernized the previous plan, providing that at age sixty-five and after twenty years of service a retiree would receive at least $40 a month entirely at company cost; retirement at sixty-five was not mandatory. He concluded his talk with a flourish that brought the audience spontaneously to its feet: he read his father's message to the 1907 dinner which had become the *Post-Dispatch* platform. His recent thinking about the platform, he explained, had started him speculating on "what would have happened had Hitler and his gang of Gestapo and super-men ever succeeded in overrunning St. Louis as they have overrun so many beautiful and innocent cities of Europe; and I couldn't help thinking that if he had ever gotten into St. Louis, probably the first thing he would have done would have been to make a beeline for the Post-Dispatch office and tear that platform to pieces."

The remainder of the evening was distinctly jovial. Pulitzer's favorite comments came from Frank A. Behymer, who had been a reporter and feature writer on the paper since 1888, fifty-six years. His account of how, as a young man, Pulitzer had worked under the "Demon City Editor" Charles E. Chapin at the *New York World* drew laughter at the end of every sentence. "There is a legend that Chapin fired young Joe for coming late to work," he began, "but I have not been able to verify that so I refrain from mentioning it. Probably it didn't happen. If it did, it was a wasted gesture on the part of Mr. Chapin, for Mr. Pulitzer, grown older, and again on the payroll, still comes in late. And nobody does anything about it." (This was, as many there knew, accurate. Pulitzer seldom showed up at his office before midday. After breakfast and a brisk walk, he had a secretary read him the morning papers and take dictation for two or three hours in his study at home.) Behymer presented the employees' gift to the publisher, a commission to have his portrait painted by New York artist Wayman Adams. The idea, kept secret from Pulitzer until the dinner, had been secretary King's. The employees had donated $5,000.[2] The portrait, showing Pulitzer holding several sheets of the yellow copy paper on which his memorandums were typed, has hung in the lobby of the newsroom floor of the *Post-Dispatch* since its completion. The likeness so pleased Pulitzer that Mrs. Pulitzer had Adams do another, this one in hunting clothes, for his summer home at Bar Harbor.

As is usual on such occasions, the evening was full of warm sentiments, typified by Behymer's words in presenting the employees' gift: "I want to say, with utter simplicity, that the gift . . . is a symbol of the friendship that exists and has always existed between you and your employees. I said 'friendship.' I know no better word. That, I think, is the outstanding quality of the Post-Dispatch family. I do not want to speak extravagantly. You wouldn't like that. But I can say, and do say, that in all the years that I have been a member of that family I have never heard an unfriendly word spoken against you. On the other hand, I have heard many, very many friendly words spoken."

At that point Pulitzer had been editor and publisher of the *Post-Dispatch* for thirty-three years, the same span — from 1878 to 1911 — that his father's forceful intellect, if not physical presence, had guided the newspaper. As engaging as the work was for both men, misunderstandings, disagreements, and some battles of will inevitably came into it. Yet, by following the lines of humanitarian concern spelled out in the platform, each maintained the confidence and respect of his employees, of the St. Louis community generally, and — under the second J.P. — of a significant national following. Several emphasized the last-named achievement during the program. "You have built better than he knew," concluded former *Post-Dispatch* cub reporter and later *World* executive editor Herbert Bayard Swope in comparing father and son.

But at the same time, as already observed, the son maintained an almost religious reverence for his father's precepts, using them whenever possible as his basis for decision. This did not necessarily resolve disagreements. The trouble was that those parental injunctions, like constitutional clauses, were subject to varying constructions, especially in prosecuting editorial policy. Even as a young man, Pulitzer had anticipated such difficulty, remarking in a letter to his father a few days after arriving in St. Louis in 1906 for his first prolonged period of training, "The editorial page, I think, will be my greatest trouble. The business and news I believe I shall be able to master."[3]

The comment was prophetic. He had no more persistent trouble in his forty-three years as editor-publisher than in working with the five men who served, successively, as his editorial page editors: George S. Johns, Clark McAdams, Charles G. Ross, Ralph Coghlan, and Irving Dilliard. All had advanced from posts of lower authority on the paper and were strong believers in its commitment to militant vigilance in behalf of the democratic process and individual freedoms. Each had a keen intelligence and interest in ideas, and each wrote well. But beyond that was the inevitable source of friction with Pulitzer: each was a distinctly singular individual whose judgments and passions were certain at times to conflict with his. The record of the succession of editorial page editors reveals a pattern of continuous concern on Pulitzer's part about two extremes: dullness and overzeal. This suggests a moderate cast of mind not always easy to anticipate; a thought process something like that of the judicial balancer who attempts to weigh the merits of competing viewpoints. When, inevitably, subjectivity on his part or an editor's — whether perceived or real — entered in, conflict was probable. Accordingly, in Pulitzer's relationship with each editor there was a measure of vexation and vicissitude.

The least complicated relationship was the first, with George S. Johns, the elder statesman previously described, well acquainted with the founding Pulitzer and a man of twenty-three years' service on the *Post-Dispatch* when "Young Joe" began his career there in 1906. Johns had enjoyed considerable autonomy from the time he joined the paper as a reporter in 1883, the year the elder Pulitzer bought the *World,* leaving St. Louis virtually for good. For years, the editorial page he directed had the reputation of being one of the most outspoken and courageous among metropolitan dailies. But by the second decade of the second Joseph Pulitzer's administration, the young publisher found it "old-fashioned, cocksure, know-it-all,"[4] and oftener than not just plain dull.

He tried, but with only limited success, to convey this to Johns, then in his fifth decade of employment. This, for example, came in 1924: "After stewing about it over night and trying to cool off, I am writing to say that I think [Harry M.] Williams' editorial advocating the erection of lightning rods to prevent forest fires, in the issue of Tuesday . . . is about the damndest fool editorial I ever read or ever hope to read, and I blame you personally for continuing to permit the paper and particularly the editorial page to be made ridiculous by editorials of this kind, practically all of which are written by Williams. I must ask you to put a stop to it."[5] Williams, advanced in years himself, was shifted to nonwriting chores on the page. Pulitzer complained later that year about an editorial on how to deal with lynchers: "Obviously, obviously, obviously, lynchers should be prosecuted. Why not say so plainly, simply, tersely and forcibly in ten double leaded lines and stop there? This is what I regard as obviously a hack type of editorial. This view is handed along not so much by way of criticism but in line with my recent promise to give you my ideas from time to time about what constitutes a stupid editorial."[6] On another occasion, Pulitzer sent to Johns an editorial page across which was written in pencil: "A very dull page." As soon as editorial writer Clark McAdams spotted the page on the absent Johns's desk, he gleefully announced its message to those in the room. He considered the page lifeless and agreed with Pulitzer that at that particular time it had harped to the point of boredom on its opposition to prohibition.[7] He obviously thought he could do better, and shortly got the chance.

Johns's retirement proved the easiest step toward Pulitzer's full maturity as editorial head of the newspaper. Johns actually stepped down in 1929, but for several years before had been relieved during frequent absences by writers Bart B. Howard and McAdams, both in their fifties. Howard had joined the staff in 1919. His shining hour came just before his retirement at age seventy, when he won the 1940 Pulitzer Prize for a series of editorials on the growing menace of German militarism. McAdams had joined the *Post-Dispatch* in 1898 and had favorably impressed young Joseph Pulitzer II during the latter's apprenticeship days. "McAdams I find to be a very bright chap," he had written his father, "stupid to talk to but very clever on paper. He should be developed."[8] He was. For more than twenty years, McAdams wrote "Just a Minute," a distinctive editorial page column of light prose and verse that was one of the paper's most popular features. Even Bovard liked it. "It is unique," he told Pulitzer. "Better than most 'columns' in its humor, it is also rich in sound and entertaining philosophy and on occasion it is very enlightening in its shrewd analysis of current events."[9]

Pulitzer valued the column too, and eventually changed his opinion of McAdams as a conversationalist, particularly after McAdams introduced the young publisher to duck-shooting at Cuivre Island in the Mississippi River northwest of St. Charles, Missouri. McAdams interested several other *Post-Dispatch* people in the sport, including Bovard, Fitzpatrick, and Coghlan. Clark and Joe, as they were known to each other, usually shared a blind, McAdams becoming adept at directing Pulitzer's limited line of vision toward the flight path of incoming birds. Pulitzer later interested his second wife in the sport, and some years they followed duck seasons all the way from Maine to the southern states as the birds migrated. Mainly because of their mutual love for the outdoors, McAdams may have been the closest personal friend Pulitzer ever had among *Post-Dispatch* employees.

Their compatibility as editor and "chief of staff," as McAdams sometimes described himself, was another matter. Without any fanfare, formal announcement, or assumption of title — most likely in deference to Johns, who still came into the office, and to Howard, who might have thought he should have been chosen — McAdams succeeded Johns in 1929. An interesting perception of his editorship has been preserved in a handwritten memoir given by McAdams's widow to the Missouri Historical Society in St.

Louis. Biased in favor of her husband and speculative as to Pulitzer's motives, it is built on the convenient assumption that Pulitzer's wealth and upper-crust social connections put him out of harmony with the platform he had pledged to uphold. Of course, it was fairly commonplace for salaried employees of newspapers and other businesses to conclude that the rich were by definition conservatives, not progressive liberals. Assuming that his wife's account accurately reflects his views, McAdams was strongly captivated by this thought with respect to Pulitzer — moreso, it appears, than were any other of the editorial page editors, though all probably harbored suspicions at times. As Laura McAdams, writing in 1936, put it: "Pulitzer himself approved of Roosevelt for President in 1932, and his New Deal as it was first set up in '33. But when he began to see that much of the legislation being passed by the new Congress was directed against the ownership class — his own class — he began to shift his position and moved off to the Right."[10]

The same issue, previously considered, was at the heart of Bovard's discontent. Like Bovard's, McAdams's major differences with Pulitzer grew out of the Depression, although — illustrating how complex this all was — he agreed with Pulitzer that Bovard's socialism was too extreme while at the same time finding Pulitzer's approach too reserved. Thus it soon developed that from Pulitzer's perspective McAdams had extremist tendencies too. This was foreshadowed — and doubtless fed McAdams's mistrust — when Pulitzer wrote of a McAdams editorial in 1928: "I don't like such phrases as 'the financial juggling of the magnates.' There seems to be an inference here that all magnates are burglars, which is not true." He became more emphatic following the stock market crash. He wrote McAdams in 1930:

> Getting right down to brass tacks, do you really believe that any one, however heartless and cold-blooded he may be, is "indifferent to the plight of industrial labor?" Has not every one, if for reasons of downright avarice if for no other, a deep interest in that subject? And did not Hoover, in all fairness, whatever the motive that prompted him, show that he was not indifferent when he tried to do what surely seemed the sensible thing of bringing the heads of

all business together at Washington? . . . Your understanding that the Post-Dispatch is still sympathetic with the unfortunate is, I hope it goes without saying, entirely correct. But sympathy with the unfortunate . . . is not a thing on which we have an exclusive copyright. And I cannot imagine anything that would in the long run do more harm to the unfortunate than going in hell bent for Federal unemployment insurance. Prohibition in comparison would be a heavenly blessing.[11]

The next year Pulitzer objected to a facetious comment in a letter to the editor that the less well-off, "not the capitalists, should finance the army and navy and give their boys to die in distant jungles that millionaires may have more millions." He thought the page should omit "all kinds of arguments that are non-sensible, illogical and occasionally vicious," adding that in this case "the reader cannot escape the conclusion that this flubdub about the millionaires represents in whole or in part the views of the editor or it would not be there. That happens not to be the case, and I must ask you to put an end to it."[12]

Not all his memorandums to McAdams were critical. He praised a 1933 editorial on the problems of industry for its moderate tone, but cautioned McAdams that he should "for goodness' sake, ask your young men to keep their shirts on. . . . The more reserved and temperate our editorials are, on this whole subject, the more convincing they will be."[13] He showed further uneasiness about McAdams in a memo written at the end of the year, as the publisher prepared to leave on a four-month world cruise: "Let me again beg you to do your best to accomplish these three objectives while I am gone," he began.

> 1.   Avoid long editorials. Believe me, you are in danger of losing readers by printing too many long, ponderous editorials. . . . The tendency is definitely growing and should be checked, and you are the one to check it.
> 2.   Try every day to get humor and satire into the page. As you well know, serious subjects can often be best handled satirically, and you are so good at it that I am sure you can help the page if you will remember this.

3.   Try to get Fitz greatly to increase his average of humorous cartoons. Too many grim, grisly pictures of death, destruction and disaster fail to do him credit and inevitably detract from the value of the occasional cartoon of this kind which he always does so very well.[14]

According to Laura McAdams's account, while "Pulitzer was traveling with a group of rich reactionaries" on the 1934 cruise, he decided to relieve McAdams of his editorship. (Pulitzer probably would have contested the inference that he was influenced by his shipmates. In a letter to his brother Herbert, he described them as "stuffy, dull and old, with just a few exceptions."[15]) She gave this as the background:

It was McAdams' belief that it was not until after his mother's death [in 1927] that Pulitzer became definitely more "class conscious" and revealed increasing signs of his social ambitions — for in her will she left him a great part of the inheritance denied him by his famous but irascible and violent tempered father. . . . [This was wrong. Following their father's will, each son received one-third of his mother's newspaper stock, each third valued at that time at $234,018. Her other assets were divided equally among all five children.[16]]

McAdams also was aware of the fact that Pulitzer's friends in the social world had for some time been trying to convince him that his paper was "in the hands of the enemy," that the editorial page was radical, red, pink or what not, and he began to wonder — will Pulitzer's Country Club associates succeed in turning him away from his former rather liberal point of view? . . .

In his conferences with Pulitzer, McAdams tried to emphasize what [Pulitzer's] father had believed in, and what . . . he stated in his platform — that the Post-Dispatch, far from being a class paper, as Pulitzer Jr. seemed now, at times, to want to make it, had been established as a class free, as well as a party free paper, devoted to the public welfare.

. . . He reminded Pulitzer that Top Hats, typifying the

so-called Vested Interests, were worn by only a small minority of the Post-Dispatch readers, while the majority of
them wore Caps . . . for Pulitzer had of late been objecting
to Fitzpatrick's Top Hat cartoons and the editorials that
went with them.

That considerable conjecture and some bitterness went into this
analysis is suggested by the fact that Ralph Pulitzer characterized
the paper's performance during his brother's absence in a highly
positive way. "The editorial page continued to be admirable," he
reported to his brother just after the cruise ended, although it had
been "at times, a little further to the Left and more indiscriminately
supporting Roosevelt than agreed with my own point of view, but a
fault (if fault it was) on the right side."[17]

Still, although J.P. had reached almost precisely the same conclusion as to the treatment of Franklin Roosevelt and some other
matters, he was annoyed. When his ship reached Hong Kong it
was met by Basil Rudd, one of his secretaries, who had reports
from all the newspaper's departments including this lighthearted
message from McAdams: "We hope you are enjoying your trip
around the world as much as we are." This went flat, he shortly
learned. "Amazed your seeming defiance my views," Pulitzer cabled
him, singling out two editorials in particular as "invidious attacks
on publishers" for which McAdams was to run an apology on
Pulitzer's return. In one of these, McAdams had written that only
a few liberal papers "have resisted valiantly the folly of permitting
the United States to become that paradise for the rich man which
the Russians say it is and that hell for the poor man that we know
it is."[18] Pulitzer continued: "Also report . . . any points on which
you have disagreed with administration. Discontinue wholesale
condemnation of dividends declared from surplus. Discontinue
demanding that government use force to compel NIRA [National
Industrial Recovery Act] compliance. Convinced such action would
destroy both government and business . . . entirely too much government aid for everybody now."[19]

At least in his attitude toward the press, McAdams was not
deterred by Pulitzer's sharp reaction. About two weeks after hearing from the publisher, he spoke at the annual Journalism Week
program at the University of Missouri in Columbia. "McAdams

studded his speech with accusations that part of the American Press is deserting public service — the protection of the people from the greed of big business and dishonest public servants — and presents instead of fearless, forthright truth, opinion and fact tainted by privilege," said a news account. It continued: " 'The press is closely integrated with wealth and privilege,' McAdams declared. 'Like government itself, it takes its color from the great financial and industrial structure of which it is a part.' "[20]

That may have been the last straw for Pulitzer. He returned to St. Louis at about the time of the speech, but waited until June to tell McAdams he was being replaced. He then invited the editor to join him for some salmon-fishing on the Restigouche. There they had a long talk, the result of which was that McAdams accepted a position as "contributing editor" with the understanding that his work would be passed on and edited by his successor, Charles G. Ross, the paper's chief Washington correspondent and a former journalism professor at the University of Missouri. Ross's Depression analysis, "The Country's Plight," previously described, matched the publisher's assessment of economic conditions more closely than those of McAdams or Bovard. Pulitzer persuaded Ross to return to St. Louis by letting him name his own salary figure, $25,000.[21]

The friendship of Pulitzer and McAdams stayed intact; when McAdams returned from Canada he told his wife nothing of what they had discussed, only that they had had "quite a session." Pulitzer wrote him within a few days: "I have often thought of our conversation, and I still believe the time will come when you will tell me that in your work as Contributing Editor you are happier than you were before. If, as I know you will do, you will stick to the ship and throw yourself whole-heartedly into helping to make Ross' position at the start a less trying and difficult one, I shall be grateful to you." McAdams replied: "What you have said to me at Brandy Brook and have since written me has given me great comfort. I am confident that in time your judgment of me will soften. A fighting editor, the only kind worth having, sometimes unpacks a wild blow; but even so, a cold blade wins few battles. My conscience is clear, however clouded my title."[22] A few days later he wrote to a friend, "I have not been kicked into the street, but I did lose my peacock feather." The editorial line he and Fitzpatrick had been following, he explained, "was too much for the owners of the paper, many of whose friends in and out of Wall Street saw their racket going overboard." Eventually, he predicted,

> I will come back. I have not forgotten that when I was a boy the state of Illinois built a monument over at Alton to Elijah P. Lovejoy. They first ran him out of St. Louis for opposing human slavery, and when he continued his fight at Alton they went up and killed him, burned his print shop and threw his press in the river. It is no fun to fight for civilization. I always think the people who do it cannot help it. They are that kind. All this, of course, is confidential.[23]

Sixteen months later, in November 1935, McAdams died of cancer at the age of sixty-one. Following Roosevelt's landslide reelection the next year, when Pulitzer had given the paper's endorsement to Republican Alf Landon, Bovard reported the electoral vote tally in this message to McAdams, which he posted on the editorial page office bulletin board: "Dear Mac: The issue is: Country, 523; Country Club, 8."[24] Recalling this several years later, Pulitzer observed: "Bovard might have added to this: 'Socialistic ticket . . . 0.' Painful though it might have been to admit, the Country Club was still eight up on the Socialists."[25]

In appointing Ross to the editorship, Pulitzer took two precautions. First, he put in writing "our mutual understanding that I retain complete and absolute power and responsibility in determining what is to be the editorial policy of the Post-Dispatch. This does not mean that I shall not invest you with a large degree of that power and responsibility, for it is my intention to do that very thing."[26] Second, the first year would be a trial period, at the end of which the appointment could be terminated, with Ross having the option of returning to Washington at no decrease in salary. It was understood that his work would be "primarily as an editor and not primarily an editorial writer" expected to write a daily editorial.[27]

In contrast to Pulitzer's working relationship with McAdams, or even with Johns, that with Ross was tranquil. Ross was not a combative person by nature; he believed less in the power of heated debate than in decision via calm, ordered reason. Perhaps his strongest trait was fair-mindedness. When Pulitzer committed the paper to Landon, Ross agreed, producing an editorial with a headline that matched its analytical approach: "For President— Not Mr. Roosevelt." The piece complimented Roosevelt for his "high-minded and patriotic endeavor to improve the lot of the common man" and conceded, "We have approved and continue to approve a substantial part of his program. . . . We do not subscribe to the vituperative criticism which has been heaped upon the President, though we believe that much of this is the result of his own too-frequent imputing of unworthy motives to his opponents." The reason for the paper's opposition, the editorial explained, was that New Deal measures were being promoted as a cure-all by a president so self-assured that he had dangerously disregarded the prerogatives of the states, Congress, and the Supreme Court. Landon wasn't mentioned until the twenty-fifth of the editorial's twenty-eight paragraphs, and never by his full name. The editorial's final sentence recommended that the "most useful weapon" against Roosevelt's excesses "is a vote for his leading opponent, Governor Landon."[28] It was hardly a ringing endorsement, but Fitzpatrick dissented from it anyway and was permitted to draw only non-political cartoons for the remainder of the campaign. "Sorry you couldn't go along with us," Pulitzer told him.[29]

Asked for his opinion of the editorial before it was published, Bovard (who would have endorsed no one, but wasn't averse to taking another lick at the President) told Ross it wasn't "tough" enough. But Ross disagreed, telling Pulitzer, "It seems to me good tactics to take a position that cannot be shelled as hyper-critical; to pitch our editorial . . . on a somewhat lofty plane; and I have in mind, too, that the Post-Dispatch for a good many months accorded Mr. Roosevelt almost undivided support."[30]

Despite the truth in what Ross said, and though he tried to counteract it, Pulitzer never was able to overcome the distrust created by his own wealth, as when a reader wrote: "I suspect that the younger Pulitzer, like Hearst, thinks more of his income taxes than of fairness to liberal readers." Calling this a "perfectly natural suspicion," Pulitzer asked Ross whether it might be answered by repeating "more than once" editorially "the old argument that 'soak-the-rich' taxes inevitably soak the poor as well? And that there is a point beyond which taxes cannot go or the result is stagnation, a check on business initiative and expansion and consequent unemployment?" He said he knew the rich had often used that line of argument against proposed tax increases, and that while he did "not believe that the point of business stagnation has yet been reached, . . . I think we are not far from it. . . . My point is that high taxes have not influenced the 'younger Pulitzer' or the editorial staff or any one connected with the Post-Dispatch except in so far as they retard or tend to retard recovery."[31]

But how does one convey such subtleties convincingly? More forcefully than the professorial Ross had been doing, Pulitzer began to think. After getting several letters "charging us with having deserted our old liberal position and having become Tory and reactionary," Pulitzer suggested that Ross might assign "Coghlan, who has been doing fine work lately," to explain "what we are trying to do: That is, preserve and restore the American form of government, and say, not apologetically but almost defiantly, that if that represents conservatism we accept the challenge and are glad to let those [who] misguidedly consider themselves liberals make the most of it." Further, there should be no hesitation about castigating "all Roosevelt's acts which tend to lead us toward centralized, one-man government and ultimately to dictatorship."[32]

As that suggests, Pulitzer's problem with Ross was almost the reverse of that with McAdams. While McAdams had been too shrill and intemperate for his taste, Ross was too well modulated. Coghlan, who had joined the editorial staff in 1925 at the age of twenty-eight after writing editorials for several years for two Louisville papers, had a much hotter temperament than Ross. Sensing Pulitzer's dissatisfaction, Coghlan asked twice during 1937 to be given Ross's job. His request, he explained, grew out of the "conviction that the page in the past few years has lacked the kind of editorship it should have. The page should be a powerful, useful, interesting force; for months on end it has been dull and spiritless, boring our readers and sapping the morale and enthusiasm of the staff."[33] The brightest periods had been when Coghlan was in charge while Ross was away. After one such interlude, Pulitzer told Ross that "Coghlan and the entire staff have done exceptionally well. The page has had the vigor and fire, and vitality and vivacity that I like to see in it."[34]

But this changed little. He complained eight months later that too often the lead editorial was a long, dull discourse on foreign affairs instead of what he thought it should be: "nearly always . . . an article in which the paper takes a very definite, positive position for or against something. . . . I should like to see you put more punch into the page. As you well know, its platform demands that it shall always be a 'fighting' page." The next month he asked Ross to "raise the tempo of the page" so it would have "one strong punch every day."[35]

Coghlan assumed greater authority during 1938. At the beginning of 1939, Ross was made a contributing editor based in Washington, D.C., and Coghlan was named head of the editorial page. Until the war started, Ross wrote a signed column two or three times a week. He also contributed the longer, analytical articles, which were his specialty, and produced several wartime series before he was tapped in 1945 by Harry Truman, his former Independence, Missouri, schoolmate, to be presidential press secretary. Ross died of a heart attack in his White House office on December 5, 1950, at the age of sixty-five. He hadn't wanted the press secretary job, which paid only $10,000, but didn't feel he could turn down the President. One of the few strongly critical stances he ever took as editorial page editor had been against the election of Truman—the Pendergast machine's candidate—to the U.S. Senate in 1934.[36]

In Coghlan, Pulitzer may have had his closest match in editorial philosophy of the five men who edited the page for him. Their working relationship during the war, stormy though it became at times, illustrates this, as does Pulitzer's comparatively gentle handling of Coghlan in the course of several of Coghlan's personal crises during the nearly ten years of his editorship. Serious though it was, the least of these was recurring tuberculosis, for which periodic hospital rest was required. Coghlan also drank heavily, was somewhat unstable emotionally, and, according to one who knew him socially, was subject to periods of severe depression, during the worst of which he felt on the verge of suicide. Pulitzer may never have known of that depression. Another factor in their compatibility almost certainly was Pulitzer's experiences with McAdams and Ross. His main reason for elevating Coghlan was to get a livelier editorial page. Coghlan had the fire in him which

Ross lacked; it was almost as though Pulitzer was riding a pendulum that had reached one extreme with Ross and was now swinging back in the direction of McAdams. He did not ask Coghlan to take an oath to the publisher's final authority, as he had with Ross.

The high point of the Pulitzer-Coghlan association and one of the peaks in *Post-Dispatch* history developed after Coghlan, Reese, Fitzpatrick, and the Pulitzer Publishing Company were charged with contempt of court on March 9, 1940. The charges were based on the publication of two editorials and a cartoon criticizing Missouri Circuit Judge Thomas J. Rowe Jr. for dismissing extortion charges against Missouri State Representative Edward M. (Putty Nose) Brady and John P. Nick, head of the St. Louis Motion Picture Operators Union. Brady and Nick had been charged with extorting $10,000 from theater owners by threatening to demand higher wage scales for projector operators. In an editorial by Irving Dilliard, the *Post-Dispatch* called Judge Rowe's dismissal of these charges "a burlesque of justice." A Fitzpatrick cartoon set in "Rat Alley"—his locale for underworld activities—supported this. On April 3, with Pulitzer in the courtroom with his editors and cartoonist, Judge Rowe handed Coghlan a twenty-day jail sentence and a $200 fine; Fitzpatrick got ten days and a $100 fine, and the company got a $2,000 fine. The judge dismissed the charge against Reese because he was not responsible for the editorial page.

An appeal was filed immediately, and the following day the paper ran a defiant editorial over Pulitzer's signature with the headline, "The Post-Dispatch Will Not Be Gagged." Said the publisher:

> For years the Post-Dispatch, striving to comply with the provisions of its founder's platform . . . has been exposing and condemning the rottenness and incompetence that festers in local administration of the law. . . . [T]he recent record of some courts and some public officials is appalling. We could fill this page with instances of defective indictments, inexcusable delays, packed juries, incredible incompetence on the part of prosecutors, and threatened, bribed or murdered witnesses. . . . If a newspaper is to be gagged by being hauled into court to answer a charge of contempt whenever a judge has felt the sting of editorial criticism, that means the end of the power of the press to tell the

people about the failures and evils of their courts. That means the end of freedom of the press.[37]

The case drew national support for the newspaper's position, which Pulitzer helped along by sending telegrams to Henry R. Luce of Time-Life and publisher Robert R. McCormick of the *Chicago Tribune.* McCormick disagreed with the *Post-Dispatch* on most things because of its Democratic tendencies and general toleration of the New Deal, but "whatever differences of opinion we may have had in the past," Pulitzer suggested, "I believe you will be interested in this case of ours as a clearcut case of a judge . . . attempting to silence the criticism of a newspaper. Issues are purely local and have nothing to do with New Deal beyond incidental fact that [the] judge is a Democratic machine made official."[38] *St. Louis Star-Times* publisher Elzey Roberts told *Post-Dispatch* advertising manager George Burbach that he thought the contempt citation "was the best thing that ever happened to the *Post-Dispatch,*" said he was sorry it hadn't happened to his paper, and "evaluated it as worth a half million dollars" to Pulitzer.[39]

Pulitzer got a lighthearted letter about the situation from Washington lawyer Harry B. Hawes, a former U.S. senator and Missouri legislator. Hawes liked a courtroom photograph the paper had printed of the *Post-Dispatch* defendants and St. Louis County Sheriff J. J. Fitzsimmons: "You are looking contented and happy, Fitz looks as serious as a pig making water; the Sheriff is getting his picture in the paper, which pleases him; but 'Big Ben' [Reese] is having the time of his life. That smile tells a real story. With Fitz and Ralph in jail, it would be equal to a long vacation for Ben. No wonder he smiles!"[40] The same photo produced this from Coghlan to J.P.: "I received an amusing telephone call yesterday from Miss Quinn of the Sheriff's office. You may remember her as the yellow-haired Hebe, the cup-bearer, who passed around the Coca-Cola and otherwise illuminated the atmosphere. Miss Quinn said: 'Say, Mr. Coghlan, I don't want to be *promiscuous,* but could you let the Sheriff have copies of last Wednesday's paper in which his picture appeared?' After taking a moment to gulp over the 'promiscuous,' I said, 'Certainly, Miss Quinn.' "[41]

The apparent confidence that they would win on appeal was justified. In June 1941, the seven-member Missouri Supreme Court unanimously reversed the convictions. To uphold them, the court said, "would be to narrow the limits of permissible criticism so greatly that the right to criticize would cease to have practical value."[42] The newspaper had a protected right to criticize Judge Rowe's actions, the court reasoned, because his dismissals meant the Nick and Brady matters were closed cases. While the newspaper's appeal was being decided, Nick and an associate were convicted in federal court of labor racketeering and sent to jail.

Coghlan rode high for the next couple of years. During the contempt case, a Washington University law professor wrote him: "The Post-Dispatch is the best newspaper in the country and you are the best editorial writer next to William Allen White."[43] (The gifted White was editor of the small-town but nationally influential *Emporia Gazette* in Kansas.) At the beginning of 1943, Coghlan became his own booster in a memo to Pulitzer:

> When I came to the Post-Dispatch, the editorial page was considered a kind of old boneyard, which it assuredly was. Bovard was then in top form and, for one reason or another, he had a contempt for the editorial page and fostered that contempt in other members of the news staff. It was partly deserved. Often the news was far out in front of the editorial page. It was better informed. It was more original. It was bolder.... I have done my best to shatter the tradition that the editorial page is a boneyard. I have tried my damndest to keep it abreast of the news, to keep it alive, to carry on the Post-Dispatch tradition of public service. Right here you will remember my faults and mistakes and I remember them, too. But I'll hazard this boast: that I have made the editorial page a part of the Post-Dispatch and not a dull and spiritless laggard, as it was when I arrived in 1925.[44]

He might have pointed to a matter then pending in state court as the freshest evidence of his claim. About a month previously he had suggested in an editorial that "on some dark night" someone should remove an old cannon from the state capitol grounds in Jefferson City and take it to a scrap-metal pile for war use. Two St. Louis tree surgeons who knew Coghlan took this as a challenge and drove a truck there with the intention of towing the cannon to a scrap pile. They were unable to move the relic, though, because it had a defective wheel. At the insistence of Missouri Governor Forrest C. Donnell, they were arrested and charged with grand larceny, even though the cannon hadn't been moved. When they disclosed the source of their inspiration and the fact that Coghlan had given them $50 for expenses, the editor was charged as a co-conspirator. After the cannon's value was determined to be $10, the charges were reduced to conspiracy to commit petit larceny. A jury aquitted all three men. "I believe this whole proceeding is ridiculous, farcical and absurd, and should have been brought in a Justice of the Peace Court if at all," the presiding judge declared.[45] "The charge has been thrown into the ashcan where it belongs," Pulitzer said in a signed editorial. He said the governor's inappropriate reaction demonstrated "the unhappy fact" that Donnell "appears to be utterly disqualified to discharge the important duties of his office."[46] The *Post-Dispatch* had opposed his election.

There was another development during 1943, of greater consequence in Coghlan's life and career. Pulitzer described it in a letter to his son in the Pacific:

> Dan Cupid has been raising quite a little hell around the office. About three weeks ago Coghlan complained about being very nervous and said he wanted to take a week of his vacation, resting up at French Lick. Three days later there appeared on the third page of the Globe-Democrat an item announcing his divorce on the usual Missouri grounds of incompatibility, indifference, etc. When I next saw him I expressed, with my tongue in my cheek, my most friendly sympathy. Although nothing was being gossiped about it, and although Mommie told me she thought I was crazy, I had a hunch that there was a lady in the case and that she was none other than Jean Lightfoot, former feature writer on the Everyday Magazine, and since August writing editorials on Ralph's staff. Although her style is too flowery and poetical to suit me, she shows some signs of being a genius, and, in the course of a few months, she has received offers from the New York Herald Tribune and the Chicago

Sun. She is about 30 years old, college educated, originally from Springfield, Mo., divorced, pretty, blonde, of medium height and distinctly smart in appearance. A few days ago Ralph told me that they are to be married in Kansas City in about 10 days. That presents a problem, for it would be difficult, if it became necessary, to fire the editor's wife, but Ralph understands that I am to feel perfectly free, as I have been doing, to criticize severely and occasionally to kill her copy. I am therefore letting well enough alone and am hoping for the best.[47]

His hope did not prevail. The marriage lasted less than eighteen months. Coghlan's drinking interfered with his work so frequently that Pulitzer decided in April 1945 not to offer the editor the usual five-year contract renewal. He told him that he had decided for the time being not to make an offer that would have raised his pay in five annual steps to $25,000, but would continue him at $20,000 for the time being. As a further precaution, he would want a clause in any future contract "providing that the company . . . is privileged to appoint an executive editor who shall act for the editor (myself) in my absence, my purpose . . . being to relieve you of the responsibilities you have several times complained about which fall on your shoulders exclusively when I am away."[48] He also docked Coghlan his share of the most recent dividend payment to "principal editors and managers."

Coghlan was contrite and full of assurances that he would again be fully productive. "The divorce from Jean . . . was absolutely necessary to recover my peace of mind and to quiet a bad conscience," he explained in a letter to Pulitzer. "The fundamental trouble with me is that ever since I married Jean I have had an unquiet mind, and no permanent marriage can be built on that basis." He said that since the divorce was filed, his son and daughter had shown him "the first real warmth I have had from them since this whole thing happened." He planned to ask his former wife "to take me back after a suitable period" because he had had "thoroughly impressed on me that she is a woman of the finest character and of innate strength and dignity. O, I have learned a lot."[49]

Pulitzer surely hoped so, but couldn't have helped recalling the empty reassurances and evasions he and Bovard had gotten several years earlier from reporter Paul Y. Anderson, who, after repeated "last chance" warnings, was fired for his alcoholism. Toward the end, when he was writing a column out of Washington, D.C., Anderson resorted to having friends do the column for him. Editors noticed the change in style and the column was stopped.[50] Things hadn't gotten this bad with Coghlan; his first wife agreed to remarriage, and even during the interlude with Miss Lightfoot he had been productive. After they broke up, she took a job elsewhere.

Reds and Rights

Coghlan was not the only troublesome editor Pulitzer had to worry about. Another was Julius H. Klyman, editor of the Sunday rotogravure section, "Pictures," the quality of which some considered on a par with, or even better than, *Life* and the *New York Times Magazine.* [1]

Klyman was not a problem drinker. He was a labor activist who some, including Joseph Pulitzer, suspected of being a Communist. The evidence was all circumstantial, having largely to do with Klyman's labor union activities and his unstoppable persistence in trying to get class-conscious topics into the *Post-Dispatch.* He had joined the newspaper as a reporter in 1922. By the early 1940s, he had been vice president of the American Newspaper Guild and remained one of the most active members of its St. Louis unit. At

that time he was also a member of the state executive committee
of the Missouri Congress of Industrial Organizations and chairman of the Missouri-Kansas CIO political action committee (PAC)
and belonged to the St. Louis Industrial Council.[2] One of his most
successful PAC activities had been to publicize a little-used Missouri law that gave employees four hours off with pay to vote in
elections.

Marxists and Marxism interested Klyman intensely. He had
gotten two interviews for the *Post-Dispatch* with Leon Trotsky,
the exiled anti-Stalinist Russian revolutionary who had been a
collaborator of Lenin's. "Trotsky lived and died a dissenter," he
wrote.[3] He might have been describing himself. Although he had a
middle-class upbringing as the son of a St. Louis silk salesman and
looked, in his immaculate suits accented by a cane and grey
homburg, "like the corporate personality incarnate," he developed
a reputation as a "radical." He wasn't interested, however, in
working for a left-wing publication. Mainstream newspapers reached
a broader audience, and besides, he confessed, "one eats better on
the metropolitan press."[4]

Before elevating him to the "Pictures" editorship in 1944, Pulitzer
had a long talk with Klyman to impress upon him his belief that
editors should be "monastic" and not take an active part in any
outside activities that might have even the appearance of compro-
mising the paper's editorial independence. In recognizing the
publisher's authority "to expect nonparticipation in outside movements," Klyman said it was his "guess that if one could express
himself through his regular professional channels, the urge to
express himself in extra-curricular fashion would no longer exist."[5]

Although that statement contained the seeds of a series of
painful future annoyances for Pulitzer, it satisfied him at the time.
The publisher did try to nail down the Communist allegation more
definitely, although before asking "Are you a Communist?" he told
Klyman to feel free not to answer if he wished. Klyman responded
that Pulitzer had asked that question two years earlier, that he had
replied negatively then, and that that "still was the correct answer."
He said he had often heard the charge but "didn't know how to
stop a few people from making accusations against me and I didn't
see that it mattered much." He said he had even heard Pulitzer
"accused of being a Red as well as a Catholic who was trying to use

the P–D as a pro-Catholic weapon."[6] (Pulitzer was an inactive Episcopalian whose children, when young, were taken to Protestant Sunday school by neighbors. A more frequently heard charge in heavily Catholic St. Louis was that the *Post-Dispatch* was anti-Catholic. It had been, for example, the city's only newspaper to publish the embarrassing story that a Catholic priest had been caught *flagrante delicto*.[7])

So it went. Pulitzer and many others considered Klyman unusually gifted in his work, but the suspicion didn't disappear. For one thing, he had told Pulitzer during that long session that "of the estimable gentlemen who make up the paper's first editorial rank, there is hardly one who has had more intimate contact with working people than paying off the maid on Saturday night." That naturally led to "a fear among the most eager and able men on the staff," where Klyman definitely placed himself, "that several of the first-string editors have conservative leanings to a degree that may overbalance the paper's past policy."[8] Klyman would sometimes rub a colleague the wrong way in his apparent efforts to check this incipient conservatism. "I am damn sick and tired . . . of Klyman . . . injecting the Marxist and CIO point of view into his criticisms," Coghlan exploded to Pulitzer in mid-1944.[9] This was because Klyman thought a book review on which Coghlan had passed was overly generous to an anti-Communist former CIO official.

What came to bother Pulitzer the most about Klyman was that "Pictures" seemed overly weighted toward issues of economic inequality, frequently in the form of commentary on the economic arrangements of various noncapitalist countries. In advising Reese to "keep a sharp eye on J.K.'s sociological convictions and his desire to do something about them," he observed: "To be sure the platform says: 'never lack sympathy with the poor,' but I submit that Pictures was not intended primarily for that purpose but was originally issued as a substitute for the old Sunday magazine and rotogravure picture sections, intended primarily to entertain, divert and interest the reader."[10] He then tried gently to make the same point to Klyman: "I think that in your enthusiasm to develop the full possibilities of pictorial journalism and in your search for the significant, serious and the important . . . you are perhaps a little too prone to overbalance the section with the serious type of feature. Let me say that in my own case . . . I am always looking forward to finding something that is distracting or relaxing or . . . in one way or another, pleasant to read."[11]

When that didn't produce the desired results, Pulitzer asked Klyman to bring his "Pictures" file to him "and let me go over it with you with a view to determining how often you have run what, for lack of a better term, we might call these 'class struggle' pages."[12] Still, the results were unsatisfactory. Saying he was "very sorry, indeed, to have to wish another important duty" on the managing editor, he assigned Reese in May 1947

> to assume personal responsibility for the objectivity of text, underlines and heads of stories appearing in Pictures which concern themselves in any way with labor. If I ever saw UNOBJECTIVE writing I find it in the underlines of the page of . . . drawings of Senators, Sunday, May 4, and in the text. The whole thing impresses me as a most naive revelation of pro-labor bias. I cannot escape the conclusion that the purpose underlying this publication was plainly to smear all those who are demanding stiff labor legislation, to label them as right-wingers, or members of the "Old Guard," and to identify all those in opposition as "progressives," "liberals," or "moderates."
>
> The whole thing involves nice questions of phrasing, construction, qualifications and emphasis. Written as they are, they add up to support the serious charge I've made of unobjective writing.[13]

When Reese confronted him with this, Klyman rejected every single charge of bias, pointing out that all the terms objected to had long been used in the news columns. "The front office thinks sister Klyman is a sinner," he retorted. "Well, you know about that business of casting the first stone. In my opinion, even the famous old P–D could occasionally get out the whiskbroom and give a tiny flick or two to the hem of its skirt." He said he had received complimentary letters from both labor and management following earlier stories and had never had a complaint about the "very great many labor stories," most of them "highly controversial," which "Pictures" had run. However, as to "the story under fire, and the approach of Pictures on controversial labor, political, economic and social subjects: I don't think you or Mr. Pulitzer need be further concerned. We'll watch it."[14]

That may have been the case for a while, but at one point during this period, Charles J. Hentschell, then the paper's production manager, recalled, Pulitzer ordered a "Pictures" press run already in progress halted and all printed copies (about 120,000) dumped. It took seven hours to prepare new plates and resume the run. The reason for the change wasn't readily apparent to Hentschell, so he asked Pulitzer the next day why he'd given the order. "The damn thing was slanted," he replied. What most impressed Hentschell was that to Pulitzer "the expense was immaterial."[15] By the end of 1947, Pulitzer concluded that it was futile to expect Klyman to change. Between August and October, "Pictures" had carried four layouts on various European and Asian countries that Pulitzer considered slanted. For example, in the presentation on Yugoslavia, he wrote Reese, "it is crystal-clear to me that the editor was trying to make the contrast between the old and admittedly backward condition of . . . Yugoslavia under the old regime with the fact that everything is really grand and glorious under the new communist setup." As for Portugal, "I was amused to observe that . . . the story informs us that it is ruled by a dictator, which of course is true, but never, never, never is that word dictator applied to dear old Mother Russia or any of her camp followers." Faced with Klyman's obvious inability to curb his leftist impulses, the publisher had concluded "that this kind of weasel-worded editorializing must and will be promptly eliminated."

But he would not fire or transfer Klyman, he said, because he "is too good a picture editor and has been with the paper too long." Instead, Reese was to instruct Klyman "to omit all subjects which have anything whatever to do with social or economic conditions . . . , or of anything which deals with the conflict of the haves and the have-nots here or abroad." He realized this would "cut the very heart out of Pictures as presently constituted" and that it would "cease to be a chronicle in picture form of serious world events" and again become "a purely feature magazine in picture form." He realized too that

This will probably break Julius' heart. However, I am very

strongly inclined to believe that if we forget world affairs
we may get a more popular section even than we now have.

We read and hear constantly about the chaos and conflict that is going on in this poor, grief-stricken world. We
read plenty of it in the columns of the Post-Dispatch. Why
not rule this type of matter out of Pictures and end for all
time what I am convinced is the reflection of a restless
mind and soul, whose sympathies are sincerely with the
underdog and who cannot refrain from letting his proletar-
ian and, as I firmly believe, his communist leanings be
reflected in the pages under his leadership.

This memo is the result of some four months' thinking
and is not a hasty conclusion.[16]

Reese was generally successful in following this directive, so
much so that Klyman tried in 1949 to foil the managing editor's
oversight of "Pictures." He proposed to Pulitzer that the paper run
a symposium on "The Arithmetic of Capitalism" along the lines of
the wartime "What Are We Fighting For?" "It is my opinion that
despite all the ups and downs and vagaries of our economy, it can
continue to work, at least as far as its arithmetic is concerned. If it
fails, it will do so because some of those who have the most to gain
through capitalism will unwittingly sabotage it—in other words,
milk the economy when they should be feeding it," he explained,
adding, "I don't share the Government's optimism concerning the
immediate future of our economy."[17] Pulitzer rejected the idea.

After Reese retired in 1951—at which time the irrepressible
Klyman asked to be named managing editor[18]—Reese's successor,
former city editor Raymond L. Crowley, continued to police
Klyman's work. "Many times in the past two years," he wrote
Pulitzer in 1953, "I have thrown out whole pages or single photos,
or required complete revision of textual matter in Pictures, in
order to avoid even the suspicion of bias in the direction which
might be expected because of Mr. Klyman's thinking."[19] Even so,
Klyman was able occasionally to sneak something by, as when
Joseph Pulitzer Jr. called his father's attention to a "Pictures" page
depicting the governmental organization of the Soviet Union. Among
other things, the copy with the photos and charts reported that
political candidates in Russia "are nominated by the Communist

Party, collective farms, trade unions and youth organizations. All citizens over eighteen years old have the vote." What the associate editor wanted to know was: "Is not the uninformed reader entitled to know that this political organization of Russia's government is theoretical? . . . That the [Council of Ministers] in practice responds to the will of the chairman, recently the absolute dictator Stalin?"[20]

During the same years as the tribulations with Klyman, Pulitzer's concern about Coghlan's performance was growing. He had noticed, he told the editor in mid-1946, that he was writing fewer editorials, "and in consequence, the page is definitely suffering."[21] That was correct, Coghlan admitted. His explanation was that, particularly since the recent sudden death of Ferd Gottlieb, he had a largely inexperienced staff whose direction took up much of his time. Moreover, this had been "a time of crashing news events, violently changing times and a raft of brand-new problems for editorial decision." He said he didn't mean to make "an invidious comparison," but "I have written more than Charles G. Ross did in placid times and with an incomparably more efficient (and larger) staff than I have had. More than that, I have established a style of editorial writing that others on the staff have copied." In accepting that, Pulitzer said he wanted to "express rather than 'imply' " one compliment: "That the editorial page of the Post-Dispatch suffers when Ralph Coghlan's editorials do not appear and that it benefits noticeably when they do appear."[22]

In the fall, Pulitzer raised a subject which ultimately led to an agreement that Coghlan could step aside from writing certain editorials—those favoring Republican presidential candidate Thomas E. Dewey, whom Pulitzer decided to support in 1948. "The thought is growing on me," Pulitzer wrote from Bar Harbor, "that Harry Truman is a flop and that it may be about time for us to say so." Coghlan replied that he could not see anything constructive in coming out so early against "the legatee of the New Deal, which we have for the most part supported." He said the Republicans had yet to offer an attractive candidate and that an anti-Truman stance now could tip the balance toward some Republicans the *Post-Dispatch* opposed in the upcoming off-year elections. "You are probably right," Pulitzer conceded, "but I must confess I have no enthusiasm for the Democrats and am hoping and praying that another Willkie will spring up among the Republicans."[23]

Matters of defense and foreign policy occupied much of Pulitzer's attention toward the end of 1946 and into the next year. "I see war coming with Russia, probably within ten years," he wrote Coghlan in August.

> I have come to believe that the human animal is not capable of establishing a brave new world. Dogs, ordinarily, are kindly, peaceable creatures, but when there is a bone to fight over, they fight. So I fear it is with human beings. I have completely lost confidence in the present leaders of the Russian people. It is easy to say that the American people don't want war, but surely that cannot be said of the people of India, of China and of the Balkans, or even of the Jews and the Arabs. There are too many fundamental differences, I fear, between the Russian way of life and the Russian way of thinking and the American way of life and the American way of thinking. Sooner or later we are bound to clash, whether it be over oil or the Dardanelles or China or something else.

He complimented Coghlan for a recent editorial "about the lethargy that prevails in this country. About all I can see that we can do about it is (a) to wake the people up, (b) to build our armed forces, and (c) to make the Russians realize that we have quit turning the other cheek and that while we are not looking for trouble and will do almost anything under the sun to avoid it, we, too, have self-respect. In a word, Russians are not good neighbors but bad neighbors and need to be never allowed to forget that we are watching them." His only hope of avoiding war, he said, would be "if we ever get the United Nations really established and really put force behind it to prevent war," but this to him seemed unlikely.[24]

About a week later, perhaps out of contemplation of Klyman's behavior, he suggested to Reese "that we work up a thoroughly well-informed piece on the proposition that American Communists are working their way into the leadership of American labor unions and that there is a certain real danger in that fact." This would have to be done carefully, to avoid the charge of "having the Commie jitters or with starting a Red scare," he cautioned, "but I can't help thinking that there must be something to this frequently-heard charge." Whoever got the assignment "should have no preconceived notions for or against the American labor movement or for or against Communism."[25]

The publisher's own notions about communism, however, were hardening. Coghlan went to Germany in early 1947 and wrote four articles that Pulitzer called "a brilliant, penetrating job of reporting." He said they reminded him "of how glibly I prescribed our occupation of Germany for one or two generations, and the methods by which we might teach them at least the beginnings of democracy. What abject fools we Americans are in pulling out of Germany, in over trusting the Russians and letting them make monkeys out of us, in slashing military appropriations, etc., etc., ad infinitum. Do you remember my father's series of editorials 'Must the Democratic Party Be an Ass?' Why not another series to be headed, 'Must We Americans Be Fools?'" He said he agreed completely with Coghlan's analysis "that instead of living in the brave new world that I was fool enough to hope for, we are now, as you say, living in two worlds. Why should we put up with any more of this Russian monkey business? We simply must let them understand that we mean business. . . . I urge that we be even tougher and less tolerant with the Russians than we have been. They simply just cannot understand tolerance or even the meaning of the word."[26]

The slippery interpretation of "tolerance" may have been the central issue of concern for the remainder of Pulitzer's editorship. The issue had both international and national ramifications that were at various times and in various ways linked with one another. It was a subject ready-made for debate at the *Post-Dispatch,* where, as Pulitzer once expressed it, "civil liberties are one of our specialties."[27] By the spring of 1948 this had resolved in Pulitzer's mind into what he called a "$64 question . . . that is concerning me night and day and day and night." The question was: "If we see civil liberties plainly about to disappear in Europe, should we not go to war for the primary purpose of hoping to preserve our own civil liberties?" He told Coghlan that he was "leaning strongly to the belief that regardless of everything that can be argued about intervention in the affairs of other countries, about the sacred right of self-determination and about respect for the choice of the majority, the right to civil liberty overshadows these other rights and that, therefore, we would be justified in going to war over the issue of preserving our civil liberties." It was a problem, he confessed, which "concerns me more, I believe, than anything that I have ever had to think about in my entire life."[28]

Coghlan replied that he did not think the United States, without "a distinct threat" to its own liberties, "would be justified in going to war to force peoples to overthrow a system that they had adopted of their own free will." He pointed out that unlike the fervently idealistic days of the American and French revolutions, the emphasis "in this rapidly changing century" is on economic security. "Lots of people argue that . . . you can't eat a ballot. This is a depressing trend in human affairs, perhaps, but the instinct for self-preservation is man's primary and most powerful one." Frankly, he concluded, he thought Pulitzer's concern was largely academic: "Aren't you torturing yourself over something that is most unlikely to happen? It is impossible for me to believe the English would forfeit their liberties, or the Scandanavians or the French." He also wanted to make the point, he added, that "if we went to war to impose civil liberties on the world, we might fail to do so and lose our own in the bargain."[29]

A civil rights issue both more concrete and closer to home shortly came to Pulitzer's attention in the form of a racist pamphlet being distributed around St. Louis. He suggested to Reese that there might be a news story in it, but the managing editor, who didn't disguise his own racism, turned it down. Pulitzer chose not to force the issue. "I concede that its value in the news columns is at least debatable," he said, and handed the matter over to Coghlan. He suggested that Coghlan reprint the pamphlet in the "Mirror of Public Opinion" space with a note calling the reader's attention to an accompanying editorial which would "again remind the Nigger-haters and those with open minds that to deny the Negro equal educational and employment rights breeds just this kind of pamphlet. . . . Here, as I see it, is a nice little example which may possibly serve to cause the Nigger-haters — and I know quite a few of them — to stop and think."[30]

While Coghlan saw eye-to-eye with the publisher on that question, their conclusions about the 1948 presidential endorsement, as already noted, were far apart. By midyear Coghlan had told Pulitzer secretary Robert A. Randolph two or three times that he was "on the verge of a nervous breakdown because of uncertainty over the course to be pursued in the coming election." He asked Randolph to convey "my confused and unhappy condition to Mr. Pulitzer," which Randolph tried to do in a letter to J.P. in Canada. "He is afraid that you are going over to the Republicans lock, stock and barrel, and that this will hurt the paper very badly," the secretary wrote. "He admits Truman is a poor president but feels it would be better to have an inefficient Truman and sound Democratic principles rather than a good administrator such as Dewey and principles that may not jibe with the Pulitzer tradition. He also feels Dewey is backed by a very dangerous political gang."[31] Pulitzer didn't agree. He suggested that Coghlan take four weeks of vacation, spending some of it in New York, where Baruch had offered to put Coghlan up in his apartment there as he sometimes did Arthur Krock, head of the *New York Times* Washington bureau, and Marquis Childs. Following the election, Coghlan wanted to tell anyone who asked that he had *not* supported Dewey. By all means, Pulitzer agreed, he should make it clear that the endorsement was Pulitzer's alone, "that you opposed it and were absent on vacation throughout the end of the campaign."[32]

Coghlan's alcoholism became worse during this time. He became irresponsible, as when he missed the first week of work in the new year to get treatment for a badly bruised toe without telling Pulitzer about the emergency or how long he would be out. He knew Pulitzer wanted to discuss their editorial approach on Truman's forthcoming State of the Union address. "This conduct suggests gross irresponsibility to which the New Year's celebration may or may not have contributed," Pulitzer recorded.[33] In this instance, as in earlier ones, Pulitzer asked Irving Dilliard to take over the assignment.

By midyear he decided Coghlan was so unreliable that he had to be replaced. Dilliard was made editor and Coghlan became a correspondent and columnist, a move much like Coghlan's succession of Ross. Coghlan continued to drink, however, and after breaking several promises to Pulitzer that he had stopped, was put on leave of absence until he was eligible for retirement benefits. Coghlan's parting words to Pulitzer were: "While you and I have had sharp disagreements, such as over the support of Gov. Dewey, I have always believed in the seriousness, honorableness, fairness

and, on occasion, even in the nobility of your course as a newspaper man."[34] At Coghlan's request, Pulitzer wrote a "To Whom It
May Concern" letter of reference, which Coghlan never used. It
began: "In my judgment Ralph Coghlan, when he is himself, is the
best editorial writer in the United States." It ended: "He was a
victim of the disease of alcoholism. That was his only weakness."[35]
After he left the *Post-Dispatch,* Coghlan did public relations work
for Presidents Truman and Kennedy and for New Jersey Governor
Robert B. Meyner. When he died at the age of sixty-eight in 1965,
he was working for the New Jersey State Democratic Committee.[36]

Time magazine described the new editor as "almost [Coghlan's]
exact opposite as a personality. Sober, earnest Irving Dilliard, 44,
an ex-Nieman fellow, has a schoolteacher's manner and a historian's
mind. Dilliard is an expert on the U.S. Supreme Court, a pen-pal of
several justices, a contributor to the *Dictionary of American
Biography.* The P–D distributed 70,000 reprints of his 'news
dispatches' (datelined Philadelphia 1787) on the adoption of the
U.S. Constitution."[37]

Dilliard had joined the *Post-Dispatch* as a reporter in 1927 and
began submitting editorials two years later. In 1930 he was invited
to join the editorial page staff and had been there from Johns
through Coghlan. "I know the problems of a whole series of
editors who preceded me," he wrote Pulitzer in a "blow your own
horn" memorandum the publisher asked him to write in 1951. "It
has been my purpose to apply this experience. As you know, I have
stood squarely for what I thought was right as the editorial opinion of the Post-Dispatch. I yield to no one in my attachment to the
principles in our founder's platform." That, he made clear, included
Pulitzer himself:

> The conduct of the page should not be and has not been
> out of any desire to please you as such. It has been to apply
> the platform. . . . This is because . . . I have recognized your
> authority but never forgotten my own responsibility. I
> have seen editorial suggestions on your yellow slips in the
> past received with resentment. It was almost as if you were
> intruding when you made an editorial suggestion. This to
> me is utterly foolish. I think an idea should be judged on
> its merits. Where it comes from does not either make it or

break it. If it tests out by the platform, fine. If it does not, then I should say to you why I think it does not.[38]

As that indicates, there had been some differences between them during the first two years of Dilliard's tenure. Their views parted particularly on questions of the application of constitutional guarantees of civil rights and liberties, especially those of expression and religion in the First Amendment. Dilliard was decidedly an "absolutist" in those matters, much along the lines of Supreme Court Justices Hugo L. Black and William O. Douglas, both of whom he knew. They believed the First Amendment's language was an impenetrable barrier against governmental disturbance of its guarantees. In contrast, Pulitzer believed there were conditions and circumstances under which the constitutional terminology should be interpreted less one-sidedly. That view prevailed during his lifetime and has been held by most members of the Supreme Court. His approach could be described as a version of Justice Oliver Wendell Holmes Jr.'s "clear and present danger" formula for drawing the line between protected and punishable speech. It is similar as well to the method of several more recent Court members who attempt to weigh free speech and other values against one another, selecting that which for them tips the balance. Absolutists think balancers are dangerously flexible in their approach to fundamental freedoms; balancers think absolutists are unrealistically rigid in theirs.

Pulitzer's reaction to the Jehovah's Witnesses compulsory flag salute cases of the early 1940s points up this difference between the two men. In 1940 and again in 1943, he complained to Coghlan about editorials agreeing with Jehovah's Witnesses who contended that compelling their children to salute the American flag in school was an unconstitutional infringement of religious freedom. The question had reached the Supreme Court. "Please . . . take me by the hand, with or without Mr. Dilliard's assistance," he directed Coghlan, "and teach me why a law requiring a child to salute the flag at the expense of being expelled from school is undemocratic. I hold very definitely to the view that that is one simple piece of good manners which the people as a whole have a right to expect from all comers, be they Masons, Baptists, Rotarians or Jehovah's Witnesses. . . . Perhaps I am hopelessly illiberal on this issue, but

I'll be damned if I can see anything to it." He instructed Coghlan, unless he could persuade him otherwise, "to move gradually away from our present editorial position in this matter."[39] He was dissuaded after Coghlan pointed out that although the Court had originally taken Pulitzer's stance, it was likely to reverse itself and agree with the paper's position in an upcoming case. It did.[40]

At the same time this was happening, Pulitzer was by and large well pleased with Dilliard's work. This was clear in the publisher's appeal to President Roosevelt to help him persuade Dilliard not to join the Army. "If ever there was a time for straight, sound thinking here at home, this is the time," he wrote Roosevelt. "Dilliard does think straight and on many an important occasion he has contributed immeasurably to straight thinking on the part of the people of this community. Do you agree with me that he should remain at his desk, and, if so, may I tell him so, or, better still, will you write him to this effect?"[41] There apparently was no answer, for Dilliard never heard anything about this.[42]

After the war, Dilliard had occasion to be complimentary in return when the Bureau of Internal Revenue sought depositions about Pulitzer's work habits from upper-echelon *Post-Dispatch* employees. In order to determine his tax liability, the government wanted to know what Pulitzer did to earn compensation paid him as a "commission" on company business. Between 1941 and June 1947, this had amounted to $565,803.[43] Pulitzer's involvement in the work of the editorial page was substantial and continuous whether he was in St. Louis or away, Dilliard testified. "He insists upon accuracy and fairness to the fullest possible extent. Sometimes the editorial writing staff disagrees with his suggestions. They always find him ready to reason and willing to listen to opposing arguments. . . . He is never dictatorial even when the final decision is his, which in the nature of circumstances it must at times be."[44]

As generally congenial as that made the work appear, it also conveys the point that a measure of discomfiture was built into the operation. With Dilliard, as with McAdams, Bovard, and Klyman, Pulitzer's differences centered on the man's zeal for certain issues. He considered Dilliard excessively interested in legal topics and their intricacies. He objected, for example, to a lengthy editorial in early 1949 because it seemed to him to have been addressed to

Dilliard's "admirers on the supreme court bench" rather than to the "average reader," who must have found it "hopelessly dull and unintelligible." His point, he said, "is this: you unquestionably enjoy a splendid reputation as a constitutional writer and historian. You not unnaturally take pride in hearing that your writings have influenced the court. BUT BUT BUT there is a limit to all things. And in taking all this space to develop this particular subject I must insist that you are writing over the heads of 99 out of 100 of our readers."[45] Several months later he wrote: "May I urge that you let up for quite a while on Bill of Rights and related subjects? I am sure that you will agree that enough is enough and that too much is likely to suggest that the page has an obsession with a particular subject."[46] In his 1951 self-appraisal, Dilliard noted that he sometimes suspected that Pulitzer thought he made "a fetish" of human rights topics. "I do not think the Post-Dispatch should have any fetish subjects," he contended. "But I do think that if it were to be more firmly attached to one principle in the platform than the others it should be to 'never tolerate injustice.' I do not mean to give it undue emphasis. I only mean that there would be a great hole in the platform without it. I think it is significant that our founder put it immediately after 'always fight for progress and reform.' "[47]

That strongly suggested there were limits of compromise beyond which Dilliard would not go. Likewise, Pulitzer had his limits, some of which had been spelled out in a memorandum reacting to a report Dilliard had given him at the end of 1949:

> I have read your able report on the Bill of Rights and the Communists with intense interest. In your last line you say: "It may not tell us where to draw the line but it warns us to stop on the safe side." This does not satisfy me. I want to see the line drawn. We cannot draw the statute, but cannot we promote the drawing of a statute that will draw the line? Especially so in view of the general agreement that a government has the right to protect itself against a plan or plot to overthrow it by force or violence. . . . As to the point of view that those in this country who worry about Communist plots are hysterical, I should like to ask them about France, Italy and all the rest. To laugh

off the danger on the theory that we are a bigger and better
country is not too convincing to me. I prefer [Supreme
Court Justice Felix] Frankfurter's attitude when he refused
to hire a Communist law clerk.[48]

Pulitzer's patience was wearing thin, and a potentially powerful
clash with Dilliard was at hand. Unlike his conflict with Klyman,
though, this dispute could not be characterized as ideological; it
was a more subtly complicated difference of opinion about the
appropriate presentation of the issue in the newspaper. It grew
out of divergent interpretations of the free speech clause as well as
varying assessments of the social and political tensions out of
which anti-Communist sentiment came. Dilliard's resolution was
almost wholly to favor free expression, while Pulitzer could not
ignore the growing fear, suspicion, and confusion this movement
had spawned. He knew the concern of many was genuinely held,
and it was to him an open question as to whether the concern was
justified. Caution seemed advisable, but Dilliard was reluctant to
apply the brakes.

A good indication of just how cautious Pulitzer had become
showed up in the summer of 1949 when he asked his son and
Samuel J. Shelton, a long-time *Post-Dispatch* reporter who had
become Pulitzer's assistant, what they thought of incorporating
loyalty oath questions, such as were being adopted increasingly by
government and business, into *Post-Dispatch* job applications.
He said he could see nothing wrong with questioning appli-
cants about past or present Communist affiliations and their opinions about American Communism and American Communists,
and he would "deny employment to any applicant who did not
answer . . . satisfactorily." His son responded that he and Shelton
thought revising the forms was inadvisable because "a communist
or communist sympathizer would unhesitatingly give a false answer"
and because personal interviews, which would henceforth be
required without exception before anyone was hired, were adequate for screening. Pulitzer decided not to add the questions to
the applications, but said he wanted them asked orally and the
"record kept in writing and signed by the respective employer."[49]
A few months later he advised Reese to drop a correspondent
who had been charged with conspiracy involving defense informa-

tion: "When it comes to Post-Dispatch correspondents with pro-Communist charges against them I believe in suspecting them of being guilty until they are proved innocent, and even then I would still be suspicious."[50]

That attitude, as well as his doubts about constitutional protection of militant subversives and his concern about Klyman's ideological commitments, was developed against a nationwide background of worry verging on hysteria about the threat of Communist subversion. In 1947 an executive order by President Truman required security checks of all government employees. That year the House Un-American Activities Committee began hearings on subversion, one outgrowth of which was the Alger Hiss perjury conviction on which opinion remained divided as to whether Hiss, a former State Department official, had passed secrets to the Russians. In February 1950, U.S. Senator Joseph R. McCarthy, a Wisconsin Republican, began his crusade to root out Communists in government and the military. Also during this period, China fell to the Communists and the Korean War began. Pulitzer's responses were derived from this context, much as his approach to black civil rights issues was influenced by his reading of society's readiness to change.

Besides that, there was counsel for editorial moderation in the existence of considerable feeling in St. Louis going back as far as the "Red Scare" period of the 1920s that the *Post-Dispatch* was a haven for Bolsheviks and fellow travelers. McAdams had alluded to this. In 1946, the *Globe-Democrat* had printed a photograph of the Soviet flag flying over the Twelfth Street entrance to the *Post-Dispatch* building on May 1, in accordance with its policy of flying the flags of allied nations on their national holidays. The competing newspaper believed that a more sinister inference could be drawn, and the *Post-Dispatch* shortly discontinued the goodwill gesture.[51] (Six years later, in 1952, Senator McCarthy drew the evil inference by waving a copy of the 1946 *Globe-Democrat* photograph before a St. Louis audience when he spoke there. "This is the only place in the City of St. Louis where you find the Communist flag being flown," he said. The *Post-Dispatch* reprinted the 1946 photograph with its account of McCarthy's speech.[52])

Dilliard, however, based his decisions solely on his interpretation of the language of the platform and the Constitution, producing a rupture with Pulitzer that never completely healed. Secure in his interpretation of "never tolerate injustice," Dilliard wrote (without consulting the publisher) a ringing denunciation of the conviction of eleven Communists in federal district court in New York in October 1949, under provisions of the 1940 Alien Registration Act, usually called the Smith Act, after one of its congressional sponsors. That law made it illegal to belong to or join any group that taught or advocated the overthrow of any government in the United States by force or violence. The editorial contended that the Communists had been convicted under this "hysterical law" for holding political opinions protected by the First Amendment. "It is not enough to say that a man teaches and advocates overthrow and therefore so incites others that the government itself is endangered," Dilliard wrote.[53] Nothing was closer to his heart than the principle involved in this case. Furthermore, he told Pulitzer, "any other editorial was unthinkable in the light of [the] platform and our application of it."[54]

Those words were written in April 1951 as part of his "blow your own horn" report. Dilliard also noted that the publisher had congratulated him for his "courage" at the time the editorial was run. But the fact was that Pulitzer did not regard the Smith Act as harshly as did Dilliard. He believed that the law, if interpreted to outlaw advocacy of overt acts rather than simply expressions of ideas and beliefs, was constitutional. In upholding the convictions in 1951, the Supreme Court made that distinction to his satisfaction but not to Dilliard's. Pulitzer had construed Dilliard's 1949 editorial to have condemned outlawing any and all kinds of pro-Communist advocacy.[55] Dilliard thought that in upholding the convictions the Supreme Court had made the same great error. And he said so—again without consulting Pulitzer, who was fishing in Canada—in a long lead editorial headed "Six Men Amend the Constitution." "Never before has such a restriction been placed on the right to hold opinions and express them in the United States of America," he wrote. "Six men have amended the United States Constitution without submitting those amendments to the states for ratification. That is the nub of this decision."[56]

When Pulitzer got back to Bar Harbor in July, he made a count of all the judges, from the trial through the Supreme Court, who had supported the convictions. "The consensus of judges, all presumably honest and intelligent men who have studied this question, appears to be ten to two," he wrote Dilliard. "Although the majority is not always right, five to one is a strong majority. This prompts me to say that if a similar or comparable case comes up I shall want to discuss it with you before we make any commitment."[57] In reality, the two men probably were not as widely divided as the majority and minority at the Supreme Court. In a memo to Dilliard in February 1950, Pulitzer had said he was impressed by an American Civil Liberties Union plan to seek amendment of the Smith Act "to permit teaching and advocacy but to prohibit actual preparations and plans clearly intended to lead to such acts of violence. . . . As I see it, this is the very crux of the entire matter, that is, how to draw the line between teaching and advocacy and deliberate planning for or committing acts of violence. In other words, when does a clear danger become a present danger?"[58] (In 1957, two years after Pulitzer's death, the Supreme Court wrote the distinction between abstract advocacy and advocacy of overt acts into First Amendment law.[59])

About two weeks before Pulitzer raised that question, on February 9, 1950, Senator McCarthy began his vilification campaign by waving a piece of paper before an audience in Wheeling, West Virginia, on which he said were written the names of 205 U.S. State Department employees who were known members of the Communist party. Once more the Dilliard and Pulitzer approaches were different. Both deplored McCarthy's methods, but Pulitzer was not at first as fully persuaded as Dilliard that the senator was an utter demagogue. He believed the charges deserved investigation "in good faith without fireworks or klieg lights on either side. The sooner the charges are proved or disproved the better off the country will be."[60] Two days after writing that, he advised Dilliard to "please go slow on Communists, minorities, subversive groups and other phases of civil rights. . . . There is danger — in my opinion serious danger — that the impression will get around that the editorial page is thinking about civil rights and of not much else. We don't want to be regarded as a public bore. Too much is too much."[61]

McCarthy, of course, was impossible to ignore, and as his forays continued over the next four years, he got considerable space in the *Post-Dispatch,* including some lengthy depth analyses. One of these, by Washington correspondent George H. Hall, appeared on the editorial title page in February 1951, accompanied by a strong Fitzpatrick cartoon and under the headline "The Sinister Alliance Between McCarthy and Taft."[62] It described how the presidential ambitions of both McCarthy and Ohio Senator Robert A. Taft were motivating them to discredit opponents by use of "the big lie method." In 1953, Pulitzer asked managing editor Crowley for a broader study of the McCarthy phenomenon:

> Last night I was challenged as to McCarthy. I was asked the familiar question—granting that McCarthy has been loose in his charges and may well have smeared some innocent people, in short, that his methods have been bad, have not the results on the whole been good? Is not his objective a worthy one and if he had not uncovered so many Communists and so many who take refuge in the Fifth Amendment and refuse to answer questions who would have done so?
>
> This reminds me of a suggestion which went by the board in the Washington Bureau that I made a couple of months ago.
>
> I should seriously like to see an article which might well quote the foregoing question and might undertake, with utmost fairness and generosity to McCarthy, to give the answers. I shall want to see the copy before it is released. I repeatedly run into people who are honestly confused, who unquestionably have been influenced by pro-McCarthyites but who are hungry for information.
>
> I happen to despise McCarthy and his methods and to deplore Eisenhower's failure to come to grips with him, and probably the writer of the piece will feel the same way. I hope, however, that he will take the utmost pains to suppress any such feelings, make the piece coldly objective, even to the extent of giving McCarthy every possible break.
>
> Even if we never print the story I shall feel that it will not mean time wasted and that it will at least give me facts and information that will be helpful to me.[63]

The result was a three-part series by the chief Washington correspondent Raymond P. Brandt, which presented McCarthy's charges one by one and then, in boldface type, reported the outcome in each instance. "For the reader's guidance," Brandt observed in the first article, "this writer, who has reported on national politics for almost 30 years, believes the 'bad' vastly outweighs the 'good' in the McCarthy record."[64] Pulitzer had suggested only two minor changes in the copy—more detail in one passage and clearer expression in another.[65]

During the televised Army-McCarthy hearings in 1954, which led to McCarthy's censure by the Senate, Pulitzer again thought the editorial page was giving the matter too much space. "Please, please, please lay off the McCarthy hearings. To me—and I believe to the great majority—they are the most terrific bore. Off hand, I should say that one editorial, one letter and one cartoon a week would be about right."[66] In December, after Dilliard ran in the "Mirror of Public Opinion" a rather tedious excerpt from the Senate's censure hearings which Pulitzer considered "a total waste of space," he directed the editor "that the words 'McCarthy' or 'McCarthyism' or any oblique reference to either shall not appear on the editorial page without my specific approval in the issues of December 7, 8, 9, 10, 11 and 12."[67]

Nearly thirty years later, author Edwin R. Bayley's selection from among Pulitzer's memorandums on McCarthy—including portions of several quoted above—was used to support the conclusion in Bayley's book *Joe McCarthy and the Press* that over the four years from 1950 to 1954 Pulitzer's messages to Dilliard "were a succession of notes that pleaded, wheedled, or demanded that the editor be kinder to McCarthy."[68] Dilliard, retired for some years and a member of the editorial board of the *St. Louis Journalism Review,* reviewed the book for that publication. "Among the many values of Bayley's research and writing is careful use of the personal papers of the late Joseph Pulitzer II," he wrote. "The Bayley book . . . shows what a first class newspaperman who turns researcher can do when he takes on a subject such as Joe McCarthy and handles it honestly and fearlessly."

Bayley did have impressive credentials. He was dean of the Graduate School of Journalism at the University of California at Berkeley when his book came out. He had been a political reporter for the *Milwaukee Journal* between 1946 and 1959. In that capacity, he had been one of McCarthy's targets, a factor that may have intensified his animus against the senator. Once, during a McCarthy appearance in Wisconsin, Bayley's book notes, he was singled out by the senator. "I'd like first to introduce a reporter in the audience, Ed Bayley from the *Milwaukee Daily Worker*," McCarthy began. "Stand up, Ed, and let the people see what a communist looks like."[69]

One memorandum quoted partially in both Bayley's book and Dilliard's review is the one to Crowley, quoted in its entirety above, which led to Brandt's highly condemnatory three-part series in 1953. Apparently assuming the book had used all of it, Dilliard said in the review, "The memo closed with the words: 'I shall want to see the copy before it is released.'"[70] In fact, the memo ran for four more sentences, which, if used, would have sharply altered, if not negated, Bayley's conclusion that Pulitzer wanted Dilliard to "be kinder to McCarthy."

Although Pulitzer was often harsh in his condemnation of McCarthy during those four years, Bayley either failed to read or ignored that information in Pulitzer's papers. In one memo, for example, the publisher seemed to counter his own advice to avoid becoming a bore about McCarthy: "What would you say," he asked Dilliard, "to our tagging him with the name Phoney Joe McCarthy and repeating, repeating and repeating it in editorials and cartoons? It might well catch on." Dilliard was cool to the idea, responding: "It is a question . . . whether he has not done so much damage and may not do so much more in the future that ridicule as a steady treatment would not be sufficient handling."[71] Dilliard wouldn't have seen another item Bayley omitted, Pulitzer's response to New York textile executive Minot K. Milliken, who sent him a book praising the senator in April 1954:

> I am having the McCarthy book you sent me read for me and marked. I fear I will not enjoy it for, as you know, I detest McCarthy as much as I detest Communism and believe his motives are unworthy, his methods thoroughly unAmerican and his early record unspeakable. Nevertheless, thanks for the thought.

He instructed the secretary he assigned to read the book "to mark
such chapters or passages as you think are most convincing and
favorable to McCarthy. I do not relish reading it but it was sent me
by a violently pro-McCarthy friend and I feel I should know something about it."[72]

Dilliard's review of Bayley's book angered Joseph Pulitzer Jr.,
much of whose training to succeed his father had consisted of
reading his father's memorandums. He was certain they did not
convey Bayley's conclusion and asked his managing editor, David
Lipman, to have a Washington bureau reporter check his father's
papers at the Library of Congress to see whether they confirmed that
belief. They did. He sent a copy of the reporter's findings and a letter
to Dilliard personally, but not to the *Review,* in which he said:

> From personal experience, I can state categorically that what
> concerned J.P. was fairness and balance in news reporting
> and responsibility and avoidance of excess in editorial
> writing. You will remember that he had displayed earlier his
> abhorrence of demagoguery by initiating a series on Dixie
> demagogues written by Rufus Terral, then detached from
> the editorial page for this assignment; it was illustrated
> with powerful caricatures by Fitzpatrick. My father's nega-
> tive attitude toward demagoguery continued and intensified.
> He detested McCarthy and despised his conduct. In my
> presence, he deplored Eisenhower's reluctance to come to
> terms with the senator's abuse of the administration and
> the Senate. There were many dinner-table conversations
> making clear J.P.'s disgust with and deep resentment of
> Joe McCarthy. . . . Bayley's coverage of J.P.'s role in the
> McCarthy issue was at best superficial and at worst lacking
> in perception and even malicious.[73]

Dilliard thanked the publisher for this information and urged that
the "fuller treatment" of the situation should be "broadly shared
so as to reach not only readers of the Journalism Review but also
many readers of Bayley's 'Joe McCarthy and the Press.' It surely
must not stop here."[74] In effect, J.P. Jr. agreed by releasing this
exchange to the author of this book.

He also released other information from his father's tenure

which had not been sent to the Library of Congress, as well as some from his own files. This explains the role of Pulitzer's most trusted assistant, Sam Shelton, in the publisher's relationship with Dilliard, the fifth and final of his editorial page editors.

Shelton was hired as a *Post-Dispatch* reporter in 1913 and served in that capacity—with a break in the 1920s to edit a trade publication in Chicago—until 1945. That August, just as the war was ending, Pulitzer tapped him to be his labor relations representative during a strike by newspaper carriers which closed all of the city's newspapers for twenty-two days. Shelton had achieved such a record for integrity as a reporter that Pulitzer was sure he would be trusted and respected by the unions. Klyman agreed, telling Pulitzer that Shelton's appointment was "a brilliant move" because "it makes all of us on the third floor [the newsroom] comfortable; we feel now that there will be clear lines of communication between the people who work for the Post-Dispatch and yourself."[75] One demonstration of Shelton's reputation for fairness had been that when Kansas City Democratic boss Tom Pendergast was sent to prison for income tax evasion in 1939, Shelton was the only reporter Pendergast would allow to accompany him on the ride with federal marshals to the penitentiary. His biggest reportorial achievement had been a series of exclusive articles in 1938 exposing corrupt practices of the Union Electric Company of Missouri. He led the paper's effort to rid St. Louis of smoke and soot, which had made it one of the dirtiest cities in the nation. The paper won a Pulitzer Prize in 1941 for its antismoke campaign.[76]

Shelton was Pulitzer's closest business confidant during the last ten years of the publisher's life and an executor of his will.[77] He was independent of any department, had direct access to J.P., and reported to him. "Under these circumstances," Shelton recorded, "he consulted me frequently about conduct of the editorial page and also about the news department, as well as about other departments." It was Shelton who recommended that Coghlan be relieved of his editorship to become a correspondent/columnist and that Dilliard be named to succeed him. About a year later he recommended Coghlan's termination.

Almost from the beginning, Shelton recalled, "J.P. had numerous occasions to be dissatisfied with Dilliard's work as editor of the page and as [a] writer of policy editorials," but at the same time he had "mixed feelings" about the man, as revealed when he wrote this to Shelton on August 2, 1952:

> While I am not altogether satisfied with the editorial page under Dilliard's editorship, I do feel that he has done highly useful work for the Post-Dispatch and that he is entitled to a salary increase. Accordingly please see to it that his salary is fixed at $20,000 a year—an increase of $2,000. I do not feel that in his case a contract is necessary. Please inform him of the increase.[78]

Pulitzer was displeased during the 1952 presidential campaign, Shelton continued, because of Dilliard's becoming "so violently a partisan of Adlai Stevenson, . . . even before J.P.'s decision committing the paper to support of Stevenson, that the paper was widely accused of bias and prejudice." He also remained unhappy with the tone of editorials on communism, and in mid-November sent this to Dilliard:

> "THE CLIMATE OF THE POST-DISPATCH EDITORIAL PAGE MUST BE ONE THAT THE COMMUNISTS AND THEIR SYMPATHIZERS WOULD FIND THOROUGHLY HOSTILE." This is a *MUST* rule and everyone who writes or edits editorial page matter, including editorials, cartoons, mirrors, book reviews and letters shall keep it constantly in mind. . . .
> . . . We have been so intent on not "burning down the house" that we have too often overlooked or appeared to be overlooking the need for "getting rid of the rats." . . .
> It goes without saying that the foregoing does NOT mean that we should close our eyes to McCarthyism and the making of reckless charges by anyone. It DOES mean that henceforth we should interest ourselves and show a continuing alert and positive interest in "getting rid of the rats."[79]

A month later he told Dilliard that "in your zeal to protect civil liberties you have a positive obsession on the subject and are always looking for a witchhunter under the bed. In this field I am far from satisfied with your conduct of the page."[80]

In 1953, Pulitzer became increasingly dissatisfied, particularly with Dilliard's handling of a Republican charge that in 1946 then President Truman had promoted Harry Dexter White from assistant secretary of the treasury to become the first American executive director of the International Monetary Fund (IMF), even though Truman knew at that time of serious accusations that White was a Communist spy and that a secret investigation of the charges was pending. White was removed from the IMF post in 1947. He died in 1948, leaving the allegations against him a matter of controversy.[81] Dilliard's 1953 editorial, Shelton recorded, "was widely construed as an effort to vindicate Harry Truman's loose handling of Dexter White and even as being sympathetic toward White himself in the face of disclosures strongly linking White with Communist espionage." Just the month before that editorial appeared, Pulitzer had written to Dilliard:

> I propose in this memo to give you a lesson in the writing of editorials defending the civil rights of questionable characters. . . . The point of the lesson is that when you are dealing with a man of questionable, or certainly of controversial reputation . . . you should always indicate to the reader that you realize that the subject of the editorial has for years been well to the left and charged with, or suspected of, being definitely sympathetic to the Communist philosophy. In other words, show the reader that you are well aware of all this and then go ahead with all the more effectiveness to defend his civil rights. Do not by omission appear ignorantly to be making a hero of him.[82]

Concluding that this had had little effect, Pulitzer became so exasperated by the end of 1953 that he asked Shelton to come up with some alternatives to the current situation. Shelton suggested two: appoint a new editor or "place someone in charge with supervisory authority, while retaining I.D. as editor." They finally settled, after several conferences with Dilliard at Pulitzer's home, on what they called a "guidance" or "tutelage" arrangement under which Shelton "would exercise an advisory function with reference to the editorial page contents."

In the course of coming to this compromise, Shelton wrote a long memorandum for Pulitzer in which he discussed Dilliard's strengths and weaknesses. On the positive side, he noted that, as editor, Dilliard "has dealt with many major issues with clarity, force and persuasiveness," including many outside the field of civil rights; that Pulitzer had commended him numerous times, both for editorials he wrote and for the page as a whole; that "he has a background of extraordinary scholarship and historical information which contributes much to the page; that he was "a tireless worker" with "zeal for the job and pride in the traditional policies of the paper"; that his character was admirable, "marked by unquestioned integrity, clean living, highest ideals of good citizenship, humanitarianism"; and that he had "established a better spirit among [his] personnel than existed before, although I recognize that administratively he becomes too much involved in details and in outside activities." (Pulitzer had commented several times that he thought Dilliard saw too many office visitors and wrote too many letters.) On the negative side, Shelton listed "immaturity of judgment, blindness to the logic of certain situations, overzealousness in devotion to 'causes,' bias of a nature to indicate partisanship, stubbornness." This was followed by a list of more than a dozen instances of differences with the publisher. For example: "I.D.'s correspondence with and visit to Hiss's lawyer on the new trial effort. An excess of zeal." Near the end, he included several "other observations" that are supportive of Shelton's reputation for fair-mindedness. "It is inevitable," he pointed out, "that you will find some editorials displeasing which other competent persons may think are praiseworthy. But you are the boss." And finally, "I am sure you recognize these points: 1. The physical burden of the day to day conduct of the page. 2. The difficulties which confront any editor in so conducting the page as to conform to your views on broad policy considerations. 3. The problem of reconciliation of an editor's honest and firm opinions on important policy matters when they may differ from your opinions."[83]

Sometime during the "tutelage" planning discussions, Dilliard told Fitzpatrick about them in connection with Pulitzer's dislike of a Fitzpatrick cartoon that made fun of Eisenhower. Apparently assuming that both Fitzpatrick and Dilliard were going to be censored, Shelton related to Pulitzer, "Fitz literally blew up. He said, 'Maybe they better get another boy' and a few other choice expressions." Pulitzer, who had known the feisty Fitzpatrick since the cartoonist joined the paper in 1913, and who hunted ducks with him regularly, wasn't surprised. "Of course, Fitz will again 'blow up,' " he replied. But, "he, like everyone else, should not have too much trouble in realizing that the editor of the paper must hold himself responsible for the mistakes of himself and of all other staff members up and down the line in his and all other departments."[84]

Robert Lasch, who had been a Rhodes Scholar, was chief editorial writer for the *Chicago Sun-Times* in 1950, when he accepted an offer to join the *Post-Dispatch* editorial page staff. He eventually succeeded Dilliard as editor and viewed at close range much of the Pulitzer-Dilliard conflict. It appeared to him that Dilliard's troubles with Pulitzer "were due to a conflict of personalities. J.P. was certainly more conservative than I.D., but other elements entered in. I suspect that J.P. felt there was a question as to whether he or Irving was running the paper—an echo of his troubles with Bovard, of whom Irving was a devout admirer. Irving had a way of running his fiercest editorials when J.P. was out of town, and this led to recriminations." The upshot was the "guidance" arrangement, which, Lasch explained, worked this way: "All editorial proofs went to Sam and he and Irving would have long telephone conversations, often close to press time, about disputed points. Irving was to have final say, but Sam was to present what he thought was J.P.'s view on specific editorials, both as to content and as to style. This was a pretty clear indication that Irving did not have J.P.'s complete confidence." Lasch said that "J.P. was never a McCarthyite. He would hardly have stood for the P-D's supporting Stevenson over Eisenhower in 1952 if he had been one. But he did share some of the concern over Communism at that period," and the disagreement with Dilliard about the constitutionality of the Smith Act "probably was one of the major differences with J.P." Reflecting on Pulitzer's overall attitude, Lasch observed: "I had the feeling that he took the famous 'platform' seriously and wanted the paper to be generally a little left of center even though he himself might be farther right. It was my impression

that he wished to be relieved of day-to-day supervision of the
page by a staff he could trust to keep the paper in line with its
tradition of independent liberalism." Lasch recalled "one amusing
note that illustrates the personality differences" between the publisher and Dilliard: "Irving had a habit of wearing no socks. One of
J.P.'s secretaries called this to his attention and J.P., according to
report, was outraged."[85] J.P. Jr.'s recollection of this was that his
father found it " 'not amusing,' and inappropriate, distasteful but not
outrageous. J.P. told me about the incident with a bit of mild dis-
approval but also with some humor involving a 'country bumpkin.'
That was his opinion of Dilliard's style and manners which he
presumably never uttered to anyone but me. He respected I.D.'s
intellect."[86]

There were relatively few times under the guidance system,
Shelton noted, when he and Dilliard were not able to reach an
understanding and Dilliard "insisted on printing material which I
could not approve." But he and the publisher anticipated trouble
toward the end of 1954, when decisions on some appeals of
anti-Communist prosecutions were expected. Pulitzer was strongly
inclined to retract Dilliard's earlier condemnation of the Supreme
Court for upholding the Smith Act and had Shelton draft an
editorial doing so. Its key sentence read: "The Post-Dispatch takes
this opportunity to make known that it approves the Supreme
Court's decision that the Smith Act is constitutional as applied in
the case of the 11 Communists prosecuted in New York, and that
its earlier views to the contrary expressed on this page were in
error."[87] After traveling from Bar Harbor to St. Louis for a
conference, Pulitzer decided to withhold the editorial for the time
being.[88] In telling Dilliard of this, he wrote:

> The Post-Dispatch will continue to protect the Bill of Rights,
> but it will recognize plainly and clearly that none of these
> rights, including freedom of speech, is absolute. With this
> recognition in mind it will be very slow in denouncing any
> new act, as it did the Smith Act, on the ground that there
> has been undue limitation of the rights guaranteed by the
> Bill of Rights. . . .
>   You, I.D., must recognize or at the very least you
> must accept my recognition of the fact that teaching and

advocating overthrow . . . is not mere abstract, philosophical, teaching and advocacy but, on the contrary, represents a deliberate planned effort and intention to overthrow the government at the first opportunity. You must recognize that the danger, although it may be argued that it is not imminent or even that it is somewhat remote, is clear and present. . . .

If you . . . can honestly and conscientiously subscribe to these principles and will express them editorially and will, by constant repetition, emphasize them editorially, I am willing to defer indefinitely and perhaps permanently publication of the editorial by S.S. . . .

Written in longhand at the bottom of the memo, probably by Shelton, is this notation: "I.D. says he is now impressed as not before by the aspect of 'clear and present danger.' "[89] But Pulitzer remained uneasy about the editorial page, especially with Shelton approaching retirement. On March 25, 1955, just five days before Pulitzer's death, Shelton wrote in his desk diary: "Discussion with J.P. on edit page. His main thought was that J.P. Jr. and I should go on a tour to try to discover a man who in time could take over as brilliantly as did Cobb of the World." Shelton asked him if he thought the arrangement with Dilliard had been worthwhile. "Very much so," Pulitzer replied. "I am relieved when you are here. [I] wish very much I had a man at the head of the edit page I trust as I do you and R.L.C. [managing editor Crowley]."[90] They planned to discuss the matter more fully later but never got the chance. (After reading this chapter in draft, Dilliard commented: "The Communist cases, the McCarthy era and all the rest added up to a difficult time for the P–D's editorial page and JP II and I.D."[91])

Under Joseph Pulitzer Jr., Shelton kept his editorial page assignment until he retired in early 1957. That October, the new editor-publisher told Dilliard he was dissatisfied with his work and wanted him to step down as editor. He asked Lasch, "bearing in mind the hazardous tenure which history has shown," to succeed Dilliard.[92] Lasch held the job until his own retirement in 1971, longer than anyone since George Johns. In 1966, he won the Pulitzer Prize for editorial writing for several editorials critical of

American policy in Vietnam. The *Post-Dispatch*'s opposition to U.S. involvement in the Indochina war dated from 1954, when the paper started a series of editorials headed "A War to Stay Out Of."[93] That year, Fitzpatrick won his second Pulitzer Prize, for his anti-intervention cartoon, "How Would Another Mistake Help?"[94] In this instance, the editor-publisher, the editorial page editor, and the cartoonist were united in their opposition to what became a great tragedy. "I am more than ever convinced that whether or not Hanoi falls and regardless of the emotions that would be stirred by Hanoi's fall, my so-called sailing orders [a reference to earlier memorandums] are still sound," Pulitzer wrote in June 1954, less than a year before his death. "I cannot conceive of any circumstances or combination of circumstances that would justify Congress's authorizing the President to 'go it alone' into Indochina. If and when the time comes I hope the P–D will not hesitate to say so plainly and very, very sharply."[95]

Dilliard left the *Post-Dispatch* in 1960 and was a lecturer at the Salzburg, Austria, Seminar in American Studies that year. In 1963, he accepted an endowed professorship in journalism at Princeton University, a post he held until 1973. He was director of the Illinois Department on Aging in 1974–75 and then retired. He won several national awards and recognitions for his support of civil liberties while at the newspaper and was invited to speak at a number of universities.

How Lasch's editorship might have gone under the second Joseph Pulitzer can only be conjectured, but it seems likely that there would have been some tense times. During the week before his death, Pulitzer asked Shelton, "Won't you try to sober up and steady down Lasch's expressions on economic subjects?" He mentioned three editorials, including one criticizing Monsanto president Edgar Queeny in a "sarcastic and almost contemptuous" way. "Lasch's tone of fairness and sincerity and moderation is very much more impressive in his conversation than it is in his editorial expressions," he observed. "It hurts me to think that we are so often right in our point of view but so often wrong—very wrong—in our expression."[96]

That may well identify the essence of the conflict with Dilliard, in contrast to the basically philosophical difference with the collectivistic Klyman. The evidence makes it appear that without the resistance of such strong-willed lieutenants as Klyman and Dilliard, Pulitzer could have committed the *Post-Dispatch* to a more stridently anticommunist stance. In all probability, the issue would have gotten less editorial attention in the paper. Yet at the same time, there is little question that, while he was open to argument, Pulitzer had the last word on the matter—both personally and by delegated authority—throughout his dealings with the two men. It is clear that overall he chose to use his power in a temperate way. More than anything else, he seemed to want to give a balanced presentation of this emotionally supercharged issue. That appears to be why, for example, he thought it was wrong to dismiss the widespread concern McCarthy had tapped, even though he disliked the senator and said so. Further, a memorandum Pulitzer wrote Dilliard in late 1951 shows that he and Dilliard were not ideologically far apart.

> I am seriously tempted somehow to nail the following to the masthead and to run it permanently:
> "If there is any principle of the constitution that more imperatively calls for attachment than any other it is the principle of free thought—not free thought for those who agree with us but freedom for the thought that we hate."[97]

That never reached the masthead, probably because, as Pulitzer anticipated in the memo, the statement would "seem to subordinate the platform." Still, the proposal is indicative of a commitment much like Dilliard's; the differences, while more than superficial, had to do with approach, emphasis, and style of expression—differences of degree. With Klyman, the differences were of both kind and degree. In Pulitzer's relationship with both men it is revealing and impressive to see the concentration with which those differences were monitored and debated. What this reveals is that it was through an almost continuous tug-and-pull process, rather than any assertion of the proprietor's prerogative by Pulitzer, that shaped *Post-Dispatch* handling of one of the most challenging controversies of Pulitzer's editorship.

Philosopher Businessman

A gainst the travail of keeping watch on editorial policy and execution, directing the business side of the *Post-Dispatch* was comparatively easy for Pulitzer. Differences were usually resolved quickly, and there were no struggles of will or ideology. While he was both liked and respected by virtually all who worked under him, differences notwithstanding, the men who carried out his business policies found him unusually impressive. Albert G. Lincoln, the company's secretary and then business manager for most of Pulitzer's career, almost idolized him. He carefully preserved in thirty-five scrapbooks the many memorandums he exchanged with the publisher, as a record of what he considered both highly effective and principled leadership. The only regret of Charles J. Hentschell, who succeeded Lincoln as business manager, was that he hadn't joined the *Post-Dispatch* earlier than 1941, so that he could have worked longer with Pulitzer.[1]

Pulitzer's success as a businessman seems attributable to three factors. First, when he became editor and publisher in 1911 the newspaper had an established record of financial success; in fact, it had failed to return a profit to its owner only once in its history — in 1897 — when the founder had relinquished control briefly to another man.[2] The company was profitable throughout the second Joseph Pulitzer's forty-three-year tenure as publisher and, as of 1991, every year since.[3] Second, the managers he inherited were experienced, capable, loyal, and forward-looking, and their successors — usually promoted from within the organization — were of the same mold. Third, Pulitzer was a competent business-man in his own right. With little apparent effort, he assumed the mantle of authority, quickly establishing himself as a working administrator who was aware of and interested in all phases of the newspaper's operations. Throughout his career, as throughout his father's, his primary interest was the journalistic phases of his work. But his memorandums show that he was also a regular follower of the paper's business development and a discerning interpreter of trends in circulation, advertising, business conditions, competition, and the operation's large human and mechanical apparatus. If anything, in the opinions of Sam Shelton and Shelton's successor as assistant to the publisher, Richard G. Baumhoff, he could have safely and perhaps more wisely spent less time on this by delegating more authority.[4]

But Pulitzer had a compelling reason for wanting his presence felt on the business side: the sales people and accountants would otherwise tend to let strictly business considerations override the newspaper's journalistic purpose. He recalled his father's saying "that when the Post-Dispatch had in one year made $365,000, or a thousand dollars a day, that was entirely too much and he asked department heads how the sum of $100,000 could best be spent for the improvement of the paper."[5] That expressed, of course, a mixture of idealism and business pragmatism, but the thumb was on the idealistic side of the scale, and it was Pulitzer's happy lot to be able to keep it there as, year after year, the profits came in. For the forty-three full years of his tenure, from 1912 through 1954, the company averaged an annual after-tax "Nelson" (the founder's code word for "Net Profit," which has continued in use) of 11.3 percent of its revenues. The highest point in that span was 18.5 percent in 1929; the lowest was 4.8 percent in 1948.[6]

Profits in the late 1940s would have been higher had Pulitzer decided to print bigger papers in order to carry all the advertising then available. But he wanted circulation gains that could be translated into higher advertising rates, instead of transitory bulges in advertising volume to move the company forward. The paper had "more business than we can carry," he explained to his son, because it was a time of "many economic dislocations and of abnormal prosperity." The main economic dislocation for the newspaper was a shortage of newsprint, forcing a choice between allocation to circulation for long-term benefit or to advertising for short-term gains. The point to keep in mind, he counseled, is that "circulation is still and always will be the life blood of a newspaper. The quality and quantity of its contents may be likened to the soul and character and personality of a newspaper." On that basis, he believed "that journalistic quality and that natural, honest circulation should . . . retrieve such temporary advertising losses as we may suffer. This policy, I know, will hurt my pocketbook but in the long run I am convinced it is the sound policy."[7]

The advice was vintage Pulitzer, virtually the same as its author had heard from his father, and represented a thread of philosophical continuity even though the elder Pulitzer had abandoned the pursuit of circulation by means of extravagant sensationalism after the Spanish-American War. The basic point still stood, in his son's opinion, that an advertising-supported American newspaper that could gain and keep readers by following a news policy of thoroughness and dependability should be able to support itself and turn a profit. He had tried to make that very point to his brothers during the final years of the *World*. Despite that failure and others, it seemed to him that most newspaper publishers understood this quite well, and he gave them high marks for purveying unbiased news. Where he parted company with many other publishers was in his sense of the newspaper's editorial mission in behalf of participatory democracy. As had his father, he considered himself more aware of this calling than most men in his position, and he worked to maintain business practices that were consistent with it.

He explained his viewpoint in late 1938 in response to the often-heard charge of New Dealers that capitalistic newspapers were essentially profit-motivated, conservative partisans of the status quo. "I think Roosevelt and his crowd exaggerate the counting room control, at least insofar as the news columns are concerned," he wrote Charles Ross. "As to their being tories, editorially, that is probably true but it probably always has been true of both the Northern Republican and Southern Democratic press with a very few shining exceptions. After all, how could you expect [*St. Louis Globe-Democrat* publisher] Lansing Ray, estimable, honest and well-meaning gentleman as he is, with his background of education in the advertising office to be anything but a business man with a business man's point of view as to the good old days of laissez-faire, and Lansing, I think, is a perfect type of American newspaper publisher, not only of today but of the last 25 or 30 years." Papers such as the *Globe-Democrat,* it seemed to Pulitzer, were "almost entirely 'free' " in their news presentation, but inadequate editorially because of "the limited horizons of [the] Lansing Rays." But then, "there never were many [Henry] Wattersons, [Samuel] Bowleses, [William Rockhill] Nelsons, even in my father's time and there are not many of them today. In a nutshell, the press reports well but cerebrates poorly."[8]

Consistent with this, he thought University of Illinois journalism school director Fred S. Siebert made "a darn good point which we should ram home to the public" when Siebert testified before the Federal Communications Commission in 1942 that it was largely a myth that advertisers could control the content of newspapers and radio. Siebert contended that there was such a diverse range of advertisers that "publishers have been independent of most pressures that might be brought upon them." Furthermore, "until newspapers became an independent financial institution it was impossible for them to resist the various pressures . . . devised by political leaders from time to time."[9]

It is striking to note how closely similar the second J.P.'s appraisal of the American press is to sociologist Michael Schudson's more recent description of the setting in which the first J.P. worked:

> This equal estimation of the editorial and news functions of the press was unusual in the late nineteenth century.

Pulitzer may have created the first modern mass-circulation newspaper, but he did so as the last of the old-fashioned editors. Most leading newspaper proprietors of the late nineteenth century were businessmen rather than political thinkers, managers rather than essayists or activists. Pulitzer cared deeply about his editorial page, but Adolph Ochs considered eliminating the *Times'* editorials altogether; Hearst looked upon the editorial page with contempt; James Gordon Bennett, Jr., toyed with dropping the editorial department of the *Herald.* [10]

Of course, Schudson added, the first Joseph Pulitzer was fully aware of the importance of entertainment to his undertakings. So was his son. As already noted, that had been a major point of difference with the haughty Bovard. But at the same time, the newspaper was spending about $100,000 a year on its editorial page when Bovard quit in 1938.[11]

In sum, while Pulitzer's general outlook did not cause him to perceive the newspaper press of his day with the same shrill alarm Clark McAdams had voiced in his antipublisher editorials of 1934, he had considerable sympathy with that view. In fact, at that time he had written his brother Ralph that he considered McAdams's editorials only "about 51% wrong" because he agreed that there are "a good many selfish publishers who use freedom of the press as a smoke screen."[12] Just three years later, shortly before the annual meeting of the American Newspaper Publishers Association, the *Post-Dispatch* ran an editorial that compared the ANPA "to the National Association of Manufacturers or the American Petroleum Institute or any other coalition of business men for the purpose of advancing the fortunes of themselves and their companies." Its bylaws, the editorial continued, showed that its purpose was "to foster the business interests of members, to procure uniformity of usage, to settle differences, to protect members from irresponsible customers, and so on. This is the language of business; it is not the language of the newspaper profession. It is the language of men engaged in manufacturing a product; it is not the language of men engaged in the high and responsible calling of writing, editing, and interpreting the news."[13]

Pulitzer saw the prestigious prizes his father had established at

Columbia University as based on ideals that were contrary to such commercial trends. In 1928, he asked Harold S. Pollard, who had been one of his father's secretaries, what he could remember the elder Pulitzer had said about the Pulitzer Prizes. "As to the newspaper prizes," Pollard replied, "I heard him say one thing many times with emphasis: 'A newspaper should be more than a first-rate newspaper, printing every day first-rate news and first-rate editorials. It should have hobbies, undertake reforms, lead crusades and thereby establish a name for individuality and active public service.'"[14] His son worked to perpetuate this view as a member for nineteen years and as chairman for fourteen of the Advisory Board on the Pulitzer Prizes, which picked the winners after juries in the various categories submitted their recommendations. There was sometimes grumbling by outside observers when Pulitzer newspapers won the awards, even though it was made plain that neither Joseph nor Ralph—who chaired the advisory board until his death in 1939—had any part in those selections. One of the newspaper's public-service Pulitzers had been shared with the *Chicago Daily News* for a highly unusual exposé of journalistic dishonesty. An investigation in 1949 by the two newspapers revealed that fifty-one Illinois editors and publishers had accepted payments totaling $480,000 a year from state coffers in exchange for printing handouts from Republican party headquarters.[15]

To help him decide whom he would support when newspaper executives were nominated to fill vacancies on the twelve-member advisory board, Pulitzer sought information on each candidate's business orientation. For example, in reporting on a list of nominees about whom Pulitzer had asked him to make inquiries in 1952, managing editor Crowley related that Paul Miller of Gannett Newspapers "is regarded as being very ambitious and more of a business office man than a reporter" and that James Cox of the *Miami Daily News* "is more interested in profits than in establishing and maintaining a high standard of journalistic excellence for his newspapers."[16] Neither man was elected. The extent to which Pulitzer may have influenced those rejections is not known, but Miller was not nominated again until 1956, the year after Pulitzer's death, when he was elected. Cox never was.[17]

Although the journalism prizes interested him the most, Pulitzer took an active interest in the other categories as well. He tried to see and read as many as possible of the plays and books under consideration each year. He voted against the winning play in 1943, Thornton Wilder's *Skin of Our Teeth,* which set a contemporary family in prehistoric times, finding it "too mystic for my feeble imagination." The drama jury, led by novelist Somerset Maugham, was unanimous in its recommendation, and Pulitzer's son, who had seen the play in Washington, D.C., before going into the Navy, told his father he "was much impressed" and thought it deserved the prize.[18] Although Pulitzer was in full agreement with the board's desire to keep the identities of prize winners secret until the official announcement time, he once couldn't resist the temptation to leak word to a recipient. "If you don't keep this secret I will have you shot at sunrise," he wrote his sister-in-law, Margaret Leech Pulitzer, Ralph's widow, in 1942. "You are likely to win the Pulitzer Prize in history this year, but for God's sake don't mention it to a single soul for we have had leaks before that have been very embarrassing to the Board."[19] Her book, *Reveille in Washington,* about life in the capital during the Civil War, did win.[20]

To some extent, Pulitzer probably rationalized his approach to the selection of advisory board members out of his own experience. Even some of the conscientious, well-meaning men in his own employ, he had found, were afflicted more or less chronically with misplaced priorities. It amused Pulitzer to recall near the end of his career that William Steigers, the business manager when he became publisher, had told him he was "committing commercial suicide" when he ordered two major department store accounts, Scruggs and Nugent's, off pages two and three to make more space for news.[21] Similarly, he found that the business office had trouble understanding the need for outspoken editorials, which were likely to alienate both readers and advertisers. As Lincoln, who had been with the *Post-Dispatch* since 1895, had put it to the publisher in 1926, "a continuation of a policy of sneering at those who oppose the Post-Dispatch on public questions, treating them with ridicule that leaves a sting, will make the work of Post-Dispatch canvassers even more difficult than it has been in the past, from this same cause." Lincoln believed it had been ill-advised for McAdams to call several St. Louis County officials under indictment for malfeasance "coyotes." After all, "the number under indictment, together with their friends, undoubtedly constitute a large body. Many of them are readers of the Post-Dispatch." Pulitzer wasn't moved. "The County, as you know, is controlled by about as venal a lot of politicians as exists anywhere," he responded. "It was these men . . . that McAdams in his editorial was calling coyotes. If you will think it over you will agree that if we were to try to get out an editorial page that did not 'sting' or offend any individuals or group of individuals it would not be a forceful page. Isn't the Globe-Democrat's page a good example of this?"[22]

Some years later, Pulitzer found it necessary to instruct Lincoln on something which, to him, was fundamental. As soon as he read a full-page advertisement promoting "National Retail Demonstration Week" in the issue of September 18, 1941, he clipped it and sent it to Lincoln with this memo:

> The enclosed advertisement fairly sickened me. It is purely and simply an editorial which does what?—which salutes the retailers for a creed which in the last analysis is a lot of hog wash [about] maintaining employment (my eye!), avoiding fake advertising (before the Federal Trade Commission gets after them!) etc. etc. etc. Why not have printed the same "salute" for the plumbers' association or the sewer cleaners' association or the banana dealers' association? The answer is, obviously, because they don't advertise. To my way of thinking it was just about the lowest example that I have ever seen of American commercialized dollar grubbing vulgarity which the retailers perpetrated and in which they persuaded the Post-Dispatch to participate.
>
> Please, please, please try to get my point of view on this thing. . . . Whenever the Post-Dispatch signs its sacred name to an advertisement it endorses the statements in the advertisement and hence the advertisement differs in no sense from the statements contained in a leading double-leaded editorial. I most seriously feel that such things grievously wound what I know you love as much as I do—the Post-Dispatch. So please forgive me but for pity's sake see to it that there is no repetition.[23]

Two years later, the publisher again counseled restraint. Lincoln

FIG. 45.   Joseph Pulitzer II at work at his desk, about 1930.

FIG. 46. *Post-Dispatch* managing editor Oliver K. Bovard at work, about 1930.

The Post-Dispatch platform, which I placed at the masthead 27 years ago, shall continue to be this newspaper's guide and its only guide.

JOSEPH PULITZER.

August 2, 1938.

FIG. 47. Sign Joseph Pulitzer II had posted in the *Post-Dispatch* newsroom following Bovard's resignation in response to the managing editor's charge that the second J.P. had abandoned the founding Pulitzer's mandate.

FIG. 48. Joseph Pulitzer II and *Post-Dispatch* business manager George Carvell (to Pulitzer's left) in a negotiation session with a Newspaper Guild bargaining committee, 1939. At far right are Julius Klyman and Betty Loeffler of the Guild.

FIG. 49. At hearing in contempt-of-court case against the *Post-Dispatch*, 1940. From left, managing editor Ben H. Reese, editorial page editor Ralph Coghlan, J.P. II, and editorial cartoonist Daniel R. Fitzpatrick. The convictions of Coghlan and Fitzpatrick were unanimously reversed by the Missouri Supreme Court in 1941.

FIG. 50. Joseph Pulitzer II opens the St. Louis showing of the German atrocity exhibit in 1945. The *Post-Dispatch* sponsored the display in a number of other cities. With his severely limited vision, the editor-publisher could read a speech only if it was printed in large block letters, as here.

FIG. 51. Joseph Pulitzer II greets Frank A. Behymer, a reporter and feature writer for the *Post-Dispatch* for 56 years, at Pulitzer's sixtieth birthday party in 1945. Managing editor Ben Reese is at the far right.

FIG. 52.   Front entrance of the *Post-Dispatch* building, late 1940s.
The competing *Globe-Democrat* and (several years later) Wisconsin Senator Joseph R. McCarthy criticized the *Post-Dispatch* for
flying the Soviet flag on one of these stanchions on May 1, 1946, in
accordance with its practice of displaying the flags of allied nations
on their national holidays. The goodwill gesture was discontinued.

FIG. 53.   *St. Louis Post-Dispatch* building, 12th Boulevard and Olive
Street, St. Louis, about 1955.

Fig. 54.   The *Weatherbird,* the Pulitzer Publishing Company's DC-3, which J.P. II used for both business and pleasure, including moving his hunting dogs to and from retrieving assignments. Purchased in 1951, it (and a smaller predecessor) was named for the *Post-Dispatch* front-page cartoon weather commentator, whose likeness was painted on the aircraft's tail.

Fig. 55.　Joseph Pulitzer III, left, and his father, whom he succeeded as editor and publisher, examine a proof copy of the *Post-Dispatch* 75th anniversary edition in December 1953.

FIG. 56. Joseph and Elizabeth Edgar Pulitzer and guest Dr. James
F. Mitchell (left), a Washington, D.C., surgeon, breakfast on the
porch at Brandy Brook, their salmon-fishing lodge on the
Restigouche River, Matapedia, Quebec, about 1930.

FIG. 57. "Liza" Pulitzer lands a salmon on the Restigouche River,
Quebec, with the help of her guides, about 1930.

FIG. 58.   Joseph Pulitzer II, guide Harry L. Felt (probably), and Chesapeake Bay
retriever "Brownie" after shooting Hungarian partridge near Findlater, Saskatchewan,
in 1932. This was Pulitzer's favorite photograph of himself.

FIG. 59. Joseph Pulitzer II (left) and his older brother, Ralph, in a duck blind at J.P. II's Illinois hunting camp in November 1934. Ralph, and for a short time their younger brother, Herbert, headed the *World* newspapers in New York following their father's death in 1911. After the *World* failed in 1931, J.P. II alone ran the *Post-Dispatch,* though Ralph and Herbert did share in its earnings.

FIG. 60. Joseph Pulitzer II and "Butch," his favorite Chesapeake Bay retriever, in a canoe on the Restigouche River, Quebec, about 1949.

Fig. 61.   Joseph Pulitzer II and his grandson Joseph Pulitzer IV, about 4 years old, aboard yacht, about 1954.

FIG. 62. *Discoverer*, a 75-foot schooner built for Joseph Pulitzer II in 1924. His means of transport around Frenchman Bay, off his summer home at Bar Harbor, Maine, until World War II, when the yacht was taken over by the Coast Guard. Each August the Pulitzers and some St. Louis friends would spend two weeks aboard her cruising the Atlantic coast.

FIG. 63. Joseph Pulitzer II and the 44-pound salmon he took while fishing the Alta River in Norway, in 1954.

FIG. 64. Fishing in Norway, June 1954. From left, Herbert Pulitzer, younger brother of J.P. II; Paris banker Georges Vernes and Mrs. Vernes; Elizabeth Edgar Pulitzer, second wife of the editor-publisher; Paris Ritz Hotel operator Charles Ritz; Mrs. Jacques Pol-Roger, sister of Mrs. Vernes; J.P. II.

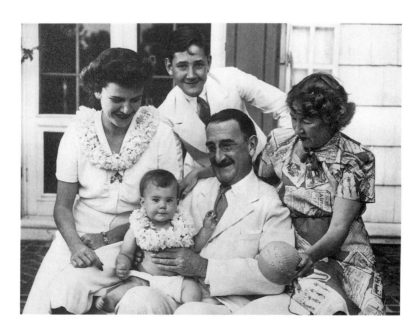

FIG. 65. Kate Davis Putnam, first grandchild of Joseph and Elizabeth Pulitzer, sits on her grandfather's lap in 1944. Looking on are her mother, Kate Davis Pulitzer Putnam (Mrs. Henry W. Putnam, later Mrs. Elwood R. Quesada), left; her uncle, Michael E. Pulitzer, center; and Elizabeth Edgar Pulitzer. The child's father, an Air Corps officer, was killed in World War II.

FIG. 66. Joseph Pulitzer IV, age 4, is flanked by his grandfather, Joseph Pulitzer II, and father, Joseph Pulitzer III, before the John Singer Sargent portrait of the first Joseph Pulitzer, in 1953.

FIG. 67. The former Elinor Pulitzer, second daughter of Joseph Pulitzer II and Elinor Wickham Pulitzer, with her husband, Dr. Louis H. Hempelmann Jr. (second from left). At far left is Charles W. Moore, a brother-in-law of Elinor Wickham Pulitzer. At far right is Lt. Gen. Elwood R. Quesada, husband of Elinor's sister, Kate Davis. About 1943.

FIG. 68.   Joseph Pulitzer IV, age 5, at his grandfather's seventieth birthday party, March 21, 1955. Joseph Pulitzer II died nine days later, on March 30.

FIG. 69.   Joseph Pulitzer III, chairman of the board (seated), and his half-brother, Michael E. Pulitzer, president and chief executive officer of the Pulitzer Publishing Company, in 1989. Behind them is the Wayman Adams portrait of their father, Joseph Pulitzer II, which hangs outside the *Post-Dispatch* news and editorial offices in St. Louis.

asked to sell four more columns of space in "Pictures" to advertisers. "I think our first objective to be kept always in mind is to MAINTAIN THE QUALITY OF OUR PRODUCT," Pulitzer replied. He believed the existing ratio of three pages of ads out of twelve, or one quarter of the section, was appropriate. "If we must hurt something, I would rather divide the hurt between circulation and advertising than hurt the goose that lays the golden egg, i.e., the Post-Dispatch newspaper."[24]

He was guided by that general rule in a variety of ways over the years. In 1937, he heartily endorsed editorial page editor Ross's plan to discard purchased material that he judged more likely to confuse than enlighten the public. "Let us live up strictly to this policy," he urged Ross. "The cost of a killed feature should not be given the slightest consideration."[25] He did not want advertising copy presented as though it were news or editorial material: "If the advertising is not worth anything to the advertiser unless it be disguised as reading matter it must be poor advertising and we should not sell it. In any event, we should not deceive and mislead the reader."[26] When the Associated Press in 1945 claimed that the first amendment made it immune from prosecution for its anti-competitive practice of denying membership to some newspapers that sought its service, Pulitzer found the argument "phony."[27] He was pleased when the U.S. Supreme Court agreed.[28] As a general proposition, he thought journalists put themselves "in bad odor when, under the guise of defending freedom of the press, they appear to be asking for special privileges."[29] When Hentschell pointed out in 1952 that a savings of between $250,000 and $300,000 a year could be achieved if the paper's news space was reduced by 5,000 columns, Pulitzer said he thought the economy would be unwise. "I believe that before long we would impair our reputation which wins us Pulitzer Prizes, with all of the intangible promotion value which that means, and would be spending some of our savings on doubtful promotion schemes. . . . After all, THERE IS a difference between reducing the size of a chocolate bar and reducing the reading contents of a newspaper."[30]

That was not to suggest that there was anything inherently evil about profit, but rather that certain compromises should be avoided. There is nothing to indicate, for example, that Pulitzer found any fault with following general practices of thrift and economy. Those qualities in longtime company treasurer James T. Keller were memorialized in a quip by "Pictures" editor and Newspaper Guild officer Julius Klyman when someone asked him one day why workmen were tearing up the sidewalk outside the *Post-Dispatch* building. "Oh, Mr. Keller must have dropped a dime out his window," Klyman replied.[31]

Pulitzer recognized, as had his father, that another legitimate way to make money and at the same time maintain one's ideals was to stay technologically current. "Let me repeat again that I want to be equipped to produce any confounded thing that any publisher anywhere at any time has ever produced or has ever thought of producing," he told Lincoln in 1940. "That means 3 or 4 color daily printing, a folded daily tabloid magazine, a small size Sunday comic book and . . . many more color pages than we are now able to produce in Pictures." He was premature but correct in predicting that color photographs soon would be "the rule rather than the exception."[32]

His most forward-looking business decision was to enter broadcasting. By 1990, the company's seven television and two radio stations accounted for 62 percent of its cash flow against 38 percent for its three daily newspapers.[33] The company's interest in wireless communication dated from 1904, when the *Post-Dispatch* sponsored a telegraphy demonstration at the St. Louis World's Fair. It sent reporters' accounts four miles, "right through buildings," from a 300-foot tower on the fairgrounds to the *Post-Dispatch* building, then at 210 North Broadway. As soon as wireless voice transmission became feasible, Pulitzer approved the creation of KSD as the radio station of the *Post-Dispatch*. The call letters were assigned by the U.S. Department of Commerce, and the station's first broadcast was on March 9, 1922.[34] The station was seen, as were virtually all the early radio stations, as a promotional adjunct to the newspaper — "a direct way," as Lincoln put it, "of getting the name 'Post-Dispatch' into homes of non-readers." It carried no advertising and for the first few years got by with volunteer entertainers. By 1925 it had to pay a few of these, and once word of that got around, Lincoln predicted, all would want to be paid and "we may probably feel urged to sell all nights to advertisers." He was doubtful that this enterprise would pay, either for the station or the advertisers, but there was "a lurking danger" that it might, he told Pulitzer in advising him to give commercial broadcasting a try.[35] He did. In 1926, KSD was among the first five stations to join the National Broadcasting Company, the first of the commercial networks, virtually assuring KSD's profitability. By 1940, the station was producing an annual operating (pre-tax) profit of more than $1.5 million.[36]

Pulitzer enjoyed radio. His favorite entertainment program was that of most Americans, "Amos 'n Andy."[37] But the medium's major importance, he believed, was its speed in transmitting news, so dramatically demonstrated during World War II. To his mind, there was something solemn and dignified about news and he wanted it conveyed in such an atmosphere, both in print and on the air. The combination of this attitude and his intense dislike of misleading and distasteful advertising caused him to call in the early 1940s for two reforms in the sponsorship of radio news. He ordered the mid-program commercial message, which he dubbed a "plug-ugly," eliminated from newscasts, and he insisted on what he considered dignified, general interest sponsors, such as oil companies, automobile manufacturers, railroads, and banks, for these programs. "The great St. Louis Post-Dispatch and its great radio station, K.S.D., should not start off the day by broadcasting vital news of the world, news upon which our civilization might depend, under the sponsorship of a woman's cosmetic, Sweetheart Soap," he wrote George M. Burbach, former *Post-Dispatch* advertising manager who had become KSD general manager, in 1943. "It is, to my way of thinking, most painfully out of keeping with the seriousness and importance of the occasion." What most annoyed him, he added a few days later, was "that I, as a man, and other men like me, do not want to start the day listening to a lot of prattle about a woman's skin, beauty, face and hands, etc. etc. etc. The sponsored product should be one of general use and of interest to both men and women."[38] When he learned that references to "underarm perspiration" and "keeping armpits dry" were being used in deodorant advertising in the *Post-Dispatch,* he ordered it killed and made it clear that the ban went for radio as well. "In a word, I don't think body stinks make pleasant reading or pleasant listening regardless of what the high-class magazines have established," he told Lincoln.[39] Eight KSD advertising contracts, representing nearly $66,000 in annual revenue, were canceled.

Most of this time, however, was resold to acceptable sponsors. While there was relatively little financial loss, Burbach told Pulitzer, the policy "will always be a sales barrier and will require more than just the ordinary sales effort."[40]

Pulitzer didn't care. After reforming KSD, he went after the networks. "I should like you to start a little extra special editorial campaign on a particular hobby of mine, . . . present news broadcasting methods," he wrote Coghlan. Attack the networks for using "plug uglies" and accepting "objectionable advertisers," he directed. "My hunch is that the American public accepts sponsoring on the theory that it has improved their broadcasts but that it objects to broadcasts which are tied up with bodily aches and pains, stomach acidity and gas, body odors, bad breath, and a thousand and one equally revolting references."[41] The editorial campaign began January 18, 1944, and attracted the attention of the news magazines and a number of major newspapers. FCC chairman Paul Porter endorsed the paper's suggestions. One of Fitzpatrick's cartoons pictured a "Radio plug-ugly" as a hog talking into a microphone. Within two months, NBC eliminated commercials in the "dead center" of newscasts, which the *Post-Dispatch* called "a stumble in the right direction," but kept what Pulitzer considered objectionable sponsors. CBS upgraded its sponsorship requirements for network news, but not for the local broadcasts of its key stations. The Blue (later American Broadcasting Company) and Mutual networks did nothing.[42] Pulitzer held to the same local sponsorship requirements for television news as for radio when KSD–TV was established.

That happened in 1947, largely on Burbach's strong belief that this would become a powerful money-making proposition. Shortly before the station went on the air, Burbach invited Pulitzer to his office to watch a fifteen-minute closed-circuit broadcast on a small-screen monitor. Pulitzer sat just inches from the screen with a magnifying glass to his good eye. He didn't say a word until the broadcast ended. Then he leaned back and said, "Well, that's the death of radio!"[43] He eventually revised this as it became clear that the main financial impact of television was on print advertising. "We should consider ourselves very fortunate to have under our roof KSD and KSD–TV," he observed on learning in 1952 that two major St. Louis advertisers, the First National Bank and Laclede

Gas Company, were spending about three dollars for broadcast advertising to every one dollar for the *Post-Dispatch.* [44]

It had taken a little chicanery on Burbach's part in the early days of KSD-TV to maintain Pulitzer's interest in staying with that medium. At first, the station operated at a deficit—about $100,000 in the first year—and in 1949 Pulitzer gave Burbach six months to get the operation into the black. By juggling the figures of KSD radio and KSD-TV and by delaying the payment of some invoices, Burbach was able to show about $1,000 profit by September 1949. From then on, the station gained steadily.[45] A little more than two years later, Burbach told Pulitzer that he expected the combined operating profits of KSD radio and television to exceed $2 million each year in 1952 and 1953. On May 15, 1953, he reported: "Our operating profit for KSD-TV last week again established a new high record of $67,898. The revenue was $86,490—also a new high record."[46] If sustained for a year, that performance would generate a $3.5 million annual operating return by the television station alone.

A couple of fortuitous circumstances fostered the success of KSD-TV. Just before World War II, the FCC allocated television channels in St. Louis to the *Post-Dispatch,* the *Star-Times,* and the CBS network. The war delayed construction, and by its end the *Star-Times* and CBS had decided to wait until color broadcasting was perfected. But Pulitzer went ahead as planned and launched KSD-TV as soon as possible after the war. When the station went on the air on February 8, 1947, as the first completely equipped postwar television station in the nation, there were only four television sets in St. Louis, including the one in Burbach's office. Shortly thereafter, the FCC froze the construction of television stations to give the agency time to revise its regulations for the medium. The freeze held for six years, during which time KSD-TV was the only station in St. Louis, then the nation's ninth largest market. For that period, it had access to the programming of all the major networks. When the time came to choose a single affiliation, the company went with NBC, with which it had been associated the longest and because of the network's tie-in with the large Radio Corporation of America manufacturing apparatus. Pulitzer had been strongly tempted to go with CBS, whose war coverage by Edward R. Murrow and programming generally he believed was superior, and because he knew and respected CBS chairman William S. Paley. But he also thought highly of General David Sarnoff, the head of RCA.[47]

Overall, he was so well satisfied with Burbach's business management of the broadcasting stations that he wrote relatively few memorandums about it. Instead, he operated mainly with Burbach as he did with his managing editor, as a journalistic shepherd and a listener-critic. He may have been the first to decry "happy talk" news delivery when he told Burbach in March 1943 that he considered one of their newscasters "totally disqualified" and advised the manager to "find some other work for him. He was telling, among other things, the first news of the serious Russian reverses and his tone of voice was that same amiable, cheerful, very very happy tone which he might have used if telling a classroom full of children that he was about to give each one of them a lollipop."[48] In 1946 he wrote: "I must protest against our 7:45 A.M. broadcast. It strikes me as a jumble of police news of very little value placed ahead of more significant news and on the whole it sounds rankly amateurish, unintelligent and not worthy of KSD or the Post-Dispatch."[49] Several times he complained about announcers who read too rapidly, as when he asked Burbach in 1954 to try to "persuade the chap at NBC who announces the world news roundup at 8 A.M. to slow down his speaking and not be quite so breathless, ala Walter Winchell. The deliberate, calm tone of Murrow is one of the several things I like about him."[50]

He hoped that television, in time, could achieve quality in both public affairs and entertainment programming—something he had not seen happen in radio. In 1949, he asked Coghlan to write an editorial about this, saying, "It will be a crime if the lowbrows who have been ruling AM broadcasting don't raise their sights and try to get just a little further away from the hogwash they have been giving the country over AM."[51] How firmly anchored he was to his newspaper foundations was apparent in a letter of complaint he wrote General Sarnoff in 1954. He was concerned, he wrote, because NBC had failed to carry President Truman's 1952 speech in which he announced that he was not going to seek reelection (about which he had complained to Sarnoff at the time) and one just the previous week by Adlai Stevenson at a Democratic rally. KSD-TV's soon-to-expire option to substitute with CBS programming had saved it, Pulitzer explained, "from being beaten on news events which any cub reporter could have anticipated as being of the first importance." He was worried about what might happen when NBC would be the station's sole supplier of national and international news:

> If we were a hash house or a plumbing manufacturer which happened to be operating a television station the situation would be different. But we are not. We are a newspaper, the St. Louis Post-Dispatch, to which the public of St. Louis and of its surrounding area looks for information quite as much as for entertainment. When our television station makes a dismal failure in covering news, the Post-Dispatch is naturally and properly charged with the same dismal failure.
>
> I do not wish to seem to presume to tell you how to run the television business but surely, in the long run, repeated failures of this kind inexorably point to loss of prestige, loss of public confidence and, in time, loss of audience.[52]

Expansion into broadcasting was not the only direction in which the company grew or contemplated growth during Pulitzer's career. Starting in the summer of 1946, the board of directors— composed of Pulitzer, his son, and the seven principal editors and managers[53]—began to consider the possibility of buying the *St. Louis Globe-Democrat*, whose publisher, E. Lansing Ray, was in his early sixties, just slightly older than Pulitzer. Ray had been ill, and his only son, whom he had expected to succeed him, had died unexpectedly. Despite these factors, Pulitzer wasn't very enthusiastic, mainly because he believed newspaper competition was best for the city. He also doubted that Ray wanted to sell, because Ray had told him recently that he would feel "lost" without his newspaper. Still, there was a rumor around that the *Globe-Democrat* was available for $12 million—which Pulitzer discounted as "whisky talk," since the paper had not earned more than "some $300,000 a year." And there was the possibility that *Star-Times* publisher Elzey Roberts might try to buy the morning paper.[54]

Mulling all this over, Pulitzer decided to stay put for the time being. In addition to his own preference for competition, he was concerned that the public might be hostile to the *Post-Dispatch* having a semi-monopoly in St. Louis. Nor could he help but recall how disastrous morning-evening-Sunday operation of the *World* had been. There was a real possibility, he believed, that the *Globe-Democrat* would "prove a money-losing millstone," just as the morning *World* had become. In any case, he told his son, "My hunch is that having to get out a morning paper would be a constant distraction, would divide our editorial energies and resources, and it might very well impair the journalistic prestige of the P–D."[55]

In 1947, with the *Post-Dispatch* becoming cramped for space, Pulitzer broached the subject to Ray of their entering into some kind of joint operating agreement, sharing a press and taking advantage of currently unused space in the *Globe-Democrat*'s considerably larger building. Just such an arrangement came to pass in 1959, after both men had died, but at that point Ray brushed it aside. "You and I," he told Pulitzer, "are both too independent and want to run our own newspapers."[56] He also said that nothing of this kind had ever been worked out in a large city, and he alluded to the problem of getting out two Sunday newspapers with one press.

With any deal with the morning newspaper foreclosed, Pulitzer was receptive when he learned in 1951 that the *Star-Times,* whose costs had been closing the gap on its revenues for several years, might be available. He did not want the *Globe-Democrat* to get it, and he had heard that Ray might be interested. Hentschell did the groundwork with *Star-Times* publisher Roberts in several secret meetings, each one at a different hotel. By May 1951 a deal appeared possible. With Hentschell in his office, Pulitzer telephoned his brother, Herbert, to see if he would be agreeable. Herbert knew almost nothing about the *Star-Times,* including that it was a six-day evening newspaper. Once he was told that, and that Hentschell expected the added circulation and advertising would produce a pre-tax profit of about $1 million, he said, "If you and Charley think it's a good deal, go ahead."[57] At that time, the *Star-Times* had about 180,000 circulation; the *Globe-Democrat* was about 10,000 ahead of the *Post-Dispatch* with 292,000 daily, but behind — 364,000 to 432,000 — on Sunday.[58]

It was almost time for the Atlantic salmon run, and Pulitzer wasn't going to miss the start of the season. He was confident that he could go to Canada while his son, Hentschell, and the lawyers completed the negotiation, but he wanted to be kept informed, particularly about the financial aspects. He authorized Hentschell to go as high as $5 million. The best means of communication was telegram. In the Pulitzer tradition, the publisher devised a code with which to keep the most sensitive information secret. He gave names of fruits and vegetables to various sums of money. "For example," Hentschell recalled, "$500,000 would be watermelon, and if it was two watermelons, it would be a million." The *Star-Times* opened the negotiations by asking $6.25 million, which Hentschell proceeded to put into code for transmission to Pulitzer. "It took me an hour to write that damn thing," he said. "You can imagine trying to decipher six million, 250 thousand into melon, squash, pickles and Christ knows what else."[59] On June 14, 1951, Joseph Pulitzer Jr. and Roberts closed the deal for $5,058,000.[60] The *Star-Times* ceased publication the next day, completely surprising the community, and Hentschell received a $5,000 bonus for his work in the transaction.[61] Mid-September figures showed that the *Post-Dispatch* had held more than 100,000 of the *Star-Times* circulation; it now had a daily advantage of about 90,000 over the *Globe-Democrat,* and 100,000 on Sundays.[62]

This was impressive, as were statistics revealing that in 1952 and 1953 the *Post-Dispatch* carried 67 percent of the advertising linage in the city's two daily newspapers.[63] But Pulitzer was somewhat ambivalent in commending advertising manager Fred F. Rowden for this level of success. "I feel I must congratulate you," he commented on learning of the 1952 gains. "This showing strikes me as certainly good enough and perhaps a little too good. Is there any showing anywhere around the country which can be compared with this 67% figure? Are there any good sized cities left with only two newspapers? How about New Orleans? This inquiry is prompted, confidentially, by my misgivings as to the future of the Globe-Democrat." Rowden replied with a list of ten two-newspaper cities showing that Milwaukee, New Orleans, and Indianapolis had a greater imbalance than St. Louis. Milwaukee and New Orleans, where the *Sentinel* and *Times-Picayune* had 75 percent of the total linage, were the most disproportionate.[64]

Shortly after buying the *Star-Times,* Pulitzer asked its now out-of-work managing editor, Norman E. Isaacs, to meet with him to discuss the implications of the purchase for the *Post-Dispatch.* Pulitzer knew Isaacs had a high regard for the *Post-Dispatch,* and the publisher didn't want to waste time discussing its strengths. He wanted Isaacs's views as the leader of his evening opposition for the past five-and-a-half years about ways the *Post-Dispatch* could be improved. He agreed with Isaacs's warning that the *Post-Dispatch* should not become even more arrogant than it had been as top dog, now that concern about being scooped by the *Star-Times* was gone. If anything, he argued, the *Post-Dispatch* had an even greater obligation to keep its vigil on local events. Pulitzer thought Isaacs had another good point in saying that the *Post-Dispatch* tended to put disproportionate emphasis on national and international coverage, as opposed to local coverage, but he was unreceptive when Isaacs said he thought the editorial page had a dull, stuffy appearance and that its makeup should be modernized. Pulitzer closed that discussion off "very quickly, without being rough," Isaacs recalled. "And he was wrong as hell about that one, because the page was really bad. But he just quickly made it clear that that was his page and he wasn't about to listen to me about it."[65] Pulitzer also told Isaacs that, as much as he respected his ability, he could not offer him a place on the *Post-Dispatch;* Crowley, recently elevated to the managing editorship, had made it clear that he didn't want Isaacs around. Isaacs said he understood, and soon thereafter became managing editor of the *Louisville Times.*

In 1954–55, Pulitzer decided that conditions to make a bid for the *Globe-Democrat* might be better than nine years ago. Ray was now seventy years old and had no heir. His paper had been in the Ray family for three generations but was now certain to go into other hands. Hentschell made five visits to Ray over a period of months, trying to interest the publisher in selling to Pulitzer, but, as he told Pulitzer, "I wasn't getting anywhere." About a week after hearing that report, in March 1955, Pulitzer called his son and Hentschell into his office. "We're going to have a visitor," he told them. Then, Hentschell recalled, David R. Calhoun, president of the St. Louis Union Trust Company, "*the* banker of the city, comes in."

"I think we have a new publisher of the *Globe-Democrat,*"
Calhoun told the three men.

"Yes?" asked Pulitzer.

"A fellow named S. I. Newhouse out of New York. I checked up
on him. He's a very reputable man. He thinks this would be a good
town for him."

"Is the deal finished?" Hentschell asked. He and the Pulitzers
knew Newhouse as an aggressive newspaper-chain maker who
had purchased the *Oregonian* in Portland a few years before.

"Yes," Calhoun answered, following this with a few pleasantries
and then leaving.

Neither of the Pulitzers said anything, but Hentschell announced
he was going home to get drunk. "That he comes in here with that
kind of finality to it just knocks me off my feet," he declared. Later
that afternoon, Pulitzer called Hentschell at home to ask how he
was feeling. "I feel ok. I've had a few drinks, but I'm not drunk," he
reported.

"Don't worry, we'll make it without the *Globe-Democrat* in spite
of Newhouse," Pulitzer consoled him.[66]

Ray had added his newspaper, his radio station, and 23 percent
of the stock in his television station to the Newhouse chain of
nine other newspapers and several broadcast properties for $6.25
million. It was agreed that Ray would remain the newspaper's
publisher, that there would be no change in its conservative-
Republican policies, and that Newhouse would never sell out to the
Post-Dispatch.[67] Ray died only a few months after the sale, and
Richard H. Amberg, in his thirties, became publisher. He modernized the *Globe-Democrat* and for several years made it a tougher
competitor than the *Post-Dispatch* had had for some time. During
the first six years of Newhouse ownership, the *Globe-Democrat*
earned a net profit of about $15 million. Part of this was the result
of tightfistedness with salary increases and Newhouse's refusal to
establish a formal pension plan, such as that at the *Post-Dispatch,*
which was considered "a national model."[68]

Perhaps the most decisive way Pulitzer maintained the quality
of his newspaper was by the way he treated its employees. Once
hired, few *Post-Dispatch* employees sought jobs elsewhere. This
was true for both the journalistic and the business side of the
operation. "In the thirty years I was in the advertising department,

I can't think of anyone who left us to go to work for somebody else," said retired national advertising manager Ben Brockman in 1984. "On the other hand, we had applications from people at the *Globe, Star,* and *Times* by the handsful."[69] Particularly before the establishment of the American Newspaper Guild in 1933, Pulitzer believed journalists generally were inadequately paid. When Columbia University president Nicholas Murray Butler suggested in 1928 that the amount of the Pulitzer Prize for reporting, among others, be reduced from $1,000 to provide more money to cover administrative costs, Pulitzer objected, saying, "Reporters need the money."[70] *Post-Dispatch* reporters, however, were an exception. An *American Mercury* article in 1931 called the paper's level of wages "remarkably high": "The day when a newspaper man had to duck up alleys to avoid an I.O.U. for a poker debt of ten dollars is definitely over so far as the *Post-Dispatch* is concerned."[71] *Post-Dispatch* news-editorial employees affiliated with the Guild in late 1938. Their first contract provided the highest minimum wages for the first four years of employment the Guild had ever gotten.[72] As that suggests, Pulitzer fundamentally supported the union movement. He even said that if he were a young reporter just starting out he would join the Guild. However, he put news-editorial workers in a different category from his mechanical and other employees. As a precaution against a pro-union taint of *Post-Dispatch* news and editorials, he opposed a closed shop, or "Guild shop," for these employees. He believed that journalists should be philosophically free to join or not join the Guild, as they wished, and that he should be free to hire and keep journalists who might not want to join the Guild or who might decide to drop out.

A Guild shop provision was rejected when the first *Post-Dispatch* contract was negotiated. The issue was raised again in the 1940 and 1942 negotiations. On both of these occasions, Pulitzer prepared a lengthy statement of his position, and in 1942 he presented it in person to a newsroom packed with employees, reiterating his basic sympathy with the idea of collective bargaining but insisting that even the remote possibility that compulsory union membership could compromise the newspaper's news and editorial independence made him adamantly against the closed shop. He countered the Guild claim that the open shop "put a premium" on staying out of the union by noting that 80 percent of eligible employees already belonged. He also pointed out that the company's contract with the American Federation of Radio Artists, to which on-air KSD employees belonged, contained a clause permitting him whenever he wished to assign any open-shop *Post-Dispatch* employee "to carry out an assignment on the radio in his capacity as a representative of the *Post-Dispatch*."[73] Pulitzer succeeded in keeping the Guild shop at bay, but in subsequent years only a few employees opted not to join the union.[74] Evarts A. Graham Jr., a Guild officer for a number of years, eventually became *Post-Dispatch* managing editor. "Guild activity . . . was never a hindrance to promotions, choice assignments or pay raises," he recalled.[75]

After Sam Shelton became his assistant in 1945, Pulitzer had little direct contact with any of the several unions with which the company was involved. "They are keeping Joe Pulitzer out of the negotiations," Julius Klyman grumbled after this practice started. "They are afraid he will give us everything we want."[76] As previously noted, Shelton had a reputation for fair play. "He was very urbane, never shouted, was always willing to listen to the other point of view," recalled attorney Morris J Levin, who as of 1985 had represented the St. Louis Guild unit for forty-five years. Mainly because of Shelton, he believed, "you had a very good ship that was run by tight management, but understanding management." He credited Shelton's pragmatism with ending a twenty-two-day shutdown of all three St. Louis newspapers in the summer of 1945. After the newspapers closed because of a dispute with carriers, some of the out-of-work employees started their own newspaper, the *St. Louis Daily News*. They considered this a "lockout" because they had not struck in sympathy with the carriers, and they wanted to be paid for the time they were involuntarily unemployed. When this group gained War Production Board approval for an allocation of newsprint — enough to print 300,000 copies of a sixteen-page daily newspaper — Shelton advised all three publishers to negotiate without delay. Agreements that included "lockout pay" were reached with all the unions in a single day. According to Levin, Shelton's approach to the publishers had been: "Look, you'd better sit down and work this thing out. It's got beyond the point of reason, and if you don't, they'll be publishing tomorrow, and they'll be a real competitor to all three of you." In addition to Shelton's sound reasoning, Levin believed, the settlement also reflected Pulitzer's own "flexibility and willingness to do what was necessary, even to eat a little crow in order to restore good relations."[77] Pulitzer might have disputed his having "eaten crow" by conceding lockout pay. In his view, explained in a signed statement published the day publication resumed, an improperly drawn law had prevented a speedy, court-supervised resolution of the issues with the carriers. He had expected the papers' closings to be brief, and he especially regretted their blackout just as the war finally was ending.[78]

The salaries of the company's nonunion executives were customarily established in contracts, usually running for five years. Again reflecting his priorities, Pulitzer once told his son: "There are basically two scales for executives, Joe, $25,000 for the journalists and $20,000 for the eighth floor" [then the location of the business office].[79] These maximums increased in time, of course, but that the publisher's formula was followed is borne out in a 1945 report showing managing editor Reese at $25,000 and business manager Lincoln at $20,000, and editorial page editor Coghlan at $21,000 and treasurer Stuart M. Chambers at $18,000. Editorial cartoonist Fitzpatrick was not an executive but was paid $25,000. Circulation manager George E. Carvell received $17,000.[80]

Over the years, Pulitzer received numerous expressions of gratitude for his compensation policies. "Frankly I do not think employers exist anywhere who have been as considerate of conscientious effort," city editor Reese wrote him in 1932.[81] An exception to that general sentiment showed up from time to time in memos from chief Washington correspondent Raymond Brandt to Reese. He wrote in 1942 that, judging from the homes and standards of living of the Washington bureau chiefs of the *Detroit News,* the *Cleveland Plain Dealer,* the *Kansas City Star,* and others, "I am certain that most receive greater compensation than I. Prestige is a valuable asset to a Washington correspondent and part of prestige in Washington depends on income."[82] He wanted his salary increased from $13,000 to $14,950. Reese bucked the request to Pulitzer, who held the line. "When the head of the Washington bureau reaches a point where his salary is approximately $1,000 a month, or $12,000 a year, he has just about reached the limit which this job will pay him," he wrote Brandt.[83]

He said the extra $1,000 Brandt was getting was in recognition of work beyond what a bureau chief usually does, such as helping cut through government red tape involved with wartime freight regulations—which affected rail transport of newsprint—and KSD's operation. By 1955, Brandt was earning $19,000, some $6,000 less than Charles Ross had received in the 1930s but a comfortable salary nevertheless.[84]

When it came to his own compensation, Pulitzer would just as soon have forgone its public disclosure from time to time, but he recognized it was news when the U.S. Treasury periodically provided information on corporate incomes to Congress. Articles about those whose incomes were among the top five or ten in Missouri, where he regularly ranked, were printed in the *Post-Dispatch*. He was the highest-paid executive in the state in 1937, 1938, and 1939—$255,000, $180,461, and $196,735, respectively. For the period 1935-46, his compensation averaged more than $200,000 a year. It averaged more than double that, $407,602, in 1952 through 1954, the last three years of his career. His income from other sources was frequently $100,000 or more.[85] While the *World* newspapers were paying dividends, he received 10 percent, as provided in his father's will, and for some years, at least, he received a relatively small annual salary of $4,160 as secretary of the *World*'s parent, the Press Publishing Company.[86] A complete record of this income does not seem to exist, but his share of 1922 *World* dividends was $14,218. Ralph would have received double that, and Herbert six times, or $85,308, but as Ralph wrote Joseph, Herbert had to pay a considerably larger sum in income tax. "It is amazing how Uncle Sam's taxes tend to equalize testamentary discrimination!" he remarked.[87]

Pulitzer's starting salary as publisher in 1912 was $20,000. After he authorized the addition of a weekly rotogravure section, which was credited for a 38,468 increase in Sunday circulation by 1915, the board of directors increased his salary to $30,000. The "Everyday Magazine," Pulitzer's idea, was added in 1917. This increased daily circulation by 20,000 within six months, and the board voted to pay him a 3 percent commission on yearly net earnings in addition to his salary. In 1920 his salary was increased to $80,000, and in 1924 to $100,000 plus a raise in commission to 5 percent. In 1927, following the commercial success of KSD and the sale in 1926 of more than 25 million lines of advertising—the seventh largest volume of all newspapers in the nation that year, and almost 15 million lines more than it sold in 1911—the board voted him a $100,000 bonus for any year in which dividends of $1 million were paid. That had happened for the two previous years and continued through 1930. The bonus arrangement was modified in 1935 to pay Pulitzer an additional $50,000 if dividends reached $650,000, and more—to a maximum of $100,000—if they were higher.[88] When much of the foregoing was assembled by treasurer Chambers into a report in 1945, Pulitzer commented that he found the report "disappointing in its failure to credit me with much of anything on the strictly journalistic as contrasted to the publishing side. . . . I like to feel, and do feel, my value to the paper has been as an editor rather than as a publisher."[89]

The fact that he served in both those capacities while his brothers worked at neither after 1931 was recognized by Ralph and Herbert and was responsible for their agreeing to various methods of reapportioning their incomes to deal with the uneven distribution of earnings under their father's will. Neither Ralph nor Herbert received salary, commission, or bonus from the Pulitzer Publishing Company. In 1927 the three brothers agreed that any earnings above $1 million would be divided equally among them. Further adjustments were made between Joseph and Herbert after Ralph died in 1939, after the company purchased the *Star-Times* in 1951, and after earnings from KSD–TV began to rise rapidly at about the same time.[90] There is no evidence of even a mild conflict among the brothers in the course of making these arrangements; Ralph and Herbert were plainly satisfied that their brother and his executives knew what they were doing. The only evidence of financial disagreement among second-generation Pulitzers was in 1913, when Edith threatened to contest her father's will on the grounds that he had suffered from "insanity as to the family." That was hardly a persuasive argument, Joseph told Ralph confidentially, against the fact that their father had "sufficient sanity to run the World as he did."[91] He suggested a compromise to increase her income to $50,000 a year, which apparently satisfied their sister.

Although Pulitzer believed his business accomplishments were unduly emphasized over his journalistic achievements in treasurer Chambers's 1945 tracing of the publisher's compensation history, that imbalance was surely overcome to his satisfaction in 1953. That June, Columbia University conferred on him the honorary degree of Doctor of Laws. The citation read:

> Son and namesake of one of America's great crusading editors; a native of this city, educated at St. Mark's and Harvard, and now in his fifth decade as an active journalist; president and editor of the St. Louis Post-Dispatch, successfully carrying out those aggressive policies in the public interest for which that newspaper has been honored through two generations; for over thirty years a valued member of the advisory board of our Graduate School of Journalism; a dedicated fearless person, whose devoted and distinguished leadership of one of the great newspapers of this country has been an inspiration to all men of his calling.[92]

Had he been there, his father might have felt obliged to challenge the accuracy of "educated at St. Mark's and Harvard," but nothing else. It was all a part of the record.

Still, the son never nurtured a thought of his having transcended his father's influence on his life. "I was expelled from St. Mark's School," he candidly told editorial writer Bart Howard in 1940, "but not many years thereafter received an honorary diploma from the Headmaster, which is one of my most prized possessions. My expulsion from Harvard came not at the hands of the college but was executed by my father, who took me by the seat of my pants in the middle of my sophomore year and sent me, an effete eastern youth, into the hinterland of Missouri—unquestionably the best thing he ever did for me."[93]

Fish, Fowl, Family, Friends

Pulitzer once remarked, "My professional life is what I live for, and I have a perfectly swell time living it and would not swap it for any other kind of life."[1] In a certain sense, he was a nonstop worker. He worked at home as well as at his office, took his files and a reader-secretary along when he migrated to Bar Harbor in the summer, had his newspaper (and usually several others) delivered to him whenever he was out of town, and stayed in such close touch with his business and news-editorial lieutenants by memo, telegram, letter, and telephone that they could never develop a sense of being outside his reach.

Yet for all his preoccupation with being editor-publisher and his correctness in claiming that this was his foremost enthusiasm, he had other interests as well. There is not a hint of anything journalistic in the bookplate he and his first wife designed. It shows a fisherman in a stream, a yacht under sail, a portion of their large and beautiful St. Louis County home, and two duck hunters in a blind at sunrise. Those were the settings in which he enjoyed the rest of his life.

Tied for first place among his avocational pursuits were salmon-fishing and duck-shooting. There is no better word than "passionate" to describe his interest in these sports. He pursued them almost his entire adult life; when he wasn't doing one or the other, he was thinking ahead to the next outing. He kept extensive records on how many fish and ducks were taken by himself and his companions by date, location, time of day, weather conditions, and equipment used. These records were typewritten and periodically bound into books that were used as reference for future planning, most of which was done with his second wife, who was as much a devotee of these activities as he. His daughter Elinor recalled that on evenings at home after dinner, "when spring came and his ever-loving salmon-fishing was going to go on in Canada, the records would come out." At that point, she added, "I took a quick powder. . . . I never heard anything so boring, but they thought it was wonderful."2

Pulitzer fished for species other than salmon, including trout, and on a few occasions tuna in waters off Nova Scotia and marlin in the Gulf of Mexico. But every June from 1927 on, the migration of the Atlantic salmon into freshwater to spawn lured him to Canada's Restigouche River, which forms the border between New Brunswick and Quebec. It was a rich man's sport. For the privilege of fishing four-and-a-half miles of the river for a month during the 1920s and 1930s, usually most of June and a few days of July, he paid $4,000 plus the salaries and subsistence of six guides who handled the canoes from which the fishing was done, and of the cooks and maids who ran the comfortable lodge in which Mr. and Mrs. Pulitzer and their guests stayed. On a few occasions, one or another of their children or other relatives joined them for a few days, but most years parties of one to four friends went up for several days of fishing while the Pulitzers fished daily — except Sundays, when fishing was prohibited by law.

The salmon were large, seldom under twenty pounds and sometimes twice that. Taking them was a learned skill, and one at which Mrs. Pulitzer, who weighed only about 100 pounds herself, became more adept than her husband, who weighed twice that. The successful taking of a salmon began with a graceful cast to attract the eye of the fish to the fly. If it took the fly, one had to sense just the right moment to tug the line and set the hook and then "play" the salmon to exhaustion by alternately giving out and reeling in the line, never allowing it to go slack. The lightweight bamboo rods were equipped to be held with both hands. When the fish became tired enough to be reeled near the canoe, it was netted or gaffed by a guide onto the shore and dispatched with a blow on the head with a rock. The duel in and over the water often took an hour or more, and the fish frequently won. It was considered a good day to "kill" four salmon in about eight hours — excellent to do better than that.

In a typical season the Pulitzers and ten guests took some 200 salmon averaging about 20 pounds, more than 100 of those caught by the hosts. The demands on skill and patience were not for everyone, but for Pulitzer the appeal was irresistible. "Ouch!" he began the letter in 1930 with which he enclosed his check to New York banker Mortimer L. Schiff, from whom he leased Brandy Brook, his favorite Restigouche lodgings, for several years. "However, here it goes enclosed herewith, and after all what is four thousand bucks compared to the solid strike of a 36 pound salmon such as came my way the year before last."[3] In another letter to Schiff, he spoke of a period at Brandy Brook as "Heaven on earth." So sacred was the annual salmon quest that he advised his children not to schedule anything important such as a wedding or birth of a child during the salmon season. They managed to keep marriages out of the way, but both of Kate Davis's daughters were born in June.

Most of the fish caught were shipped fresh to friends, family, and *Post-Dispatch* and other business associates. During the 1937 season, for example, seventy-two fish were given away. Among those receiving what one frequent recipient described as "a little baby coffin"[4] containing a salmon that year were Burbach, Lincoln, Ross, Brandt, and Coghlan of the *Post-Dispatch,* Ralph and Herbert Pulitzer, Mrs. William Randolph Hearst, Mrs. Vincent Astor, and Mr. and Mrs. Eugene Williams, the Pulitzer's usual August yachting companions. Another year, St. Louis department store presidents Frank M. Mayfield of Scruggs, Vandervoort-Barney, and Morton D.

May of Famous-Barr, received fish. The recipients often gave a luncheon or dinner party at which the salmon—briefly—was the centerpiece. For a number of years, Burbach hosted a salmon luncheon for KSD broadcasting employees at the Missouri Athletic Club.

Irving Dilliard was perhaps the most resourceful of all those who received a salmon. "It may interest you to know that the boxes in which you ship your salmon make up with almost no waste at all to splendid sawbucks," he once wrote Pulitzer. "On knocking it to pieces I found that it had exactly what was needed, with little more than the ends of the box to spare. If you were of a mind to you could print instructions and a diagram for turning these boxes into sawbucks after removal of the salmon—if you think your friends are woodpile enthusiasts." There was only one "hitch," he confessed. After nailing the sawhorse together "I found that the stencil, 'J. Pulitzer' is prominent in black letters. It looks as if I had swiped yours."5 That probably amused Pulitzer, but he thought President Truman showed "damn bad manners" in 1945 when he had press secretary Charles Ross thank J.P. for the fish he sent the White House rather than writing a note himself. "I have a special feeling for salmon," Pulitzer wrote Ross, "and think that if a salmon is considerate enough to get himself hooked and shipped to the White House, he deserves more consideration."6

The 1949 salmon season proved to be one of the most interesting to Pulitzer. When it had ended, he wrote a long letter about it to his brother Herbert, whom he seldom called by his given name but addressed either as "Tony" or "Doc." He liked this letter to "Dear Doc" so well that he had it set in type and sent copies to friends. The high point of the season for Pulitzer had been catching a 41-pound salmon, but a more unusual episode involved Butch, the Chesapeake Bay retriever he had recently purchased and kept with him in the canoe while fishing. One day Pulitzer made a bad cast, hooking the cap of one of his guides and then swinging it into the water. "When the cap drifted by Mr. Butch, he could not resist it," Pulitzer recounted. "He promptly leaped overboard after it. As the cap drifted down, Butch went swimming madly after it, barking loudly all the way. He finally caught up with it and promptly clamped down on it. Fortunately he did not hook himself, but Butch had the cap and I had not a 70-pound salmon but a 70-pound dog. . . . This doesn't sound funny but it had all three of us in hysterics."[7] Pulitzer kept the line taut until both the dog and canoe came ashore, and the retriever dutifully returned the cap to its owner.

Pulitzer loved dogs and usually owned several at a time, but Butch unquestionably was his favorite. Back in St. Louis County a few years after the cap incident, Butch delivered to the front door of the Pulitzer home between twenty and thirty possums over a six-week period. Surprised that there were so many of these creatures in the vicinity, and considering the dog's enterprise "something of an accomplishment," Pulitzer wrote Werner O. Nagel of the Missouri Conservation Commission about Butch's exploit and asked where on Pulitzer's wooded property the possums might live. "On one evening he delivered three of them and on another two," he wrote. "His expeditions seldom require more than half an hour. The possums are seemingly not hurt and, after 'playing possum' for fifteen or twenty minutes and lying on the door mat seemingly dead, they invariably disappear." Nagel replied: "It seems to me that Butch has done two things; demonstrated an unusual and highly individual ability, and shown that there are a lot of possums in your vicinity. This performance of his is an entirely new one in my experience." He said it was unusual for a dog not to kill or at least injure the possums—"a tribute to a tender mouth, as well as to unusual industry in retrieving." But it was not unusual for there to be so many possums where trees and undergrowth provided attractive habitat, he explained.[8]

Butch had to stay behind in 1954 when Herbert invited his brother and wife to join him and several friends for salmon-fishing on the Alta River in Norway. Herbert had purchased a lease on this choice water when it was vacated the previous year on the death of the Duke of Westminster. The others in the party were Paris banker Georges Vernes and his wife; Mrs. Vernes's sister, Odette Pol-Roger; and Charles Ritz, son of the founder of the Ritz Hotels who operated the Ritz in Paris. Ritz was an avid trout fisherman who had invented the "parabolic" fly rod and had an interest in the largest fishing tackle factory in France. Pulitzer, as he had done almost a decade earlier during the trip to conquered Nazi Germany, kept a diary of this adventure, which he had privately printed and distributed to friends. The sixty-eight-page booklet, with twenty pages of photographs, provides a more intimate glimpse of the publisher than anything else he committed to paper. It begins: "To Liza, who, as my companion, has dropped many a high mallard and has landed many a wild salmon, and who was high rod on this trip, this diary is lovingly and gratefully dedicated." Following that is this prefatory note:

> This document, dear reader, let it be understood at the first, does not concern itself with prunes, prisms or power politics. It relates exclusively to the Atlantic salmon of Norway and will tell only about the fish, the whole fish and nothing but the fish.[9]

It is, however, more wide-ranging and revealing than that note suggests. Pulitzer began his description of those in the party by saying, "I feel that I need not describe my brother, Tony, beyond saying that he is 58 years of age; that he was a U.S. Navy flyer in the United States and overseas in the first World War, and, after being refused admission in our Air Force because of defective vision, he served with the R.A.F. in Europe during the second World War; that he is a man of great courage, and that he is an enthusiastic and excellent shot and angler."

The fishing in Norway was done at night, which at that time of year in that latitude (235 miles above the Arctic Circle) never became dark. The members of the party slept most of the day, breakfasted in the late afternoon and then began fishing. There was a break for tea and toast at 8:00 P.M. and a picnic on the shore at midnight, after which fishing was resumed. They usually returned to their lodgings between three and five o'clock in the morning and had cheese and crackers "and a Scotch highball or two, without ice" at 6:00 or 7:00 A.M., before retiring. A Danish cook, French butler, Italian chauffeur, and Norwegian guides served the party, all of whom Pulitzer liked except John, the guide assigned him. "John, at 71 years, is too old for this tough job," he recorded. "Indeed, he is sometimes cranky and shows no interest in the fishing. I have not enjoyed his company. To get the most out of fishing you have to like your guide and I do not like this old codger."

Although Pulitzer was sixty-nine himself at that time, people who knew him would not think the comment amiss. He never thought of himself as old, and preferred people twenty and thirty years younger for social friends. He found them vibrant and lively, his daughter Elinor recalled, in contrast to his contemporaries, especially those preoccupied with what he called " 'The Deadly Ds: Disease, Domestics and Dependents.' If he sat next to a woman at dinner who talked about the Deadly Ds it just bored him to extinction."

The talk at Alta was predominantly of salmon, never a dull topic to Pulitzer. In just under five weeks, the party took a total of 232 fish along eighteen miles of water. The salmon were somewhat larger than those taken from the Restigouche, averaging 22½ pounds. Among his total of 44 fish, J.P. had a 43-pounder and a 44-pounder. Liza caught 61 fish, one weighing 42 pounds. Herbert had 54, including a 41-pounder. Ritz took the biggest salmon, 48½ pounds. There were some slow fishing days, and days on which Pulitzer lost more than he caught. "I fear the Alta River valley is still echoing a short, four-letter word that I find myself using loudly whenever I lose a fish, and that is often," he confessed. "According to my best information, the French equivalent is *merde!*" While in Norway, he received the *Post-Dispatch* regularly—four days after publication—but made no record of anything in it bringing forth a similar expression of distress.

The last ten days of the trip were spent touring the Scandinavian capitals of Oslo, Stockholm, and Copenhagen. The diary of this period is a mixture of travelogue and commentary, with a few passages reflecting some ingrained private prejudices and insensitivities typical of those times. In Oslo, they saw Thor Heyerdahl's replica of the prehistoric Polynesian ocean raft *Kon-Tiki* and several whaling ships, and Pulitzer called on the editors of both the Labor and Conservative party newspapers. All this interested him greatly. The Conservative editor told him there were too many newspapers in Norway, with two in every small town and a dozen in Oslo. He also said that his paper had three chief editors. "Why they don't spoil the soup, I fail to understand," Pulitzer commented.

Stockholm offered a variety of experiences. Pulitzer had an adventure of sorts when it took him two hours and visits to both a bank and a travel bureau to get about $30 worth of Norwegian money changed into Swedish currency. With it he bought tickets for a sightseeing boat. That evening they went to a vaudeville show, which he described in some detail:

> In one act a young Negress, with a flashing smile, does a hula hula dance. She has a tassle attached to her brassiere over each breast and has an amazing ability to make them whirl in first one and then the other direction. Ditto one on her backside, where her tail once was not so many hundreds of years ago! The other act is by Herbert some one or other. He is a very tall, well built Negro, with a flashing smile, dressed in immaculate white dinner coat. He has a wonderful bass voice and delicate, sensitive, artistic fingers and hands. He sings spirituals and *Old Man River* and is applauded enthusiastically. A young, flat-chested blonde comes up from the audience and hands him a bouquet of tired carnations and he kisses her lightly on the cheek and remarks, "Stockholm, that's the place for me." He did sing very beautifully.

The following day he observed several men asleep on stone steps in the city. "This seems to reflect on their claims of welfare housing and no slums," he commented, "but they are probably Sunday morning drunks." The next day he called on Marcus Walenberg, a banker. Marquis Childs, who had written a book about Sweden, had given him a letter of introduction. Walenberg, who spoke "perfect English with some American idioms like 'nigger in the woodpile,'" told him Sweden's welfare economy worked fairly well, although he thought full employment resulted in "featherbedding" to the extent that it decreased production. The banker predicted that Indochina eventually would go Communist. In the afternoon, the Pulitzers visited their chauffeur's apartment, which he described in detail. "It is *extraordinary, "* he began. On an income of about $1,900 a year, $400 of which went for rent, the chauffeur got a living room, kitchen, and bedroom—in which the man, his wife, and his six-year-old son slept—plus a bathroom with tub and shower and a small balcony "used for sunning themselves and for drying laundry; central heating and hot water. *No one* could ask for more." With certain exceptions, it went without saying.

That evening the Pulitzers dined with U.S. Ambassador and Mrs. John M. Cabot and several others at the ambassador's residence. He found Cabot less than enthusiastic about Swedish economic arrangements. "He makes the point that at home our slums and our housing shortage are due not only to the greed of the real estate lobby but to the greed of the building unions as well," Pulitzer recorded, adding: "In St. Louis we know something about this with our racketeering and skullduggery." He noted that the other diners were attachés and their wives from around the United States who had served in many other foreign posts, and commented: "I can discover neither fairies nor Pinks among them." He found the residence "charming," but the embassy nearby an "ultra-modern steel and concrete glass monstrosity that looks like a boiler factory."

The embassy in Copenhagen, where they flew the next day and saw Ambassador Robert D. Coe, was no better. Pulitzer said he hoped the federal agency that approved architects' plans for embassies "can be persuaded to get away from the ultra-modern. There is nothing typically American about it. A Williamsburg house would, I think, be very much more appropriate." In contrast, he found Edvard Eriksen's famous *Mermaid* "by far the most beautiful sculpture we have seen in Scandinavia." As for those countries as a whole:

> I have the impression that there is much to avoid but a very great deal to admire in the social welfare states of Norway, Sweden and Denmark. Among other things, even though they live within a stone's throw of the U.S.S.R., they believe in political freedom and are not afraid to permit the continued existence of a Communist Party. Norway, Sweden and Denmark all have their weak and unimportant Communist Parties. Here in the United States, as I write this, we are about to outlaw our Communist Party.

Perhaps the most remarkable thing about Pulitzer's Scandinavian diary is its visual detail. A reader unaware of his handicap would never suspect that the author had only partial sight in one eye. That was just as he wanted it to be. In some ways, most likely as a form of compensation, he emphasized the visual. He had a keen interest—greater than most men, certainly—in the beauty of flowers. There always were cut flowers in his homes, and even in his fishing and hunting lodges. When economizing at Bar Harbor one year, he had his gardener decide whether it would be less costly to buy rather than raise the one to two dozen vases of flowers the leased cottage required each week. There was no thought of curtailing or doing without this visual accent; he chose to enjoy whatever sight was left rather than bemoan that which was gone. After agreeing to turn over the *Discoverer* to the Coast Guard in 1942, he wrote that he would appreciate being a passenger on the boat for two or three patrols: "I say as a passenger for the reason that my eyesight is so limited that I would be of little or no use, for I am unable to read ordinary type and I am unable to see the points of a compass."10

His family never heard him speak with such candor about his handicap. Part of the reason, no doubt, was that he did not want to become the object of pity his father had made himself by continually calling attention to his blindness and other infirmities. He went out of his way to avoid this. When his son Michael was about ten years old, he asked his father to come out to the yard and hit a few baseball pitches, a virtual impossibility for someone with no depth perception, but Pulitzer didn't mention this and agreed to try. Michael pitched a few times, and his father swung but always missed. "Hey, you're not very good at this, are you?" Michael remarked. "No, I guess I'm not very good at it," was the reply.

Those who knew how poorly he could see marveled particularly at his interest in, and ability at, shooting. The conditions had to be right. It was almost impossible for him to sight a bird in bright sunlight, but he could distinguish the shape of an incoming bird against an overcast sky. Ducks are usually the most plentiful in such climatic conditions. He had what his physician son-in-law Louis Hempelmann Jr. called "tubular vision" in his right eye; by his mid-thirties the left was completely blind. Yet with neither depth nor peripheral perception, he could see quite well at a distance, "as long as it was straight ahead." Liza, his usual shooting companion, would help him line up a shot with such brief instructions as "Mark left, Joe," or "Mark at two o'clock." Close work was nearly impossible, but at times he would struggle, with the aid of a magnifying glass, to read ordinary type, but, Hempelmann recalled, "he had to hold the paper just a couple of inches in front of his eye."

Part of the explanation for his skill with a shotgun probably is that he had vision in both eyes when he learned to shoot and only gradually suffered greater impairment. As a younger man, he shot a variety of game birds in the field, including pheasant, quail, partridge, prairie hens, and doves. This required faster visual reaction than shooting ducks or geese from a stationary blind. His favorite photograph of himself was taken in September 1932 in Saskatchewan, Canada, where he and Clark McAdams hunted Hungarian partridge. With him in the photo is Brownie, a Chesapeake Bay retriever he bought during the trip. He had a portrait painted from this photograph by artist Wayman Adams in 1945 shortly after Adams completed the one commissioned by *Post-Dispatch* employees which hangs at the *Post-Dispatch.* As late as 1937 he took part in a pheasant shoot on private lands in Hungary, but this was under controlled conditions, where "beaters" flushed the birds from heavily stocked fields within close range of the shooters. More than 10,000 birds were killed in ten days by six guns on that trip. The birds were the property of the Hungarian government and were sold to restaurants throughout Europe.[11]

Pulitzer's interest in duck-shooting began about 1910, near the time of his first marriage, when Clark McAdams introduced him to the sport at Cuivre Island in the Mississippi. For some years he traveled annually with his first wife and some St. Louis friends to Texas to shoot ducks.[12] Before long, there were years in which he followed the duck migration through the hunting seasons from Maine to the southeastern states. The earliest shooting he was able to get in some years was at sea ducks, hunting from a somewhat perilous perch on a ledge of Egg Rock in Frenchman Bay off Bar Harbor. It is doubtful that his first wife ever shot with him, but his second wife was with him for the majority of his duck-shooting, most of which was done at two private locations: Bath, Illinois, where they had a small, comfortable house they called "The Shack," and Stuttgart, Arkansas, where they first leased an entire floor of the Riceland Hotel for themselves and guests and then a large furnished house during the duck season. For a number of years he also maintained a small place, where he usually shot only with his wife or other family members, at Chandlerville, Illinois.

The Illinois and Arkansas seasons were back-to-back, providing sport from late October into early January. Pulitzer's shooting places were readily accessible from St. Louis, particularly if travel was by air. In 1946 the *Post-Dispatch* acquired a twin-engine Beechcraft that could carry up to five passengers. It was replaced in 1951 with a fourteen-passenger DC-3. Both craft were named *Weatherbird,* after the *Post-Dispatch*'s cartoon weather commentator who appears daily on the newspaper's front page. An 8-foot-high "Weatherbird" reading a copy of the *Post-Dispatch* with the KSD microphone and KSD–TV transmitting tower at his sides adorned the second plane's tail structure.[13] Most of the time the plane was used to take reporters, photographers, and company executives to out-of-town assignments, but Pulitzer used it for his recreational travel as well. There were times, in fact, when the plane's only passenger besides the pilots was a dog being transported to or from a retrieving job.

The plane was a great convenience and a large expense. When the cost of operating the smaller craft reached $50,000 a year in 1948, business manager Hentschell recommended selling it and using commercial flights.[14] Pulitzer's response was to keep it until he bought the larger craft three years later. He especially enjoyed the DC-3, which cruised at 175 miles an hour and was comfortably appointed, including radio and television receivers, a well-stocked bar and galley, and sleeping berths for two, which the Pulitzers used frequently. In effect, the *Weatherbird* served Pulitzer as the yacht *Liberty* had his father. After he had the airplane, it was not unusual for him to return to St. Louis from Bar Harbor once or twice during the summer for a few days' work at the *Post-Dispatch.*

Duck-shooting at Stuttgart, the main event of the shooting season, was another costly proposition. Starting in 1934, Pulitzer hunted there on several reservoirs owned by rice farmer Frank A. Freudenberg, who gradually increased his holdings to about 1,000 acres, most of which was reserved for the season for the exclusive use of Pulitzer and guests.[15] The reservoirs stored water for the rice crop, and the combination of the water and the rice attracted migrating ducks most years by the hundreds of thousands. On some days, people who hunted there with the Pulitzers recalled, the sky was literally black with what seemed a never-ending stream of ducks. Most of the birds were mallards, considered the best-tasting wild ducks because they feed on grains rather than fish. Pulitzer paid the cost of creating several hundred acres of new reservoir over the years in exchange for his hunting rights. The annual cost of Arkansas shooting during the 1930s and 1940s was about $7,000. This included the payment to Freudenberg and the cost of all provisions and help. A 1943 article in the *Arkansas Gazette,* headlined "Pulitzers Are Hunters Deluxe," noted: "During the depression it was a common sight to see a row of Negroes waiting at the rear door of their residence to receive the leftover food from their lavish hospitality." Of the Pulitzers, it said: "Though of a retiring and unassuming type, they are affable and democratic and well-liked in Stuttgart."[16] In 1948, Pulitzer was one of the judges in Stuttgart's annual national championship duck-calling contest, and in 1951 he arranged KSD–TV coverage of the affair.[17]

Some years, especially as they got older, the Pulitzers spent virtually the entire Arkansas season, including Christmas, at Stuttgart, entertaining guests brought in by train or plane for long weekends. In other years they divided each week during the duck season between St. Louis and Stuttgart. They almost never mixed social friends and employees when they entertained, and they usually socialized with company people only at Stuttgart. Several *Post-Dispatch* executives liked to hunt ducks and were invited to Stuttgart several times each season. For several years this group included Hentschell, advertising manager Fred Rowden, sports editor J. Roy Stockton, and Fitzpatrick. Hentschell recalled that the daily routine at Stuttgart never varied when this group was there. Pulitzer was the first to rise—about four o'clock in the morning—and went around to the bedrooms calling, "Good morning, Gentlemen, get up!" They ate a hearty breakfast prepared by Matilda Dwyer, wife of Pulitzer's estate manager and chauffeur, and then drove out to the reservoirs. There they were met by locally hired guides—one guide to each pair of hunters—who rowed them in boats to their blinds. Decisions on who would hunt from which of several blinds were made the night before. The shooting began at sunrise and ended, usually, about 10:30 A.M. The hunters returned to the house for the day's main meal, which often included duck expertly prepared by Mrs. Dwyer.

The time away from the blinds was partly social, partly business. Pulitzer used the time to question his executives about their work—particularly, Hentschell and Rowden recalled, their assessments of the business operation. This wasn't nerve-racking, but it wasn't particularly relaxing either, Hentschell said. "He was a great guy, but don't you tell him anything if you don't know it. If you don't know, say you don't know but you'll find out. He'd throw twenty questions at you for one little statement you made, so you damn well better know what you're talking about. He was completely thorough." Rowden agreed: "You'd better be careful in what you told the man because I don't think he ever forgot anything."[18] The variation in this pattern when the party was strictly friends was that, on returning from hunting, Pulitzer usually spent an hour or more talking by telephone to people at the *Post-Dispatch*. The Pulitzers usually took a midafternoon nap, and the guests could do the same, play cards, or amuse themselves as they liked.

About 4:30 P.M. there was a "happy hour" featuring martinis. "I didn't know it at the time, but Mrs. Pulitzer always made the guts of the martinis," Hentschell said. "She put vermouth in the bottle, then filled it up with gin and sealed it. Oh, boy, they were good. I'd say four to one." Martinis made Fitzpatrick garrulous, and he would monopolize the dinnertime conversation. The morning after one such performance, Pulitzer asked Hentschell, "Do you suppose we can do something about Fitz's longwinded speeches?" "Yes," Hentschell replied, "I have a very marvelous idea." It involved a conspiracy with the Pulitzers and Stockton:

> So that night at dinner, Mr. Fitzpatrick was buttering away on a long bun and he started off on whatever the hell it was—"and Washington, mumble, mumble, mumble, . . . " and about the third "mumble" I said, "You know, Mr. Pulitzer, we ought to shoot the west [reservoir] tomorrow." I broke in as rudely and crudely as I could. It almost knocked Fitz off his feet to think that someone had the audacity to interrupt him. He looked indignantly at me. . . . J.P. responded, "I'll have to think it over, but we might want to change." Then, after giving a few more looks, Fitz

started going on again, still buttering his roll—he must have put a pound of butter on the goddam thing. Then Liza sprightly spoke up: "Do you know, Roy, I think you do the best shooting with that automatic pump instead of the over-and-under." Fitz just mumbled to himself, and he didn't say a goddam word the rest of dinner. . . . And Mr. Pulitzer he just thoroughly enjoyed the damn thing.

"Fitz and I didn't get along exactly together," Hentschell confessed, probably because he usually voted Republican and the cartoonist seldom, if ever, did. "But I loved the old stiff, and enjoyed knowing him." That evening ended, as usual, with most of the party retiring by 9:00 P.M.

On the day Pulitzer's retriever, Butch, made his first appearance at Stuttgart, he was flown in and taken to the leased house by *Weatherbird* co-pilot George N. Sayers. Pulitzer asked Sayers to bring the dog into the house, which he did. As soon as his leash was removed, Butch became so excited that he romped all around the living room, upsetting a sofa and a coffee table. Pulitzer bellowed "Ed!" and Dwyer took the animal into the backyard and tied him on a long leash. Dinner was served shortly thereafter, but was interrupted when Dwyer came in to report that Butch had gotten loose and run away. The hunters quickly finished eating and divided up into several search parties. Sayers and Fitzpatrick started walking down a railroad track. "You know, George," Fitzpatrick observed, "this has to be the best-paid dog hunt in history!" The search proved unnecessary. When the hunters returned to the house, Butch was sitting on the back porch.[19] Another dog—Mrs. Pulitzer's black miniature poodle, Agony—also usually was with them. He had belonged to their daughter, Elinor, but she and her husband could not keep him when they moved into an apartment. They had picked the name because of their long indecision about what breed of dog to get. Agony growled at people he didn't know well. Fitzpatrick depicted his personality in a charcoal drawing of the poodle dressed in a dinner jacket and bow tie with the caption "Mr. Agony to you, Stockton!" Paintings of Butch and Agony in circular frames hang in what was Pulitzer's study at the Bar Harbor home now used by his children.

The number of ducks shot by the Pulitzers and guests during

the seasons in Illinois and Arkansas each year could easily top 2,000, although there was considerable variation due to weather, fluctuations in the duck population, the length of the season, and allowable limits. A record of the years 1940 to 1953 at Stuttgart shows 1940 as the best year, with 2,119, and 1951 the lowest, with 585. The average over those years was 1,139. After the limit dropped to four per hunter per day in 1947, the regulation was circumvented by licensing the guides, who did not shoot, and assigning a limit to each of them. With the kind of shooting Stuttgart often afforded, a limit of four might be taken in half an hour or less. Birds taken over the limit were accounted for in the shooting records as "lost."[20] This did not amount to the carnage it might at first seem. As a writer in *The American Field*, a sportsmen's publication, observed of Pulitzer's Arkansas practices in 1936: "Offhand, I'd estimate he spent a good many thousand dollars of benefit to the State Game Department and the town and community. He quit shooting every day at 10:30 A.M., rested his place regularly, and I doubt if his total bag (much of which went to hospitals and poor people) exceeded 1,500 ducks, probably less." He noted that if the area had been opened to the public on a daily fee basis, twenty or more guns would kill many more birds. Therefore, "Mr. Pulitzer was a benefactor for 1935's ducks."[21]

As that suggests, Pulitzer had some differences with the conservationists. He had no quarrel with most of the basic regulations, such as bag limits, the length of seasons, and protection of such scarce species as the wood duck, nor did he have any objection to the registration of firearms—he owned seventeen shotguns—when U.S. Attorney General Robert H. Jackson proposed it in 1940. "I am perfectly willing to comply, just as I have to register my automobile, and just as the doctor has to register any narcotic prescription which he gives me," he told Coghlan for editorial guidance.[22] But he had little patience with conservationists, "who are either sentimentally ignorant or else determined to stop the killing of all birds." Many of these people, he had found, belonged to the Audubon Society. In 1936, he asked Ross to write an editorial opposing an Audubon call for stricter protection of the Dakota duck breeding grounds. Even though that area was drought-stricken, he contended that it represented only "a comparatively small proportion of the entire American and Canadian breeding area." He also advised that "this proves again that the Audubon Societies are not so much concerned with conservation but rather with the stopping of killing of all game. Like the anti-vivisectionists and the prohibitionists, they are cranks."23 A decade later, he asked Coghlan to break their rule against planted letters to the editor by running this one by Pulitzer, signed "Duck Hunter":

> The United States Fish and Wildlife Service continues to tell us duck hunters that ducks are disappearing fast. Perhaps they are. Many of us look with suspicion on their figures and findings. Some years ago this service, then known as the Biological Survey, was assisted by a group of sportsmen who co-operated with it and met with it in Washington to recommend shooting regulations. Two St. Louisans who served on this civilian board were the late Clark McAdams of the Post-Dispatch and Edwin H. Steedman, chairman of the board of Curtis Manufacturing Co., both expert hunters with sane views as to conservation. When this civilian board was in existence, hunters generally felt that they had a friend in court and that the decisions of the government's biological survey would not be purely those of "bureaucrats" trying to make a showing and to keep a couple of jumps ahead of the overzealous ladies and gentlemen of the Audubon Society. This civilian board, for some reason, was discontinued. Why not re-establish it and to that extent at least give the hunters a break?

Coghlan published the letter.24

In all of Pulitzer's years of shooting, there apparently was only one serious firearm accident. In 1951, while his eldest daughter, Kate Davis, was shooting at Stuttgart with her husband, retired Air Force Lieutenant General Elwood R. Quesada, the safety catch on his gun failed and it discharged, hitting her in the left forearm.25 It was feared at first that she might lose the use of her hand, but after seven weeks of hospitalization in St. Louis, she regained its full use. After the sudden, tragic death of his first wife, this seems to have been the most traumatic event in Pulitzer's life. "I have been distraught over what might have been a terrible tragedy in my family," he wrote Bernard Baruch a few days after the accident, apologizing for not having responded sooner to a letter from Baruch, and enclosing a newspaper clipping about the accident.[26] He visited Kate Davis every day she was in the hospital—more undivided attention than she had ever had from him. "It was one of the greatest times of my life," she said many years later. "This accident gave me a chance to be with my father. I'd never been alone with him."

This was true, generally, for all of the children, especially for the daughters and younger son. When they were small, all four children were cared for by nurses and governesses, and as they grew older they were often supervised and taken places by members of the household staff while their parents were in adult company. They clearly understood that Daddy was not to be disturbed when he was working in his study at home. By the time Michael, born in 1930, was growing up, the *Post-Dispatch* had achieved substantial stature and Pulitzer was deeply involved in its direction. As a boy, Michael recalled, "my perception of him was as an autocrat and a very powerful man. He worked at home with secretaries, and he was always behind doors." He thought they had a good relationship, "but I wouldn't say it was a close relationship at all." He said he felt closer to his mother, "though again not terribly close." Elinor said she and her father became very close when she was an adult, but as a child she had found him somewhat remote. "Well, Daddy as a family man left something to be desired," she commented. Michael had a great companion, though, in his father's chauffeur and "man of all work" Edward Dwyer, who took him to movies and ball games as a child. Dwyer always took his own family to Bar Harbor in the summer, and Dwyer's namesake son, who was called Buster, was one of Michael's playmates.

Like his elder half-brother, Michael went to St. Mark's, starting when he was twelve. Both sons graduated from Harvard, Joseph Jr. in 1936 and Michael in 1951—Michael sooner than usual because he skipped a form at St. Mark's. He was introduced to newspaper work in 1947, when he accompanied a *Post-Dispatch* reporter to the site of the Centralia, Illinois, mine disaster and wrote a first-person account of this experience for the St. Mark's magazine.[27] His father arranged for him to work for four weeks at the *Louisville Courier-Journal* in the summer of 1950, expecting that he would enter newspapering. But after earning a bachelor's degree the following year, Michael decided to take a law degree at Harvard. His father was disappointed that he chose law over journalism, but he didn't want to force the issue. "I have often said that I would never drive a son of mine into the newspaper business who did not have a strong taste and even a passion for it," he wrote Michael in 1951.[28] Kate Davis believed he felt this way because her grandfather had virtually compelled her uncle Ralph to become a newspaper publisher even though he had neither the inclination nor temperament for it. She recalled her father telling her that "Ralph had been miserable" because he "couldn't handle the hurly-burly existence of deadlines and tough guy reporters and people in the composing room—all the things that go on at a paper." This is supported in a letter Ralph's second wife, Margaret Leech Pulitzer, wrote her brother-in-law in 1937. He had asked her whether she thought Ralph would mind if he were no longer designated a vice president of the Pulitzer Publishing Company, as he had been for years even though he had no actual responsibility. "You know, as I do, that Ralph undervalues himself and thinks that he has no ability at all," she replied, "and I suppose that, to a person of this type, any withdrawal of position or title appears to be a confirmation of his own sense of inadequacy in a way that would never occur to more confident people." She concluded, "While the title probably means nothing whatever to him, its withdrawal might cause him unhappiness—which he would never admit."[29] The title was retained.

Michael was working for a Boston law firm when his father died, but the following year he quit and became a reporter at the *Courier-Journal*, where he worked for four years. He then joined the *Post-Dispatch*, working as a reporter both in St. Louis and at the Washington bureau. He became assistant managing editor in 1968, and when the company bought the *Arizona Daily Star* in Tucson in 1971, he became its editor and publisher. He kept those positions and became a periodic commuter to Arizona after returning to St. Louis in 1978 to become associate editor of the *Post-Dispatch*, the position his half-brother eventually held when their father was editor and publisher. The two sons have worked closely since that time. As of 1991, Michael was president and chief executive officer of the Pulitzer Publishing Company and Joseph

Jr., whose career is described in the following chapter, was chairman of the board.

The daughters also went to private schools—Mary Institute in St. Louis and then Foxcroft School in Middleburg, Virginia. Elinor also attended The Stuart School, a junior college in Boston, for two years. Both were introduced to society at debutante parties. Their parents did not encourage them to earn bachelor's degrees, and neither did. When Kate Davis was about 20, Pulitzer did arrange for her to spend a week making the rounds with a reporter in order to give her a broader understanding of society. They visited a mental hospital, the morgue, the jail, and a public hospital, where she saw a baby die. She also spent a week sitting in on cases with a social worker. Then someone suggested that she attend a hanging in Belleville, Illinois, but "Daddy put his foot down" and she did not go. He arranged the other things, he told her, "because we lived in the country, all protected and lovely, and he wanted me to see how people really lived." Elinor didn't get the same opportunity because, she speculated, her father was preoccupied with the war when she reached the same age.

Because the children had been born between 1913 and 1930, their age differences, as might be expected, tended to pair off the two older and two younger siblings as companions of one another when they were growing up. Joseph Jr. and Kate Davis had gone away to school while Elinor and Michael were still quite young. As teenagers, young Joe and Kate Davis spent several summers in Europe. This meant, for one thing, that there were relatively infrequent gatherings of the entire family for meals. Kate Davis remembered that when she was still living at home the family dinners for four—the two older children and their parents—were impressive, formal affairs that began at 8:15 P.M. "We dressed for dinner. My stepmother was in a tea gown, a long, flowing robe, and a favorite diamond pin." Her father wore either a smoking jacket or a dinner jacket and his black patent leather pumps. "I didn't realize until sometime later what humdrum dinners most people had," Kate Davis said. "We had extremely civilized dinners. He'd grown up in a very civilized family, lucky enough to have people to wait on them. He never wanted to lay eyes on a leftover. One night you had lamb, the next night you had beef, the next night you had chicken. You never had hash or stew or God knows what else. It was all brand new. And it was always served with candles and fresh flowers on the table and his glass of red wine." The dinner conversation revolved around that day's *Post-Dispatch.* "If you hadn't read the paper, you were out of it. Mommie [her stepmother] used to shut herself up in her room in the afternoon when the paper had arrived and study the paper." For the most part, the topics were current events, not trivia. "We never talked about people except interesting people. We never said, 'Oh, Maisie's divorced,' or how they fixed somebody's hair or, 'Did she run off with the postman?' Gossip bored him."

Elinor recalled that when she became a part of these dinners it was usually just three of them, and her father sometimes would discuss things that were happening at the office, some of them confidential, although he did not explicitly identify them as such. Yet it "was absolutely understood that this was not to be talked about and it was the best training in the world for a young girl. You learned how to keep your trap shut, and this has been a great help always. . . . It wasn't done for the purpose of getting our reactions, it was more thinking aloud."

The Pulitzer home was the scene of many a dinner party for friends over the years. These were black tie affairs usually for twenty to thirty guests which featured happy conversation, laughter, and a good deal of drinking, mostly of martinis in stem glasses, one frequent guest recalled, "no pussyfooting around with on-the-rocks."[30] Pulitzer also "adored champagne," and often brought home a group of friends in the wee hours for scrambled eggs and champagne served by butler Albert Gould after they had been partying at the St. Louis Country Club, which abutted his property. Four who were often in the group were the Wallace H. Smiths and the Thomas W. Pettuses. Mrs. Smith's nickname was "Kelse," and she and Mrs. Pettus ("Zeekie"), both beautiful, were particular favorites of Pulitzer's at dinner parties and at Stuttgart. Pulitzer dubbed Wallace Smith, a well-known oil painter, "Wallingford." Often when they were at a country club dance, Smith recalled, Pulitzer would say, "Wallingford, tell me where the fair Johanna is. Pick her out for me. I want to talk to her a bit." Smith would point out a lady and Pulitzer would introduce himself if he didn't already know her, "dance her around the floor for a while and then take her over and talk to her and joke with her and make his kind of love, which didn't amount to much."[31] He could find a pretty woman on his own too; it was frequently remarked, in fact, that despite his visual limitations, "he could spot a pretty woman at two hundred paces." Kate Davis remembered watching him more than once locate a woman on the dance floor at the Bar Harbor Club to whom he wanted to talk. He put his right arm out in front of himself, "as a sort of fender-offer. He'd walk right through the dancers until he got over to the girl he wanted to talk to, and then cut in on her." Occasionally these flirtations upset her stepmother, even to the point of tears, but the marriage never was in serious trouble. For her part, Kate Davis remarked, "Mommie didn't look at a flea after she married Daddy."

By all accounts, both of Pulitzer's marriages were strong and loving, and if anything, the second was more secure than the first because of Liza's absolute devotion to her mate. She did whatever he wanted to do whenever he wanted to do it. "I'm his Chinese wife," she once told the Smiths. She could be ready to go on a spur-of-the-moment shooting or fishing trip without a word of complaint. She had grown up and spent nearly all her time in the city of St. Louis, and until she married Pulitzer at the age of thirty-five—her only marriage—had enjoyed indoor activities, such as bridge and doing fine needlework. For a time she had worked in a smart dress shop, where the salesgirls were served afternoon tea by a maid in a black uniform. But she readily took to outdoor life, learning to ride horseback, shoot, and fish, and—apparently by force of will—trained herself not to become seasick on the yacht. On chilly Bar Harbor mornings she would faithfully join her husband for a dip in the frigid bay before breakfast. Pulitzer thought cold baths were healthful and invigorating, and she too became a believer in them. Writing to a man who was arranging a hunting trip for them in 1938, Pulitzer advised him: "My wife and I are accustomed to camp life in the woods, eating out of tin plates, sleeping in sleeping bags, no toilet conveniences, etc., so please take that into consideration. . . . If the shooting justifies it, we will go anywhere and take our chances."[32]

The difference between the two wives, in Kate Davis's view, was that Kate Davis's mother "wasn't as single-minded as my stepmother. . . . I don't know whether she liked to hunt or not, but I know she liked to go dancing, and she liked to go to New York.

She never would have been the companion that Mommie was. She had too much of a spirit of her own." She undoubtedly had a large number of friends and admirers, Joseph Jr. concluded, because of the many people who told him — some as late as twenty-five years after her death — that they had known and admired her and could describe her personality in detail. An oil portrait of her, smiling, in an evening gown, hung in the dining room of the Pulitzer home throughout Pulitzer's life. Some of his friends — though they never told him so — thought this was inconsiderate of his second wife. But she plainly had no objection. Nor did she change or rearrange the home's interior decor, which largely reflected the taste of the first wife. Pulitzer liked things the way they were because he could find his way around the house with ease, and she didn't want to disturb that. This also suggests that she was keenly sensitive to the feelings of the three children who had lost their mother. There somewhere exists, because several interviewed sources including her son recalled it, a short story by St. Louis poet-playwright-screenwriter George R. O'Neil about the portrait of Elinor Wickham Pulitzer. O'Neil had known the lady and wrote a story he titled "Immortal Laughter," about a dinner party at Lone Tree Farm after the second marriage. The dramatic point of the story came when there was a lull in the conversation and peals of laughter burst forth from the painting as if to signify a comment on the proceedings. It may have been mockery or mirth. Presumably each of those in the room drew his or her own conclusion.

The Pulitzers were, of course, frequent guests at the homes of others, both in St. Louis and at Bar Harbor. They attended several costume parties at the home of investment broker Joseph L. Werner and his wife and also shot with them at Werner's private lodge and at a club to which he belonged. Pulitzer especially enjoyed the costume parties the Werners gave. At a "tacky party" he appeared in red "long-johns" and wore a clashing red beard. At another, held on Werner's fortieth birthday at the exclusive, conservative Log Cabin Club — to which Pulitzer did not belong and because of his newspaper's leanings would not have been asked to join — Pulitzer came as General Ulysses S. Grant and his wife as a Southern belle.

Pulitzer frequently was among people whose political philosophies were anathema to those espoused in the *Post-Dispatch* but who nevertheless enjoyed his congenial, outgoing personality. Still, there were times of strain. As one woman, who was the wife of Claude T. Porter, owner of the Porter Paint Company in St. Louis when Pulitzer knew them, put it: "The *Post-Dispatch* was not popular with, it sounds arrogant to say, 'our group.'" She remembered being at a party attended by the Pulitzers at the Deer Creek Club, a small, informal club that Pulitzer and some of his St. Louis Country Club friends had started. This was just after the *Post-Dispatch* had endorsed Roosevelt in 1932. "Everyone was just so mad at them," she recalled. "They were just kind of isolated." She also remembered the effect of the paper's refusal to shield the prominent from negative publicity: "If anything came out that should be printed, it was printed. I can't remember incidents, but I can remember people being infuriated."[33] She was certain that Pulitzer had gained his social access to these people because his first wife was from an old St. Louis family. "She offered him the opportunity to get into the St. Louis Country Club and all that," she said. "She was his hand up the social ladder, there's no doubt about it."

Her view and that of the Smiths differed somewhat as to whether Pulitzer's Jewish ancestry through his father caused resentment on the part of some members of the country club, which rarely admitted Jews. She thought his marriage to Elinor Wickham, plus the fact that St. Louis has long had a distinguished Jewish population, overcame that. But Smith, who knew Pulitzer only after his second marriage, believed the publisher sensed an anti-Semitic coolness toward him at the club, because some members definitely harbored that prejudice. Smith remembered the Pulitzers being there as part of larger parties rather than as a couple expecting to meet some friends. The children, however, enjoyed the club's facilities regularly. Elinor remembered that she "practically lived there," playing tennis and swimming, and also that on more than one occasion one of the Pulitzer retrievers loped over from their place and plunged into the club's pool. "That made them so furious because it meant they had to empty the pool, clean the pool, refill the pool. I think Daddy got the bill for those, I'm not sure."

Elinor said she once raised the question of anti-Semitism with her father "and he got so tense, not angry, but just terribly tense.

And put it all off. . . . It was one of those things [his eyesight was another] that you just didn't talk about." Not with a youngster, apparently, but with a close friend he wasn't above repeating a Jewish joke. "You probably have heard the one about the Jew who said it was too bad that Harry Truman wasn't a Jew," he said in a note to Bar Harbor neighbor W. Seward Webb in 1951. "On being asked why, his reply was to the effect that if Truman had been a Jew he wouldn't have failed as a haberdasher and, hence, would never have become President."[34] The fact was, as telling that joke suggests and his elder son observed, "he was quite positive in wanting to be identified with the Christian world, because he called himself in *Who's Who* an Episcopalian." When the children were small, he recalled, his parents "were very casual about where we went to Sunday school, and some neighbor took us down to I think it was the Presbyterian church. They didn't seem to care whether it was one church or another. They just said, 'Give the kids a little religion and that's fine.' But there was no structured thing, except at St. Mark's School. That was a church school — an Episcopal church school — which one could take seriously or not."

Kate Davis said the topic of anti-Semitism came up indirectly in 1939, when she planned to travel to Europe aboard the North German Lloyd liner *Bremen* to go skiing in Austria. Demonstrators angered by Nazi persecutions of Jews and others had picketed the ship when it docked in New York Harbor in November 1938.[35] Her father suggested that she book passage on a different ship. "You know I never mix business with family," he explained, "but in this particular case I feel I should ask you not to go across on the *Bremen*. . . . We have a great many Jewish advertisers, and the fact that my daughter went over on that boat would indeed be insensitive to their beliefs," he explained. He didn't insist that she change, but let her know that doing so "would be helpful to these people and to the paper." Of course, she changed.

His daughter's description of how he approached this matter is consistent with many descriptions of his personality by people who knew him. Powerful and confident though he was, he was almost formally courteous and never bombastic, as his father often had been. The former Mrs. Porter remembered that when several men were in a group at a party "having a big argument, my Charlie would say, 'Now let me tell you something!' He knew, and he was going to tell them. I never heard Joe do that. I think everybody who worked for him loved him." Mrs. Pettus, whose husband was head of Scullin Steel Company, said almost the same thing: "My husband Tommy used to needle Joe all the time, and he just loved it; he just ate it up. . . . He never, at any time, got mad, and he could have, because Tommy would say, 'What about that editorial in your damn paper? What have you got to say about that?' And he was always right there with an answer. Tommy never let up on him, and Joe never resented it."[36]

It appears true that no employee who got to know Pulitzer failed to develop an affection for him. James Lawrence, an editorial writer during Pulitzer's tenure and a guest at Stuttgart several times, said his theory about this was that Pulitzer's wealth and his poor eyesight "shut him off from what you might call the common people, and he knew it. And he would drag people into his office and even down at Stuttgart and really put them through an inquisition trying to find out what people really thought about things. He made a real effort to do this." He once asked Lawrence for his opinion of a national health insurance proposal of President Truman's. "And he said something like, 'Jim, how does the average fellow out there making let's say $3,000'—which was average money in those days—'what does he do if he gets hit with a big operation or something?' He wanted to know how people dealt with these things. So he really was a very fine newspaperman and a very fine gentleman, and I really wound up loving the old boy."[37] Of course, the *Post-Dispatch* and broadcasting stations employed more than 2,000 people, many of whom didn't know what Pulitzer looked like. He once boarded the elevator to go up to his office. "Take me straight to three," he said to the operator. "Who do you think you are—Mr. Pulitzer?" she replied. "That's who I am," he answered.[38]

That he was a somewhat less than enthusiastic country club member also meshes with other opinions, even if this was not because of a sense of anti-Jewish prejudice. All his children agreed that beyond a point the social circuit bored him and that yachting, fishing, and hunting provided irresistible means of escape. He wrote numerous letters over the years declining invitations, explaining that the dates conflicted with one or another of his outdoor activities. That doctors had told him healthful outdoor exercise should slow the deterioration of his eyesight provided an additional justification, but he never used "doctor's orders" as an excuse. He confined most of his indoor social activity to the winter. For many years the Pulitzers gave a large open house party on Christmas afternoon at which both invited and uninvited guests appeared. But it eventually came to be burdensome and was abandoned in favor of spending the holidays at Stuttgart. Above all, as Joseph Jr. remembered it, his father "was quite determined . . . to have fun in life as well as having a responsible and important career. You could still have a lot of fun, and he loved a good time."

— 25 —

Looking Toward the Future

On Saturday, April 2, 1955, Raymond Crowley walked slowly out of Christ Church Cathedral at 1210 Locust Street in St. Louis. Tears were spilling down his face. This surprised *Post-Dispatch* photographer Louis L. Phillips, who was going into the church. "I never thought he was the type who could cry over anybody or anything," he said of the uncompromising managing editor.[1]

Crowley was one of many who emerged from the cathedral in tears that day. He had just paid his last respects to Joseph Pulitzer II, who had died at his home shortly after 11:00 P.M. on March 30, three days before. An aneurysm in his main abdominal aorta had hemorrhaged. His last word was an instinctive "Ed!"—a call for his faithful Edward Dwyer. Mrs. Pulitzer telephoned Dwyer at his home nearby and Dr. Samuel B. Grant, Pulitzer's physician, who arrived quickly. Grant checked the publisher's vital signs, then looked at Dwyer and shook his head. He knew there was no hope, but summoned an ambulance to take Pulitzer to Barnes Hospital, where he was pronounced dead at 11:45 P.M. He was seventy years and nine days old.

The word of his death came with stunning suddenness to almost everyone. He had worked a full day, as usual, leaving his office about 7:00 P.M. Charles Hentschell had seen him shortly after lunch. He was chewing antacid tablets, three or four at a time, and seemed uncomfortable, but the business manager didn't think this indicated anything serious. "Boy, those things are going off like firecrackers!" Hentschell remarked. "I chew a lot of them," Pulitzer replied. By the end of the day, it was clear to secretary Arch King that Pulitzer was not feeling well. "He had his head on his desk, and Ed Dwyer, the chauffeur, came in and [Pulitzer] said, 'I think I'll go home.'" He was watching television with his wife after dinner when he slumped over in his chair.

Most of the top-echelon *Post-Dispatch* people had been told of Pulitzer's death by shortly after midnight. Crowley and others came into the office, hours earlier than usual, to begin planning the paper that would announce his passing. There was not a great deal to be done. Pulitzer's obituary had been written and set in type several years earlier—"I feel some delicacy about editing my own obituary," he had remarked at the time[2]—and the photographs to accompany it had been selected. Only the most recent details had to be added. Yet the desks in the newsroom gradually filled. Unable to sleep, Hentschell went in about 3:00 A.M., going first to the newsroom. "There probably were thirty men there, key men of the whole staff," he recalled. "It was the quietest thing. It was absolutely incredible that so many men could work without saying anything. They were so immersed in their thoughts of that great guy, just as I was."[3] Of immediate concern was that the morning *Globe-Democrat* should not print the news first; it should come from the *Post-Dispatch*. And it did.

Pulitzer's death was a shock to Dr. Grant, who had known him for years, but did not come as a complete surprise. For two years he had seen the publisher's health decline. In February 1953, a benign tumor was removed from his stomach. The aneurysm was discovered at that time but did not seem to be life-threatening. Almost exactly a year later, a benign colon polyp and his appendix had been removed uneventfully.[4] Pulitzer went fishing in Canada in June as usual and then to Norway. A more worrisome condition showed up in the fall of 1954. Tests revealed partially obstructed blood flow through the right carotid artery to the head. The tests were ordered after Pulitzer experienced several episodes of transient blindness in his functioning right eye in October and November. One of these occurred while he was duck-hunting at Chandlerville, Illinois. It passed, and he shot well thereafter.[5] But the condition was serious; there were no surgical techniques at that time to eliminate the obstruction. "The outlook for this condition was not good," said Grant's son, Dr. Neville Grant, who reviewed his father's records of Pulitzer's case, "although unpredictable in any individual case."[6]

Except for his eyes, for which he took injections of tuberculin for years as a means of slowing their deterioration,[7] Pulitzer had enjoyed robust health until 1953. The discovery of the stomach tumor frightened him. Shortly after he learned surgery would be necessary, he called Shelton, Hentschell, and Crowley into his office. "You've heard me talk about what to do if I should be hit by a streetcar," he reminded them. "Well, I'm going to be grazed by one next week. I am to have a stomach operation. . . . I want you men to consider what I should do—have I overlooked anything?" In a memorandum of the meeting, Shelton recorded that while the physicians were optimistic about the outcome of the surgery, they had told Pulitzer that "anything could happen." He continued:

> He was concerned as to whether Joe Jr. was competent to carry on. What did we think? He mentioned Joe's shyness. All three of us have a high regard for Joe and told him so—we thought Joe would respond well if full responsibility fell on him. I said to JP he could be sure we would back up Joe. I said: "Joe Jr. will be here and whatever the outcome may be you can be sure all three of us will do everything we possibly can to help him." This so affected JP that tears came to his eyes, he turned his chair away from us and for some minutes wept silently.[8]

After he regained his composure, Pulitzer told the three men he was concerned that his brother Herbert might "place too low a value" on his job if his son were to inherit it, and all three assured him that they had "a full appreciation of the value of the job of heading up a business of this size and so closely related to the public interest." The next day Pulitzer cabled Herbert in France, asking him to approve Hentschell as Pulitzer's successor as trustee of the Newspaper Trust (then himself, J.P. Jr., and Herbert) should that become necessary. He also asked for assurance that his son would receive "ample and generous compensation for heavy responsibilities" if he became president of the company. Herbert agreed, and flew immediately to St. Louis to be with his brother.[9]

After the surgery, Pulitzer went to Florida to recuperate. While there, he wrote Shelton: "I sometimes chuckle over my performance in my office with you and Charlie and Ray. You were right. The streetcar did miss me but my back side still reminds me that it was a damn close shave."[10] On his return to St. Louis, his executives gave the publisher an elaborate "welcome home" dinner at the University Club of St. Louis. On the front cover of the printed menu was a smiling likeness of Pulitzer drawn by Fitzpatrick; the back cover contained the signatures of all those who attended.[11] Just as the dinner began, Pulitzer proposed a toast, mindful that two of his broadcasting executives were present: "With apologies to Brother Burbach and Brother Grams, I want to drink a toast to the noblest profession of all, journalism." The words were spoken in such a way, Grams remembered, "that you knew he really meant it."[12] The festivities lasted well past midnight. "Is there any more bubbly, Charlie?" Pulitzer asked Hentschell at intervals.[13]

After the carotid artery obstruction was discovered late the following year, Pulitzer summoned Shelton to his home. "I am not in good shape," he confided, explaining that only he, his wife, and Dr. Grant knew this and that it was to be kept "graveyard secret." He said he might have to consider some degree of retirement, but hoped he could continue at least his duties as editor, perhaps giving up some of those as publisher. He wanted Shelton's advice on what to do. "This comes to me cold," Shelton replied. "I am not sure just what I would advise after deliberation." Pulitzer suggested that he meet with Dr. Grant and immediately telephoned the physician to authorize him to discuss the case with Shelton, calling him "one of my most trusted associates, whose advice I value."[14] Shelton saw Dr. Grant several days later. He was told that Pulitzer came close to having a stroke but that the condition was treatable with an anticoagulant. Blood tests would be necessary over a period of time to establish the effective dosage. Dr. Grant believed Pulitzer should cut back on his workload but remain actively involved in the *Post-Dispatch*. He thought the publisher had an expectancy of another ten or fifteen years "if he will take care of himself." On that basis, Shelton advised Pulitzer the following day to "delegate more operational details to others" but not resign from any of his jobs because, under his physician's care, the outlook was "very good, for a good many years."[15]

Nevertheless, Pulitzer was prepared for the inevitable. The most important preparation had been under way for years: his eldest son's training for eventual succession. Joseph Pulitzer III was forty-one when his father died. He had worked for the Pulitzer Publishing Company since his graduation from Harvard in 1936, gradually being given greater responsibility. This was broken only by his three years in the Navy during World War II. He had been vice president of the company and a trustee since his uncle Ralph's death in 1939, and associate editor of the *Post-Dispatch* since 1948. His training had differed from that of his father in that he and his father were able to be physically together much of the time, and he was able to observe the editor-publisher at work. "Ask Jody to come in," secretary King remembered Pulitzer saying countless times when he wanted to discuss something with his son or to include him in a meeting.

As has been noted, Pulitzer would not have insisted that his son follow him as head of the company had the young man begged off. But at the same time he hoped it would not come to that, and to an important degree the wish was its own fulfillment. His father never commanded him to enter journalism, Joseph Jr. said, "but he gave me the options that were open to me and I naturally wanted to carry on in the company because the cousins were all in the east and they were not interested, and I was obviously next in line to succeed if I could take over. I felt the third generation thing. I felt it was important to try." Pulitzer also told him that "if

he proved himself to be the right man to head the Post-Dispatch"
he was sure that in time "he could look forward to earning $100,000
a year," Pulitzer's base salary. His son responded that he was
"more than willing to take his chances in the future, stand on his
record and prove that he will be worth that amount." Relating this
in 1950 to his brother Herbert, who presumably would eventually
have some say in setting his nephew's compensation, Pulitzer
commented, "I, for one, think this is a fair attitude which does
him credit and I hope you will think the same."[16]

The third Joseph Pulitzer majored in fine art at Harvard, becoming deeply interested in modern painting and sculpture. This was
an interest difficult for his father to apprehend, both because of
his poor eyesight and because of his limited appreciation of the
impressionistic and the abstract. His tastes ran toward Currier
and Ives prints and other natural depictions, especially of boats
and birds. But Elizabeth Pulitzer recognized her stepson's interest
as a significant pursuit, worthy of encouragement. It was her idea
to remodel the former "Clemenceau room" of their home into a
space that would provide a suitable background for the art Joe had
begun to collect.[17] He bought his first major painting in 1936,
Amedeo Modigliani's *Elvira Resting at a Table*. He has since
become "one of America's top 100 collectors" and has given a
number of pieces to the St. Louis Art Museum.[18]

His father, Joseph Jr. remembered, teased him about his art
"because he couldn't see it. But he was amusing. He couldn't
possibly understand the pictures I bought and he said so." Pulitzer
once chided him: "I think that you're being taken in by those
shrewd New York dealers." To which his son replied, "Well, I
studied art at Harvard. I'm doing the best I can."

Several years later, there was this exchange:

"Joe, how did you know how to buy PEEcass-o?"

"Well, I studied art history at Harvard. You remember that you
gave me an education at Harvard and I studied art history."

"Oh, they taught about PEEcass-o at Harvard?"

"Yes, he's one of the giants of our century." That seemed to
impress his father, Joseph Jr. recalled. "He thought it was quite
remarkable that I had chosen 'PEEcass-o.' I think he was pleased
that I had chosen independence and had done that without any
guidance from family or anyone." Joseph Jr. believed that his

grandfather, had he retained his sight, might have become a serious collector. "After all, he picked two great artists to do him. One was [sculptor Auguste] Rodin—I have him in my office—and the other was [painter John Singer] Sargent [also in his office]. Those are great artists—often underappreciated. When I was in college, Rodin was hardly even taught and Sargent was disparaged as a sort of a fashionable portrait painter, and now that's all been reevaluated and these names are giants. But he picked the right people. I don't know how he did it."[19]

Despite its strong attraction, Joseph Jr. knew while he was learning about it that art "would be an avocation—a very great interest, which it has been—but I wasn't going to do it professionally." His preparation for his career in journalism began in earnest in 1935, when he spent four weeks during the summer as a reporter at the *San Francisco News*. "Whether he has any aptitude for journalism, I do not know," Pulitzer had written *News* editor W. H. Burkhardt in arranging the assignment. "I should much prefer that he be given no special consideration as to hours, discipline, etc.," Pulitzer added, "and indeed I should rather see him given if anything the worst of it, for the sooner he realizes how very little he knows and how much he has to learn, the better."[20] It was clear from that and from a letter he sent the boy's summer camp director ten years earlier, when his son was eleven years old, that Pulitzer wanted to discourage a life of leisure: "He needs to learn to stand up under gruelling physical exercise and of overcoming physical fatigue, discomfort, exposure, anything and everything to make him realize that a soft life is really not worth living. If you can awaken these instincts in him, I feel that you will be doing him and myself the greatest possible service."[21] Twenty years later, in suggesting a "Pictures" layout to Julius Klyman, the publisher commented: "In this day and age with the evils of excessive wealth and of the maldistribution of wealth so much in the public mind, I always find it interesting to see a man rise to a highly useful position in spite of the disadvantages of excessive wealth. Nelson Rockefeller appears to be such a man."[22] He almost certainly took some satisfaction in his own case as well, and hoped his sons would lead similar lives.

In the fall of 1936, after Joe returned from a postgraduation vacation in Europe, Pulitzer put him in the charge of Washington bureau chief Raymond Brandt with instructions that he was to become familiar with the bureau's work and accompany Marquis Childs on upcoming presidential campaign trips. "Let me remind you that Joe is a shy youth with absolutely no knowledge of politics or of current history here or elsewhere. He has a certain undeveloped facility for writing," he wrote Brandt. "I hope you and Childs will run his legs off, see to it that he does thoroughly what you assign him to do, give him perhaps a chance to do a bit of descriptive writing here and there whenever there may be an opportunity for it, and in general try to teach him the whys and wherefores of newspaper work and of American politics." There was to be "no special consideration as to hours, days off or other conditions of labor," but he suggested that Brandt try "to convince him that his first plunge into politics will not be the terrifying ordeal that he imagines."[23] The facility for writing that Pulitzer had mentioned is evident in a letter he wrote his father two months later, when he was back in St. Louis:

> We've been having a very hectic debutante season here with parties three or four times a week. Somehow I manage to rip myself from bed at quarter to seven. If it weren't for the routine I wouldn't be able to do it.
>
> Mrs. Kauffman approached me at a party looking as if she had discovered a new religion and said, "I've discovered Fascism. I'm a Fascist—pronounced Fahcist—They're marvelous." I told her I hoped you'd hear her say that when you got back, but it made no difference; she continued to murmur Fahcist wistfully as she disappeared into an eddy of people.[24]

The day after the election, in which Joe voted for Roosevelt and his father for Landon,[25] Childs wrote the "frank report on Joe" Pulitzer had asked him to submit after the campaign. "I think that Joe wants to be genuinely interested in newspaper work and I feel that he will eventually overcome a certain diffidence toward public affairs that he now has," Childs wrote. "He has a preeminent interest in ideas, and therefore, as he well realizes, most people, particularly those who do not speak his own language, bore him. He is timid about making requests and seeking people out, but no more than many beginning reporters." Childs thought he also needed to develop a stronger appreciation of the need for accuracy in names, addresses, spelling, "and those details which are acquired through routine reporting," and to gain a fuller understanding of national affairs.[26]

On his return to St. Louis, Joe began a period of observer-apprenticeship in the business department. "I spent about two weeks with Mr. Keller going through his files pretty thoroughly and listening to long sad lectures on the mounting expense accounts of the paper," he wrote his father, who was out of town.[27] He was given a desk in the business office, and treasurer Keller was pleased with the young man's attentiveness. "He professed delight at my interest in reducing extravagance and waste," he noted in a lengthy report to his father. He quoted the treasurer as saying: "I'm tickled to death to see you getting into these things. . . . You're the only person around here who pays any attention to me. I have to keep hollering all the time." Keller apparently drew some comparisons between the *Post-Dispatch* and the defunct *World,* for the young man commented that "Mr. Keller's hollering, as he calls it, has no doubt kept us from such terrible waste as the Press Publishing Co. witnessed with their series of business managers and executives all maintained at huge salaries." During this period he also spent time with the business, circulation, and advertising managers. "The first thing that strikes an observer or newcomer in the business office is, as you have often said, the loyalty of the men," he reported. "They are all proud of the paper as a newspaper with character and independence and enjoy seeing it as a successful enterprise."[28]

Gratifying though that was to Pulitzer, he did not want his son to become overly enthusiastic about business matters. His first concern was that he develop the critical abilities of an editor who could function as a reader-critic and keeper of the paper's platform. He turned to Bovard, then approaching the denouement of his differences with the publisher, for an assessment of the young man's potential. He had reason to think that the managing editor would be harsh; several years earlier, after Bovard had a chat with Joseph Jr., he told Pulitzer he thought the young man should "stick to his violin." Pulitzer didn't attach any real importance to that crack—"[Joe] improvises very well on the piano but not the violin," he later told Reese[29] — and asked Bovard to teach his son about news operations and to critically evaluate some of his work. "The editor is only a student of journalism," Bovard commented disparagingly after Pulitzer sought his opinion of Joe's work in editing several issues of the Sunday magazine. "In my opinion, editing cannot be learned by cramming." However, "He might have done much worse. I doubt that any of the other young men of his age on the staff would have done much better."[30] Bovard left the paper within a few months, and Joseph Jr. gained most of his experience in news under managing editor Reese and city editor Crowley.

Also, from about 1937 on, Joseph Jr. was given access to copies of his father's memorandums, the same material from which the bulk of this biography is drawn. Looking back after thirty years as editor-publisher himself, he said he considered this the most important part of his training. The memos revealed the scope of the job and were as well a form of indoctrination in his father's principles and priorities, especially his emphasis on the news and editorial aspects of the job. J.P. Jr. probably saw at least some of the memorandums about himself, such as one to his uncles Ralph and Herbert at the end of 1938. With it, Pulitzer sent three examples of his son's journalistic work. "I had been concerned about his showing too much interest in the business end of the shop but here, I think, are three little evidences of interest in the journalistic end which I find encouraging," he wrote.[31] As the years passed, Joseph Jr. became surer of himself and expressed his point of view on certain matters. "What was your reaction to the strong language and vulgarity quoted in the article 'An Intimate Study of Dixie Demagogues'?" he asked his father in 1946. "I thought it marred an otherwise vivid, provocative piece." Pulitzer responded that he thought the language was "so very typical and so very characteristic of them that I felt it was justified. As a matter of fact, I personally oked to Reese the spelling out of the words 'sons-of-bitches.' My judgment may have been at fault, but that was it."[32]

By the late 1940s, Joseph Jr. was preparing lengthy reports during his father's summer absences. These showed his involvement in the full range of the company's activities. One from 1947, for example, reported that after publishing a three-article series by "a top State Department advisor identified mysteriously as 'X' " — but who was known in Washington circles to be George F. Kennan — he had suggested a series of profiles on little-known foreign policy planners and administrators. Three of these had been done. On the editorial page there had been "no disagreements on matters of policy . . . in contrast to the spot I was in a year ago when R.C. [Coghlan] still had hopes that Russia could be sold on international cooperation and I felt that Russia's actions indicated otherwise." He had negotiated salary contracts with Brandt, Hentschell, and Dilliard and reported that wage settlements had been reached with all the mechanical unions and, after some resistance, the paper handlers. Newsprint, on which he had reported separately, continued to be "one of our vexing problems" because of manufacturing and allocation difficulties. Advertising for June was up 36 percent, "a greater gain than our competitors combined," and a decision had been made to raise certain retail and classified rates. This was expected to bring in an additional $260,000 annually. Circulation was in the usual summer slump. He and treasurer Chambers were looking into ways to cut certain costs that were running 24 percent above the previous year, and final plans for KSD expansion were nearly ready. He said the KSD–TV broadcast of the U.S. Open Golf Championship from the St. Louis Country Club "made a very favorable impression on me. I am convinced that this medium has inherent dramatic possibilities which will result in ultimate financial success."[33]

That, as earlier related, proved true. As the company grew larger and continued to prosper, and as he and Herbert grew older, Pulitzer saw a problem not far over the horizon. The Newspaper Trust, which their father had established by his will, would expire when the last second-generation son died. Since 1936, as grandsons of the first Joseph Pulitzer had come of age, the stock of the Pulitzer Publishing Company had become scattered among seven adult grandsons, and two more were soon to come of age. Most had no interest in the business beyond the dividends they received. Unless something was done to counter this dilution, interfamily differences could develop and destroy the *Post-Dispatch* as two Joseph Pulitzers had conducted it. Other once-prosperous and influential family-owned newspapers, finding themselves in the same circumstances, had either shrunk in value, merged, sold out, or gone out of business. The *Minneapolis Tribune* and *Indianapolis News* had failed for that reason. On the other hand, the *Chicago Tribune,* the *New York Daily News,* and the *Milwaukee Journal* had maintained continuity of sound management by reorganizing to place voting rights in the hands of trustees.

In 1950, at Pulitzer's direction, the Pulitzer Publishing Company was reorganized in this way. A Voting Trust was established to take effect on the expiration of the Newspaper Trust. That happened when Herbert died in 1957. Nearly all the stock was put in the control of five voting trustees: the chief executive officer, the managing editor, the business manager, the treasurer, and an individual elected by holders of stock in the trust.[34] This arrangement functioned until the mid-1980s. At that time, a group of minority stockholders, including Pulitzer's two daughters plus one grandson and six great-grandsons of the founding Pulitzer, decided they wanted to sell their shares if they could get considerably more than the $25,000 book value stipulated in the voting trust arrangement. This group held nearly 43 percent of the stock. The majority group, headed by Joseph Jr., Michael Pulitzer, and their cousin David E. Moore — the only surviving son of the late Edith Pulitzer Moore — had 57 percent. After the two sides were unable to agree on a price, the minority sought an outside buyer for their shares. For $10 million they sold an option on them to Michigan developer A. Alfred Taubman. In turn, Taubman hoped to interest the majority shareholders in selling out to him. He made offers of $500 million and then $625 million for the company, which the majority rejected. Instead, after some legal maneuvering by both sides, they agreed to buy back the minority's shares at about $80,000 each, for a total of $185.9 million, if Taubman would relinquish his option. He did, selling it back to the minority for $16 million.[35] On December 11, 1986, the Pulitzer Publishing Company made an initial public offering of stock in order to raise funds to partially repay money it had borrowed to redeem the shares.

This resolved what had threatened to end nearly 108 years of Pulitzer journalism in the United States. Looking ahead, the majority group created a new Voting Trust composed, like its predecessor, of company directors and other senior managers.[36] Under this "consolidation of ownership," as the company's first annual report to shareholders described the 1986 changes,[37] the Voting Trust retains virtually full policy control while the public shareholders have minimal voting rights. As a measure against future divisiveness within the controlling group, and as a means of discouraging takeover attempts from outside, the company's new Voting Trust Agreement goes to much greater lengths of legal language than the 1950 version to define what the third Joseph Pulitzer calls "the ethical and moral reasons for its procedures."[38] While the old agreement spoke only of providing "for the continuance of trustee management in order to secure continuity and stability of policy and management of the Post-Dispatch,"[39] the new one reads:

> The Trustees, in connection with the exercise of their judgment in determining what is in the best interest of the company and its stockholders, shall give due consideration to the effect of their actions on the editorial and publishing integrity and the character and quality of the Company's newspaper and broadcasting operations, and all other relevant factors, including, without limitation, the social, legal, and economic effects on the employees, customers, suppliers and other affected persons, firms and corporations and on the communities and geographical areas in which the Company and its subsidiaries operate or are located and any of the businesses and properties of the Company or any of its subsidiaries, as well as such other factors as the Trustees deem relevant. In addition, the platform of the St. Louis Post-Dispatch printed daily on the editorial page as the statement of the principles of its founder, Joseph Pulitzer, should be considered by the Trustees in assessing the public service aspects of journalism.[40]

In that language are echoes of the founder's injunction in his will that the *World* was to be operated "as a public institution, from motives higher than mere gain."[41] He was just as explicit when it came to the *Post-Dispatch,* admonishing his son Ralph in 1907, when the eldest son became president of the Pulitzer Publishing Company, "I beg you again and again to use your influence in spending money liberally on the paper and checking the tendency of managers simply to conduct the paper for money-making. That shall not be the primary object although I certainly wish that not a single dollar should be wasted by sheer stupidity. . . . [T]he P.D. should spend more money."[42]

On March 31, 1986, at the age of seventy-two, Joseph Pulitzer Jr. retired as editor and publisher of the *Post-Dispatch* after thirty-one years in those positions. He remained as chairman of the board of the company. Two of his top executives succeeded him: William F. Woo, who had been editor of the editorial page, became editor, and Nicholas V. Penniman IV, formerly general manager, became publisher. This marked the first time in its history that the *Post-Dispatch* was not headed by a Joseph Pulitzer. Joseph Jr.'s son, Joseph Pulitzer IV, was thirty-five years old and held the title of "vice president, administration" when his father stepped down as editor-publisher. "His education continues," publisher Penniman said of the fourth J.P. at that time.[43] While a detailed appraisal of Joseph Pulitzer Jr.'s third-generation stewardship remains to be made, in the opinion of Evarts A. Graham Jr., who served more than a decade as *Post-Dispatch* managing editor under him, it will reflect favorably: "I know that in St. Louis he's regarded as a hopeless dilettante who really only cares about art; doesn't give a damn about the newspaper. But the fact is that both as a businessman and as a newspaper editor he's been great."[44]

When the second Joseph Pulitzer's life ended, the company consisted of three entities—the *Post-Dispatch*, KSD radio, and KSD–TV, all in St. Louis. By 1991, it owned three daily newspapers, seven television stations, and two radio stations. These properties were in Missouri, Illinois, Arizona, North and South Carolina, Pennsylvania, New Mexico, Nebraska, Kentucky, and Louisiana.[45] The company's prosperity and growth are one measure of its success, but not—it is apparent in the vision of its proprietors— the most important.

Nine days before his death, on his seventieth birthday, March 21, 1955, a luncheon was given for Pulitzer at the Statler Hotel in St. Louis. It was attended by his immediate family, including his son and five-year-old grandson, and twenty-five employees, each of these the person with the longest service in his or her department. On behalf of all employees, Daniel Fitzpatrick, the senior man on the editorial page, presented Pulitzer with a bound copy of reproductions of March 21 *Post-Dispatch* front pages from each of the forty-three years of Pulitzer's career. It also contained a hand-lettered tribute to the philosophy by which he led. "In our experience you have always treated your associates and subordinates with the consideration you yourself would expect if the situation were reversed," it said. "If you are exacting in your requirements, as you must be, you have never breached the rule of courtesy in being so. Your respect for a man because he is human and needs a certain pride in himself, includes a respect for his ideas."[46]

Several years before this, Pulitzer had the pleasure of reading what amounted to a tribute to his pragmatic side. It came from one of the several previously mentioned depositions by persons closely familiar with his work habits to the Internal Revenue Service attesting to the legitimacy of the publisher's compensation. "It is an axiom of journalism that a paper retains its supremacy in its own field for twenty-five or thirty years," but seldom beyond that, wrote former *Post-Dispatch* reporter and *World* executive editor Herbert Bayard Swope in noting that the *Post-Dispatch* was an exception to this rule. The credit belonged "almost wholly" to Pulitzer, he said, "including his ability in the selection of men." In his view, the qualities of the first Joseph Pulitzer had been "reborn, invigorated, broadened and deepened by the zeal and energy" of his namesake son. He noted the competitive superiority of the *Post-Dispatch* in St. Louis and credited its domination of the evening field for keeping Hearst, "who contemplated doing so on several occasions," from buying or starting a newspaper in St. Louis. "I cannot pay a higher eulogy to Joseph Pulitzer [II] and the Post-Dispatch," he concluded, "than to say that had the elder Pulitzer lived and had he given his attention to the paper, instead of divorcing himself from it, he would not have been able to make a better paper than the Post-Dispatch is today."[47]

Roy A. Roberts, president of the *Kansas City Star*, went even further in one of scores of tributes which came in following Pulitzer's death: "Frankly, I think he left a greater impress on American journalism than did his illustrious father."[48] That is possible, but the second Joseph Pulitzer is not likely to have appreciated the compliment. He'd have brushed it aside with perhaps his favorite homely phrase, which he usually credited to an anonymous friend, "I do the best I can for a fellow with my shaped head." He saw the purpose of his professional life as a continuity of commitment to liberal, independent journalism in a constitutional democracy, not as a competition with his father's contributions. He would more readily have accepted the comparisons in his favor between the *Post-Dispatch* of his tenure and other newspapers of his time; there was precedent for those in the case of his father and contemporaries. Just such a comparison was suggested when staunchly conservative *Chicago Tribune* publisher Colonel Robert R. McCormick died on April 1, 1955, a little more than twenty-four hours after Pulitzer. "It will take a few years to show whether Mr. Pulitzer has passed along a going concern to his son," said the *Christian Century.* "We think the chances are that he has. But in the case of the *Tribune,* we expect much of the color and editorial punch to fade rapidly from its embattled columns. It is hard to see how the triumvirate of competent but run-of-the-mill staff members who have inherited direction of the paper's policies could possibly continue the erratic and unpredictable forays by which 'the Colonel' made such a dent on his city and his time." These two deaths virtually ended personal journalism in the United States, the commentary continued, a development many would applaud as a check on "the temptations inherent in too much power." Yet the trend toward journalism as big business, "nurtured by today's enormous costs of publishing a big city newspaper, may be more dangerous than the personal journalism it is displacing," it observed. "The newspaper which operates with an unwavering eye on the auditing department, seeking profit by catering to the prejudices of the community until it makes the world picture appear a reflection of the community's own ignorance and pettiness, can have a deadening effect. And whatever the journalism of the Pulitzer-McCormick brand may have been, it was not deadening."[49]

In accordance with Episcopal church practice, there was no eulogy at Pulitzer's funeral, but expressions of sympathy and praise covering nearly two pages of the newspaper attested to his distinctive contributions[50]—a presentation Pulitzer almost certainly would have considered "slopping over." He had done what he could to curtail this by suggesting the shortening and simplifying of an early draft of his obituary. He preferred something plain. "If somehow you could establish my identity more clearly as an active newspaper man, contributing with suggestions, criticism, editing and occasional rewriting, to the news, feature and editorial contents of the paper from day to day, I should like to see that done," he advised its author, reporter Carlos Hurd.[51]

Those words were incorporated into the obituary, followed by an explanation of how Pulitzer's memorandums on yellow paper "eternally, or so it seemed" kept his editors alert by politely raising questions "that could not be shrugged off unless the recipient checked carefully to make sure he knew all the answers." The flurry of "yellow slips," it continued, "was the only yellow journalism they knew."[52] A more eloquent remembrance appeared a few days later in an editorial signed by Joseph Pulitzer Jr. It began: "A flame of integrity was extinguished at the death of my father, Joseph Pulitzer, but its light will always radiate to newspaper men of conscience everywhere." The editorial pledged that the words of the founding Pulitzer's platform "are a monument of granite which the tides of time will never efface."[53]

At its first meeting following Pulitzer's death, the Advisory Board on the Pulitzer Prizes, which had unanimously elected Joseph Pulitzer Jr. its new chairman, adopted a memorial resolution written by Arthur Krock describing Pulitzer as one who "steadily enhanced" the "great newspaper tradition" he had inherited thereby leaving at the end of his life "a greater heritage — shining personal character, humility in possession of power, and compassion for the unfortunate. He hated cant, sham, injustice and corruption and was incapable of any of these. He was one of the few gifted with both humor and a sense of consecration."[54]

Two items by Pulitzer, one a memorandum and the other an unsigned editorial, convey such a personality. The memorandum was to editorial page editor Ralph Coghlan in 1944, written after Pulitzer read a column he didn't like:

> As a constant reader of the Post-Dispatch let me say that I for one would love to see the P-D take the hide off Edgar Ansel Mowrer's highhat insinuations that American boys who want to get back to the corner drug store and their fathers have lost their forefathers' sense of adventure. That, very frankly, got my goat. My firm and confident belief is that we are a damn sight more likely to find that brave-new-world right here in the U.S.A. than in Communist Russia

or so-called liberal Europe, and that one of these days they will be coming around and knocking at our back door to find out how in the hell we did it. I submit that the Henry Kaisers and the Henry Fords and the President [James B.] Conants [of Harvard] and the sulfa drugs and penicillin researchers (even though penicillin was discovered in England) and the Franklin Roosevelts and the Harry Bridges and even the John L. Lewises all possess a sense of adventure and plenty of it. Every now and then Mowrer with his Phi Beta Kappa key and his Pulitzer Prize and in spite of his frequently brilliant writing, gives me a pain in the neck. This is one of those times. Forgive me.

In a postscript, he added: "If you want to break your rule and run this as a letter under an anonymous signature, go ahead." It appeared three days later, initialed "T.E."[55]

The editorial was short—282 words in two paragraphs—run in a subordinate position on February 19, 1947, under the headline "U.S.A. Calling U.S.S.R.":

Hello, Russia. This is the voice of the U.S.A. We mean to tell you the truth, the whole truth and nothing but the truth. (Melody: "Turkey in the Straw.") We've got two governors in Georgia. How come? We don't know, but it's a fact, nevertheless. We have a Senator by the name of Bilbo who likes to call us Americans kikes, dagoes, niggers, etc. One of our favorite pastimes in Congress is what we call the filibuster—where a man gets up and reads Shakespeare and the Sears-Roebuck catalog for a week or more at a time. We are likely to freeze to death when John L. Lewis calls a coal strike and to starve to death when the railroads, trucks and the merchant marine go on strike. Our electric lights and power are likely to be turned off at any time. Scientists tell us that we have a good man in [Atomic Energy Commission chairman David E.] Lilienthal, but the politicians are getting ready to liquidate him. Our Protestants fight our Catholics, our Catholics fight our Protestants and nearly everyone fights our Jews. We lynched a Negro in South Carolina only the other day. Our literacy rate and

our murder rate are the highest in the world. We hold a
great many elections but we don't vote. Our school buildings are the finest in the world, but we will soon have no
teachers.

In spite of all these confusing contradictions, we like it
over here. We like to do as we please and we have no doubt
that some day we will work things out in this, the land of
the free and the home of the brave.[56]

The editorial was selected by the State Department for broadcast
abroad by the Voice of America.[57]

Following his funeral, which was attended by about five hundred persons, Pulitzer's body was cremated, as he had instructed.
He had explained his reason for wanting this done to *Weatherbird*
co-pilot George Sayers the previous year: "As you know, Liza is my
second wife, and I had children both by her and my previous wife.
Because both of these women were so much to me in my life, I feel
that I should not be laid to rest beside one and not the other. . . . I've
decided that I'm going to avoid that problem and ask you to spread
my ashes from the airplane." He asked that this be done in the
vicinity of the whistling buoy off Egg Rock in Frenchman Bay,
the place he always considered the "coming home point" of his
cruises, preferably on a bright, sunny day. Sayers agreed, saying he
hoped it would be many years before this was necessary. Pulitzer
"just smiled and handed me a yellow memo," Sayers recalled. It
said that Sayers and *Weatherbird* pilot John Matthews were to
have jobs in the Pulitzer Publishing Company for as long as they
wished, even if the aviation department should be discontinued.

The ashes were scattered from a camera hatch in the plane's
baggage compartment by Elizabeth Pulitzer on June 4, 1955, a
stormy, turbulent day. Also in the plane were Pulitzer's sister
Edith (Mrs. William S. Moore), his son Michael, and secretary
Arch King. During the flight, Michael told King that he planned to
leave the Boston law firm for which he was working and become a
newspaperman, fulfilling his father's wish. Mrs. Pulitzer's ashes
were scattered in the same place following her death in 1974 at the
age of eighty-four.[58] So were those of Mrs. Moore, who died at age
eighty-eight in 1975.[59]

Ten months into his new job as directing head of the company,

Joseph Pulitzer Jr. delivered the first Joseph Pulitzer Memorial Lecture at the Columbia University School of Journalism. His new responsibilities were "not lightened, you may be sure," he observed, "by the realization that both my predecessors were men of extraordinary endowment, intellectually and morally":

> But if there was one quality that was passed on it was that tradition of conscience, or, more specifically, a conscientious attitude toward the service of the press to the public.
>
> Reflection about a newspaper leads inevitably to thoughts of the larger social context in which it operates and with which it should have an organic connection. My father thought of the *Post-Dispatch* as an instrument for promoting democracy, popular government being for him not just a desirable system but the only system that places no limits on human achievement.[60]

Both in that speech and in the signed editorial on his father's death, the third J.P. pointed out that the newspaper's civic commitments were not all that he intended to carry forward. While opinion would "be strong for what we believe to be right, and equally strong against what we construe to be wrong," he pledged in the editorial, "we also know that laughter is a joy and we hope we will entertain."[61] To be sure, the laughter and joy in living of which he wrote was much more his legacy from his father than his grandfather, and it equipped him with an optimism that may have been his greatest help. Just a week after assuming his new responsibilities as editor and publisher he wrote this:[62]

THE BOSS

A comedy in one act

By Joseph Pulitzer Jr.

The time: The present—morning
The place: A dressing room bath
The cast: Joseph Pulitzer Jr., an editor
            Joseph Pulitzer IV, a schoolboy

As the curtain rises, the editor is shaving; the schoolboy is twirling his cap, waiting for the school bus.

THE SCHOOLBOY: Daddy, Grandfather Joe went to heaven.

THE EDITOR: Of course.

THE SCHOOLBOY: The boys on the bus said the boss of the Post-Dispatch went to heaven.

THE EDITOR: Yes, Joe, that is true.

THE SCHOOLBOY (*still twirling his cap*): Then who is now the boss at the Post-Dispatch?

THE EDITOR: I am now the boss.

THE SCHOOLBOY (*dropping cap and, with incredulity mingled with awe*): YOU are the boss?

THE EDITOR: Yes.

THE SCHOOLBOY (*reflectively*): Then you are the boss of the AIRPLANE.

The editor nods.
The schoolboy smiles radiantly, and at the sound backstage of an automobile horn, exits running.

Curtain.

Abbreviations

The following abbreviations are used in the notes:

AB	Alfred Butes
AGL	Albert G. Lincoln
ARK	Arch R. King
ASVB	A. S. Van Benthuysen
BHR	Benjamin H. Reese
BMB	Bernard M. Baruch
CFH	Carlos F. Hurd
CGR	Charles G. Ross
CJH	Charles J. Hentschell
CM	Clark McAdams
CU	Papers of Joseph Pulitzer I, Rare Book and Manuscript Library, Columbia University, New York City
EEP	Elizabeth Edgar Pulitzer
FDW	Florence D. White
FFR	Fred F. Rowden
FG	Ferdinand Gottlieb
FRO	Frank R. O'Neil
GEC	George E. Carvell
GMB	George M. Burbach
GSJ	George S. Johns
HBS	Herbert Bayard Swope
HOG	Harold O. Grams
HP	Herbert Pulitzer
HSP	Harold S. Pollard

ID	Irving Dilliard
JHK	Julius H. Klyman
JP	Joseph Pulitzer
JPII	Joseph Pulitzer Jr. (II)
JPIII	Joseph Pulitzer III ("Jr.")
JTK	James T. Keller
KDP	Kate Davis Pulitzer (mother of JPII)
LC	Papers of Joseph Pulitzer I or papers of Joseph Pulitzer II (microfilm copy), Manuscript Library, Library of Congress, Washington, D.C.
MEP	Michael Edgar Pulitzer
MHS	Missouri Historical Society, Jefferson Memorial Building, Forest Park, St. Louis, Missouri
MWC	Marquis W. Childs
NGT	Norman G. Thwaites
OKB	Oliver K. Bovard
P–D	Materials held in the office of Joseph Pulitzer III, morgue, or storage files of the *St. Louis Post-Dispatch,* St. Louis, Missouri
PYA	Paul Y. Anderson
RC	Ralph Coghlan
RL	Robert Lasch
RLC	Raymond L. Crowley
RLS	Richard L. Stokes
RP	Ralph Pulitzer
RPB	Raymond P. Brandt
SMC	Stuart M. Chambers
SS	Samuel J. Shelton (always signed his initials as "SS")

Notes

Chapter 1
The Heir Unapparent

1. Samuel W. Tait Jr., "The St. Louis Post-Dispatch," *American Mercury*, April 1931, pp. 403–412; Jack Alexander, "The Last Shall Be First," *Saturday Evening Post*, January 14, 1939, pp. 5–7 and ff.; Roger Butterfield, "The St. Louis Post-Dispatch — Pulitzer's Prize," *Collier's*, December 16, 1950, p. 25 and ff.

2. JPII to JPIII, May 18, 1949. Papers of Joseph Pulitzer II, Library of Congress, microfilm reel 88, frame 187. Hereafter, these papers are identified by correspondents, date, the repository initials "LC," and microfilm reel and frame numbers.

3. See Chapter 19.

4. See Chapter 22.

5. JP to JPII, October 8, 1908, Papers of Joseph Pulitzer (I), Rare Book and Manuscript Library, Columbia University, New York City. Hereafter these papers are identified by correspondents, date, and the repository initials "CU."

Chapter 2
Life with Father

1. JP to William C. Steigers, May 13, 1889. From files at the *St. Louis Post-Dispatch* opened to the author by Joseph Pulitzer III. Hereafter, materials from these files will be designated P-D.

2. *New York Evening World*, October 10, 1889, p. 1.

3. *New York Times*, October 11, 1889, p. 2.

4. Ibid.

5. A detailed story of the senior Pulitzer's life with his secretaries was written by one of them: Alleyne Ireland, *Joseph Pulitzer: Reminiscences of a Secretary* (New York: Mitchell Kennerley, 1914).

6. Don C. Seitz, *Joseph Pulitzer, His Life and Letters* (New York: Simon and Schuster, 1924); W. A. Swanberg, *Pulitzer* (New York: Charles

Scribner's Sons, 1967). Unless otherwise noted, biographical details in this chapter are from those biographies of the senior Pulitzer and from William Robinson Reynolds, "Joseph Pulitzer" (Ph.D. diss., Columbia University, 1950), and the *St. Louis Post-Dispatch,* Commemorative Edition on the 100th Anniversary of Joseph Pulitzer, April 6, 1947.

7. Swanberg, *Pulitzer,* pp. 38–39. That both of JP's parents were Jewish was determined in 1985 by András Csillag, a Hungarian scholar who researched records in the city and county of Pulitzer's birth and other Hungarian archives. He verified that Pulitzer's mother was born to a Jewish family in 1823 at Pest and in 1838 married Philip Pulitzer, who was born in 1811 in Mako. He noted that in the United States "it is accepted as fact that his father was a Hungarian Jew and his mother an Austrian-German Catholic," even though Hungarian scholar Edmund (Odon) Vasvary had identified his mother's origin as Hungarian-Jewish in *Lincoln's Hungarian Heroes* (Washington, D.C.: Hungarian Reformed Federation of America, 1939), a book about the participation of Hungarians in the U.S. Civil War. Vasvary concluded that American scholars had overlooked his work and in large part ignored Pulitzer's Hungarian origins. See András Csillag, "Pulitzer József makói származásáról," A Makói Múzeum Füzetei 46 (Mako, 1985). An English translation by Erika A. Goldberg ("Andras Csillag, 'The Hungarian Origins of Joseph Pulitzer,' Publication of the Museum of Mako, No. 46, 1985") was prepared for Joseph Pulitzer III (P-D). A condensed version of this monograph, also by Csillag, was published as "Joseph Pulitzer's Roots in Europe: A Genealogical History," in *American Jewish Archives,* April 1987, pp. 48–68.

8. The usual practice of recruiting agents was to trade only the immigrant's passage for his willingness to serve, the agent collecting the bounty for himself on arrival. Pulitzer circumvented that stratagem by jumping ship, swimming ashore, and collecting his bounty.

9. Selwyn K. Troen and Glen E. Holt, eds., *St. Louis* (New York: New Viewpoints, 1977), p. xxi.

10. Seitz, *Pulitzer,* p. 52.

11. Ibid., p. 90.

12. Quoted in ibid., p. 91.

13. Originally the *Post and Dispatch,* but soon after hyphenated.

14. Piers Brendon, *The Life and Death of the Press Barons* (New York: Atheneum, 1983), p. 86.

15. George Juergens, *Joseph Pulitzer and the New York World* (Princeton: Princeton University Press, 1966), pp. vii–viii, 4.

16. Reynolds, "Pulitzer," p. 469.

17. Transcription of shorthand dictation, undated (approx. 1889), P-D.

18. Alleyne Ireland, "A Modern Superman," *American Magazine,* April 1912, p. 670.

19. Roy T. King, "The Joseph Pulitzer Family," genealogical chart compiled May 1976, P-D. Only the girls were given middle names.

20. Transcript of interview with Louis M. Starr, October 7, 1954, Oral History Collection, Columbia University, p. 72 (hereafter Oral History interview of JPII); JPII to Jack Alexander, approx. November 4, 1938, p. 3, LC, reel 3, frame 389.

21. Ralph Pulitzer, *New York Society on Parade* (New York: Harper and Brothers, 1910).

22. Felix Webber to his wife, November 14, 1894, among Webber's letters from 1894 to 1899, owned by Joseph Pulitzer III, P-D. Hereafter identified as."Webber letters".

23. Quoted in Reynolds, "Pulitzer," p. 621.

24. JP to KDP, December 12, 1900, CU.

25. HSP to JPII, April 11, 1928, LC, reel 140, frame 407.

26. JP to KDP, 1894 (date incomplete), CU.

27. Oral History interview of JPII, p. 15.

28. JP to KDP, 1894 (date incomplete), CU.

29. JPII to JP, approx. 1892, P-D.

30. In his biography, Swanberg concluded that JP's symptoms of alternating periods of furious activity with fatigue, insomnia, and irritability would by mid-century have been diagnosed as manic-depressive psychosis. But he also noted that both he and the psychiatrist he consulted on the question were "wary of the couch school of biography" and agreed "that judgments of a man long dead must be made with caution." Swanberg, *Pulitzer,* pp. 145, 420.

31. Claude Ponsonby to KDP, December 23, 1889, P-D.

32. JP to KDP, December 23, (1889), P-D.

33. JP to KDP, January 1, 1890, P-D.

34. Dr. Weir Mitchell to JP, December 15, 1891, P-D.

35. Webber letters, September 27, 1894.

36. Ibid., October 6 and December 17, 1894.

37. Ibid., December 9, 1894.

38. Ibid., January 2, 1895.

39. JP to KDP, undated (approx. 1886), P-D. (Transcription of dictation taken in shorthand.)

40. Swanberg, *Pulitzer,* p. 217.

41. Reynolds, "Pulitzer," p. 615.

42. Oral History interview of JPII, pp. 3-4.

43. Telephone interview with Marquis W. Childs, May 31, 1984.

Chapter 3
"Make a Real Man Out of Him"

1. Quoted in Swanberg, *Pulitzer,* p. 162.
2. Oral History interview of JPII, pp. 4–5.
3. *The Best Private Schools, 1915,* Sargent's Handbook Series (Boston: Porter E. Sargent, 1915), p. 32.
4. Oral History interview of JPII, pp. 8–9.
5. Quoted in Reynolds, "Pulitzer," p. 623.
6. See Csillag, "Pulitzer" (Chapter 2, n. 7, above).
7. Oral History interview of JPII, pp. 17–18.
8. Seitz, *Pulitzer,* p. 19.
9. KDP to JP, September 27, 1903, CU.
10. JPII to JP, March 12, 1900, CU.
11. Interview with Mrs. Elwood R. Quesada, daughter of JPII, June 19, 1984, Washington, D.C.
12. Transcription of dictation taken in shorthand, November 24–29, 1901 (recipient not identified), P-D.
13. Ibid.
14. JPII to JP, (probably 1901), CU.
15. James W. Barrett, *The World, the Flesh, and the Messrs. Pulitzer* (New York: Vanguard, 1931), p. 47.
16. RP to JP, 1907, CU.
17. JPII to JP, April 9, 1901, CU. Hereafter, for items from JPII to his father, only the date and the repository are noted.
18. Webber letters, December 12, 1894.
19. Ireland, "Modern Superman," pp. 215–216.
20. Webber letters, December 22, 1894.
21. Ibid., October 14, 1894.
22. June 23, 1902, CU.
23. June 6, 1902, CU.
24. Swanberg, *Pulitzer,* pp. 206–207.
25. Edwin Emery and Michael Emery, *The Press and America,* 5th ed. (Englewood Cliffs, N.J.: Prentice-Hall, 1984), pp. 288–295, 311–313.
26. JP to unidentified recipient, transcription of shorthand notes, undated (1903), P-D.
27. January 24, 1903, CU.
28. JP to D. W. Woods, telegram, February 4, 1903, P-D.
29. Pulitzer Code Book, P-D.

Chapter 4
Newspaper Apprentice to Harvard Man

1. FDW to JP, January 25, 1903, CU.
2. JPII to JP, January 29, 1903, CU. Unless otherwise indicated, all items in this chapter are from the son to his father.
3. FRO to JP, February 17, 1903, CU.
4. February 19, 1903, CU.
5. January 24, 1903, CU.
6. February 12, 1903, CU.
7. February 25, 1903, CU.
8. February 27, 1903, CU.
9. February 12, 1903, CU.
10. Ibid.
11. February 26, 1903, CU.
12. March 3, 1903, CU.
13. March 10, 1903, CU.
14. Ibid.
15. February 9, 1903, CU.
16. Eventually, when the son was publisher, much of such advertising was banned from the *Post-Dispatch.* Daniel W. Pfaff, "Joseph Pulitzer II and Advertising Censorship, 1929-1939," *Journalism Monographs,* no. 77, July 1982.
17. Undated (1903), CU.
18. February 27, 1903, CU.
19. March 6, 1903, CU.
20. March 13, 1903, CU.
21. JP to RP, March 23, 1903, CU.
22. May 30, 1903, CU.
23. September 27, 1903, CU.
24. JP to JPII, September 29, 1903, CU.
25. January 20, 1904, CU.
26. January 21, 1904, CU.
27. January 28, 1904, CU.
28. JP to W. C. Steigers, July 19, 1881, P-D.
29. February 2, 1904, CU.
30. February 4, 1904, CU.
31. February 8, 1904, CU.
32. February 11, 1904, CU.
33. Oral History interview of JPII, p. 11.
34. Quoted in unaddressed, unsigned memo, February 4, 1904, CU.
35. February 29, 1904, CU.
36. Undated (approx. April 1904), CU.
37. May 19, 1904, CU.
38. August 20, 1904, CU.

39. September 27, 1904, CU.
40. Undated (approx. October 1904), CU.
41. November 10, 1904, CU.
42. Ibid.
43. November 23, 1904, CU.
44. JPII to KDP, December 2, 1904, CU.
45. December 9, 1904, CU.
46. December 17, 1904, CU.
47. RP to JP, undated (approx. January 15, 1905), CU.
48. January 25, 1905, CU.
49. FDW to JP, August 31, 1905, CU.
50. Emery and Emery, *The Press and America,* p. 295.
51. Pfaff, "Joseph Pulitzer II."
52. February 16, 1905, CU.
53. February 27, 1905, CU.
54. February 1, 1905, CU.
55. April 28, 1905, CU.
56. December 8, 1905, CU.
57. February 27, 1905, CU.
58. William W. Nolen to JP, October 14, 1905, CU.
59. Undated (approx. December 1905), CU.

Chapter 5
J.P. Takes Charge

1. November 20, 1905, CU.
2. Diary, with 1905 materials (date incomplete), CU.
3. November 20, 1905, CU.
4. Oral History interview of JPII, p. 20.
5. JPII to Butes, January 31, 1906, CU.
6. AB to JPII, February 1, 1906, CU.
7. February 18, 1906, CU.
8. February 23, 1906, CU
9. February 28, 1906, CU.
10. March 12, 1906, CU.
11. March 14, 1906, CU.
12. Hurlbut to JP, March 8, 1906, CU.
13. Hurlbut to JP, March 19, 1906, CU.
14. March 26, 1906, CU.
15. Ibid.
16. Oral History interview of JPII, p. 19.
17. February 23, 1906, CU.

18. Henry Adams, *The Education of Henry Adams* (Boston: Houghton Mifflin, 1927), pp. 54–55.

19. May 25, 1906, CU.

20. June 4, 1906, CU.

21. June 12, 1906, CU.

22. "Report on Last 3 Months' Work. J.P. Jr.," undated (1906), CU.

23. Theodore Dreiser, *A Book About Myself* (New York: Boni and Liveright, 1922), pp. 467, 485.

24. With "Stories Written by J.P. Jr. for Evening World During Spring of 1906," undated (1906), Scrapbook of Joseph Pulitzer II, P-D.

25. *Charles E. Chapin's Story* (New York: G. P. Putnam's Sons, 1920), pp. 224–229.

26. Memorandum "To Father," August 4, 1906, P-D. There is an often-published anecdote to the effect that Pulitzer sent Joseph to St. Louis in 1906 bearing this message to editorial page editor George S. Johns: "Dear Mr. Johns: This is my son Joseph. Will you try to knock some newspaper sense into his head? J.P." (Alexander, "The Last Shall Be First," p. 72). However, this memorandum does not include Johns among those Pulitzer designated as his son's tutors. It says: "I am to go out there and attach myself more particularly to O'Neil. I am to tell him: 'I am out here to learn something in case something happens to my Father. Teach me as much as possible without my becoming a bore.' O'Neil is therefore first choice; Taylor 2nd, more especially for mechanics and Wants (his great specialty); 3rd Bovard for news [indicating, interestingly, that Pulitzer rated him ahead of managing editor Dunlap]; 4th Dunlap; 5th Murphy; and last but not least Keller, a very valuable man, the Shaw [J. Angus Shaw, treasurer of the *World*] of the P.D. Also 7th Lincoln, a wonderfully earnest fellow, who has his whole heart in his work." Johns is mentioned occasionally in the young man's correspondence to his father but never identified as his supervisor. Still, in a memoir, Johns's son recorded that J.P. Jr. "had worked in all departments directly under Johns's personal supervision for years." Orrick Johns, *The Time of Our Lives* (New York: Stackpole Sons, 1937), p. 161.

27. Swanberg, *Pulitzer*, p. 243.

28. August 14, 1906, CU. Most of the originals of the surviving letter and diary pages are at Columbia University. Carbon copies of originals apparently lost were found at the *Post-Dispatch* and filled in some of the gaps. These are designated P-D.

29. The two morning dailies were the *Republic,* with 100,271 daily and 121,412 Sunday circulation, and the *Globe-Democrat,* with 138,672 and 173,279, respectively. *American Newspaper Annual and Directory* (Philadelphia: N. W. Ayer and Son, 1906, 1907).

30. James W. Markham, *Bovard of the Post-Dispatch* (Baton Rouge: Louisiana State University Press, 1954), pp. 1–3.

31. April 15, 1906, CU.

32. August 20, 1906, CU.
33. JP to JPII, August 19, 1906, P-D.
34. August 20, 1906.
35. AB to JPII, September 6, 1906, P-D.
36. JPII to AB, September 8, 1906, CU.
37. September 8, 1906, P-D.
38. October 1, 1906, CU.
39. JP to JPII, undated (approx. September 15, 1906), P-D.
40. October 1, 1906, P-D.
41. October 9, 1906, CU.
42. Swanberg, *Pulitzer,* p. 334.
43. Oral History interview of JPII, pp. 39–40.

Chapter 6
Pleasure and Pain

1. Clippings in JPII scrapbook, P-D; two reports from unidentified papers, both dated November 17, 1906, are in the *Post-Dispatch* morgue. Several of the stories state that the young man's first blow struck Hearst.
2. *New York Times,* November 25, 1906, p. 1.
3. December 19, 1906, CU.
4. JP to JPII, December 20, 1906, P-D.
5. December 25, 1906, CU.
6. November 30, 1906, CU.
7. November 30, 1906, P-D.
8. December 12, 1906, CU.
9. FRO to JP, December 15, 1906, CU.
10. January 22, 1907, CU.
11. January 15, 1907, CU.
12. Ibid.
13. FRO to JP, January 29, 1907, CU.
14. "Anniversary Birthday Dinner Given by Joseph Pulitzer, April 10, 1907," pp. 13, 41–42, P-D.
15. April 13, 1907, CU.
16. Harry Wilensky, *The Story of the St. Louis Post-Dispatch* (St. Louis: St. Louis Post-Dispatch, 1981), p. 4.
17. Alexander, "The Last Shall Be First," p. 72.
18. December 6, 1906, CU.
19. December 15, 1906, CU.
20. January 15, 1907, CU.
21. January 18, 1907, CU.
22. FRO to JP, January 29, 1907, CU.

23. January 23, 1907, P–D.
24. February 15, 1907, CU.
25. April 23, 1907, P–D.
26. KDP to JPII, May 2, 1907, P–D.
27. May 13, 1907, CU.
28. JP to JPII, May 27, 1907, P–D.

Chapter 7
In Love

1. JP to JPII, May 29, 1907, P–D.
2. "Conversation with Andes, J.P. Jr.," June 5, 1907, P–D.
3. RP to JPII, March 8, 1907, P–D.
4. March 9, 1907, CU.
5. JPII to RP, March 9, 1907, P–D.
6. JP to RP, March 21, 1907, P–D.
7. October 15, 1906, CU.
8. November 30, 1906, P–D.
9. December 12, 1906, CU.
10. JP to JPII, December 5, (1906), P–D.
11. JP to RP, (1905), P–D.
12. November 19, 1906, CU.
13. December 2, 1906, P–D.
14. April 9, 1907, CU.
15. Undated proof (1907), P–D.
16. FRO to JP, April 26, 1907, CU.
17. Undated (1907), CU.
18. FRO to JPII, August 27, 1907, CU.
19. Hartley Davis, "Joseph Pulitzer: Father of Modern Journalism," *Broadway Magazine,* December 1907, P–D.
20. JPII to RP, April 24, 1907, P–D.
21. RP to JPII, April 26, 1907, P–D.
22. Samuel H. Adams, "The Great American Fraud," *Collier's,* June 8, 1907; "Apropos Medical Potash," undated (1907), P–D.
23. JPII to RP, September 30, 1907. Papers of Joseph Pulitzer (I), Library of Congress, Washington, D.C. Hereafter these papers are identified as JPI Papers, LC.

Chapter 8
Hopes and Hazards

1. March 11, 1907, CU.
2. May 9, 1907, CU.
3. February 11, 1908, CU.
4. February 4, 1908, P–D.
5. See Markham, *Bovard.*
6. February 11, 1908, CU.
7. The Press Publishing Company published the *World.*
8. February 4, 1908, P–D.
9. JP to JPII, February 17, 1908, P–D.
10. February 27, 1908, CU.
11. JP to OKB, July 23, 1908, CU.
12. OKB to JP, July 25, 1908, quoted in Markham, *Bovard,* p. 69.
13. September 7, 1908, P–D.
14. September 14, 1908, P–D.
15. Ibid.
16. JP to JPII, October 4, 1908, CU.
17. OKB to JP, October 2, 1908, P–D.
18. October 19, 1908, P–D.
19. JP to JPII, February 20, 1908, P–D.
20. February 11, 1908, CU.
21. JP to JPII, February 20, 1908, P–D.
22. Arthur Billing to JPII, April 25, 1908, P–D.
23. April 1, 1908, P–D.
24. May 15, 1908, CU.
25. May 29, 1908, CU.
26. April 17, 1908, P–D.
27. Telephone interview with C. Wickham Moore, nephew of Elinor Wickham Pulitzer, October 5, 1985.
28. September 14, 1908, P–D.
29. October 19, 1908, P–D.
30. Quoted in Alexander, "The Last Shall Be First," p. 73. Alexander says this happened in 1908, but Joseph's letters in early 1909 seem to place it in March, near his twenty-fourth birthday.
31. March 18, 1909, P–D.
32. March 21, 1909, P–D.
33. March 29, 1909, P–D.
34. "Last Will and Testament of Joseph Pulitzer," April 15, 1904, and codicils dated March 23, 1909, January 17, 1910, May 11, 1910, and July 12, 1911, pp. 9, 30, 32, 33. P–D.
35. JP to RP, June 25, 1909, JPI Papers, LC.

Chapter 9
New Responsibilities

1. JP to JPII, August 31, 1909, P-D.
2. JP to JPII, and JP to Elinor Wickham, August 31, 1909, P-D.
3. JP to JPII, June 1, 1909, P-D.
4. *New York Times,* August 25, 1909.
5. NGT to JPII, October 8 and 11, 1909; "Diary up to Date," September 21, 1909, P-D.
6. Swanberg, *Pulitzer,* pp. 344–346: "She was one of the biggest private yachts ever built, 65 feet longer than J. P. Morgan's second *Corsair* and only a few feet shorter than *Corsair III,* . . . twice as expensive as [former *New York Herald* publisher] James Gordon Bennett's *Lysistrata.* . . . [S]he had every imaginable comfort for a blind man sensitive to noise—smooth teak decks with no bolts or projections, a huge cabin for Pulitzer sealed by thick carpeting, double bulkheads, double doors, double portholes. . . . His immense four-poster bed bristled with bell cords of different lengths so that he could call the major domo, captain, head butler, chief steward or physician. . . . The yacht had a crew of 60 men, plus his own personal staff, and had a coal capacity for 6,000 miles. Wireless equipment was purposely omitted so that he could escape the messages that excited him. . . . The yacht . . . gave him *complete control.* It was an absolute monarchy, he was king and the 75 employees were his subjects. He took great pride in his very own seagoing vessel and in the thought that she emancipated him from his dependence on White Star to get him across the ocean."
7. Edith Pulitzer to JPII, November 6, 7, [1909], P-D.
8. JP to JPII, November 22, 1909, P-D.
9. "In reply to Mr. Pulitzer's Mem. dated December 16, 1909," P-D.
10. January 3, 1910, P-D.
11. Markham, *Bovard,* p. 88.
12. JP to JPII, May 6, 1910, P-D.
13. January 4, 1910 (erroneously dated 1909), P-D.
14. January 5, 1910, P-D.
15. March 18, 1910, P-D.
16. March 28, 1910, P-D.
17. *New York Times,* April 11, 1910.
18. JP to JTK, May 8, 1910, P-D.
19. Last Will and Testament, codicil of May 11, 1910, P-D.
20. JP to JPII, May 6, 1910, P-D.
21. On page one of the *New York Times,* May 26, 1910.
22. Unidentified clipping dated June 2, 1910, *Post-Dispatch* morgue.

Chapter 10
On Trial

1. James N. Primm, *Lion of the Valley* (Boulder, Colo.: Pruett Publishing Co., 1981), pp. 366–367.
2. November 7 and December 3, 1910, P-D.
3. August 31, 1910, P-D.
4. September 9, 1910.
5. JP to JPII, September 18, 1910, P-D.
6. Seitz, *Pulitzer,* pp. 332–333.
7. OKB to JP, October 13, November 1, and November 30, 1910, CU.
8. JP to JPII, November 23, 1910, P-D.
9. "Memo on Political Interviews," October 4, 1910, P-D.
10. NGT to JPII, October 4, 1910, P-D.
11. Postscript, JP to JPII, November 19, 1910, P-D.
12. NGT to JPII, October 4, 1910, P-D.
13. JP to JPII, November 19, 1910.
14. December 19, 1910, P-D.
15. RP to JPII, December 22, 1910, P-D.
16. While they were looking forward to two dinners his mother was giving to introduce Elinor to some people their age, he wrote: "Entre nous formal N.Y. society has few charms for either of us. As Seward Webb [Ralph's brother-in-law] said the other night, 'They are all frozen faces.' " January 17, 1911, P-D.
17. December 12, 1910, P-D.
18. *Post-Dispatch,* December 18, 1910.
19. *World,* November 10, 1911.
20. December 27, 1910, P-D.
21. The episode is described in detail in Swanberg, *Pulitzer,* pp. 359–390, and Seitz, Pulitzer, pp. 352–385.
22. January 4, 1911, P-D.
23. December 13, 1910.
24. JP to JPII, January 11, 1911, P-D.
25. January 23, 1911.
26. December 13, 1910, P-D.
27. Undated (approx. 1910), P-D. He also reported here: "There is little or no drinking in office hours and every man seems to feel that he has got to work to hold his job. The credit for originating this reform is due Chapin."
28. *New York World,* November 6, 1911.
29. January 23, 1911, P-D.
30. After someone pointed out that President McKinley's assassin had a copy of the *Journal* in his pocket when he shot the President in 1901, Hearst changed the name of the paper to the *American.* Even though the Hearst paper was much more reckless than the *World,* Joseph's

memorandums to his father in 1911 show that the *American* was watched carefully and often admired for its enterprise by *World* men.

31. JP to JPII, cable and letter, both February 28, 1911, P–D.

Chapter 11
The Founder's Last Year

1. NGT to JPII, February 28, 1911, P–D.
2. March 1, 1911, P–D.
3. Ibid.
4. April 3, 1911, CU.
5. April 25 and May 4 and 17, 1911; OKB to JP, May 8, 1911, CU.
6. JP to JPII, November 19, 1910; January 18, 1911, P–D.
7. May 4 and 17, 1911, CU.
8. May 29, 1911, CU.
9. JP to JPII, June 21, 1911, P–D.
10. JP to JPII, June 27, 1911, P–D.
11. June 30, 1911, P–D.
12. June 23, 1911, CU.
13. FDW to JP, June 26, 1911, CU.
14. "Report of Talk with White," August 13, 1911, P–D.
15. JP to JPII, September 7, 1911, P–D.
16. Elizabeth Jordan, "The Passing of the Chief," *New Yorker,* December 18, 1937, pp. 59–61.
17. *World,* October 30 and November 1 and 3, 1911.

Chapter 12
St. Louis for Good

1. *World,* November 6, 1911.
2. June 14, 1911, CU.
3. Interview with Ben L. Brockman, April 27, 1984, St. Louis, Missouri.
4. "Report of Talk with White," August 13, 1911, P–D; Memorandum of July 14, 1939, LC, reel 68, frame 495.
5. JPII to JTK, October 7, 1938, LC, reel 68, frame 500.
6. JP to RP, August 5, 1910, JPI papers, LC.
7. Markham, *Bovard,* p. 95.
8. Orrick Johns, *Time of Our Lives* (New York: Stackpole Sons, 1937), p. 140 and passim.

9. Address by GSJ, December 19, 1923, P-D.

10. December 16, 1909, P-D.

11. *Post-Dispatch,* October 8, 1916.

12. JPII to KDP, January 22, 1916, P-D.

13. *Post-Dispatch,* October 9, 1916.

14. Interview with Mrs. Edward L. Dwyer, widow, July 20, 1985, St. Louis, Missouri.

15. JPII to Don C. Seitz, March 24, 1922, P-D; Charles A. Perera, M.D., *May's Manual of Diseases of the Eye,* 21st ed. (Baltimore: Williams and Wilkins, 1953), pp. 199–202.

16. Oral History interview of JPII, pp. 158–159.

17. Unfortunately, we do not know exactly what the hereditary relationship might have been, or any other details of the diagnosis and treatment of the brothers, because the records of their care by Dr. Wilmer, once in the Johns Hopkins Medical Archives, have been lost or destroyed.

18. JPII to KDP, September 29, 1918, P-D.

19. *Post-Dispatch,* June 28, 1916, and August 14, 1918.

20. Markham, *Bovard,* pp. 132–133.

21. Ibid., p. 134.

22. *Post-Dispatch,* June 4, 1917.

23. Unidentified clipping dated June 6, 1917, P-D.

24. Unidentified clipping dated November 16, 1916, P-D.

25. Unidentified clipping dated 1913 in P-D morgue.

26. *Globe-Democrat,* July 5, 1918.

27. Oral History interview of JPII, p. 80.

28. Alexander S. McConachie, "The 'Big Cinch': A Business Elite in the Life of a City, St. Louis, 1895–1915" (Ph.D. diss., Washington University, St. Louis, 1976), pp. 111–128.

29. Oral History interview of JPII, p. 80.

30. McConachie, "The 'Big Cinch,' " p. 127.

31. "The Joseph Pulitzer Prize," April 16, 1918, P-D.

32. JPII to AGL, January 12, 1922, P-D.

33. JPII to AGL, October 12, 1924, P-D.

34. Telephone interview with Norman E. Isaacs, October 2, 1984.

35. AGL files, January 12, 1922, P-D.

Chapter 13
Triumphs and Tragedies

1. *Post-Dispatch,* December 1 and 2, 1922.

2. *Post-Dispatch,* December 3, 1922.

3. *World,* March 14, 16, and 17, 1925; *Post-Dispatch,* March 16, 1925.

4. McAdams to Laura McAdams, March 18, 1925, Clark McAdams papers, Missouri Historical Society, St. Louis, Missouri.

5. Interview with Mrs. E. R. Quesada, June 19, 1984, Washington, D.C.

6. Clemenceau to JPII, April 25, 1925, P-D.

7. Ralph Pulitzer, *Dreams and Derisions* (Privately printed, 1927).

8. JPII to Mrs. Fred W. Allen, April 13, 1925, LC, reel 8, frame 202.

9. JPII to RP, April 1, 1925, LC, reel 7, frame 394, and to the Rev. William G. Thayer, April 24, 1925, LC, reel 20, frame 275. Interviews with Kate Davis Pulitzer Quesada, June 19, 1984, Washington, D.C., and JPIII, July 17, 1984, Ladue, Missouri.

10. "On Board Discoverer," June 14, 1925, LC, reel 151, frame 129.

11. JPII to GSJ, February 5, 1926, LC, reel 72, frame 154.

12. JPII to KDP, May 27, 1926, LC, reel 156, frame 359.

13. Mrs. William C. Weir to author, February 27, 1985.

14. Telephone interview with Dr. and Mrs. Louis H. Hempelmann Jr., July 5, 1984.

15. Mrs. Anderson (Katryna) Dana to EEP, July 30, 1945, LC, reel 11, frame 138.

16. Telephone interview with JPIII, August 16, 1984.

17. *Post-Dispatch,* July 30, 1927.

18. After Joseph inherited it following Ralph's death in 1939.

Chapter 14
Days of the Summer Palace

1. See Swanberg, *Pulitzer,* p. 194; Ireland, *Pulitzer,* pp. 212-213; *Bar Harbor Record,* January 16, 1895, and March 17, 1897; JPII Papers, "Fire Insurance Analysis, Chatwold," September 13, 1935, LC, reel 105, frame 55. Unless otherwise noted, the material that follows is drawn from reels 104-107 and 151-152 of the JPII Papers (LC).

2. Interviews with Mrs. Lawrence Lymburner and Mrs. Frank Doyle, August 12, 1985, Bar Harbor, Maine.

3. ARK to author, June 19, 1987.

4. Interview with Mrs. Matilda Dwyer, July 20, 1985; St. Louis, Missouri; telephone interviews with Dr. William A. Gould and John A. Gould, September 30, 1985.

5. Interview with Mrs. Thomas Pettus, April 25, 1984, Ladue, Missouri.

6. Eugene Williams to JPII, August 16, 1945, personal correspondence at "Beechcroft," Bar Harbor, Maine.

7. JPII to Field and response, May 30, 1927, and JPII to Field, June 3, 1927, both in LC, reel 105, frames 59, 65.

8. *Post-Dispatch,* June 13, 1945, and July 5 and October 12, 1946; interview with Mrs. Quesada, June 19, 1984.

9. "Bar Harbor: 40 Years Later," *Down East,* September 1987, p. 103.

10. JPII to J. Hampden Robb, March 10, 1942, LC, reel 106, frame 557.

Chapter 15
Editor and Censor

1. Alexander, "The Last Shall Be First," p. 72.

2. OKB to JPII, September 5, 1924, P–D.

3. Telephone interview with Norman E. Isaacs, October 2, 1984.

4. ID to Paul C. Patterson, May 16, 1943, LC, reel 52, frame 280.

5. JPII to GSJ, May 2, 1927, and GSJ to JPII, May 3, 1927, LC, reel 72, frames 178–179.

6. JPII to GCJ, March 24, 1921, LC, reel 72, frame 43.

7. JPII to GCJ, July 9, 1921, LC, reel 72, frame 65.

8. JPII to GSJ, January 21, 1920, LC, reel 72, frame 16.

9. JPII to GSJ, March 28, 1928, LC, reel 72, frame 214.

10. JPII to GSJ, April 27, 1926, LC, reel 72, frame 155.

11. JPII to GSJ, February 19, 1926, LC, reel 72, frame 141.

12. JPII to RC, November 16, 1939, LC, reel 44, frame 21.

13. OKB to JPII, October 12, 1935, LC, reel 37, frame 496.

14. Irving Dilliard, "Mr. Bovard: A Great Managing Editor, A Complex Man," *Page One,* October 1948, p. 12.

15. OKB to JPII, July 28, 1936, LC, reel 37, frame 107.

16. Markham, *Bovard,* pp. 97–103.

17. Memo by SS, August 10, 1951, LC, reel 75, frame 27.

18. Ernest Kirschten, *Catfish and Crystal* (Garden City, N.Y.: Doubleday, 1960), p. 384.

19. Markham, *Bovard,* pp. 111–116.

20. *Post-Dispatch,* August 14, 1938.

21. BHR to James W. Markham, January 23, 1952, LC, reel 18, frame 33.

22. Paul Y. Anderson, "Bovard of the Post-Dispatch," *St. Louis Star-Times,* August 1, 1938, LC, reel 37, frame 264.

23. JP to OKB, November 14, 1921, and OKB to JPII, November 16, 1921, both in LC, reel 36, frames 104, 72.

24. HBS to JPII, December 28, 1950, LC, reel 20, frame 27.

25. OKB to JPII, August 18, 1925, LC, reel 36, frame 212.

26. JPII to GSJ, December 31, 1924, LC, reel 72, frame 108.

27. Florence R. Beatty-Brown, "The Negro as Portrayed by the St. Louis Post-Dispatch from 1920–1950" (Ph.D. diss., University of Illinois, 1951).

28. JPII to OKB, January 2, 1920, LC, reel 36, frame 12.

29. JP to OKB, February 18, 1920, LC, reel 36, frame 21.

30. OKB to JPII, February 27, 1920, LC, reel 36, frame 17.

31. JPII to OKB and reply, March 11, 1935, LC, reel 37, frame 50.

32. JPII to OKB, March 12, 1935, LC, reel 37, frame 510.

33. Unless noted otherwise, what follows is presented in different form in Pfaff, "Joseph Pulitzer II and Advertising Censorship, 1929–1939," *Journalism Monographs,* no. 77 (July 1982). Reproduced by permission of the Association for Education in Journalism and Mass Communication.

34. J. Cassell to JPII, December 13, 1913, LC, reel 27, frame 54.

35. Associated Advertising Clubs Special Bulletin, November 20, 1916, P–D.

36. *Post-Dispatch,* March 17, 1925.

37. Interview with Ben L. Brockman, April 27, 1984, St. Louis, Missouri.

38. "Financial Resume of the Pulitzer Publishing Company, 1920–1947," P–D.

Chapter 16
The *World* in Decline

1. Richard Kluger, *The Paper: The Life and Death of the "New York Herald Tribune"* (New York: Alfred A. Knopf, 1986), p. 257.

2. William H. Boyenton, "Origins of Advertising Censorship in the New York Newspapers," *Journalism Quarterly* 19 (June 1942), 138–149.

3. Frank McCabe to JPII, October 24, 1930, LC, reel 23, frame 298.

4. JPII to McCabe, October 29, 1930, LC, reel 23, frame 297.

5. JPII to Clifford P. Smith, December 14, 1928, LC, reel 7, frame 455.

6. JPII to RP, August 8, 1925, LC, reel 7, frame 391.

7. Under Cobb, there was close coordination between the news and editorial operations in the prosecution of the paper's reform-minded crusades. Lippmann and Swope generally tried to stay out of one another's way. E. J. Kahn Jr., *The World of Swope* (New York: Simon and Schuster, 1965), p. 233.

8. Correspondence between RP and Don C. Seitz, and RP to JPII, between July 21, 1920, and August 14, 1922, LC, reel 22, frames 19–31.

9. New York: Simon and Schuster, 1924.

10. JPII to RP, February 28, 1925, LC, reel 7, frame 382.

11. N. R. Hoover to JPII, April 11, 1925, LC, reel 7, frame 389.

12. JPII to RP, April 13, 1925, LC, reel 7, frame 387.

13. Ibid., frame 386.

14. JPII to RP, November 7, 1925, LC, reel 7, frame 395.

15. Breshnahan to RP, November 11, 1925, LC, reel 7, frame 397.

16. FDW to RP, November 19, 1925, LC, reel 7, frame 402.

17. *New York Times,* December 22, 1925.

18. RP to JPII, November 24, 1925, LC, reel 7, frame 400.

19. "Gross Income, Profits, U.S. Taxes, Dividends, Average Circulation, 1888-1925," LC, reel 7, frame 406.

20. JPII to RP, January 28, 1926, LC, reel 7, frame 408.

21. RP to JPII, January 29 and February 1, 1926, LC, reel 7, frames 411-412.

22. JPII to RP, February 4, 1926, LC, reel 7, frame 408.

23. JPII to FDW, July 1, 1926, LC, reel 103, frame 367.

24. JPII to RP, May 30 and October 15, 1927, LC, reel 7, frames 431, 434.

25. RP to JPII, October 27, 1927, LC, reel 156, frame 341.

26. JPII to RP, December 6, 1926, LC, reel 7, frame 415.

27. Barrett, *The World, the Flesh,* p. 75.

Chapter 17
The *World*'s Fall

1. The accounting basis used is not identified, but figures compiled in subsequent years show a 16 percent net profit of $1,084,664 for the *Post-Dispatch* in 1922. "Financial Resume of the Pulitzer Publishing Company, 1920-1947," P-D.

2. Undated, unsigned memorandums, probably by JPII and JTK in early 1927, LC, reel 23, frames 213-219.

3. Interviews with JPIII and MEP, April 23, 1984, St. Louis, Missouri.

4. JPII to RP, February 28, 1927, LC, reel 7, frame 418.

5. RP to JPII, March 4, 1927, LC, reel 7, frame 420.

6. *Editor and Publisher,* March 22, 1930, p. 10.

7. JPII to HP, March 25, 1930, LC, reel 23, frame 102.

8. Quoted in Kahn, *World of Swope,* p. 309.

9. Villard to McAdams, March 6, 1928, Clark McAdams Papers, Missouri Historical Archives.

10. RP to JPII, May 15, 1928, LC, reel 7, frame 438.

11. JPII to RP, May 17, 1928, LC, reel 7, frame 436.

12. RP to JPII, May 21, 1928, LC, reel 7, frame 440.

13. Wrote Morris Markey in the *New Yorker* of March 14, 1931,

p. 42: "The Page Opposite Editorial, rather than the front page, became the goal of every dreamy cub in the land. This was wholly admirable — but the stories in the news columns began to be ridiculously bad. . . . Whatever befall, a newspaper must purvey the news, and the *World*, during the declining years, purveyed its news fitfully, inaccurately, and often a little stupidly." See also Walter Lippmann, "Two Revolutions in the American Press," *Yale Review* 20 (March 1931), 439.

14. JPII to RP, September 28, 1928, LC, reel 7, frame 446.

15. Barrett, *The World, the Flesh,* pp. 81–82.

16. JPII to RP, February 1, 1930, LC, reel 23, frame 155; memo by RP, February 10, 1930, LC, reel 23, frame 144. Oral History interview of JPII, pp. 90–91.

17. JPII to HP and RP, January 31, 1930, LC, reel 23, frame 153.

18. JPII to ASVB, January 31, 1930, LC, reel 23, frame 200.

19. N. R. Hoover to HP, April 8, 1930, LC, reel 23, frames 124–128.

20. John F. Green to JPII, January 29, 1930, LC, reel 23, frame 165.

21. John G. Jackson to JPII, January 28, 1930, LC, reel 23, frame 170.

22. Judson, Green, Henry, and Remmers to JPII, January 27 and 31, 1930, LC, reel 23, frames 162, 172.

23. HP to JPII, February 8, 1930, LC, reel 23, frame 111.

24. "Memo re Luncheon in New York, January 15th 1930," LC, reel 23, frame 211.

25. Memo by JPII, February 7, 1930, LC, reel 23, frame 160.

26. FDW to HP, August 20, 1930, LC, reel 23, frame 207.

27. J. F. Breshnahan to HP, August 20, 1930, LC, reel 23, frame 209.

28. FDW to JPII, August 25, 1930, LC, reel 23, frame 108.

29. Meyer Berger, *The Story of the New York Times, 1851–1951* (New York: Simon and Schuster, 1951), pp. 369–372.

30. Ibid., pp. 369–370.

31. JP to JPII, August 25, 1930, LC, reel 23, frame 108. A similarly contradictory version of events is related in Gerald W. Johnson's "biographical study" of Ochs, *An Honorable Titan* (New York: Harper and Brothers, 1946), pp. 294–296. It says Ochs was "astonished" when the Pulitzers offered to sell him the morning and Sunday *World,* asking $10 million, and that Ochs was not at all interested, but he did propose the employee buyout scheme, in which Herbert "exhibited no interest."

32. As were some others, although their terms and just when they were put out is not clear. JPII to John G. Jackson, March 9, 1931, LC, reel 23, frame 456. The *Post-Dispatch* reported on February 27, 1931, that "Frank Gannett, publisher of the Brooklyn Eagle and of other newspapers, William Griffith of the New York Enquirer and David J. Stern of the Philadelphia Record and Camden Courier all made offers for the Worlds," but no mention of these offers was found in the correspondence on the subject in the papers of JPII at either LC or P-D.

33. JPII to HP, September 25, 1930, LC, reel 23, frame 84; Alexander Troup to JPII, October 9, 1930, LC, reel 23, frame 91.

34. JTK and ASVB to JPII, August 25, 1930, LC, reel 23, frame 118.

35. Kahn, *World of Swope,* pp. 344–346.

36. W. R. Hearst to Arthur Brisbane, October 19, 1930, LC, reel 23, frame 133.

37. Memorandum by John G. Jackson on meeting of November 19, 1930, LC, reel 23, frame 135.

38. Peter Greig to JPII, March 19, 1930, LC, reel 23, frame 100.

39. Kahn, *World of Swope,* pp. 308, 342.

40. The deal with Scripps-Howard was the immediate payment of $500,000 and another $500,000 within 90 days, $2 million in notes, and the final $2 million contingent on the profits of the *World-Telegram.* See *Post-Dispatch,* February 27, 1931.

41. Quoted in ibid.

42. "Memo by J.P.," undated (approx. March 1, 1931), with the notation that it was shown to Howard on March 26, 1931 (LC, reel 23, frame 448). The memo also said: "He had weeks to come to us and did not come. He showed business irresponsibility last summer when he made a firm offer of $10,000,000 one day and withdrew it a few days later, explaining that he could not raise the money." Publicly, Block denied that he had been acting in Hearst's behalf in the matter. *Post-Dispatch,* February 26, 1931.

43. There are accounts of this in Barrett, *The World, the Flesh,* and in James W. Barrett, ed., *The End of the World* (New York: Harper and Brothers, 1931).

44. In Barrett, *End of the World,* p. 216.

45. Gay Talese, *The Kingdom and the Power* (New York: World Publishing Co., 1969), pp. 14–15, 215. Johnson's *Honorable Titan,* pp. 295–296, claims that had Ochs not been in Hawaii at the time of the sale, he would have testified in surrogate's court that the *World* was worth "not less than $5,000,000" and that he was prepared to raise as much as $3 million, "provided the property were turned over to men who would maintain it." Johnson continued: "That would have blocked the sale and probably would have saved the *World.* But he was in Honolulu."

46. *Post-Dispatch,* February 27, 1931.

47. Barrett, *The World, the Flesh,* p. 59.

48. Statement by JPII before members of the American Newspaper Guild, approx. 1942, LC, reel 30, frame 464.

49. Oral History interview of JPII, pp. 91–94.

50. Ibid., p. 95.

Chapter 18
Exit Bovard

1. JPII to RP, February 18, 1931, LC, reel 23, frame 431; "Valedictory," initialed "OKB," LC, reel 23, frame 439.

2. "Letter to the Editor," February 28, 1931, quoted in James W. Markham, "Bovard of the Post-Dispatch" (Ph.D. diss., University of Missouri, 1952), p. 171. Markham's book of the same title, previously cited, is drawn from this thesis. The book manuscript was subject to the approval of Mrs. Bovard, and at least partly for that reason is not as candid or detailed as the thesis, although this letter is there too. Many details not specifically attributed in this chapter are from this source.

3. "The Post-Dispatch," *The Nation,* December 9, 1928, pp. 675-676.

4. *Post-Dispatch,* November 10, 1945.

5. Marquis W. Childs, *Sweden, The Middle Way* (New Haven: Yale University Press, 1936), and *This Is Democracy* (New Haven: Yale University Press, 1938).

6. JPII to RP, May 18, 1932, LC, reel 7, frame 517.

7. OKB to JPII, undated (approx. July 1931), LC, reel 36, frames 548-550.

8. Charles G. Ross, "The Country's Plight," *Post-Dispatch,* November 29, 1931.

9. OKB to JPII, September 7, 1931, LC, reel 36, frame 534.

10. OKB to JPII, September 21, 1931, LC, reel 36, frame 534.

11. JPII to OKB, October 28, 1933, and OKB to JPII, October 31, 1933, both in LC, reel 37, frame 26.

12. OKB to JPII, March 6, 1936, LC, reel 37, frame 82. A few months later, annoyed by what he considered Lippmann's inability to interpret matters of constitutional law accurately, he suggested to Pulitzer that the " 'hired hands' be required to enlighten and entertain the customers on other topics." OKB to JP, June 4, 1936, LC, reel 37, frame 65.

13. OKB to JPII, July 18, 1932, LC, reel 36, frame 551.

14. JPII to RP, May 18, 1932, LC, reel 7, frame 517.

15. JPII to OKB, July 1, 1936, LC, reel 37, frame 52.

16. OKB to JPII, July 20, 1936, and JPII to OKB, July 25, 1936, LC, reel 63, frames 142, 163.

17. *Post-Dispatch,* October 4, 1936.

18. JPII to CGR, October 19, 1936, LC, reel 65, frame 60.

19. JPII to OKB, June 16, 1937, and OKB to JPII, June 21, 1937, LC, reel 37, frames 418-419.

20. OKB to JPII, March 6, 1936, LC, reel 63, frame 181. The book was *Congress, the Constitution, and the Supreme Court* (Boston: Little, Brown, 1925).

21. OKB to FDW, March 24, 1938, quoted in Markham, *Bovard,* p. 366; JPII to OKB, July 28, 1936, LC, reel 37, frame 452.

22. JPII to OKB, March 12, 1937, LC, reel 37, frame 137.
23. OKB to JPII, March, 1937, LC, reel 37, frame 141.
24. JPII to OKB, December 28, 1937, and OKB to JPII, December 29, 1937, LC, reel 37, frame 136.
25. OKB to JPII, February 19, 1938, LC, reel 37, frame 249.
26. OKB to JPII, August 6, 1937, LC, reel 37, frame 173.
27. OKB to JPII, February 3, 1938, LC, reel 37, frame 320 (the thesis is reproduced between frames 314 and 344).
28. GMB to JPII, June 30, 1937, and OKB to JPII, July 19, 1937, LC, reel 37, frames 144–147.
29. JPII to OKB, May 30, 1938, LC, reel 37, frame 606.
30. OKB to JPII, June 18, 1938, LC, reel 37, frames 602–605.
31. JPII to OKB and reply, July 23, 1938, LC, reel 37, frame 569.
32. OKB to JPII, May 13, 1938, LC, reel 37, frame 263.
33. Markham, *Bovard*, p. 365.
34. In 1938, the company's revenues fell nearly $750,000 from the previous year. "Financial Resume of the Pulitzer Publishing Company, 1920–1947," P-D.
35. *Post-Dispatch*, July 30, 1938.
36. August 2, 1938, LC, reel 37, frame 267.
37. Transcript of interviews of Reese (BHR) by Louis M. Starr during the spring and summer of 1954. Oral History Collection, CU, p. 41.
38. OKB to PYA, January 11, 1938, LC, reel 101, frame 528.
39. *St. Louis Star-Times*, August 1, 1938.
40. OKB to JPII, August 3, 1938, LC, reel 37, frame 278.
41. JPII to OKB, July 26, 1938, LC, reel 37, frame 276.
42. JTK to JPII, July 14, 1939, LC, reel 68, frame 496.
43. JPII to FDW, April 5, 1922, LC, reel 50, frame 384.
44. Papers of JPII, LC, reel 68, frames 460, 495; Basil G. Rudd to JPII, September 20, 1938, P-D.
45. "U.S. Lists High Newspaper Salaries," *Editor and Publisher,* January 18, 1936, LC, reel 68, frame 520.
46. Markham, *Bovard*, pp. 374–384.
47. CGR to JPII, September 30, 1938, LC, reel 37, frames 552–554.
48. *Post-Dispatch*, November 14, 1954.
49. Markham, *Bovard*, p. 360.
50. Interview with Ben L. Brockman, April 27, 1984, St. Louis, Missouri.

Chapter 19
Life After O.K.B.

1. JPII to BHR, July 15, 1939, LC, reel 68, frame 489; JPIII to JPII, February 2, 1951, P-D.

2. Oral History interview with BHR, pp. 3, 95.

3. OKB to JPII, August 3, 1938, LC, reel 37, frame 280.

4. BHR to James W. Markham, January 23, 1952, LC, reel 18, frame 33.

5. Oral History interview with BHR, pp. 76–77.

6. "Man over Legend," *Time,* April 16, 1951, p. 78.

7. Carlos F. Hurd, "O. K. Bovard Resigns from Post-Dispatch," *Editor and Publisher,* August 6, 1938, p. 20.

8. BHR to JPII, July 30, 1938, LC, reel 92, frame 429.

9. James Lawrence to author, February 26, 1987.

10. JPII to RP and HP, April 11, 1939, LC, reel 7, frame 640.

11. Paul Y. Anderson, "The Greatest Managing Editor," *The Nation,* August 13, 1938, pp. 142–143.

12. "Memo by J.P.," November 10, 1938, LC, reel 72, frame 418.

13. JPII to RP and HP, April 11, 1939, LC, reel 7, frame 640.

14. RPB to JPII, August 22, 1938, and JPII to RPB, August 24, 1938, both in LC, reel 102, frame 14.

15. JPII to BHR, August 29, 1938, LC, reel 92, frame 472.

16. JPII to BHR, November 14, 1942, LC, reel 93, frame 327.

17. JP to *World,* November 1, 1899, JPI Papers, LC. The notations at the bottom of the memo read: "Received: Nov. 2, Understood: yes, Executed: Quietly."

18. JPII to BHR, March 12, 1941, LC, reel 93, frame 152.

19. JPII to BHR, November 15, 1945, LC, reel 94, frame 181.

20. Quoted in JPII to BHR, December 18, 1938, LC, reel 92, frame 418.

21. JPII to BHR, February 26, 1947, LC, reel 94, frame 564.

22. Roger Butterfield, "An Editor Must Have No Friends," *Colliers,* December 23, 1950, p. 47.

23. JPII to Owen Bryant, January 15, 1951, LC, reel 9, frame 173. Ben L. Brockman, the paper's national advertising manager for many years, told this story: The business people decided it would be a good idea to build a new printing plant on Duncan Avenue because papers printed there could be delivered more quickly in the western section of the city. At a meeting shortly after the new plant opened, someone asked how much speedier the delivery had become. The answer was that it was actually slower because of the time it took to get the mats rolled downtown out to the new plant. "Well, this really got Pulitzer upset. That cost them a barrel of money to put up that plant." At that point James T. Keller, the longtime penny-pinching treasurer, said to the publisher: "I've

been telling you all along you ought to sit down with these guys and find out what's going on in your goddamn newspaper!" Shortly thereafter the new plant was closed. Interview with Ben L. Brockman, April 27, 1984, St. Louis, Missouri.

24. JPII to BHR, April 10, 1939, LC, reel 92, frame 596.

25. JPII to BHR, December 6, 1939, LC, reel 92, frame 499.

26. Telephone interview with Norman E. Isaacs, October 2, 1984.

27. JPII to BHR, March 28, 1947, LC, reel 94, frame 551.

28. Baumhoff, *Story,* p. 41.

29. JPII to BHR, March 6, 1939, LC, reel 92, frame 613.

30. JPII to BHR, February 8, 1943, LC, reel 93, frame 580.

31. BHR to Kent Cooper, November 9, 1942, LC, reel 93, frame 131.

32. JPII to BHR, February 4, 1946, LC, reel 94, frame 337.

33. "Memo to Mr. Reese," February 14, 1944, LC, reel 94, frame 39.

34. JPII to BHR, October 14, 1943, LC, reel 93, frame 472.

35. JPII to BHR, January 30, 1939, LC, reel 92, frame 619.

36. JPII to BHR, April 12, 1945, LC, reel 94, frame 263.

37. JPII to BHR, June 4, 1940, LC, reel 93, frame 57.

38. Interviews with Mrs. Thomas Pettus, April 25, 1984, Ladue, Missouri, and Mrs. Charles Allen Thomas, July 20, 1985, Clayton, Missouri.

39. JPII to BHR, September 10, 1942, LC, reel 93, frame 355; JPII to RC, September 16, 1944, LC, reel 45, frame 333.

40. His compensation as publisher alone was in the $250,000-plus range during the Depression and as high as $502,000 before. He also usually received $100,000 or more in investment and other income. Furthermore, he spent the lion's share of what came in each year. See "Savings and Income in Prosperity and Depression, 1928–1933," LC, reel 105, frame 558; Alexander, "The Last Shall Be First," p. 6.

41. JPII to BHR, January 17, 1944, LC, reel 94, frame 170.

42. JPII to BHR, May 26, 1947, LC, reel 94, frame 468.

43. JPII to BHR, August 6, 1947, LC, reel 94, frame 428.

44. JPII to BHR, October 4, 1947, LC, reel 94, frame 514.

45. JPII to BHR, June 1, 1950, LC, reel 95, frame 311.

46. JPII to BHR, November 14, 1946, LC, reel 94, frame 363.

47. *Post-Dispatch,* February 13, 1954; and Interview with Mrs. Charles Allen Thomas (formerly Mrs. Claude Tillinghast Porter), July 20, 1985, Clayton, Missouri.

48. JPII to BHR, undated [1939], LC, reel 92, frame 570.

49. JPII to JPIII, November 27, 1943, LC, reel 6, frame 72.

50. JPIII to JPII, July 3, 1941, LC, reel 88, frame 214.

51. JPII to JPIII, July 9, 1941, LC, reel 88, frames 214–215.

52. Quoted in Swanberg, *Pulitzer,* p. 376.

53. Beatty-Brown, "The Negro," pp. 233, 277, 294.

54. JPII to BHR, May 8, 1949, P-D.

55. Interviews with Mrs. Elwood R. Quesada and Mrs. Lawrence

Lymburner, August 12, 1985, Bar Harbor, Maine. As a young man, he had used the word "nigger" a few times in letters to his father, evidently because the senior Pulitzer had no objection and probably used the term himself. An acceptance of black stereotypes is suggested in the way he concluded a feature-story suggestion for an interview with Roosevelt's valet: "Perhaps he is a dull Negro with no ideas; if so, don't bother." JPII to BHR, March 18, 1941, LC, reel 93, frame 143.

56. JPII to William S. Moore Jr., April 29, 1941, LC, reel 2, frame 274.

57. JPII to RC, October 6, 1942, LC, reel 44, frame 520.

58. JPII to RC, January 17, 1944, LC, reel 45, frame 245.

59. Interview with Ben L. Brockman, April 27, 1984.

60. Quoted in Beatty-Brown, "The Negro," p. 284.

61. Ibid.

62. Interview with Richard G. Baumhoff, August 12, 1983.

63. JPII to RC, February 8, 1945, LC, reel 45, frame 477.

64. JPII to BHR and response, June 3, 1941, LC, reel 93, frame 121.

65. Beatty-Brown, "The Negro," p. 285.

66. Byron J. Dietrich to JPII, February 3, 1947, LC, reel 85, frame 229.

67. JPII to GEC, February 11, 1947, LC, reel 85, frame 228.

68. *Post-Dispatch,* June 11, 1948.

69. JPII to BHR, May 18, 1944, LC, reel 94, frame 143.

70. JPII to BHR, April 20, 1945, LC, reel 94, frame 249.

71. JPII to BHR, February 5, 1947 (marked "not sent"), P-D.

72. *APME Inc. 1948* (New York: Associated Press, 1949), p. 35; Telephone interview with Norman E. Isaacs, October 2, 1984.

73. RC to JPII, July 10, 1944, LC, reel 94, frame 126.

74. JPII to Donald Grant, March 27, 1950, P-D.

75. Donald Grant to JPII, April 28, 1950, and JPII to Grant, April 29, 1950, both in LC, reel 70, frame 207.

76. Interview with Richard G. Baumhoff, August 12, 1983; Wilensky, *Story,* p. 25.

77. John Gunther, *Inside U.S.A.* (New York: Harper and Row, 1947), pp. 351–353.

78. *Brown* v. *Board of Education of Topeka, Kansas,* 347 U.S. 483 (1954).

79. Richard G. Baumhoff, "Problems of the Negro," *Post-Dispatch,* April 9, 1950.

80. JPII to ID, November 29, 1954, P-D.

Chapter 20
World War II

1. Seitz, *Pulitzer,* pp. 201–207.

2. JPII to CGR, March 7, 1938, LC, reel 96, frame 231.

3. JPII to CGR, May 25, 1938, LC, reel 96, frame 162.

4. JPII to RC, September 13, 1938, LC, reel 43, frame 522.

5. JPII to RC, September 6, 1938, LC, reel 43, frames 527–528.

6. BHR to JP, September 13, 1939, LC, reel 92, frame 558.

7. ID to AGL, September 13, 1939, LC, reel 52, frame 197.

8. September 15, 1939, LC, reel 92, frame 556.

9. JPII to RC and BHR, September 28, 1939, LC, reel 92, frame 654.

10. RC to BHR, undated (probably September 26, 1939), BHR to JPII, September 26, 1939, both in LC, reel 92, frame 654.

11. After Marshall's death, his widow married Vincent Astor at the Bar Harbor home of Joseph and Elizabeth Pulitzer on October 8, 1953. Brooke Astor, *Footprints* (New York: Doubleday, 1980), p. 275.

12. JPIII to author, June 5, 1987.

13. *Post-Dispatch,* September 13, 1939; Interview with Mrs. Elwood R. Quesada, August 12, 1985, Bar Harbor, Maine; Papers of JPII, LC, reel 5, frames 3–54.

14. JPII to CGR, May 18, 1940, LC, reel 96, frame 345.

15. BHR to MWC, May 22, 1940, LC, reel 102, frame 583.

16. JPII to RC, May 24, 1940, LC, reel 63, frame 484.

17. JPII to GMB, June 19, 1940, LC, reel 25, frame 204.

18. *Post-Dispatch,* June 11, 1940.

19. RC to JPII, June 12, 1940, LC, reel 63, frame 466; ID to RC, undated (probably June 13, 1940), LC, reel 63, frame 452; *Post-Dispatch,* June 14, 1940.

20. RC to JPII, June 13, 1940, LC, reel 63, frame 456.

21. JPII to RC, June 17, 1940, LC, reel 63, frames 436–437.

22. JPII to BHR, June 16, 1940, LC, reel 93, frame 56.

23. JPII to RC, June 22, 1940, LC, reel 63, frame 431.

24. JPII to FG, July 10 and 26, 1940, LC, reel 69, frames 589, 595.

25. JP to BHR, July 29, 1940, LC, reel 93, frame 39.

26. Ronald Steel, *Walter Lippmann and the American Century* (New York: Random House, 1980), pp. 384–385.

27. "Memo of conversation with Walter Lippmann," September 16, 1940, LC, reel 63, frame 526.

28. Steel, *Lippmann,* p. 385.

29. RC to JPII, September 13, 1940, LC, reel 63, frame 151.

30. "Notes on U.S. and War," September 17, 1940, LC, reel 63, frame 531.

31. *Post-Dispatch,* September 3, 1940.

32. *New York Times,* September 4, 1940.

33. JPII to RC, September 20, 1940, LC, reel 63, frame 512.

34. Ibid., frame 513.

35. Memos dated October 19, 23, and 26, 1940, LC, reel 65, frames 236–263.

36. *New York Times,* October 13 and 14, 1940.

37. RC to JPII, January 18, 1941, LC, reel 44, frame 338.

38. JPII to RC, January 24, 1941, LC, reel 64, frame 253.

39. JPII to FDR, January 23, 1941, LC, reel 64, frame 35.

40. JPII to RC, May 22, 1941, LC, reel 64, frame 7.

41. BHR to JPII, May 23, 1941, LC, reel 64, frame 11.

42. JPII to RC, May 27 and June 2, 1941, LC, reel 64, frame 354, and reel 44, frame 286.

43. JPII to RC, July 25, 1941, LC, reel 44, frame 472.

44. RC to JPII, August 21, 1941, LC, reel 44, frame 464.

45. JPII to RC, August 23, 1941, LC, reel 44, frame 462.

46. JPII to H. T. Meek, September 11, 1941, LC, reel 102, frame 79.

47. Margaret L. Coit, *Mr. Baruch* (Boston: Houghton Mifflin, 1957), p. 523.

48. BMB to JPII, May 9, 1941, LC, reel 64, frame 367.

49. MWC to JPII, July 6, 1943, LC, reel 103, frame 11.

50. MWC to JPII, September 20, 1943, LC, reel 103, frame 6.

51. BHR to JPII, May 23, 1941, LC, reel 64, frame 11.

52. JPII to MWC, January 14, 1942, LC, reel 103, frame 80.

53. MWC to JPII, January 30, 1942, LC, reel 99, frame 410.

54. *New York Times,* April 10, 1972.

55. JPII to RC, February 3, 1942, LC, reel 44, frame 422.

56. JPII to RC, February 6, 1942, LC, reel 44, frame 421.

57. JPII to RC, February 20, 1942, LC, reel 44, frame 413.

58. *Post-Dispatch,* March 4, 1942.

59. JPII to MWC, April 10, 1942, LC, reel 103, frame 72.

60. Interview with Mrs. A. Mervyn Davies, widow, September 21, 1984, Wilton, Connecticut.

61. JPII to FDR, January 18, 1943, LC, reel 6, frame 101.

62. Interview with ID, April 28, 1984, Collinsville, Illinois.

63. JPII to RC, September 23, 1942, LC, reel 44, frame 528.

64. RC to JPII, September 25, 1942, LC, reel 64, frame 421.

65. David A. Shannon, *Twentieth Century America* (Chicago: Rand McNally, 1963), p. 486.

66. JPII to RC, November 18, 1942 (marked "not sent"), LC, reel 64, frame 566.

67. JPII to ID, July 29, 1942, LC, reel 52, frame 247.

68. *Post-Dispatch,* February 18, 1942. The evidence that Pulitzer was the author was found in JPII to RC, March 20, 1942, LC, reel 57, frame 13.

69. Outline by JPII, February 9, 1943, LC, reel 103, frame 444.

70. "What Are We Fighting For?" (*Post-Dispatch* booklet, 1943), p. 3, P–D.

71. JPII to BHR, January 25, 1943, LC, reel 103, frame 435.

72. "What Are We Fighting For?" p. 42.

73. Edgar M. Queeny to JPII, April 1, 1943, and JPII to RC and reply, April 2, 1943, LC, reel 103, frames 546–548.

74. JPII to RC, September 16 and October 25, 1944, LC, reel 45, frames 333, 358.

75. JPIII to JPII, April 17, 1943, LC, reel 6, frame 90.

76. JPIII to ARK, December 3, 1944, LC, reel 6, frame 103.

77. "Pulitzer," *St. Louis,* August 1987, p. 28.

78. Telephone interview with David E. Moore, May 14, 1987.

79. JPII to JPIII, January 18, 1943, LC, reel 6, frame 101.

80. JPII to JPIII, May 24, 1943, LC, reel 6, frame 89.

81. Telephone interviews with Dr. and Mrs. Louis H. Hempelmann Jr., July 5, 1984.

82. *New York Times,* November 22, 1968.

83. Unless otherwise noted, the material on war correspondence is drawn from Anne R. Kenney, " 'She Got to Berlin': Virginia Irwin, *St. Louis Post-Dispatch* War Correspondent," *Missouri Historical Review* 79 (July 1985), 456–479.

84. RPB to JPII, January 26, 1944, LC, reel 102, frame 244.

85. RLS to JPII, September 6, 1944, LC, reel 99, frame 436.

86. *Post-Dispatch,* March 11, 1945.

87. JPII to Virginia Irwin, November 17, 1944, LC, reel 71, frame 648.

88. Memorandum by SS, August 10, 1951, LC, reel 75, frame 27.

89. Quoted in Kenney, "She Got to Berlin," p. 477.

90. JHK to JPII and response, July 27 and 30, 1945, LC, reel 80, frames 292–293.

91. *Post-Dispatch,* May 20, 1945.

92. JRS to JPII, May 25, 1945, LC, reel 80, frame 432.

93. *New York Times,* May 23, 1945.

94. JPII to RC, December 26, 1944, LC, reel 45, frame 131; August 17, 1944, LC, reel 64, frame 514.

95. JPII to RPB, November 16, 1945, quoting telegram to Eisenhower, LC, reel 102, frame 259.

96. JPII to Lindsay Hoben, June 18, 1945, LC, reel 80, frame 397.

97. JPII to FG, June 5, 1945, LC, reel 80, frame 308.

98. JPII to FG, June 4, 1945, LC, reel 70, frame 45.

99. Eugene Williams to JPII, August 16, 1945, personal correspondence at "Beechcroft," Bar Harbor, Maine.

Chapter 21
Joys and Sorrows

1. Several sources on the 1945 dinner: Transcript of remarks and menu, P-D; JPII to JPIII, March 31, 1945, LC, reel 6, frame 130; interviews with ARK, Mrs. Elwood R. Quesada, CJH, HOG, and letter from Elbert A. Talley, June 16, 1983, all of whom attended.

2. Oral History interview with BHR, 1954, CU, p. 114.

3. JPII to JP, August 20, 1906, CU.

4. JPII to RC, November 19, 1939, LC, reel 44, frame 21.

5. JPII to GSJ, July 20, 1924, LC, reel 72, frame 104.

6. JPII to GSJ, December 31, 1924, LC, reel 72, frame 108.

7. RC to JPII, November 10, 1938, LC, reel 43, frame 588.

8. JPII to JP, undated (1906?), P-D.

9. OKB to JPII, undated (probably 1921), LC, reel 50, frame 390.

10. Laura McAdams in Papers of Clark McAdams, Missouri Historical Society (hereafter MHS).

11. JPII to CM, September 1, 1930, LC, reel 78, frame 105.

12. JPII to CM, May 12, 1931, LC, reel 78, frame 169.

13. JPII to CM, September 9, 1933, MHS.

14. JPII to CM, December 28, 1933, MHS.

15. JPII to HP, May 31, 1934, LC, reel 149, frame 290.

16. Heber Smith to JPII, December 30, 1927, John G. Jackson to JPII, June 23, 1933, and undated wire service account (1927), all in LC, reel 156, frames 311, 251, 421.

17. RP to JPII, April 30, 1934, LC, reel 7, frame 587.

18. Post-Dispatch, February 22, 1934.

19. JPII to CM, April 14, 1934, MHS (punctuation supplied).

20. Telegram to Post-Dispatch, May 9, 1934, LC, reel 78, frame 196.

21. Ronald T. Farrar, Reluctant Servant (Columbia: University of Missouri Press, 1969), p. 112; Memo by CGR, May 29, 1934, P-D.

22. JPII to CM, July 2, 1934, LC, reel 78, frame 236; CM to JPII, July 8, 1934, LC, reel 78, frame 200.

23. CM to Gene(?), July 20, 1934, MHS.

24. Markham, Bovard, p. 173.

25. JPII to Jack Alexander, November 7, 1938, LC, reel 8, frame 492.

26. JPII to CGR, May 31, 1934, P-D.

27. Memo by CGR, May 29, 1934, P-D.

28. Post-Dispatch, September 27, 1936.

29. Farrar, Reluctant Servant, p. 125.

30. CGR to JPII, undated (September 1936), LC, reel 65, frame 99.

31. JPII to CGR, September 22, 1936, LC, reel 65, frame 92.

32. JPII to CGR, September 20, 1936, LC, reel 65, frame 95.

33. RC to JPII, September 2, 1937, LC, reel 43, frame 568.

34. JPII to CGR, February 15, 1937, LC, reel 96, frame 146.

35. JPII to CGR, November 3 and December 29, 1937, LC, reel 96, frames 112, 115.

36. Farrar, *Reluctant Servant,* pp. 121, 156, 226.

37. *Post-Dispatch,* April 4, 1940.

38. JPII to R. R. McCormick, March 13, 1940, and JPII to H. R. Luce, March 12, 1940, both in LC, reel 75, frames 463, 480.

39. GMB to JPII, April 3, 1940, LC, reel 75, frame 553.

40. Harry B. Hawes to JPII, April 19, 1940, LC, reel 13, frame 236.

41. RC to JPII, April 11, 1940, LC, reel 75, frame 525.

42. Quoted in Baumhoff, *Story,* p. 26.

43. Tyrrell Williams to RC, March 12, 1940, LC, reel 75, frame 468.

44. RC to JPII, January 16, 1943, LC, reel 93, frame 590.

45. *Post-Dispatch,* February 4 and 5; April 2, 1943.

46. *Post-Dispatch,* February 5, 1943.

47. JPII to JPIII, November 27, 1943, LC, reel 6, frame 73.

48. JPII to RC, April 16, 1945, LC, reel 45, frame 421; "Salary History of Mr. Coghlan," April 10, 1945, LC, reel 68, frame 701.

49. RC to JPII, June 14, 1945, LC, reel 45, frame 411.

50. RPB to JPII, February 3, 1938, LC, reel 101, frame 519. Less than a year after leaving the *Post-Dispatch,* Anderson, age forty-five, committed suicide. Markham, *Bovard,* p. 106.

Chapter 22
Reds and Rights

1. JHK to BHR, April 10, 1947, LC, reel 94, frame 467.

2. Clipping, "Donkey and Elephant," undated (approx. 1944), LC, reel 72, frame 566.

3. Julius Klyman, "Leon Trotsky," in *Dictators and Democrats,* ed. L. Fernsworth (New York: Robert M. McBride, 1941), p. 213.

4. JHK to JPII, February 16, 1944, LC, reel 72, frame 559. Telephone interviews with Morris J. Levin, June 26, 1985, and another source who asked not to be identified, October 5, 1984.

5. JHK to JPII, February 16, 1944, LC, reel 72, frame 559.

6. JHK to JPII, May 31, 1944, LC, reel 72, frame 558.

7. Telephone interview with Morris J. Levin, June 26, 1985. Such stories clearly had no detrimental effect on circulation. Readers bought more than 1,000 extra copies one day in 1882 when the paper reported that a priest was suspected of fathering a child. Julian S. Rammelkamp, *Pulitzer's Post-Dispatch, 1878–1883* (Princeton: Princeton University Press, 1967), p. 171.

8. JHK to JPII, February 16, 1944, LC, reel 72, frame 559.

9. RC to JPII, July 7, 1944, LC, reel 72, frame 554.

10. JPII to BHR, February 5, 1945, LC, reel 73, frame 120.

11. JPII to JHK, April 14, 1946, LC, reel 73, frame 115.

12. JPII to JHK, January 17, 1947, LC, reel 73, frame 82.

13. JPII to BHR, May 9, 1947, LC, reel 73, frame 55.

14. JHK to BHR, undated (approx. May 10, 1947), LC, reel 73, frame 54.

15. Interview with CJH, May 5, 1984, St. Louis, Missouri.

16. JPII to BHR, November 18, 1947, LC, reel 73, frame 170.

17. JHK to JPII, July 29, 1949, LC, reel 73, frame 233.

18. JHK to JPII, March 21, 1951, LC, reel 72, frame 680.

19. RLC to JPII, March 30, 1953, LC, reel 72, frame 615.

20. JPIII to JPII, March 10, 1953, LC, reel 72, frame 617.

21. JPII to RC, July 18, 1946, LC, reel 45, frame 643.

22. RC to JPII, July 20, 1946, and JPII to RC, July 23, 1946, both in LC, reel 45, frames 642, 657.

23. JPII to RC, September 20, 1946; RC to JPII, September 23, 1946; and JPII to RC, September 30, 1946, all in LC, reel 45, frames 626, 625, 616.

24. JPII to RC, August 24, 1946, LC, reel 45, frame 635.

25. JPII to BHR, September 3, 1946, LC, reel 94, frame 380.

26. JPII to RC, July 24, 1947, LC, reel 46, frame 78.

27. JPII to BHR, December 29, 1949, LC, reel 95, frame 134.

28. JPII to RC, April 1, 1948, LC, reel 54, frame 555.

29. RC to JPII, April 2, 1948, LC, reel 54, frame 554.

30. JPII to RC, May 27, 1948, LC, reel 46, frame 210.

31. Robert A. Randolph to JPII, June 24, 1948, LC, reel 46, frame 209.

32. JPII to RC, July 22, 1948, and November 9, 1948, both in LC, reel 46, frames 209, 195.

33. "Memo for file," January 4, 1949, LC, reel 46, frame 170.

34. RC to JPII, September 26, 1950, LC, reel 46, frame 371.

35. JPII to To Whom It May Concern, August 4, 1951, and RC to JPII, December 19, 1951, both in LC, reel 46, frames 367, 366.

36. *New York Times,* October 19, 1965.

37. *Time,* July 4, 1949, p. 49. Dilliard has written nearly one hundred articles for the *Dictionary of American Biography,* including articles on Ralph Pulitzer, Joseph Pulitzer II, Clark McAdams, Paul Y. Anderson, Charles G. Ross, and Oliver K. Bovard. Originally published in the *Post-Dispatch* in 1937, Dilliard's reconstruction of the secret Constitutional Convention, "Building the Constitution," is still available. More than 500,000 copies have been distributed. It was reprinted in the *Post-Dispatch* during the spring and summer of 1987, fifty years after it first appeared, to mark the Bicentennial of the Constitution.

38. ID to JPII, April 5, 1951, LC, reel 56, frame 492; Interview with ID, April 28, 1984, Collinsville, Illinois.

39. JPII to RC, January 9, 1943, LC, reel 57, frame 104.

40. RC to JPII, January 12, 1943, LC, reel 57, frame 99. In the first case, *Minersville School District* v. *Gobitis,* 310 U.S. 586 (1940), the Court voted 8 to 1 in favor of the compulsory salute. This was reversed, 6 to 3, in *West Virginia State Board of Education* v. *Barnette,* 319 U.S. 624 (1943).

41. JPII to FDR, June 3, 1943, LC, reel 52, frame 282.

42. ID to the author, May 20, 1987.

43. SMC to JPII, July 24, 1947, LC, reel 40, frame 242.

44. Sworn deposition by ID, May 27, 1947, LC, reel 40, frame 230.

45. JPII to ID, January 19, 1949, LC, reel 52, frame 453.

46. JPII to ID, November 9, 1949, LC, reel 54, frame 539.

47. ID to JPII, April 5, 1951, LC, reel 56, frame 492.

48. JPII to ID, December 19, 1949, LC, reel 52, frame 383.

49. JPII to JPIII, July 23, 1949; JPIII to JPII, August 10, 1949; and JPII to JPIII, August 13, 1949, all in LC, reel 84, frames 258, 257, 256.

50. JPII to BHR, March 17, 1950, LC, reel 95, frame 346.

51. *Globe-Democrat,* May 2, 1946; JPII to JPIII, August 2, 1950, all in LC, reel 38, frame 636.

52. *Post-Dispatch,* November 1, 1952.

53. *Post-Dispatch,* October 16, 1949.

54. ID to JPII, April 5, 1951, LC, reel 56, frame 492.

55. JPII to SS, February 2, 1954, LC, reel 53, frame 502.

56. *Post-Dispatch,* June 5, 1951.

57. JPII to ID, July 23, 1951, LC, reel 55, frame 138.

58. JPII to ID, February 24, 1950, LC, reel 54, frame 538.

59. *Yates* v. *United States,* 354 U.S. 298 (1957).

60. JPII to ID, March 13, 1950, LC, reel 58, frame 188.

61. JPII to ID, March 15, 1950, LC, reel 54, frame 537.

62. *Post-Dispatch,* February 18, 1951.

63. JPII to RLC, July 7, 1953, LC, reel 58, frame 156.

64. *Post-Dispatch,* August 23, 1953.

65. JPII to RLC, July 25, 1953, LC, reel 58, frame 156.

66. JPII to ID, April 30, 1954, LC, reel 58, frame 113.

67. JPII to ID, December 6, 1954, LC, reel 58, frame 107.

68. Edwin R. Bayley, *Joe McCarthy and the Press* (Madison: University of Wisconsin Press, 1981), p. 139.

69. Ibid., p. 271.

70. Irving Dilliard, "Pulitzer II Shielded Joe McCarthy, Says Author," *St. Louis Journalism Review,* April 1983, p. 13.

71. JPII to ID, March 5, 1954, and ID to JPII, March 11, 1954, both in LC, reel 58, frames 124, 118.

72. JPII to Minot K. Milliken, and JPII to Robert A. Randolph, April 26, 1954, LC, reel 58, frames 114, 116.

73. JPIII to ID, June 7, 1983, P–D.

74. ID to JPIII, June 13, 1983, P-D.

75. JHK to JPII, September 17, [1945], LC, reel 72, frame 698.

76. *Post-Dispatch,* August 29, 1976.

77. James V. Maloney to author, August 24, 1987.

78. SS to JPIII, January 2, 1957, P-D. The August memo is also in Pulitzer's papers at LC, reel 68, frame 613.

79. JPII to ID, November 19, 1952, LC, reel 55, frame 92.

80. JPII to ID, December 20, 1952, LC, reel 55, frame 84.

81. David Rees, *Harry Dexter White: A Study in Paradox* (New York: Coward, McCann, and Geoghegan, 1973), pp. 10-11, 377.

82. JPII to ID, October 30, 1953, LC, reel 53, frame 262.

83. SS to JPII, February 16, 1954, P-D.

84. SS to JPII, April 9, 1954, and JPII to SS, April 10, 1954, both in LC, reel 53, frames 459, 458.

85. RL to author, May 18, 1985.

86. JPIII to author, July 24, 1987. Lasch and the third Joseph Pulitzer, despite having worked together harmoniously until Lasch's retirement, also had differing perspectives on the J.P. II–Dilliard conflict about McCarthy. After reading the account related here, Lasch commented: "With due respect to J.P. Jr.'s spirited defense of his father, it seems to me clear that J.P. did want the paper to go easy on McCarthy. Why else would he tell I.D. to omit McCarthy comment for a week? He was being bugged by his conservative friends and wanted to rein in I.D." To which J.P. Jr. had this rejoinder: "It was not 'Go easy on McCarthy,' it was 'Go easy on the reader.' If you overdo to excess, it will bore readers to death." As to Lasch's comment about J.P. being influenced by conservative friends, he observed that "in an environment of wealth, Bar Harbor, Republicanism, it is human nature to assume that that contact would erode [my father's] principles." He said he felt certain it never did. RL to author, August 4, 1987; JPIII to author (by telephone), September 9, 1987.

87. "For the Smith Act," September 14, 1954, LC, reel 61, frame 447.

88. Part of his reason for doing so may have been that Dilliard had reported that most law journal commentators had supported his view. Against this, however, Pulitzer told Shelton, he considered the heavily lopsided judicial support of the convictions more compelling. JPII to SS, September 8, 1954, LC, reel 61, frame 470.

89. JPII to ID, September 16, 1954, P-D; without notation in LC, reel 61, frame 446. In this connection, it is interesting that prior to being hired, Lasch had told Pulitzer that he, like Dilliard, thought the Smith Act convictions were unconstitutional and should be overturned by the Supreme Court. Pulitzer apparently was satisfied that he and Lasch would not clash on this issue, because Lasch had added: "Communists do not believe in civil liberties, but in a democracy they should nevertheless be permitted to enjoy them within the limits of the 'clear and present danger' doctrine. People who believe in democracy should fight

Communists by contesting their control of union movements, political parties and governments, not by suppression." Lasch to author, August 20, 1987.

90. SS to JPIII, January 2, 1957, P-D. "It is an interesting speculation . . . whether my editorship would have been any smoother than Irving's under JP, had he lived," Lasch commented on reading this. "If he really intended to send Sam on a national hunt for a replacement, perhaps he had already counted me out." RL to author, August 4, 1987.

91. ID to author, June 27, 1987.

92. JPIII, "Memo for file," October 1, 1957, P-D.

93. *Post-Dispatch,* May 5, 1954.

94. *Post-Dispatch,* June 8, 1954.

95. JPII to ID, June 19, 1954, LC, reel 56, frame 99. Two earlier memos are in LC, reel 56, frames 104, 131.

96. JPII to SS, March 24, 1955, LC, reel 75, frame 265.

97. JPII to ID, November 9, 1951, LC, reel 53, frame 3.

Chapter 23
Philosopher Businessman

1. Sworn deposition by AGL, May 16, 1947, LC, reel 40, frame 216; Interview with CJH, May 5, 1984, St. Louis, Missouri. There was an interval of several months between Lincoln and Hentschell when circulation manager George E. Carvell acted as business manager.

2. The loss in 1897 came about in an unusual way. In 1895, the elder Pulitzer, then absorbed in guiding his New York newspapers, sold for $80,000 a one-sixth interest in the *Post-Dispatch* to Colonel Charles H. Jones and gave Jones full editorial control of the paper. Jones fired a number of Pulitzer's trusted employees, whereupon Pulitzer sued to regain control of the paper, but lost. In 1896, Jones supported William Jennings Bryan's free silver campaign while the *World* opposed it. After Bryan was defeated, the disappointed Jones sold his share in the *Post-Dispatch* back to Pulitzer for $80,000 plus one-sixth of the profits earned during his control. This transaction wiped out any earnings for the Pulitzer Publishing Company for 1897. Baumhoff, *Story,* p. 4.

3. "Pulitzer Publishing Company 1989 Annual Report," p. 5; 1986–1988 Annual Reports.

4. Interview with Richard G. Baumhoff, August 12, 1983, Carmel, California; SS to JPII, April 9, 1948, LC, reel 98, frame 295.

5. JPII to Jack Alexander, November 7, 1938, LC, reel 8, frame 495.

6. "Financial Resume of the Pulitzer Publishing Company," 1912–1955, P-D.

7. JPII to JPIII, July 15, 1947, LC, reel 68, frame 194; JPIII to author, July 24, 1987.

8. JPII to CGR, December 21, 1938, LC, reel 99, frame 112.

9. JPII to BHR, February 3; *Post-Dispatch,* February 15, 1942, LC, reel 93, frame 408.

10. Michael Schudson, *Discovering the News* (New York: Basic Books, 1978), p. 98.

11. JPII to RC, September 3, 1940, LC, reel 44, frame 386.

12. JPII to RP, May 8, 1934, LC, reel 7, frame 586.

13. Quoted in Silas Bent, *Newspaper Crusaders* (New York: McGraw-Hill, 1939), p. 41.

14. HSP to JPII, April 11, 1928, LC, reel 140, frame 407.

15. Sam B. Armstrong, *The Story of the St. Louis Post-Dispatch* (St. Louis: St. Louis Post-Dispatch, 1962), p. 42.

16. RLC to JPII, February 20, 1952, LC, reel 137, frame 219.

17. John Hohenberg, *The Pulitzer Prizes* (New York: Columbia University Press, 1974), p. 236 and passim.

18. JPII to JPIII, May 24, 1943, and JPIII to JPII, April 17, 1943, both in LC, reel 6, frame 89.

19. JPII to Margaret L. Pulitzer, March 18, 1942, LC, reel 7, frame 8.

20. Hohenberg, *Pulitzer Prizes,* p. 160. In 1960 she won another Pulitzer Prize for *In the Days of McKinley.*

21. JPII to GMB, February 29, 1952, LC, reel 91, frame 97.

22. AGL to JPII, September 27, 1926, and JPII to AGL, October 5, 1926, both in P-D.

23. JPII to AGL, September 21, 1941, P-D.

24. JPII to AGL, August 23, 1943, LC, reel 29, frame 517.

25. JPII to CGR, March 10, 1937, LC, reel 61, frame 114.

26. JPII to GMB, September 15, approx. 1930, LC, reel 29, frame 473.

27. JPII to RC, April 6, 1943, LC, reel 45, frame 85.

28. *A.P.* v. *U.S.,* 326 U.S. 1 (1945).

29. JPII to RC, February 20, 1946, LC, reel 45, frame 549.

30. JPII to CJH, May 22, 1952, LC, reel 39, frame 17.

31. Interview with JPIII, July 17, 1984, Ladue, Missouri.

32. JPII to AGL, September 2, 1940, P-D.

33. 1989 Annual Report, p. 5.

34. Telephone conversation with James V. Maloney, April 4, 1991.

35. AGL to JPII, February 25, 1925, LC, reel 29, frame 53.

36. "The First Forty," KSD booklet, 1962, P-D. "Memo on Mr. Pulitzer's Activities," undated (probably October 1945), LC, reel 40, frame 199.

37. Interview with Mrs. Elwood R. Quesada, June 19, 1984, Washington, D.C.

38. JPII to GMB, April 21 and 26, 1943, and GMB to JPII, July 3, 1944, all in LC, reel 91, frames 316, 331, 296.

39. JPII to AGL, November 18, 1943, LC, reel 91, frame 302; JPII to GMB, December 17, 1943, LC, reel 88, frame 563.

40. GMB to JPII, June 3, 1946, LC, reel 91, frame 279.

41. JPII to RC, September 4, 1944, LC, reel 88, frame 554.

42. *Post-Dispatch,* March 16, 1945.

43. Interview with HOG, May 5, 1984, Chesterfield, Missouri.

44. JPII to CJH, May 9, 1952, LC, reel 88, frame 447.

45. Interview with HOG, May 5, 1984; telephone interview with Don Schomburg, June 15, 1987; *Television Age,* April 1954, pp. 23–24.

46. GMB to JPII, May 29, 1952, and May 15, 1953, both in LC, reel 88, frames 441, 435.

47. Interview with HOG, May 5, 1984; *Television Age,* April 1954, p. 25.

48. JPII to GMB, March 10, 1943, LC, reel 91, frame 326.

49. November 20, 1946, LC, reel 91, frame 278.

50. JPII to GMB, January 18, 1954, LC, reel 91, frame 338.

51. JPII to RC, February 7, 1949, LC, reel 46, frame 158.

52. JPII to General David Sarnoff, March 12, 1954, LC, reel 91, frame 490.

53. Managing editor, editorial page editor, treasurer, and business, broadcasting, advertising, and circulation managers.

54. JPII to JPIII, July 29, 1946, and September 30, 1946, both in LC, reel 88, frames 204, 199.

55. JPII to JPIII, July 17, 1946.

56. JPII to GEC and "The Cabinet," April 28, 1947, P-D.

57. Interview with CJH, July 16, 1984, St. Louis, Missouri.

58. *P-D Notebook,* July 1951, p. 1, P-D; *American Newspaper Annual and Directory* (Philadelphia: N. W. Ayer and Son, 1951).

59. Interviews with CJH, May 5, 1984, and July 29, 1984, St. Louis, Missouri.

60. "Agreement," June 14, 1951, P-D.

61. JPIII to JPII, October 8, 1951, LC, reel 30, frame 75.

62. SS to JPII, September 14, 1951, LC, reel 75, frame 31; *American Newspaper Annual,* 1952, 1953.

63. FFR to CJH, January 9, 1954, LC, reel 30, frame 197.

64. JPII to FFR, July 21, 1952, and FFR to JPII, July 25, 1952, both in LC, reel 30, frames 115–116.

65. Telephone interview with Isaacs, October 2, 1984.

66. Interview with CJH, May 5, 1984, St. Louis, Missouri.

67. *New York Times,* March 24, 1955.

68. Richard H. Meeker, *Newspaperman* (New York: Ticknor and Fields, 1983), pp. 166–167, 191–192. But then conditions began to change. Both St. Louis newspapers went through difficult times during the next two decades—particularly the *Globe-Democrat,* which was sold in 1984 and went out of business in 1986 after 134 years of publication. Between 1959 and 1979, the *Globe-Democrat* and the *Post-Dispatch* entered into a series of cost-cutting and profit-sharing agreements under the federal Newspaper Preservation Act, until severe losses by the *Globe-Democrat*

created conditions under which the Justice Department compelled Newhouse to sell the newspaper in 1984 rather than suspend publication. However, under a contract between Pulitzer and Newhouse, the two agreed to share equally in the profits or losses of the *Post-Dispatch* for at least fifty years. Newhouse has no say in any aspect of *Post-Dispatch* operation. For seven months in 1989 and 1990, the *Post-Dispatch* met competition in the form of the tabloid *St. Louis Sun,* the creation of second-generation media baron Ralph Ingersoll II. The *Sun,* closely patterned after the Gannett group's *USA Today,* failed to attract sufficient circulation or advertisers or to define itself editorially. *Post-Dispatch,* January 27, 1984, and October 30, 1986; "A Chronology of Increasing Post-Globe Cooperation," *St. Louis Journalism Review,* January 1984, pp. 6–7; "Sun Closing Shocks Staff, St. Louis," *St. Louis Journalism Review,* May 1990, p. 1.

69. Brockman interview, April 27, 1984, St. Louis, Missouri.

70. JPII to Nicholas M. Butler, April 28, 1928, LC, reel 137, frame 249.

71. Samuel W. Tait Jr., "The St. Louis *Post-Dispatch,*" April 1931, p. 409.

72. Alexander, "The Last Shall Be First," p. 75.

73. "A Statement by Joseph Pulitzer, February 13, 1942," P–D.

74. Telephone interview with Morris J. Levin, June 26, 1985.

75. Evarts A. Graham Jr. to author, July 18, 1953.

76. Louis L. Phillips to author, June 22, 1984.

77. Telephone interview with Levin, June 26, 1985.

78. *Post-Dispatch,* September 7, 1945.

79. Telephone interview with JPIII, June 17, 1986.

80. "Employees Earning $10,000 or More a Year," November 26, 1945, LC, reel 68, frame 460.

81. BHR to JPII, May 17, 1932, LC, reel 68, frame 554.

82. RPB to BHR, May 19, 1942, LC, reel 102, frame 142.

83. JPII to RPB, May 29, 1942, LC, reel 102, frame 141.

84. "1952 Personal Contract Expirations," January 9, 1952, LC, reel 68, frame 616.

85. *Post-Dispatch* morgue files, various dates between January 6, 1936, and February 6, 1949; James V. Maloney to author, undated [1986]; "Savings and Income in Prosperity and Depression, 1928–1933," LC, reel 105, frame 558.

86. JPII to J. Porter Henry, May 17, 1944, LC, reel 40, frame 187; JPII to ASVB, January 31, 1930, LC, reel 23, frame 200.

87. RP to JPII, March 22, 1922, P–D.

88. "Memo on Mr. Pulitzer's Activities," May 26, 1946, LC, reel 40, frames 199–203; "Financial Resume of the Pulitzer Publishing Company, 1920–1947," P–D.

89. JPII to SMC, November 1, 1945, LC, reel 40, frame 35.

90. Agreement in envelope dated November 15, 1927; Dell B. Stafford to JPII, April 14, 1954, P–D.

91. JPII to RP, March 7, 1913, P–D.

92. Citation by Grayson Kirk, vice president and provost of Columbia University, June 5, 1952, P–D.

93. JPII to BBH, May 23, 1940, LC, reel 71, frame 211.

Chapter 24
Fish, Fowl, Family, Friends

1. *Post-Dispatch,* March 31, 1955.

2. Telephone interview with Dr. and Mrs. Louis H. Hempelmann Jr., July 5, 1984. Unless otherwise indicated, family information in this chapter comes from this and other interviews with the children of JPII.

3. JPII to Mortimer L. Schiff, February 10, 1930, LC, reel 122, frame 23. Unless otherwise noted, items on fishing come from reels 122, 123, and 124 of the JPII Papers.

4. Interview with Mrs. Thomas Pettus, April 25, 1984, St. Louis, Missouri.

5. ID to JPII, March 4, (1948?), LC, reel 52, frame 536.

6. JPII to CGR, July 28, 1945, Truman Library, Independence, Missouri (courtesy of Julian S. Rammelkamp).

7. JPII to HP, July 31, 1949, P–D.

8. JPII to Werner O. Nagel, April 17, 1953 and reply, April 21, 1953, LC, reel 134, frame 363.

9. Joseph Pulitzer, *We Go Fishing in Norway* (Privately printed, 1954), p. 1.

10. JPII to Lt. Cmdr. Roy G. MacPherson, June 6, 1942, LC, reel 152, frame 34.

11. Telephone interview with Mrs. Martha Love Symington, May 3, 1984; Mrs. Joseph L. Werner to author, November 19, 1984.

12. JPII to KDP, December 29, 1918, P–D.

13. Telephone interview with George N. Sayers, August 28, 1984; *P–D Notebook,* March 1954, pp. 9–11, P–D.

14. CJH to JPII, April 2, 1948, LC, reel 71, frame 77.

15. Unless otherwise noted, the material on hunting comes from LC, reels 125–128 (JPII Papers).

16. *Arkansas Gazette,* September 21, 1943, LC, reel 126, frame 433.

17. JPII to GMB, October 9, 1951, LC, reel 91, frame 11.

18. Interviews with FFR, April 27, 1984, and CJH, May 5, 1984, St. Louis, Missouri.

19. Telephone interview with Sayers, August 28, 1984.

20. Interview with CJH, May 5, 1984.

21. Nash Buckingham, "A Duck Hunter's Viewpoint," *American Field*, June 27, 1936, p. 685, LC, reel 125, frame 32.

22. JPII to RC, June 6, 1940, LC, reel 44, frame 214.

23. JPII to CGR, August 6, 1935, and July 19, 1936, LC, reel 96, frames 18, 58.

24. JPII to RC, January 15, 1947, LC, reel 99, frame 296; *Post-Dispatch*, January 24, 1947.

25. *New York Times*, December 12, 1951.

26. JPII to BMB, December 20, 1951, LC, reel 9, frame 343.

27. Michael E. Pulitzer, "Centralia Mine Disaster," *The Vindex*, 1947, pp. 143–144, LC, reel 7, frame 286.

28. JPII to MEP, May 17, 1951, LC, reel 7, frame 355.

29. Margaret Leech Pulitzer to JPII, April 5, 1937, LC, reel 7, frame 597.

30. Interview with Mrs. Thomas Pettus, April 25, 1984, Ladue, Missouri.

31. Interview with Mr. and Mrs. Wallace H. Smith, April 24, 1984, Ladue, Missouri.

32. JPII to Walter Peacock, March 18, 1938, LC, reel 128, frame 197.

33. Interview with Mrs. Charles A. Thomas, July 20, 1985, Clayton, Missouri.

34. JPII to W. Seward Webb, May 6, 1951, LC, reel 8, frame 103.

35. *New York Times*, November 15 and 16, 1938.

36. Interview with Mrs. Pettus, April 25, 1984.

37. Telephone interview with James Lawrence, May 4, 1984. Lawrence was editor of the editorial page when he retired in 1987 after forty-eight years with the *Post-Dispatch*.

38. Interview with Lionel Horton, May 22, 1986, St. Louis, Missouri.

Chapter 25
Looking Toward the Future

1. Louis L. Phillips to author, June 22, 1984. Unless otherwise noted, the information on Pulitzer's health during the last two years of his life comes from interviews with JPIII, CJH, and ARK.

2. JPII to Carlos F. Hurd, May 15, 1947, LC, reel 5, frame 73.

3. CJH interview, May 5, 1984, St. Louis, Missouri.

4. Neville Grant, M.D., to author, August 20, 1984; JPII to HP, February 5, 1954, P-D; JPII to HBS, March 16, 1954, LC, reel 20, frame 6.

5. JPII to Samuel B. Grant, November 20, 1954, P-D.

6. Grant to author, August 20, 1984.

7. Interview with Dr. and Mrs. Louis H. Hempelmann Jr., July 5 and 6, 1984, Bar Harbor, Maine.

8. Memorandum by SS, January 29, 1953, P-D.

9. JPII to HP, January 30, 1953, and HP to JPII, January 31, 1953, both in P-D.

10. JPII to SS, March 1, 1953, P-D.

11. Menu, University Club of St. Louis, May 9, 1953, P-D.

12. HOG interview, May 5, 1984, Chesterfield, Missouri.

13. CJH interview, May 5, 1984, St. Louis, Missouri.

14. Memo by SS, December 7, 1954, P-D.

15. Memo by SS, December 13, 1954, P-D.

16. JPII to HP, February 2, 1950, P-D. He had started at $20 a week in 1936. Fifty years later, as chairman of the company, his compensation was $706,470. JPIII to author, September 29, 1987; "Proxy Information and Statement," Pulitzer Publishing Company, April 2, 1987, p. 6, P-D.

17. Telephone interview with W. Julius Polk Jr., October 4, 1985.

18. "Pulitzer," *St. Louis Magazine,* August 1987, p. 28.

19. Interview with JPIII, July 17, 1984, Ladue, Missouri.

20. JPII to W. H. Burkhardt, April 30, 1935, LC, reel 5, frame 644.

21. JPII to William Goodall, January 12, 1925, LC, reel 5, frame 174.

22. JPII to JHK, February 6, 1945, LC, reel 73, frame 20.

23. JPII to RPB, September 23, 1936, LC, reel 5, frame 687.

24. JPIII to JPII, December 3, 1936, LC, reel 88, frame 71.

25. Alexander, "The Last Shall Be First," p. 75.

26. MWC to JPII, November 4, 1936, LC, reel 5, frame 679.

27. JPIII to JPII, December 3, 1936, LC, reel 88, frame 71.

28. JPIII to JPII, July 20, (1937), LC, reel 88, frames 18–32.

29. BHR to James W. Markham, January 23, 1952, and JPII to BHR, January 28, 1952, both in LC, reel 18, frames 34, 32.

30. OKB to JPII, March 25, 1938, LC, reel 88, frame 12.

31. JPII to RP and HP, December 24, 1938, LC, reel 88, frame 5.

32. JPIII to JPII and reply, May 27, 1946, LC, reel 88, frame 202.

33. JPIII to JPII, July 11, 1947, LC, reel 68, frame 195.

34. "Outline of a Trustee Management Plan Proposed for the Pulitzer Publishing Company," May 18, 1950, P-D. In 1950, these individuals were Pulitzer, Benjamin H. Reese, Stuart M. Chambers, Charles J. Hentschell, and attorney John G. Jackson.

35. *Post-Dispatch,* October 5, 1986; *New York Times,* April 13, 1986.

36. These are Joseph Pulitzer Jr., chairman; Glenn A. Christopher, vice chairman; Michael E. Pulitzer, president; David E. Moore, director; Ken J. Elkins, senior vice president—broadcasting operations; Nicholas G. Penniman IV, senior vice president—newspaper operations; Ronald H. Ridgeway, senior vice president—finance; and William F. Woo, editor of the *Post-Dispatch.* The three grandsons of the founder—the two Pulitzers and Moore—control 93.7 percent of the voting power in the company.

"Pulitzer Publishing Company Proxy and Information Statement," April 2, 1987, pp. 2–3.

37. "Pulitzer Publishing Company, 1986 Annual Report," p. 4.

38. JPIII to author (by telephone), November 30, 1987.

39. "Outline of a Trustee Management Plan" p. 1.

40. "Statement of Policy," Voting Trust Agreement, Pulitzer Publishing Company, October 24, 1986, pp. 2–3.

41. Will of Joseph Pulitzer, April 16, 1904, and codicils, p. 13, P–D.

42. JP to RP, February 2, 1907, JPI Papers, LC.

43. "Pulitzer Retires, Appoints Penniman, Woo," St. Louis Journalism Review, February 1986, p. 6.

44. Telephone interview with Evarts A. Graham Jr., December 1, 1987.

45. "Pulitzer Publishing Company, 1989 Annual Report," p. 5.

46. P–D Notebook, April 1955, p. 13, P–D.

47. Sworn deposition by HBS, May 26, 1947, LC, reel 40, frame 235.

48. Post-Dispatch, April 1, 1955.

49. "Pulitzer, McCormick, and the Daily Press," Christian Century, April 20, 1955, p. 470.

50. Post-Dispatch, April 1, 1955.

51. JPII to CFH, May 15, 1947, LC, reel 5, frame 73.

52. Post-Dispatch, March 31, 1955.

53. Post-Dispatch, April 4, 1955.

54. Quoted in John Hohenberg, The Pulitzer Prizes (New York: Columbia University Press, 1974), p. 231.

55. JPII to RC, April 15, 1944, LC, reel 45, frame 186; Post-Dispatch, April 18, 1944.

56. Post-Dispatch, February 19, 1947.

57. Sworn deposition by ID, May 21, 1947, LC, reel 40, frame 230.

58. Sayers interview, August 28, 1984; Sayers to author, September 10, 1984; Funeral instructions of Joseph Pulitzer, February 3, 1954, P–D; Post-Dispatch, September 4, 1974.

59. Post-Dispatch, April 7, 1975; David E. Moore to author (by telephone), October 5, 1987.

60. Joseph Pulitzer Jr., A Tradition of Conscience (Privately printed, 1965), pp. 53–54.

61. Post-Dispatch, April 4, 1955.

62. "The Boss," April 7, 1955, P–D.

Index

ST. LOUIS PO

The Only Evening Newspaper in St.

Vol. 97. No. 245. (67th Year). ST. LOUIS, TUESD

VICTORY OFFICIA

WAR IN EUROPE FORMAL

POST-DISPATCH REPOI

VIRGINIA IRWIN ARRIVES WITH ROAR OF BATTLE STILL IN THE AIR

One of First Three Americans to Enter Nazi Capital — Vivid Description of Adventurous Trip—Sees German Dead on Sidewalks.

By VIRGINIA IRWIN
A War Correspondent of the Post-Dispatch.

This is the first of three on-the-spot reports from Berlin by Virginia Irwin. The second will be published tomorrow, the third on Thursday.

(Copyright, 1945. Pulitzer Publishing Co.)

BERLIN, Germany, April 27.—I am one of the first three Americans to enter Berlin. After a fantastic journey northward, after we crossed the Elbe River where the Rus-

She Got to Berlin

VIRGINIA IRWIN

Post-Dispatch war correspondent who, when advised by her editors some time ago to return home when she had enough, cabled: "I want to stick it out until I get to Berlin." She made it. A writer for the Post-Dispatch magazine section for 10 years, Miss Irwin joined the Red Cross 22 months ago. After serving in England for nine months she rejoined this newspaper as a correspondent and has followed the fortunes

CHURCHILL SA RATIFICATION SURRENDER OCCUR IN BE

Germans Agree to in Planes and Intact — Any F Resistance Wil Treated as Bandit

LONDON, May 8 (AP).
Minister Churchill toda
claimed complete victory
rope and Gen. Dwight D
hower's headquarters in P
nounced that hostilities wo
mally end at 11:01 o'clock
central European time (5:0
St. Louis time, and 12:01
May 9, British double
time).

Shattered Germany's u
tional surrender "will be
and cofirmed at Berlin"
Churchill said.

Churchill summoned his
to a battle to the finish
Japan, reminding the Brit
"Japan, with all her treach
greed, remains unsubdued.

Kennedy's Dispatch Conf

Churchill, officially bear
yesterday's exclusive disp
Edward Kennedy of the
ated Press, said the Germ
ulation occurred at Gen.
hower's headquarters at R
2:41 a. m. Monday (7:41 p.